PARTISANAS

PARTISANAS

WOMEN IN THE ARMED RESISTANCE TO FASCISM AND GERMAN OCCUPATION (1936–1945)

Ingrid Strobl

AK Press
Edinburgh, Oakland, West Virginia

Partisanas: Women in the Armed Resistance
to Fascism and German Occupation (1936–1945)
by Ingrid Strobl

© 1989 Fischer Taschenbuch Verlag, Frankfurt am Main.

This edition © 2008 AK Press

ISBN 9781904859697
Library of Congress Control Number 2007928343

Library of Congress Cataloging-in-Publication Data
   A catalog record for this title is available from the Library of Congress.

British Library Cataloguing-in-Publication Data
   A catalogue record for this title is available from the British Library.

Published by:

AK Press	AK Press	Kate Sharpley Library
P.O. Box 12766	674-A 23rd St.	BM Hurricane
Edinburgh, Scotland	Oakland, CA	London, England
EH8 9YE	94612	WC1 3XX

Translation: Paul Sharkey
Cover Design: Chris Wright
Design and layout : JR

Special thanks to Freddie Baer for years of work and for her great help in
getting this book published.

Printed in Canada on acid-free, 100% recycled paper with union labor.

CONTENTS

Dedicated to Fifi, Zala, Truus, Dina, Chayke, Niuta and all the others.

For Martina Domke, Peter Neff, Monika Richarz
and Monika Tessadri-Wackerle,
without whose assistance this book would never have been possible. And a
special thanks to Paul Sharkey for his careful and wonderful translation.

Martha Ackelsberg

Foreword

This book reclaims the stories—too-frequently unknown or ignored—of women who were active in anti-fascist resistance movements in Europe before and during World War II. It represents the fruits of many years' work by Ingrid Strobl, tracking down female participants in resistance movements in Spain and (especially Jews) in Eastern and Western Europe. First published in German in 1989, the book was issued by Virus Editorial (in Spanish) in 1994. Its publication now in English makes this fascinating material available to a considerably wider audience.

Ingrid Strobl is clearly fascinated by women who "broke the mold" of expected female passivity, and did so outside of any explicitly feminist context. The reader will find repeated references to the ways these women shattered both the stereotype of the allegedly-passive, home-bound, traditional woman, and of the supposedly resigned or non-resisting Jews who "went like sheep to the slaughter." Most, if not all, of those she interviewed were quite young at the time of their involvement, and were members either of the Communist or Young Socialist Parties, of the Jewish Labor Bund, or the Zionist youth movement. Strobl interweaves their individual stories with the broader story of the relevant movements, and follows these with a final chapter that explores, more explicitly, what impelled the women to act, and what kept them going.

"What else could I have done?" one after another of these women responded, when Strobl asked them why they did what they did. "What enabled them," she asks, "to break with their lives, their education, their role, with everything that was considered *normal* for a woman, to continually risk their lives in dedicating themselves to stealing guns, placing bombs, or attempting to assassinate people? What impelled them to abandon their parents, their homes, their lives, everything that was familiar, to spend their nights in the trenches, to suffer hunger and cold in partisan camps covered with snow, fleeing from one safe-haven to another?"

While her interviews reveal some common themes, they cannot, of course, tell us *why* some women took these steps, seeing "no other way," while others did not. We do know that most were young, most came from political (i.e. socialist or communist or zionist) families and had been involved in political activities even before the war, many were Jews. Each had a strong sense of justice. In addition, Strobl points out that roles for women—whether in pre-Civil War Spain, or in pre-World War II France, Holland, Germany, Yugoslavia, or Poland—were quite limited. They were expected to marry, have children, and raise them. At most, if they were connected to left-wing organizations, they might serve in a sort of women's auxiliary to the movement. Thus, she claims, participating in resistance movements offered "the only possibility to escape the limited and sordid rhythm of a predetermined feminine destiny." Whether through the Communist Party, the Bund, or the Zionist movement in the ghettoes of Poland, participation in the resistance provided unique opportunities for nonconformity, for connecting with those who shared one's revolutionary ideas, and for acting together to create a new world. It was, she insists, "the only human, dignified, way out." Some participated for their parents; all did it for themselves. And, she argues, they also acted as a way to exact revenge on those who had destroyed their families, friends, and communities. Vengeance may not be an emotion we associate with women; but Strobl argues that vengeance was a powerful motivator for almost all of them.

The stories are compelling; we get to know these women, share their histories, their fears, their triumphs. We learn about aspects of (women's) lives during this period that are largely hidden from mainstream histories. This reclaiming, then, fills in some important gaps in available histories, and in our understandings of resistance. And yet, at the same time, Strobl, herself, leaves some questions unanswered. She never quite defines a "partisan" or "fighter against fascism," although it is clear that she includes in this book only those who literally took up arms against fascist armies and/or occupiers. Some recent scholarship to define resistance *only* as armed resistance,[1] thereby ignoring many of the equally-critical activities (mostly undertaken by women) that enable resistance movements (armed or unarmed) to function.[22] On the other hand, Strobl's point in here is that women *did* participate in these movements—*even in armed resistance*—and that their contributions ought not to be forgotten.

In addition, her interviews and analysis focus almost entirely on those who were members of, or otherwise connected to, Communist or Socialist parties (the one exception being the radical Zionists of the Hechalutz groups in Poland). While it is certainly true that Communist Parties were critical to the mobilization and support of resistance in many of these situations, this focus leads her—at least in the context of the Spanish Civil War—to downplay or distort the role of anarchist groups in the anti-Franco resistance, both during and after the War. She acknowledges the gap in the Spanish material—indicating that it was impossible for her to find anarchist women to interview.

Nevertheless, the book perpetuates certain myths, despite her apparent efforts to question them. She *understates*, for example, the degree to which anarchist organizations did support efforts toward women's equality (for example, many unions cooperated with the apprenticeship programs organized by the anarchist women's organization, Mujeres Libres) at the same time that she sometimes *over*states the nature of Mujeres Libres' critiques of conventional women's roles, claiming, for example, that Mujeres Libres "attacked the family," or criticized the militia women. She is aware—and refers repeatedly to the fact—that the Communist Party played a counter-revolutionary role in the Spanish Civil War, minimizing the social revolution that was happening within the Republican camp, and, indeed, actively destroying collectives and attacking both anarchist and Trotskyist groups; yet, at the same time, one could easily get the impression from the book that it was *only* the Communist Party that truly supported women on the front-lines. Still, if the book is read together with other recent works, it does provide

---

1. See, for example, Dalia Ofer and Leonore Weitzman, eds., *Women in the Holocaust* (New Haven: Yale University Press, 1998); Jane Slaughter, *Women and the Italian Resistance, 1943–1945* (Boulder, CO: Arden Press, 1997); Jane Hart, *New Voices in the Nation: Women in Greek Resistance, 1941–1964* (Ithaca: Cornell University Press, 1996).

2. Strobl herself wrote of those activities, including the rescue of children and youth, in her book *Die Angst kam erst danach. Jüdische Frauen im Widerstand 1939–1945* (The Fear Came Later: Jewish Women in Resistance, 1939-1945).

important new information and perspectives on this important, but still largely understudied, era.[33]

Indeed, the issues raised by the book—the ways women, in struggling together with others for broader freedoms, were effectively *required* to challenge traditional roles, and the ways those challenges were resisted, accepted and/or incorporated—take on ever more resonance in the contemporary world. For, of course, women have been active in armed resistance not only in Europe, but also in Algeria, Kuwait, Iraq, Palestine, Nicaragua, Argentina, Peru, and Mexico. The list goes on, but attention to the ways women's participation shapes broader movements and changes the lives of those women is still relatively uncommon. If this book highlights those questions again, and leads others to explore further the multiple dimensions of resistance and its multi-layered impacts on participants, it will make a further, and continuing, contribution both to scholarship and to political struggle.

---

3. For some alternative perspectives, see, for example, Anna Delso, *Trois cents hommes et moi: Etampe d'une révolution* (Montréal: La Pleine Lune, 1989) and *De Toda la Vida* (All our Lives) [video recording], Lisa Berger and Carol Mazer (New York, NY: Cinema Guild, 1986).

Introduction to the 2008 edition

Resistance – What's that?

I - Relativizing the Absolute

"Resistance" is one of those terms that, although seemingly clear-cut, is in reality difficult to define. What is resistance? Who defines it? What conditions have to be met in order for one to identify or recognize it? Which, and whose, interests stand behind the label?

A very recent example makes clear how resistance is defined differently by groups with divergent interests: On the German left it was consistently a positive and respected option for political action. However, the understanding of resistance varied according to political direction. The unions understood resistance to mean something completely different than, for example, the radical left. Cadre organizations counted only organized actions by organized groups as resistance, while social revolutionaries saw the marginalized as entitled to an almost *a priori* right to resistance. The federal state, on the other hand, denied any connection between leftist radical actions and resistance, and instead defined them as criminal or terrorist. Actions and attitudes recognized in the West as being related to resistance were denounced in the GDR as rowdyism.

I'm not going to state authoritatively what resistance is. That would be simply impossible. The best we can do is eliminate certain delusions and then open our eyes and ears to what, up to now, has been ignored, excluded, and devalued. The long-fostered delusion that resistance is something good, and that the actions of the "bad guys" cannot be characterized as resistance, is obsolete. What is good, what is evil? The widely accepted minimum consensus implies: It is good to assist others. It is evil to harm others. However, resistance often consists of killing others—aggressors, occupiers, dictators. Moreover, since the European Enlightenment, resistance has been defined in military and, in the most narrow sense, political terms. Everything else, even that which some considered deserving of the label, is of secondary importance. It is unnecessary to add that what was, and is, meant by the latter has been principally the resistance-oriented behavior of women.

In that sense, good and socially valuable acts of resistance involve taking the lives of, or otherwise harming, others—the enemies. Actions that save lives or make survival easier for others—children, the persecuted, those in hiding—are trivialized as purely individual acts. Furthermore, actions that are calculated to save or improve the lives of the enemy are denounced as collaboration or treason. In short, resistance cannot even be defined on the basis of a minimal moral consensus.

Must we conclude that resistance eludes the moral criteria of good and evil? Is resistance always whatever anyone chooses to declare it to be? When a term is applied in such diverging and contradictory manners, it becomes an empty shell that can be applied to virtually every action, from the most banal to the most criminal. The SS-units that fought behind enemy lines against the allied troops marching into Germany, declared their murderous actions to be resistance. In certain circles they are still seen as such today. Those responsible for terror attacks against civilians—like those on the World Trade Center, commuter trains in Madrid, and the London underground—maintain that these were acts of resistance. And this assertion meets with the approval of hundreds of thousands, if not millions. Neo-Nazis, who find pleasure in mistreating people they define as non-Aryan, call themselves the "national resistance," also with the approval of segments of the population.

Must we accept this? Or should we resist these interpretations of resistance? I propose that the term alone communicates nothing about its content. It remains simultaneously ambiguous and empty when nothing is said about who resists whom, and with what motives and methods. It is always necessary to question who recognizes what actions as resistance and why.

One generally accepted criterion for resistance is organization. This usually means political or military organization, but potentially also social, ethnic, or religious. Unlike political organizations and associations, unstructured groups and individuals are rarely defined as resistance in historical research. The Cologne Edelweiss Pirates, for example, a loose association of proletarian and sub-proletarian youth who hid forced laborers and skirmished with the Gestapo, were only recognized in recent years—reluctantly—as a resistance group. And acts of resistance by women, which were neither recognized nor corresponded to prevailing moral perceptions, have simply been ignored up to the present. Even more, those who allude to them are suspected of being frivolous, apolitical, and amoral, or of making the resistance banal or even dirty.

The following are two examples that serve to represent many others: During the Paris Commune, prostitutes supplied the insurgents with food. Male revolutionaries found this embarrassing or even insulting. They feared for their good reputations. The woman revolutionary, Louise Michel, in contrast, respected the helpfulness of her female comrades-in-arms. Yet no one ever called it "resistance."

In some French brothels, prostitutes hid Jews and resistance fighters. The same women also served, as it was their job, the officers of the occupying German troops. They risked their lives when they provided safe houses for the persecuted, and those who they saved are still thankful today. Nonetheless, their practical solidarity was never described as an act of resistance.

I have researched the subject of women for many years—in particular, Jewish women in the resistance. Over the course of those years, I realized that I had also fallen under the influence of the popular hierarchization of resistance. At first, I had only been interested in women's participation in armed resistance. They were, in my view, the younger sisters of the women revolutionaries that I revered and wanted to know as much about as possible. The only women of the resistance known at that time were, however, all said to have participated in the so-called "passive" resistance. They had hidden people, typed and distributed pamphlets, and listened to the BBC or Radio Moscow, passing what they learned on to others. I nonetheless had the feeling that there were also women who had transported bombs rather than pamphlets, who had fought with weapons in their hands. It was their history that I wanted to tell. It was to them that I wanted to express my respect. My research revealed that they did really exist. I wrote a first book about these women and researched further.

One of my personal heroes was Sarah Goldberg, who had been the radio operator of the Rote Kapelle in Belgium and had—after the suppression of this organization—become affiliated with the Jewish partisans in Brussels. I was in the process of preparing an exhibition on the Jewish resistance for the Jewish Museum in Frankfurt and visited Sarah to get more information and, most of all, photos and other objects. We had become friends by then, and she was helping me to find more material for the exhibition, as well as other people to interview. She said, "You definitely have to interview Yvonne Jospa, and all the other women who rescued children." I would rather not admit this here, but I hesitated. The exhibition was supposed to be about the "real resistance." Fortunately, my esteem for Sarah got the better of my ideological stubbornness.

For Sarah's sake, I conducted an interview with Yvonne Jospa. Under the aegis of the CDJ, the Jewish self-protection committee in Belgium, she had been responsible for the rescue of Jewish children and youth. As a result, I began an intensive learning process that led to a fundamental change in my mindset. I eventually researched *all* variations of the resistance of Jewish women for my book, *Die Angst kam erst danach. Jüdische Frauen im Widerstand in Europa* (The Fear Came Later: Jewish Women in the Resistance in Europe). I realized that the women who had organized and conducted the rescue of children and adolescents had probably provided the most important and, in any case, most effective form of resistance.

I asked the women I was interviewing: How did you preserve your own humanity in the midst of the inferno of the Shoa? Where did you find the courage to resist in such a hopeless situation, and how did you deal with your fear? What did the women who killed people in armed attacks feel?

The more than sixty women I interviewed for the book answered these questions with an unexpected openness, and with deep reflection and humility. The fact that their participation in the resistance has been largely overlooked in written history did not surprise them much. Only a few of them had corrected the false picture by publicizing their memoirs. And some of the women who had participated in the rescue of children even implicitly agreed with the historians, explaining, "But we didn't put up any resistance. We only took care of the children, and that was just natural. We simply couldn't allow them to be deported."

They had internalized, to some degree, the still-binding hier-archization of resistance into an "active," military category and a "passive" category that includes everything else. This hierarchical ranking is one of the most important reasons for the exclusion of women from the research and historiography of resistance against German policies of occupation and extermination. This categorization, which is completely divorced from reality, proves to be—when one investigates the conditions, processes, and content of the Jewish resistance—both unproductive and obstructive. More helpful and appropriate to the object/subject of research, I recommend, is replacing the paired terms "active" and "passive" with the terms armed, humanitarian, material, and political resistance—and avoiding any hierarchization of these frequently interwoven aspects.

II Appreciation of the Concrete

Jewish women were involved in all forms and formations of the resistance. They were activists in urban brigades, the ghetto underground, and partisan units. They printed and distributed the illegal press; they forged papers; they transported weapons and themselves participated in armed actions. They organized underground movements and ghetto uprisings; they were political cadres and—rarely—military commanders of armed groups. They found hiding places for Jewish children and youth, brought them to these hiding places, provided them with clothing, money, food, and with forged documents and encouragement over months and sometimes even years. They smuggled groups of these children and youth across the Swiss border and they accompanied illegal transports of boys and girls over the Pyrenees to Spain, and from there to Palestine.

Within the framework of the armed resistance, the task of liaison work and scouting was the women's domain. An important reason for this division of responsibilities lay in the fact that women were able to move more freely and inconspicuously. They were checked less often than men, and they even succeeded in actively using gender-specific patterns of behavior against the adversary. Thus, female couriers for the resistance occasionally got German officers to tuck their suitcases full of weapons in the luggage rack of the train or to carry them through a round-up at a train station. Other women used their pregnancy or motherhood as camouflage, tying pistols around their stomachs and transporting illegal printed material in baby carriages. The women liaisons arranged illegal quarters, food, and clothing for the members of resistance groups. They maintained contact between groups and commanders, and among the individual group members. They scouted targets to be attacked and observed potential victims. They procured weapons and explosives and transported them to the location of the attack. Without them, the armed groups would not have been able to carry out their actions.

Like liaison work, the actions to save children were above all the responsibility of the women. It was mostly very young women, often social workers, nursery school teachers, members of the Jewish Scout, or Zionist Youth movements. They took on, without any relevant experience, work that was both full of responsibility and dangerous, and which cost some of them their lives. They brought children and youth out of the country or hid them in cloisters, boarding schools, holiday colonies, sanatoriums, or with private individuals. They compiled coded lists so that they would be able to find the children again after the liberation. As far as possible under the circumstances, they took care, not only of children's safety and their physical needs, but also of their psychological well-being. They transported letters back and forth between children and their parents; they thought up stories when letters from the deported parents no longer came. And they knew that, despite all of their efforts, they could not take away a child's loneliness, solitude, fears, and doubts.

Some of these women not only risked their lives, but also knowingly sacrificed them for their charges. Marianne Cohn, for example, was imprisoned along with children she had brought to the French-Swiss border only a few weeks prior to the liberation. The resistance offered to liberate her from the prison. She refused, although she had been horribly tortured. She did not want to risk the lives of the children. She assumed, probably correctly, that they would be killed in revenge for her flight. And she hoped that the Allies would liberate the prison before the children could be deported. This is what happened, although she herself was raped and beaten to death before they arrived.

The majority of the women (and men) entered the resistance through membership in a social or political group. It was different for those who were not already organized, or at least active on the periphery of an organization, to gain access to resistance groups that had sealed themselves off to avoid infiltration and detection. But not all members of a political or social organization became affiliated with the resistance.

Why some did and others did not is difficult to reconstruct today. The memories of the women, as far as the question of their motives is concerned, are influenced by the emotions and experiences of the decades that lie between their youth and the present.

Former Communists, for example, who turned away from the Party after the war and towards their Jewish roots, have a tendency to see their motives, in retrospect, as specifically Jewish. Those who remained loyal Party members, insist that they fought exclusively as Communists and not as Jews. Many women, however, say that, for them, both factors were mixed together. Ida Rubinstein, who fought as a Jewish-Communist partisan in Toulouse, said: "I entered the resistance on purely political grounds. But, because I am a Jew, I had a double motivation." Survivors of the Jewish-Communist resistance in France also point out that the young women and men who were able to escape the first big round-ups in Paris in July 1942, but whose parents and siblings were seized and deported, joined the resistance for this reason.

The women who worked for social or educational institutions found themselves in a situation in which social work and/or childcare was transformed into resistance. Also, the young women who were active in the Zionist Youth or the Jewish Scouts in Western Europe, grew into their resistance work almost naturally without making, at least at the beginning, a conscious decision. Denise Lévy, for example, one of the leaders of the Jewish Scouts, was informed one day that a round-up of her foreign charges was imminent, so she had to find hiding places for them. Those hidden could not, in turn, survive long without forged papers, so she therefore began to produce forged documents. One thing led to the other. When asked about her motives, Denise Lévy said: "We could not allow the children to be detained. Being detained meant being deported. We didn't know at the time exactly what happened to those deported, but simply being deported was enough. We unconditionally wanted to prevent that."

If one asks female Zionist activists who fought in Poland about their motives, most of them answer that they did not want to end up in the gas chamber, that they wanted to resist, to avenge those who had been murdered. All these reasons, however, only became important to them after the first large liquidation actions, only when they realized that the Germans would actually annihilate the whole Jewish people. Before that lay the period of the German invasion, the ghettoization, and the liquidation of the first ghettos. The foundations of an under-ground movement were laid during this time. The young women, who later fought in the ghetto uprisings and with the partisans, had already then decided to work illegally. The reasons why they did so are no longer clear to them, or are simply no longer important. For them, there is a blurring of before and after: The hell in which they lived and acted after the beginning of the "final solution" overlay almost everything that had come before.

Many of the former Jewish liaison women I interviewed em-phasized that, for the success of their work, a combination of quick-wittedness and instinct was decisive. Sarah Goldberg, for instance, remembered one situation, in which "in the midst of panic" she did the right thing, although afterwards it remained incomprehensible, even to her, how she had come up with the idea to act in such a way. While she was conducting an assignment for her group of Jewish partisans in Brussels, she noticed that a known informer was coming towards her from the other end of the street. "Ahead of me were two Belgian policemen. I said to the two of them, 'Please keep going,' and I pressed myself between them. They wanted to know what was going on and I said, 'Please simply keep moving'—as if they had arrested me. But they still wanted to know what was happening, so I said: 'Listen, I am a Jew and there in front of us is an informer.' The two of them then put me in between them and went with me in that way past the man. When the danger was past, one of them said he was going to take his lunch and the other said, 'Mademoiselle, if you need anything please come to me, I work in the commissariat of Foret.'"

This story not only makes clear that segments of the Belgian police sympathized with the resistance, or, at least, were against the anti-Jewish politics of the Germans, it also shows that a disciplined, experienced, and canny illegal like Sarah Goldberg "functioned" in this case without having to deliberate. Where this ability came from is something she cannot explain. However, she and other women who have similar memories of reacting spontaneously and instinctively, above all, in seemingly hopeless situations, guess that this behavior possibly occurred more often with women than with men. At the same time, it should be kept in mind that conduct like that described by Sarah Goldberg would probably not have worked for a man: The policemen would very likely have reacted negatively or aggressively to a similar request from a man. The intuitive behavior of the women presumably often corresponded to an unconscious protective instinct in the man involved or to his desire to impress a pretty young woman.

The female Jewish couriers occasionally consciously employed these gender-specific ways of reacting in their work. In her book on the Jewish resistance in France, Anny Latour tells a typical story about the legendary boldness of Betty Knout, a sixteen-year-old courier for the Armée Juive. She was quite often in transit with two suitcases full of weapons. The railroad bridge over the Loire had been destroyed, so, in order to reach Paris, it was necessary to get off the train on one bank, cross another bridge on foot, and take a train on the opposite bank. A German officer saw how the petite young woman was hauling the two suitcases and offered to carry them for her. When he lifted them up, he was astounded by the enormous weight and asked Betty Knout what she had inside of them. Butter? Cheese? Ham? She smiled at him conspiratorially and said, "Psst! It's submachine guns." In response the German officer burst out in resounding laughter and, amused, carried the entertaining young woman's two suitcases to the other bank of the Loire and onto the train waiting there.

The cockiness of this young woman, who gained her first experience with illegal activities in the resistance, is less astounding than the instinctual reactions of experienced communist militants like Sarah Goldberg and Yvonne Jospa. The latter also remembers "crazy" incidents that she cannot logically explain. Once, she learned there was an opportunity to house a larger group of Jewish children in a holiday colony. To do so, she had to take charge of the group at a specific time at the Gare du Luxemburg train station in Brussels. When she received this message, it was already too late to arrive on time. Jospa nonetheless got on the streetcar. She went forward to the driver and said, "Monsieur, I must be at the Gare du Luxemburg at such and such time." The driver accelerated and did not halt at any of the upcoming stops, so that she arrived punctually at the train station. "I don't know why I acted in such a way and I don't know why he reacted as he did," she said. "We both probably followed an instinct. He knew immediately that I was not a normal passenger who was simply in a hurry. And I knew, apparently subconsciously, that I could appeal to him. However, why this was so, I cannot say."

The Polish-Jewish resistance fighter Chaika Grossman, in turn, remembers one of Vitka Kempner's reactions that was based on pure feeling: She told her landlady in Vilna that she and her friends were in reality Jewish: She no longer wanted to treat the woman, whom she quite liked, "like a fool." A risky undertaking that nonetheless proved to be the right one. The landlady valued the trust that had been put in her, and in the future helped the young liaison woman for the Jewish resistance with her work.

What is interesting about these experiences is less the fact that the women had control over what they called "instinct," for lack of a better term, than the fact that they allowed themselves to yield to this instinct. Such "illogical" and "emotional" behavior was at odds with the necessity, which they themselves also recognized, of revolutionary discipline and self-control. The fact that they allowed themselves to listen to their emotions, "instincts," and "intuition," also corresponds to other departures they made from the rules of conspiracy. They met with friends and comrades, although this was strictly forbidden; they took care of and visited their parents in hiding, although this also often contradicted the security rules; occasionally, they went secretly to the cinema; they even allowed, when it seemed right to them, orders from the leadership that they were supposed to relay, "to fall by the wayside." They practiced what "Nicole" called "illegality in the illegality."

I think that it was precisely this occasional, situational "lack of discipline" that gave them an inner freedom in a situation without freedom—that their occasional breaks with inflexible principles, even when they also shared them, enabled them, in the face of mass murder, to put up resistance against an inhuman adversary without themselves becoming inhuman.

For many female and male activists, the "Morality of Resistance" consisted of not completely sacrificing their humanitarian principles for the sake of efficiency, of "not becoming like the enemy." Chaika Grossman tells of a heated discussion within the "Mejdalach," the entirely female Jewish underground group in Bialystok. At issue in this debate was whether they should, with the help of the partisans, undertake a bomb attack in a residential area almost exclusively inhabited by members of the German security apparatus and their families. They finally rejected this action because they wouldn't only be killing men from the Gestapo and SS, but their wives and children as well.

The somewhat older and politically or pedagogically more experienced men and women in the Jewish resistance were also aware of the possibility that their younger comrades might be bestialized and lose their ideals. For the most part, there were few opportunities during the war to purposefully work against this danger. Rachel Cheigham reports that her brigade, the Armée Juive in Nice, which conducted assassinations of informers, held regular meeting with its members in order to steady the young women and men: "They were still so young and they had to kill. It is not easy to kill someone. And it does not leave one unscathed. We did not want them to become criminals."

Ingrid Strobl
2007

A Brief History of
a Protracted Investigation

We had only to ask for Fifí, Fidela Fernández de Velasco Pérez advised on the phone. Her nickname was Fifí. Her house was on the outskirts of town and thus somewhat hard to locate, but we shouldn't have too much trouble. Finding it proved a lot easier than it had been to track down Fifí's whereabouts up to that point. Before I set off on the trip to Madrid to conduct the initial interviews for this book, my friend from Madrid, Pilar Panes Casas, who would later act as my interpreter, had conducted some initial soundings. In every single interview with old Communists who had lived through the Civil War and who had been pressed for the addresses of women who had fought on the front lines, the name of Fifí had cropped up. "Yes, Fifí had been on the front," Pilar was told everywhere she went. And Fifí had done other dangerous things. But no one was willing to supply her address. When Pilar pressed them about this curious reserve, they merely told her that Fifí was very much her own woman, that Fifí was something of a mannish woman. Which merely prompted Pilar to be all the more to persist with her inquiries. When I reached Madrid, we still had no idea where Fifí was living. After several phone calls to all parts of Spain, and only two days before I was due to depart, we succeeded: Fifí was living in a little house in the sierra around Madrid.

When we got there, Fifí was at the top of a collapsible ladder, tools in hand. She was repairing her roof. The little house, built with her own hands, seemed solitary amid the rocks, a good fifteen-minute walk from the village. Fifí shared these quarters with a stray cat that deigned to let her feed it and sometimes stroke it. On that particular day, arriving to find that Fifí had visitors, it spat and disappeared. Fifí set some wine on the table and sat there without saying a word. She was not pleased that we had brought along a tape-recorder, but she nonetheless let me take it out of my bag. Pilar explained that we wanted to ask her some questions and now she wanted to know the reason we were so interested. Nobody had ever taken the trouble before.

The question and answer session began. It lasted a lot longer in Fifí's case than in the cases of the other women with whom I later spoke. For one thing, the others were all delighted that someone was taking an interest in this period of their lives, but at the same time they showed themselves to be extremely skeptical about my intentions and motives. Fifí sat opposite us, as stiff as a poker, in her work trousers, her hair short, bushy, and graying, wearing neither jewelry nor make-up, but alert, intelligent, and wary. A few hours and two bottles of wine later, the ice was well broken. Fifí made her explanations, allowed us to press her persistently and also responded to the most delicate questioning, albeit off the record at that point. By the end of our chat we were fast friends. Even though we were not Party members, she saw us as young comrades with whom she could be truthful. We honestly admired her. From that day forth, the ambition that kept me working on this book was that it should be worthy of Fifí.

What I would never have imagined even in my wildest dreams is that my chapter on Spain would feature Communists almost exclusively. I had made the trip to Madrid intending to interview primarily anarchists. I had studied the Spanish Civil War in some detail and I knew how important a part the anarchists had played and how suspect or questionable the Communists' part had been. I knew that the anarchist revolution had been brutally crushed by the Communist Party of Spain, that it had locked up and tortured anarchists and Trotskyists in the Stalinist jails of the GPU (the political police of the CPSU). I had studied the theories and activities of the Mujeres Libres, the anarchist feminists who had demanded women's liberation immediately, contrary to the line of the Communists, who had given the war primacy over all social issues.

When I arrived, Pilar confessed that she had yet to track down a single female anarchist from those days for an interview. We would have to make an effort over the coming days, since the national congress of the CNT was meeting in Madrid and former female fighters exiled in France would be attending. In addition, we could also ask at the offices of the Mujeres Libertarias, the organization that had taken over from the legendary Mujeres Libres. We were enormously disappointed. No, the women had not taken part in the fighting, we were told by everyone we spoke to, because anarchism was a pacifist movement. And why did we have to be so obsessive about these women? Female anarchists had a very creditable record in children's education, in tending the wounded, in organizing the people's kitchens, in every aspect of genuinely women's work. After three days of making inquiries and asking questions again and again, and being more and more brazenly skeptical, they finally sent us on our way with a prospectus on the care of nursing mothers. Regrettably, we never established any contact with the more left-wing and more feminist sectors which, of course, existed inside the organization.

Nor can it be said that the endeavor was child's play where the Communists were concerned either. But for the tenacity of Pilar, a portion of this book would never have been written. The current functionaries of the PCE (Spanish Communist Party) persistently argued that the real Civil War heroines at that stage had fought on the political front, in the field kitchens and in the infirmaries. When they eventually consented to supply us with a few addresses, it was not without a measure of pride. And, after some initial diffidence, the old women fighters too were, frankly, enthusiastic. Somebody was showing some interest in them at last, because of their having fought on the front like a man and not in spite of that.

The book *Der Himmel ist blau. Kann sein. Frauen im Widerstand Österreich 1938–1945* (The Sky is Blue, Perhaps: Women in the Austrian Resistance 1938–1945) was published in 1984. Three of the antifascist women interviewed in that book had joined the armed resistance as partisans with Tito's Liberation Army. The military resistance in annexed Austria was not as significant when set alongside the political resistance. The Carinthian Slovenes were virtually the only ones to offer any meaningful armed resistance to the Nazis. They fought in the ranks of the Titoist partisans and were a real thorn in the Germans' side. I had discovered that there were lots of women in the Yugoslavian Liberation Army, and I set about looking for Austrian women to interview. Quite by accident, I bumped into Helena Verdel at the Austrian Resistance Documentation Center; she was working on a comprehensive study of the Slovene resistance. Helena, herself a Slovene, was very wary, as were her colleagues. For years they had been at work with very little financial backing but with great commitment to shedding light upon the silenced history of the Slovene partisans of Carinthia. Up until a few years ago, except for them, nobody had any interest in those people. But now a few reporters were showing up to interview Helena and her colleagues, write their articles and pass themselves off as experts in the field of Slovenian antifascism. "I am quite fed up with it," Helena told me as she considered whether I too was one of that breed. When she made up her mind to help me, she helped me a hell of a lot more than I could ever have dared to hope. She organized my trip to Carinthia and smoothed over all of the obstacles so that I might talk with Zala. Johanna Sadolsek, whose partisan name was Zala, was the ideal person to speak to, we promptly agreed.

Zala is also one of the women who recounts her life story in *Der Himmel is blau. Mag sein*. I had a meeting with Lisbeth N. Trallori, one of the four authors of the book and film *Küchengespräche mit Rebellinnen* (Kitchen Chats with Rebel Women) and Zala also showed up. Here, too, I found nothing but support and solidarity. Not a hint of that jealous competition that is normally found between writers and historians, no misgivings about my plagiarizing the findings of her research.

Lisbeth N. Trallori made available to me a copy of the lengthy interview that she herself had conducted with Zala for that book and film, an interview of which only a fragment later saw publication.

The next stop was Klagenfurt. There to meet me was Mirko Messner, one of the team on Helena Verdels' project and editor of the bilingual review, *Kladivo*, in Carinthia. He took me as far as Lobning, where Zala lives; in the car, he gave me a detailed and enlightening run-down of the history of Carinthia's Slovene population, a tale of discrimination, rebellion, and disappointments. He briefed me on the postcard countryside of southeastern Carinthia: here, on this very mountain, there was an important partisan base-camp; over there, guerrillas arrived from Yugoslavia through that pass; over yonder, beyond that summit, a battle was fought against the Germans.

Zala placed wine and some salt pork on the table and scrutinized me closely through her big spectacles. These days she cannot make a living from farming, being too sick and too weary for that. Risking her life in the fight against fascism in her younger days and ruining her health for good had not earned her any gratitude; quite the opposite. "These days there is no honor attached to having been a partisan," she says. Which is why, for decades, she said nothing, as did all the other women. Now, getting on in years, she can see no reason to be ashamed of what she did. The others ought to be ashamed, the ones who did nothing or even collaborated with the Nazis. Her small holding, heavily-mortgaged at one time, was rebuilt through great effort on her part, after the war; these days she runs a guest house. "Yes, German visitors too," she says. "But the ones I like best are the Dutch. Many of them were in the resistance too and many a time I sit down with them and we chat into the early hours."

A few years ago, they screened the film *Das Mädchen mit den roten Haaren* (The Red-haired Girl) on television. I missed it on that occasion, but had read a synopsis of it. It was about a young girl who had taken up arms to fight the Germans, a real-life figure whose life story was told in a book of the same name—now a movie. That was my only lead on the participation of women in the armed resistance in the Netherlands. I made contact with Mies Bouhuys, who I knew as the writer of a children's book about Anne Frank. I spoke to her warily about my project. Warily because I had in the interim become familiar with the standard reaction of all the people I had approached: "Women in the armed resistance? No, you'll get nowhere with that. There weren't any." Mies Bouhuys heard me out patiently and then said: "One of my best girlfriends was in a special squad that bumped off high-ranking SD and Gestapo officers. Would you like to talk to her?" Of course I did! Mies collected me from the station in Amsterdam. She could not have been kinder to me, acting as my driver and tourist guide. She introduced me to other female and male friends of hers who had been in the resistance and drove me out to Venhuizen, where Truus Menger, the woman I was keen to interview, lives.

In the little house that Truus shares with her husband, daughter, and son-in-law, there was coffee and cake waiting for us. On the walls there were photographs, a guitar that Truus had salvaged from the war, an oil painting, and a picture of a young woman with thick, wavy hair. "That's Hannie Schaft," Truus explained, "the third woman in our team. There's a book about her and a film called *The Red-haired Girl*."

Truus' sculptures were all over the house. Some years after the war, she had decided to become a sculptress and since then had been working as an artist of some repute. After our conversation, she brought me into the studio that she had set up in an old shed. As evening fell, Truus took me back to Amsterdam, and on the way we stopped off to see her sister

Freddie, the third legendary figure in the feared Truus-Freddie-Hannie trio so frantically sought by the Germans. Freddie, like Truus, had married a former comrade-in-arms and was sitting in front of the television with her grandchildren. "No, absolutely no trouble at all," she assured us and she fetched us some glasses and a few bottles of beer. She invited us to make ourselves comfortable and asked what I wanted to know, although she was sure that Truus would have told me the whole story already. The two sisters took turns at carrying the conversation, dredging up anecdotes about the most trivial and amusing aspects of their super-terrorist days, when they headed the Gestapo's most-wanted list. But when they began to talk about their lives since the liberation they became more serious again. For the first time, Freddie's husband butted in to the conversation: "Have you told her how we were persecuted as Communists?" he asked Truus. Yes, that she had. In the course of our chat, conducted in English, they used the German expressions Neonazis and Berufsverbot (a West German legal ordinance passed by the Social Democrat government under which active Communists or anarchists could be barred from certain occupations in the public sector, such as teacher, postman, etc.) They were keen to find out if today's German youth were different, and were hoping for a resounding assurance that they were.

While dining in Amsterdam later, Truus told me: "You know, every time I set eyes on Germans of my own age, I can't help wondering what they were doing at that time." Once, she went camping in the south of France with her husband. Alongside them, a slightly older German couple erected their tent, friendly sorts who would invite them for coffee now and again. Truus and Pit decided to swallow their prejudices, and stayed on for dinner at the Germans' place. "And as the time wore on, and we had a few drinks, the conversation started to turn towards the war. The husband had been in Russia and the wife talked about the nighttime air raids. And then he said to us: 'You Dutch were the lucky ones. You didn't have to go through what we did. You only had the occupation to put up with.'"

The route to Nancy passed through Paris and Geneva. By then I had given up any chance of interviewing a fighting woman from the French resistance. Several conversations in France had not led to anything concrete. I had staked everything on Rita Thalmann, a professor at the University of Paris, a feminist and expert on the Third Reich. When I eventually managed to track her down, she readily agreed to help me. Shortly before, I had been reading an article in *Le Monde* where the initials MOI were used for the first time. According to that article, the MOI, or Main d'Oeuvre Immigrée, had been one of the most active resistance groups in France, comprised mainly of Jewish immigrants from eastern Europe. Nothing was said about the women members of the group, but this was nothing new to me, and was no impediment to my beginning to make inquiries in that direction. Whenever I mentioned the MOI to Rita Thalmann, she needed no further explanation. Unsolicited, she gave me the names of two women who had fought with that organization. "And I'm sure there must be more," she added, taking that for granted. But I would have to have a word with Herbert Herz, a childhood friend of hers who had been in the MOI and who was currently working on a history of the group. She did not hesitate at all before supplying me with his address and a letter of recommendation. By then, I was used to such small tokens of help and unconditional support, but even so I was taken aback and grateful. Herbert Herz suggested that we meet up in Nancy with his friends, the ex-resistance fighters Dina and Henri Krischer. Which is how I was able to speak with Dina at some length and consult her extensive archives as well.

Dina and Henri received me with a cordiality that made me feel abashed. I am Austrian, and at the time the world was in turmoil over the Waldheim affair. Anyway, people like the Krischers had known well before the Waldheim business that Austria had not been an innocent casualty of Nazi Germany and that Hitler had learned his anti-Semitism in Vienna.

The only thing that the Krischers knew about me was that I came with a recommendation from Rita Thalmann and Herbert Herz—Herz's knowledge of me being confined to a telephone conversation we'd had. They would just have to trust me as far as all the rest went. We spent the morning of our first day putting questions to one another. We chatted about Waldheim and Le Pen. I talked to them of my work on the resistance by the Jews in eastern Europe and about the women I had interviewed thus far. That afternoon, Dina ordered me to cancel my hotel reservation. She prepared a bed for me in her work room. She cooked for me as if I were a queen. And when we were not sitting over a meal, she was continually feeding me sweets. For two days and one night, Dina and Henri, Herbert Herz and Jacquot Szmulewicz told me all about their struggle against the Germans. And about how that struggle had been marginalized following the liberation; about the great difficulties they'd had in their efforts to rescue that struggle from oblivion and silence and to organize an archive on the MOI groups in the south of France. Friends, former comrades-in-arms, were invited to help fill in the details that the Krischers could not quite recall. When I volunteered at one point that perhaps they were growing tired and that I felt guilty about working them so hard and putting them to so much trouble, Henri replied by telling me: "You know, we're always delighted if anybody shows any interest in our story. But you're the first one to have come from Germany. That is a special joy for us."

It was in the German weekly, *Der Spiegel*, that I came across her photograph: A gallows with three people hanged from it. To the right and left, a man, and in the middle a young woman. Three Minsk partisans, the caption at the foot of the photograph read, the woman a Jew whose name has not yet been verified. I redoubled my determination to include the resistance in eastern Europe in my book as well. But my project was continually in danger of foundering for lack of material. I knew, of course, that there had been an uprising in the Warsaw ghetto and I took it for granted, as ever, that women too had played an active part in the rebellion. The photograph in *Der Spiegel* confirmed that supposition, but that still left the problem of the lack of written documentation. Mere hypothesis is not enough for a well-founded historical inquiry. But I was still obsessed with the matter. In the end I turned to Monika Richarz, director of Germania Judaica in Cologne. Although skeptical, she was patient enough to go through her library catalogue with me. And, in fact, we turned up a few book titles in English that seemed fairly promising. I had finally come to the end of the line.

I was now faced with a demanding jigsaw, but it was worth the trouble. A world I had never even suspected opened up before my eyes, the world of ghetto uprisings, partisan bands in the Polish forests, a resistance about which no one in the country, with the exception of a few insiders, had even the slightest notion. It was about the time when I was spending all day at Germania Judaica in Cologne that WDR—German television's channel three—screened a film about the Vilna partisans, *Die Partizanen von Wilna*, directed by Aviva Kempner and Josh Waletzky. Straightaway, I wrote to Aviva Kempner who wrote back immediately and sent me the addresses in Israel of the women survivors who had fought in the ghetto. It was around the same time that a three-volume *Anthology on Jewish Armed Resistance* appeared in the United States, news passed on to me by Monika Richarz. It supplied the final pieces of the jigsaw.

The object of the present book is to offer an historical introduction and analysis of the part played by women in the armed resistance. I should also like it to pay tribute to history's unknown heroines: Fifi, Zala, Truus, Dina, Chayke and Niuta. And all the others.

Ingrid Strobl
Cologne 1994

The Three-Fold Stigma

Warsaw: one elderly man, three young men in determined poses, armed with rifles, hand grenades, knives, and stones—fighters. Before them, a colleague fallen in the fray. Behind, a woman in surrender. Breast exposed, cradling a child in her arms, she is no fighter; she is a symbol. The symbol of Jewish resistance, of the rebellion in the Warsaw ghetto against the might of the German assassins. The monument stands upon a huge swathe of greenery on the site of the former ghetto which the Germans razed completely after crushing the uprising. The front part of the monument shows a battle scene: the rear, the deportation of defenseless victims. An endless stream of women, old men, and children shuffling along, shoulders hunched, heads down, shuffling towards their deaths. A single child turns towards the onlooker, gazing into the future. The child is male.

On January 11, 1943, SS Reichsführer Himmler, wrote to SS Obergruppenführer Krüger, the head of security with the Generalgouvernement, to order the Warsaw ghetto destroyed by February 15. On January 18, SS troops accompanied by Latvian and Lithuanian auxiliary troops, and by Polish police, entered the ghetto with tank and machine-gun.

Although it had long known that just such a "big Aktion" was in the offing, this early morning incursion caught the ZOB, the Jewish resistance movement, off guard. Only some of its female and male fighters managed to snatch up their weapons, but their reaction was swift. When the Germans passed by the workshops in Gesia Street on the southern boundaries of the central ghetto (what the Germans termed the "leftover ghetto"), a hand grenade landed in the midst of their troops. This was the signal for battle to be joined. The grenade had been thrown by a woman, Emilia Landau, a member of the left-wing Zionist Hashomer Hatzair's youth organization.[1] Some weeks previously, Emilia Landau and two male colleagues had killed Jakob Leijkin, the ghetto's police delegate, one of the most feared of the Nazis' collaborators.[2] Emilia

1

Landau was not by any means the only woman involved in the armed ghetto uprising, nor was she the only one to play a significant part in it. Female participation in the fighting was on such a massive scale that, six years on, in 1949, SS Gruppenführer Jürgen Stroop, the still bewildered divisional SS and police general, the butcher of the rebels, was telling his cell-mate in Warsaw's Mokotow prison:

> The third thing...that held my attention [was] the Jewish women's participation in the fighting. I mean the groups organized by the *halutzeh* movement.[3]

> Those girls were not human; goddesses or demons they may well have been. They had the sangfroid and dexterity of circus Amazons. They were often shooting away with both hands at the same time. To the end, they fought stubbornly and with tenacity.[4]

Such was the terror they struck in the heroic members of the SS that the latter made up their minds not to jail these women, but to dispatch them then and there like wild animals. Stroop says:

> And they were especially dangerous at close quarters. One of these *halutzeh* girls, when arrested, initially gave the impression of being as meek as a lamb: but, lo and behold, when one of our soldiers passed within a few paces of her, she fetched a concealed hand grenade from under her skirt and in a flash tossed it into the middle of the SS group, and that was just one instance!... In this situation, it was only to be expected that we should sustain fatalities and casualties on our side, which is why I issued the order that no attempt was to be made to take these women alive, that under no circumstances should they be allowed to get too close, and that they should be dispatched at a safe distance by machine-gun.[5]

St. Genis-Laval, France: A commemorative plaque upon a wall: "Jeanine Sontag. Heroine of the Bataillon Carmagnole-Liberté of the FTP-MOI, murdered on this spot on 20-8-1944."

A law student at Strasbourg, Jeanine Sontag was nineteen years old when she joined the Communist partisans in Lyon. Being Jewish, she joined the MOI (Main d'Oeuvre Immigrée, the organization made up of immigrant workers from a variety of nations, a high percentage of them Jewish). In the summer of 1944, the Lyon branches of the FTP-MOI, known as the Carmagnole, were driving the Germans to despair. On a daily basis, they blew up factories, warehouses, garages, and vehicle depots, executing Gestapo and SD (Security Service) officers, and holding up firms whose owners were collaborating with the Nazis. By night, they derailed trains. Jeanine Sontag was not the only female member of the unit, which may well have been the most effective in the entire French resistance. On July 3, in broad daylight, a dozen MOI activists raided the Gambetta garage. Among the raiders was Jeanine Sontag, nicknamed Jeannette. But the raid was a failure, the garage was cordoned off by the GMR (Groupe Mobile de Réserve, the French anti-terrorist unit): the activists attempted to escape across a narrow plank to an adjacent rooftop. Jeannette was wearing some cheap wooden shoes, which proved her downfall: she slipped and fell and hurt herself and was arrested. On August 20, after weeks of torture, she was executed alongside 120 other resistance fighters in St. Genis-Laval.[6]

Haarlem, Netherlands: The statue, the work of a woman, stands four meters high and represents a woman. It symbolizes the role of women in the Dutch resistance to the German occupation. But this extraordinary monument also represents an actual person, Hannie Schaft, a student, twenty-three years old at the time she died.

On March 26, 1945, as on so many other occasions, Hannie was out cycling. This time, hers was a comparatively innocuous mission. It was not—as it had customarily been—the killing of a Gestapo officer or a traitor. On this occasion, she was merely moving a new edition of the underground Communist newspaper *De Waarheid* (The Truth). But, as usual, Hannie was carrying a handgun. Ever since she had gone underground, she had not taken a single step without a gun. Hannie wore her hair short and black and she was wearing glasses with plain lenses, since the whole of Holland was plastered with posters showing her photograph. The Germans were searching for the "red-headed girl," one of the most feared of the terrorists.

On this March 26, with liberation only a few weeks away, Hannie ran into a German patrol which promptly arrested her. Her colleagues tried in vain to free her. Her friend and comrade-in-arms, Truus Menger, tried relentlessly to rescue her, right up until she learned of Hannie's death.[7] Truus Menger, one of the most active female fighters in the

Dutch armed resistance, would, in time, become a sculptress. When a competition was launched in 1983 for a monument to be raised to Hannie Schaft's memory, Truus Menger entered, along with 119 other sculptors, and she won. Knowing first hand what women had contributed to that unequal struggle, she was able to raise a monument to the memory of her friend, a symbol of all the female fighters. She regards the four meters as scarcely adequate.

There are two myths that have survived stubbornly for decades: that the Jews went like lambs to the slaughter and that women, although they may have performed various tasks auxiliary to the resistance, played no part in the armed struggle. Even some Jewish historians (Raoul Hilberg, for one) deplore the minimal resistance offered by the millions murdered.[8] And non-Jews wonder, not without a touch of cynicism: why did they do nothing to defend themselves, if there were so many of them?

Rita Thalmann presented a paper to a symposium of the Association for Research into Contemporary Jewish History on her latest research into the matter of women in the French resistance. Of seventeen works dealing with the role of women in the resistance, thirteen have appeared since 1971, which is to say, since the first significant stirrings of French feminism. Of the four that appeared prior to then, three were written between 1945 and 1947.[9]

The same can also be said of Polish, Hebrew, and Yiddish bibliographies. Works in which the role of women is expressly mentioned or underlined were written by eyewitnesses or actual participants in the years right after the liberation, when memories were still fresh and accurate.[10]

A few decades later, by which time feminist studies had been established in the United States and there had been a general change of consciousness with regard to women, a few authors of Jewish-Polish origins began to attract more and more attention with their historical studies written in English and concentrating upon the importance of women in the Jewish resistance context.[11] Generally speaking, though, hardly any book from a Jewish pen fails to make some mention of the matter of women's participation in the resistance. The survivors of the mass slaughter who have to battle against the myth of their passivity, are proud of their fighting women.

The bibliography in German on the topic of the armed resistance is very sparse. Bernhard Mark's book on the Warsaw ghetto uprising, published in the former German Democratic Republic, is one of the few exceptions known to us.[12] In the Federal Republic of Germany everything has been shrouded in silence for upwards of forty years. Those few historical works that deal with women in the resistance focus solely upon the resistance within the Reich. Since there was—with few exceptions—virtually no armed resistance in Germany, this aspect is barely touched upon in the important accounts by Hanna Elling, Margarete Schütte-Lihotzky, Gerda Szepansky and the panel of Viennese authors Berger, Holzinger, Podgornik and Trallori.[13]

I am not aware of any detailed study of organized armed resistance in the European nations occupied by Germany and the former Soviet Union. The bibliographies I have used are (with the exception of a few books published in the now-defunct German Democratic Republic) mostly in French or English (a fair proportion of them translations from the Polish, Yiddish, or Hebrew), or in Dutch, Spanish, or Serbo-Croat (in English translation).

But even in the countries directly affected, it sometimes took decades before pertinent works could see the light of day. A sizable segment of the active resistance is doubly stigmatized: being Jewish and Communist. In western European countries, from France to the Netherlands, immediately upon their return from exile (usually in London) after the liberation, the governments wasted no time before launching their counter-offensives: the importance of the Communist resistance was side-stepped and even silenced. Later, with the Cold War, those who had but recently emerged from clandestinity found themselves the victims of persecution again. The western powers, knowing of the Communists' decisive part in the fight against the Occupation and for liberation, were afraid of the influence that these sadly unappreciated heroines and heroes might exercise over the population. The thought of a great success or victory by Communist parties in elections in the liberated nations was something that they found unbearable. The official tributes to the heroic figures of the liberation focused upon the domestic military forces of the exiled governments, upon the French Forces of the Interior for instance, or else upon the Dutch military forces under the command of Prince Bernhard.[14]

But in Israel, too, in the context of official Jewish historiography, the role of the Jewish Communist fighters was ignored rather than highlighted. To date, the partisans of the MOI have not been regarded—or at least have only been so regarded with reservations—as belonging to the Jewish resistance.[15] This is because, although many MOI members were Jewish immigrants and although a few subgroups were made up almost exclusively of Jews who spoke to one another in Yiddish and published their newspapers in that tongue, they were not organized specifically as Jews (the way the Zionists were), but rather as Communists.

The tale of the MOI is a tale of tragic oblivion, because even their own colleagues failed to show them gratitude for the struggle they waged. Nobody could have ignored the fact that many of the terrorists most feared by the Nazis bore such unlikely French names as Szmulewicz, Grzwacz, Puterflam, Fingerweig, and Bancic. And this did not quite fit in with the nationalism peddled during those final years of the war, when the Communist Party of France, reneging upon its earlier internationalism, decided to demonstrate that it was at least as patriotic as De Gaulle's followers; these Jews, most of them not even French Jews, but Polish, Hungarian, Rumanian, and Armenian immigrants, suddenly became a blemish on this newly devised image. Some MOI leaders, whose existence could not so easily be ignored, were urged to swap their surnames for French ones.[16]

A similar tragedy was played out in the Soviet Union and in Poland. Thousands of Jewish women and men had joined the partisans and had set up partisan units of their own, had fought for years and paid a countless toll of lives in the struggle. And, in spite of everything, scarcely any mention was made of their part. Not until many years later was it discovered that many of the partisan leaders were Jews.[17] In Poland, the anti-semitism of much of the population endured after the defeat of the German occupation forces. Initially, so as not to aggravate this anti-semitism, and, later, during the anti-semitic campaign under Gomulka—who harnessed the sentiment for political-party purposes—the Polish party kept quiet about the Jewish population's unparalleled role in the partisan struggle and in the ghetto uprisings.[18]

The myth that the Jews did not lift a finger to avoid extermination was systematically woven and soon came to be regarded as historical fact. The Communist resistance could not be so easily ignored in the post-war western states, but it did not form part of the official historical record taught in the schools and universities, the contents of which are transmitted through popular novels and displayed in TV movies.

Street-fighting against the rebel military.

In the Federal Republic of Germany, the armed resistance to the German occupation has been hushed up for another, more telling reason. In any event, what furnished the popular theme in newspaper articles, films, and television documentaries was the French resistance. But, here too, the focus of interest was on persecution: Espionage, detention, torture, and deportation to the concentration camps have a much higher profile than resistance activities, which is scarcely surprising, in that these activities were directed against Germans. German soldiers travelled on the trains that the partisans derailed. The officers of the German security service that Dutch resistance fighters gunned down in the streets were German officers. The troops who perished in a partisan ambush in the forests of Lithuania were their own brothers, fathers, and grandfathers.

An historical inquiry taking account of the armed resistance in the occupied countries in Europe has to keep repeating one thing: these women and men were fighting against Germans. It is a fact that many of the soldiers dispatched to fight Hitler's war were not in agreement with their mission and derived no satisfaction whatsoever from it: they feared the Red Army's partisans and their superiors and were also afraid to desert. But, whereas the struggle against the Red Army was at least out in the open, the partisans mounted surprise attacks, popping up unexpectedly, opening fire, derailing the train, and vanishing again. No one could tell when or where they might pop up again out of nowhere.

And, above all, the common or garden-variety German army sergeant who—without ever having had the chance to choose for himself—had been stationed in France, Belgium, or the Netherlands, had to regard the resistance as his worst enemy. Even as he was square-bashing in his barracks in Lyon or Grenoble, a bomb might suddenly explode in the ranks, and this while the troops were sauntering victorious through a quiet country that had surrendered. He was not on the front lines here, and yet here was the enemy suddenly confronting him.

Female and male, the armed fighters were conscious of this fact. Internationalists as they were, they understood that many of these German soldiers were simple workers like themselves. In their attentats, they were very selective in the choice of their targets: SD officers, Gestapo officers, SS officers, collaborators, and traitors.

In eastern Europe and in the Soviet Union, the situation of the partisans was very different. They were faced by an army that was laying their country waste, murdering people, and razing entire towns. As a rule, an ordinary soldier played no part in the implementation of the *Endlösung*—the systematic extermination of the Jewish population—but, by his presence, he stood as guarantor for it. Every yard that the German army had to retreat spelled hopes of survival for the few Jews still successfully hiding out in the cities and forests of Poland, the Soviet Union, and Lithuania. Every army unit obliged to busy itself with fighting the partisans was another unit denied the front lines.

The women and men whose parents, children, and siblings were incinerated in the crematoria at Treblinka and Auschwitz, or who were obliged to use their own hands to dig the ditch into which they would be tumbled by a volley of machine-gun fire from their killers, could show no consideration to one of the members of the German army who performed his duty to perfection by ensuring the flawless operation of that colossal murder machine, even though he might not be happy to be in this strange land, freezing in blizzards, and having to open fire upon folk in the opposing trenches who might well have been quivering with fear just as much as he was.

What this means is that the mere fact of being a Communist or Jew was often reason enough for one to be ignored in the historiography of the resistance. Being a Communist Jew virtually guaranteed that one would be ignored utterly by the official histories, east or west. Being a woman, even when it carried no additional stigma, was likewise reason enough for one to be simply invisible, and most of the women dealt with in this book were Jews or Communists to boot. Some were both.

Ideology aside, the prevailing idea then and, to some extent, now was that women and fighting are mutually exclusive. In recent years, thanks to the efforts made by feminists in the writing of her-story, which is to say, the history of the female population, it has proved possible to secure acknowledgment of the fact that women made a decisive contribution to the fight against fascism and national socialism. Interviews with former activists and historical research have shown that the infrastructure underpinning all manner of resistance was the handiwork primarily of the women. It was the women who moved and were partly responsible for the printing of illegal publications. The women carried and distributed anti-regime leaflets and stickers. The women sabotaged the armaments plants. The women hid partisans and other underground fighters, looking after the feeding and maintenance of them. All of these activities were subject to persecution and were punished severely with deportation to a concentration camp or, in many instances, with death. Thousands of women were executed for their support of the resistance, thousands perished in the concentration camps or as a result of torture, or took their own lives for fear that they might not withstand the torture and thereby betray other people. The enemy never made any distinction between the leading light and the ordinary general-purpose girl.

Any activity in the resistance carried infinite risks, terrors, continual changes in domicile, utter discretion, and very often, loneliness and the constant risk of losing one's life. And, whereas the active fighter, when arrested, might still try to defend himself with his weapon, the unarmed woman with her shopping basket filled with illegal handbills was utterly at the mercy of her pursuers.

The position of the Austrian and German Communists working in France and in Belgium under the auspices of the so-called *Travaille Allemande* (TA) was particularly precarious: their task was to strike up friendships with German soldiers in order either to wheedle significant war intelligence out of them or to persuade them to desert.[19] It was not uncommon for these women to risk their very honor and, although nobody acknowledges it, it cannot be ruled out that they may well have been despised by their own colleagues for this very reason. After the war, many of these female TA workers suffered the people's wrath. All that their neighbors knew was that they had been going with Germans—on which basis they were labelled collaborators and subjected to verbal abuse in the street.[20]

From the working woman who let her apartment be used as a hiding place for clandestines to the TA agent, all of these women performed quintessentially female roles which, when all is said and done, implied no breach with the traditional womanly role. They took care of the housework, the food, and other menial tasks. They did what women were allowed to do. One exception was the functionaries who shared in the policy decision-making, albeit only rarely from really high-up posts. But the ones who really made a complete break with the woman's realm were the fighters who took on the enemy with guns in their hands.

There is hardly any information about them because scarcely any (male) historians could even imagine that they could have existed. Even when female partisans and women fighters are mentioned in the reports of survivors, the facts and the details are left out. Even when survivors specifically refer to these women, their allusions are then ignored, because they do not fit in with expectations, because the male historian himself looks upon such conduct as unbecoming of women and believes that to mention women bearing arms is to cast aspersions upon the underground group in question. In the interviewing of former resistance members, it is an automatic reflex to seek out only the males. Rarely does it occur to anyone to ask the woman serving the coffee during the interview if, perhaps, she too... Not that the women themselves speak up. They keep quiet for lots of reasons: out of feminine modesty, because they do not want to seem self-important, because they never learned to speak up for themselves, because they themselves regard themselves as insignificant, because they have been embittered by the responses of their own comrades-in-arms. Spanish women frontline fighters told me that even in their own party they were looked upon as prostitutes. The blue overalls, the militians' suit of honor, once donned by a woman, become the livery of the outcast. Other former fighters have taken to their hearts the established image of what constitutes femininity. They insist that, even if they belonged to an armed unit, they never actually fired a shot. And, until such time as they gain some more confidence, they will not say how things really were. Women like the Frenchwoman Dina Krischer of the MOI who told me: "The Germans used to call us terrorists. And terrorists we were, in fact. We wanted to strike terror into the Germans. To get them to clear out once and for all, to end the killing once and for all." But the number of women who speak in such terms is small. But all of the old fighters with whom I spoke at greater length were agreed upon one thing. Fifí, who fought on the front in the Spanish civil war, put it like this: "I am happy to have done what needed doing at the time. And in similar circumstances I would do the same again."

In 1947 a book appeared in New York called *Blessed is the Match*. American journalist Marie Syrkin had travelled to Palestine to interview survivors of the Polish and Lithuanian ghettos about their struggle and their life. The book that she wrote on the basis of these conversations with partisans and underground fighters of both sexes was the first to deal emphatically with the female side of armed resistance. And, for a long time, the last. Vera Laska's study *Women in the Resistance and Holocaust* was published in Connecticut in 1983, wherein the author refers to a number of instances of women who played a part in the resistance's armed struggle. But such cases are in a minority in the book, which offers the first panoramic insight into the involvement of women in the resistance in Europe. Meanwhile, a number of articles and autobiographies have come out, most in Hebrew or in Yiddish, and, some of them, later, in English translation. A few books on women's activities against the occupation in Italy, Yugoslavia, Greece and the Soviet Union may be found in the appropriate specialist archives and libraries, sleeping peacefully like Sleeping Beauty.

Whereas in western history books—with the exception of Jewish history—active female fighters are all but ignored, the attitude of Soviet historiography is more ambivalent. During the war and immediately after it, many of the former female partisans and Red Army soldiers were awarded the highest decorations and their names were listed in the appropriate bibliography. But while these women helped drive the invaders from their country at the risk of their own lives, dressed in filthy, threadbare uniforms, famished and exhausted, Olga Mischakowa, secretary of the central committee of the Communist Youth organization, declared in an interview in 1944: "Soviet women must try to make themselves as attractive as nature and good taste will allow. After the war they must dress like women and move like women... Girls must be told to behave and move like girls and, to that end, they will probably have to be made to wear very tight skirts that force them to walk gracefully."[21] Nowhere is there any reference to how repatriated partisan women reacted, assuming they did, to this affront to their entire existence.

The position of other women, from Toulouse to Haarlem, was not much different. Some married former comrades-in-arms, others returning first to the parental home—in which case they just got on with their lives. Those women who had been leading a clandestine existence, with precarious support from the Party or other organizations, during the years when others were completing their schooling now found themselves in dire economic straits. They had to contend emotionally with a milieu that did not understand them, labelled as they were as mannish women in a world where traditionally feminine values were in ascendancy yet again. In every country, employment positions were filled by repatriated soldiers, prisoners of war, and men returning from penal servitude in Germany. Women were restored to their household role. There were quite a few of them who willingly embraced this course, out of exhaustion and the necessity of finally living a normal life—which is how they vanished from the scene. With only a few exceptions, they did not settle down to write books, did not struggle to secure the positions that were due them in the Party hierarchy, nor did they attend meetings of the veterans' organizations. They withdrew into silence and no one tried to make them talk. The exceptions, the ones who found a publisher for their books, the ones who did rise to a position of importance in the Party, the ones whose testimony was placed on record, merely served to confirm the rule.

Thus far, we have not been able to search through the mountains of existing bibliographies, the scattered elements, the jigsaw pieces, that may finally allow us to piece together a modest portrait of a woman combatant. It takes a lot of detective work just to find survivors to whom questions can be put. To the women I was able to speak to in the Netherlands, France, Austria, and Spain, I was also able to put personal questions about their childhood years, their origins, their motives, and their life since the war. To begin with, many of them could not even understand such questions. In each and every conversation, they first regaled me with the official version of the facts, starting with their entry into the underground organization, the frontline militia, or some partisan unit and ending with the defeat of the Germans, or, in the Spanish case, with the ending of the Francoist dictatorship. When I pressed them about the reasons why they opted for that course of action, they replied: "But what else could we have done?" It was only after a lot of talk, after a few glasses of wine, and after they had subjected me, the interviewer, to a sort of interrogation that a proper conversation emerged.

In setting out the struggle of Jewish women in eastern Europe and the Soviet Union, I have had to confine myself to the existing bibliographical record. I was forever running up against the same problem: in most of the books in Yiddish, and even though each of the women may be named, not a word is said about their lives or only a very perfunctory outline is provided. Whereas, when it comes to the male commanders we get their origins, political evolution, and line of work, the women are mentioned only in relation to some specific operation before dropping out of sight again. In virtually every book on the Warsaw ghetto, we find at least a cursory outline biography of the ZOB commander, Mordecai Anielewicz. Concerning his wife Mira Fuchrer, also an active member of the ZOB, who also lived in the leadership's hideout (which relatives were not allowed to enter, even if they were themselves members of the leadership) we find, at most, the information that she perished in the hideout alongside her husband and others. Since the women were not in command, there was no interest in presenting them as personalities. But there were some women who rose to command a battalion and we know no more about them than we do about a mere militant. Then again, we get the personal histories of men who held no particular leadership position. But, in order to piece together the story of Niuta Tejtelbojm, one of the most effective and daring fighters in the Warsaw resistance, I have had to bring together pieces of the jigsaw from four separate books.

Even though, in spite of my intensive inquiries, I have assuredly been able to collect information on only a fraction of women's actual part in the armed, military resistance to fascism and German occupation, the picture that it suggests is impressive. From Madrid to Bialystok, from Belgrade to Amsterdam, there were women who took up arms to fight the fascist invaders. The following examples may offer an initial overall impression of the phenomenon:

- The first sabotage operation in Lithuania was carried out by a woman. Nineteen-year-old Vitka Kempner, a member of Vilna's underground Jewish organization, the FPO, spent three days keeping watch on the rail line out of Vilna, then managed to smuggle a bomb out of the ghetto and, with the aid of two male comrades, placed it on the tracks, where, on July 8, 1942 it blew up a train carrying German troop reinforcements.[22]
- Halina Mazanik, a member of the underground organization in Minsk, worked as a maid in the home of the feared commissar-general for Belarus, Wilhelm Kube, who had made his name as a specialist in atrocities. On September 21, 1943, Halina Mazanik placed a bomb under Kube's bed. It killed him.[23]
- For weeks at a time, women sentenced to penal servitude in an arms plant in Auschwitz surreptitiously smuggled out explosive materials that they passed on to Roza Robota, a member of an underground group inside the concentration camp. Roza Robota, in turn, passed this dangerous merchandise to the crematorium special commando, thereby making it possible for them to revolt and blow up one of the murderous ovens.[24]
- For months, Sima Perston, aged twelve, guided people from the Minsk ghetto by surreptitious routes to the partisans in the forest. She carried a pistol on her at all times, in a concealed pocket. When asked what she would do in the event of her being taken unawares, she answered: "Have no fear. They won't take me alive."[25]
- Rosario, known as *la Dinamitera*, was assuredly the only female dynamiter on the front in the Spanish civil war. Dynamiters manufactured hand grenades with which the ill-equipped republican troops fought the fascist aggressors. One such grenade, which she had made for herself, blew off her right hand.[26]
- Parisienne, Marie-Madeleine Fourcade, mother of two, was the only woman to lead an important Gaullist resistance unit. She was the head of the Alliance espionage network known to the Germans as "Noah's Ark" because its members all used animal names as code names. The Alliance had a membership of 3,000 and was the first defense organization to brief the Allies on the manufacture of V-1 missiles at Peenemunde. Not until the last moment did the Germans discover that the "gang leader" for whom they were frantically search-

ing was a woman. And, at the start, even her British superiors had no idea that they were not dealing with a man.[27]

· Upwards of 100,000 women belonged to Tito's partisan army in Yugoslavia. On August 25, 1942, the first of several women's battalions was established. Slovene textile worker Pavle Mede Katarina commanded the women's section of the Pohor battalion. In January 1943, she was killed in action against the Germans on Pohorje mountain.[28]

· In issue No. 14 of the news bulletin *Feind-Nachtrichtenblatt* (News-Sheet on the Enemy) of July–August 1944, published by the high command of Army Group E in occupied Greece, a report on the "gangs" states: "The formation of women's sections has been broadly confirmed. These are almost always crack groups of twenty to twenty-five women. They are trained in the use of rifle and machine-gun. It appears that any slight or insult to these women is punished with the utmost severity (the death penalty). In Thessaly, there are mounted EPON women's sections which mount guard on villages and distribute antifascist propaganda."[29]

· On May 18, 1942, the Herbert Baum Group, which was made up of Berlin Jews, mounted a bomb attack on Goebbels' propaganda exhibition, "The Soviet Paradise." It was one of the few armed feats of the German resistance. Three of the group that planted the bomb were men and four were women.[30]

· Daily briefing No. 3 from the Gestapo command in Cologne states: "It came to light on 10-12-1944...that members of a gang had taken refuge in a street near the main Greek market. Upon entering the basement premises, officials met with resistance from within. An assault team made up of local officials took action against the bandits, using machine-guns and hand grenades... In the course of the operation a long sought after chief killed himself, one gang member and a woman were found dead and another woman was arrested."[31]

· Even in the jaws of death there were women who resisted. A group from the Hotel Polski arrived in Auschwitz on October 23, 1943. In a treacherous ploy organized to perfection, the Gestapo had issued an appeal to Jews in hiding in Warsaw to report to the Hotel Polski, with a promise that they would be allowed to emigrate to South America. Many swallowed this lie and emerged from the relative safety of their hideouts, only to be shipped from the hotel to the gas chambers in Birkenau. This transport included an actress or dancer (the sources mention both occupations) by the name of Horowitz. In the changing room outside the gas chamber, the commander of the chief SS platoon, Schillinger, notorious for his sadism, ordered her peremptorily to strip immediately. The woman picked up her clothes and flung them into his face, grabbing his pistol and shooting him in the belly. Schillinger died shortly afterwards on his way to hospital. Horowitz also opened fire on SS man Emmerich, but the latter recovered from his injuries. In the commotion that followed the woman's completely unexpected action (she acted alone as far as we can tell), lots of prisoners aped her example, disarming the guards posted there and the fighting carried on until they ran out of ammunition. Only then did the SS—camp commandant Hoss had arrived in person to mop up this catastrophe—get them to back down.[32]

Resistance in Western Europe

Spain

"I didn't come to the front to give it the once over with a cleaning rag in my hand."

On July 18, 1936, the date on which the fascist military mutinied against the Spanish Republic's Popular Front government, sixteen-year-old Rosario Sánchez Mora set off for school as she did every day. She was a girl from the provinces who had moved to Madrid to learn dressmaking at the Centro Cultural Aida Lafuente, a trade school run by the Unified Socialist Youth (JSU). On July 20, a gang of young men arrived at the school, bringing pencils and paper, and classes were interrupted so that they might say a few words about the import of the military coup and the necessity to put up ferocious resistance to it. At the conclusion of his harangue, the young Communist orator asked those present to offer themselves as volunteers. He said *"voluntarios,"* meaning male volunteers, rather than *"voluntarias."* Rosario Sánchez Mora relates: "I looked around and realized that, naturally, there were women only in our dressmaking class. So I raised a finger and timidly asked: Can we women sign up as well? 'Yes' the young man told me. Then put me down. 'Sure, *compañera,* we'll be getting in touch.' And he did." At eight o'clock the next morning, Rosario boarded the lorry that was to ferry her out to the front.[33]

The fascist officers' coup attempt had not only thrown the political situation into disarray, but had upset the day-to-day lives of the population with its traditional distinctions between the social roles of each sex, something particularly rigid in Spain. Sixteen-year-old girls swapped their dresses for the military uniforms of the militias, slung a rifle over their shoulders, and took off for the war. Housewives lent a hand to the efforts to organize the social lives of the populace. During those first days and weeks following the outbreak of the war, a revolution within the revolution took place. With disbelief, all of the witnesses would later describe how the women adopted a new way of acting, something that seemed all the more startling, in that this was Spain.[34] The vast majority of Spanish women labored under the dictatorship of poverty, Church, and husband. Up until the advent of the Republic in 1931, they had virtually no rights, were paid poverty wages, and had no organization to look out for their interests.[35] In practice, even the anarchists whose program called for equal rights for women never lifted a finger, even within the unions, much less at a personal level.[36]

Most Spanish women at the beginning of the 1930s were still putting in eighteen hours working in the fields for poverty wages. Female workers were exploited with impunity in small firms, at work in their own homes, or in the homes of others. The introduction of the eight-hour-work day, as introduced by the republican government in 1931, and the simultaneous establishment of a social security system did most of them no good at all; these measures benefited only the workers in large firms and industries—where the work force was predominantly male. Generally speaking, female workers received no sort of social assistance, the costs of which were borne by their employer, not even if it could be demonstrated that they were the sole breadwinner.[37] Only the Divorce Law brought them any benefit, in that they could now leave an unduly violent husband—in theory at least. In practice, very few women would have dared take that step, which meant exposing themselves to the risk of being looked upon and treated as a prostitute and having to eke out a living on the meager wages paid to women. The legislation passed against prostitution turned out to be plainly legislation against prostitutes, which is to say, against a considerable number of women who found themselves obliged to earn their living that way, or to add a little to their meager earnings through occasional prostitution.[38]

With the victory of the Popular Front or with the war triggered by the coup d'etat of July 1936, the circumstances of Spanish women underwent a radical change. The men went to the fronts, the women stepping into the jobs that they had left vacant, and this very fact allowed them to reach a fresh appreciation of themselves. All of a sudden, they were being asked to display qualities and aptitudes which, for centuries, they had been denied, and they were being depended upon. In terms of legislation, scarcely anything changed the lot of women, although the anarchist Federica Montseny, Minister of Health, did manage to push through the decriminalization of abortion. The collectivization of social life in anarchist Barcelona, for instance, was exclusively in the hands of the women. The Swiss woman, Clara Thalmann, who had come to Spain in 1936 and then thrown in her lot with the woman fighters, describes the situation in the Catalan capital thus: "Women who previously had looked after their own family now had decision-making power: The flour reaching the bakery would have to produce so much bread. They organized street checkpoints and pricing, in concert with the Control Commission which stepped in to deal with difficult cases. Otherwise, the women did it all themselves."[39] And they did it well. Clara Thalmann again: "For as long as the women and the workers maintained checks there was a daily bread supply. Unlike in every revolution and every war where poor administration is the problem when it comes to food supply. And prices were stable. It was not until January 1937...when the Catalan government ordered...small firms handed back to their owners and wrested from these 'savages' that prices climbed, and queues and the black market appeared."[40]

In the view of the government and the Communist Party, the savages were the anarchists. The latter had insisted that the fight against fascism be conducted alongside the fight for social revolution, contrary to the wishes of the other parties who argued: First, win the war, then—depending on each of their programs—bourgeois democracy, the revolution, or whatever. And, bringing up the rear—if included at all—the emancipation of women. Whereas the Communists appealed to women to put their own interests on the back burner and concentrate all of their efforts upon the war, the anarchists championed immediate liberation for women. For the menfolk of the CNT-FAI this was merely a theoretical concession, but for the women organized in the Mujeres Libres group, it was a very serious matter.

Mujeres Libres grew out of a group launched in April 1936 with an eye to the publication of a magazine: the group was regarded as an autonomous grouping within the CNT-FAI anarchist constituency. Its program looked well beyond what women had thus far dared to demand. They attacked the family, the repression of women behind closed doors, the institution of prostitution (but not prostitutes). One faction even repudiated motherhood as a defining factor in the life of women and called for social recognition for women who had exercised the option not to have children. One of the central demands of the Mujeres Libres was the entitlement of women to paid work—naturally in the context of equal pay for both sexes. From sex education to education of children, there was no topic that was not tackled by the Mujeres Libres. Their thinking had a great impact, committees were set up in every city and their numbers grew to some 20,000, but through its publication *Mujeres Libres*, the group reached out to a much wider female audience.[41]

The most serious competition that the Mujeres Libres faced came from the group Mujeres Antifascistas, an organization that, according to its statutes, was open to all women, but which was in fact led and dominated by the Communist Party. Mujeres Antifascistas had been set up on the basis of the group Mujeres contra la Guerra y el Fascismo (Women against War and Fascism) that the Communist Party had launched in 1933. They published the review *Mujeres* and organized young girls in the Unión de Muchachas (Girls' Union). The number one priority in their program was the declaration of war on fascism (they were for the Republic), and all women simply had to defer to this. For propaganda purposes, they eulogized motherhood: Dolores Ibarruri (*La Pasionaria*) above all was forever invoking women's maternal instinct.[42] In line with the Party's tactics, Mujeres Antifascistas repeatedly attempted to form a sort of Women's Popular Front, which the Mujeres Libres vehemently opposed. The latter imagined, not without some reason, that, given the ferocity of the Communists' competition with the anarchists—by whom they were far outnumbered—that they would first be amalgamated, only to be sidelined after that.

In a statement formally rejecting the proposal from Mujeres Antifascistas that the two organizations amalgamate, Mujeres Libres vigorously criticized the (propaganda) policy of the Communists: "What shall it profit us if a new kindergarten is opened or a few cans of milk more or less are distributed to antifascist mothers? The effrontery of combining this type of simple everyday activity with more spectacular demonstrations is not without a precedent that we would do well to remember; it is not so long ago that the church organization Caritas was buying itself converts with a cotton blanket or an item of clothing."[43]

Both organizations played an important part in Spanish political life during the civil war. And, above all, they afforded women an attention that they themselves would previously have found inconceivable. The reason was plain: their labor-power was needed, as was their willing participation in the organizing of reserve troops, the victualling of the rearguard and civilian life, and soon enough, their boundless disposition to self-sacrifice; for which reasons the eyes of the menfolk quickly settled upon their female comrades. Lucia Sánchez Saornil, one of the founders and chief editors of the *Mujeres Libres* review spotted this ploy with imperturbable perspicacity. The critique that she wrote for her colleagues in her memoirs as early as 1935 had lost none of its validity—quite the opposite, in fact—by the autumn of 1936, by which point the collaboration of women had become the number one issue: "There are many male comrades who honestly desire to see women collaborating in the struggle. But this wish is not matched by a fresh outlook on woman. The comrades want her to collaborate so as to help encompass victory all that much more easily, at a strategic moment so to speak, but without sparing a single moment's thought for the autonomy of women and without for a moment ceasing to look upon themselves as the center of the universe."[44]

Mujeres Libres, on the other hand, sought real change, and they knew that once the war was over—which is to say that once the revolution was victorious—they would have to press on with the struggle, with even greater intensity, because by that time they would be forcing women out of their jobs again and sending them back to the home.

Even so, the climate had changed, palpably. No matter what men and the officials from Mujeres Antifascistas might have been saying, women, whether anarchists or Communists, and even those of them who belonged to the leftist POUM party (which was in opposition to the Communist Party), were grabbing their taste of freedom and savoring it, and were not mending their ways. Clara Thalmann recalls: "In Barcelona the ethos was different from what it had been before—I had known the city back then. Previously, it had been impossible for a woman to venture out into the street alone... Now women could be seen...sitting in the cafés, chatting, with their rifles across their knees... Women were, all unexpectedly, free. All of a sudden it came to you—they too are showing an interest in all sorts of things."[45] Franz Borkenau writes in his memoirs on Spain that in Barcelona the women suddenly started to wear trousers, something that would previously have been unthinkable. In Madrid, he saw the gusto with which women threw themselves into making collections on behalf of Socorro Rojo (Red Aid), brandishing their collecting tins and popping into the cafés to chat and hold discussions with complete strangers.[46]

Women were "the backbone of the resistance."[47] They served on committees, set up military hospitals, nursing posts, organized the defenses of homes and streets, distributed not just food, but munitions and intelligence, as well, and sewed uniforms and procured bandages and medicines, whatever was needed.[48] But they did not confine themselves to these tasks that women are accorded and ask of themselves in wartime; they picked up rifles themselves and enlisted for frontline service. And, in the early days and weeks, nobody stood in their way. Although it was harder for them than for the men to get their hands on what few weapons were around, once they had secured one of these much sought-after firearms they, like their male comrades, clambered aboard the lorries ferrying them out to those areas or districts where there was fighting to be done. When the fascists attacked Madrid in November 1936, they were repelled by numerous militia-women. A women's battalion fought on the bridge in Segovia with considerable success, and on the Northern front, near Getafe, the women fighters were the very last to withdraw.[49] These battles involved not only the anarchists—whose organization initially proved indifferent to the question "should women serve on the front?"—but lots of young female Communists. These young women, most of whom were little older than sixteen, did not give a damn what task the Party assigned them in its official declarations. The Unified Socialist Youth organization embracing both Communists and socialists, to which most of them belonged, not only raised no objections to their appetite for the fight but, as in the case of Rosario Sánchez Mora, went so far as to recruit them for frontline action. The greatest hurdle that these girls and young women had to overcome in the first stages of the war was their own parents. Rosario Sánchez Mora recalls: "I told no one that I was going off to war. If I had, they would never have allowed me to go. The people I was living with would never have let me go without my father's permission. They would have done all in their power to stop me. And the same was true of the other women. The lorries pulled out a few minutes behind schedule and some of the women would urge the driver: Come, shake a leg. Otherwise my mother may show up and take me by the ears."[50]

But by November the situation was changing. More and more militia women were pulled back from the front lines and transferred to the rearguard for laundry, sewing, or ironing duties. George Orwell recalls that there were still a few militia women around in December, but that now they were no longer being acclaimed the way they were when the war started. Quite the opposite. The men were now beginning to laugh at their female comrades.[51] Half a year later, by July 1937, their participation in life on the front ended completely. An English anarchist review summed up the overall situation during the second year of the war thus: "The counterrevolution has triumphed."[52] Be that as it may, the Communist Party, with its motto of "First, win the war: then we shall see," triumphed over the anarchists who wanted to win the war and make the revolution simultaneously. The urban and agricultural collectives were dissolved, and the militias were converted into a regular army with distinctions of rank and a sliding pay scale, and with its own military code of discipline, hierarchy, and jurisdiction. The days of unrestrained freedom, self-management, and self-discipline were no more. Alongside the restructuring of the army, a decree was made public prohibiting women from frontline service. Female militia members were fetched from their trenches, many of them weeping with anger as they were forced to board the buses that would carry them back into the rearguard.[53]

No one could understand them, not even Mujeres Libres, who were now preaching social service to their members. An article carried in the July 1937 (No. 10) edition of *Mujeres Libres* must have read like brazen betrayal and cynicism to the militia women. For a start, it spoke in terms of eulogy of women from all callings playing their part in the resistance, of even dressmakers taking up the rifle: "The dressmaker stood up against the tyranny of the needle so as to make her dreams of adventure a reality." Leaving to one side the fact that this suggests she was thought of as incapable of acting upon a political motive, even her dreams of adventure were promptly snatched from her, so that she might again be thrust back under the needle's tyranny. Except that now, instead of elegant dresses, she was to stitch uniforms: "And she offered her young life, awash with youthful dreams, in the first days of the heroic struggle in which every man was a hero and every woman a match for a man. But courage is not everything in this protracted, ongoing struggle between two classes hating each other to death. Woman, taking this to heart, revised her thoughts and realized that street skirmishes are far removed from the methodical, routine, desperate strife of trench warfare. So with this in mind, and acknowledging her own value as a woman, she opted to swap rifle for industrial machinery and her appetite for the fight for the tender soul of WOMAN."[54]

It was not everyone who shared this enthusiasm for the tender soul of woman: some women did manage to stay on with their units. They fought to the finish, until they were wounded, captured, or killed. It is hard to speak of exact figures. Clara Thalmann reckons that women accounted for two percent of the militias, but nobody mentions how many of them stayed on in the army.[55] In units where anarchists were in the ascendancy, the ban on women was never quite enforced completely.[56] The Communist Rosario Sánchez Mora, who was her unit's *dinamitera* (*dinamiteros* made the bombs with which the poorly-equipped republic troops fought), still claimed in 1987 that women were never expelled from the front lines, that she had never heard a thing about this, nor had she ever wanted to credit it.[57] POUM activist Mika Etchebéhère, who commanded a column, was not merely expelled but formally promoted to captain, thus becoming the only female superior officer in the regular army, so far as we know. Only later on was she stripped of her command and seconded to the staff.[58]

Mika Etchebéhère's war memoirs, *La guerra mia*, are a unique document. Not only does she describe her own activities and the battles in which she fought along with her column, but she also offers her ongoing reflections upon her part as a woman in this extremely unconventional situation. The news that there was a woman on the front with a troop unit had spread throughout the country. The conclusions derived from this fact varied. Some women concluded that the column would be the best place for them. Thus, one fine day two girls showed up, eager to place themselves at her disposal. One of them, Manolita, explained the reason why: "I belong to the Pasionaria column but I would rather stay here. There they were never willing to let us girls have a gun. We were only good for washing dishes and doing the laundry... I am told that in your column the militia women have the same rights as the men, that they need not stick to the dishes or the laundry. I did not come to the front to give it the once over with a cleaning rag in my hand. I've scoured enough pots for the revolution already!"[59]

Mika actually had succeeded in introducing equitable shares of women's work for men and women. The men had gone along with this, although not always without some grumbling or, at any rate, making a great song and dance about this peculiar practice. When one of the most elderly fighters grumbled that this was some revolution, what with the men washing the socks, Mika retorted: "You said it. You freely elected me your captain, regardless of the fact that I am a woman. If we get through this war alive, we shall talk of all these things in more detail. For the time being, thanks a lot for washing my socks. I would never have had the nerve to ask."[60] Which is how things were left.

Her men actually insisted that she retain command, and were proud of their lady captain, who everyone looked upon with awe as a curious phenomenon. Even high-ranking generals detoured to the sector of the front where Mika's unit was to see the marvel for themselves. Mika's soldiers knew that they owed a lot of their celebrity to their being led into battle by a woman—and, as these troops fought with such courage, they were held up as example to the rest. In the event of anyone's daring to carp about the situation or poke fun at it, Mika's men had their answer down pat: they "have a female captain with more balls than all the male captains in the world."[61]

The lady captain with balls knew that she was a sort of anomaly: "What am I to them? Neither man nor woman, I suppose, a sort of special breed of hybrid." And yet, a woman too. "Their woman, an extraordinary woman, pure and strong, whose sex can be forgiven as long as she does not play on it."[62] And Clara Thalmann states: "On the front, we women (were) a sort of neutered breed."[63] The Communist Julia Manzanal, her unit's political commissar, cropped her hair and bandaged up her breasts. In her khaki uniform, she looked like a boy and people even nicknamed her such. She relates how, only once, at a dance during a holiday from the front lines, she donned a dress—and her comrades failed to recognize her at first. And she herself was gripped by panic at that point and was afraid lest the men might now see her "in a different light.'"[64]

On those grounds, Mika Etchebéhère completely refused to venture out during the few days' break she enjoyed from the front, days that her comrades spent in the bars and drinking dens. "I was barred from doing so by my status as an unblemished woman who did not know the meaning of fear, a special woman. So I had no option but to bury myself in the reading of a military training manual that I strove to commit to memory."[65]

Not only did she turn away from worldly delights, but she forbade herself to show any hint of weakness, knowing that would promptly be construed as indicative of womanly weakness. During the siege of the cathedral in Siguenza, where her column had dug in along with the town's inhabitants, she denied herself even a minute's sleep, while peremptorily ordering her men to sleep in shifts.[66] After a bloody engagement, she felt herself close to collapse, but mustered the last of her strength to keep control: "And, lest I start screeching, I said nothing. My arms felt leaden and a metal chain constricted my neck, the worst fear in my life held my stomach in a knot and rose in my throat, my heart pounded, making my breasts quiver and my pulse strongly in my ears and exploding inside my forehead. Some last vestige of farsightedness impelled me to take Ernesto's arm. I had to go on, I had to make it to shelter, I must not collapse, I must not scream, it was almost over, tomorrow was at hand and I would have time to myself...I would be able to strip away the strong woman mask and cry myself to sleep."[67]

Only in one particular way did Mika behave as a woman was expected to behave. She fretted more, and with greater solicitude, than her male fellow officers about her men having food to eat and reasonably good medical care. She even went so far as to tend the injured soldiers herself as if she was their mother, joking sarcastically: "Have any of you ever laid eyes on a male captain doling out cough syrup to his soldiers in the midst of war, in a trench a hundred and fifty meters from the enemy lines? Dosing the sick with spoon and bottle as if it were the most natural thing in the world, and they swallowing it the same way."[68] Elsewhere, she commented tersely: "Once again, I am a captain-mammy tending to her soldier-children."[69] She hardheadedly analyzes the ambivalence of her position: "I cannot help smiling at the thought of the bond connecting me to my militia troops. I protect them and they protect me. They are simultaneously my children and my father. They worry about my not getting enough food and sleep, and at the same time, it seems like a miracle to them that I can stand up to the inclemencies of war as well as, or better than, them. All of their thinking about women has been turned upside down...they look upon me as an exception and, on the basis of my being their officer, they feel somehow superior to the other fighters."[70]

Towards the end of 1938, when foreign governments were openly gambling upon a fascist victory—and were starting to amend their policy accordingly—at a time when her fighters were stumbling from defeat to defeat and yet would not give in, Mika experienced her own personal defeat in the midst of widespread military reverses. She was visited by a battalion commander who got straight to the point: "'I want to put something to you, señora captain. I am asking you to hand over your company to another officer and to join me as my battalion adjutant.' My first reaction was one of bitterness mingled with a flash of anger. What they are trying to do, I told myself, is to strip me of the command of my company by tempting me with a phony promotion which, though it sounded very pompous, would in reality condemn me, to all intents, to inactivity."[71] She dug in her heels, but then realized that "further discussion was pointless. I had to accept the position or go back to Madrid. I did not want to join the rearguard. Which means that I accepted the challenge."[72]

Mika Etchebéhère survived the war and managed to escape from Spain when it was overrun by the fascists. Clara Thalmann managed to flee, after some time spent in a jail of the GPU—the Stalinist secret services—as someone who was doubly suspect: suspected of being a Trotskyist and of having fought alongside the anarchists. Nor was she by any means the only woman to suffer such an absurd fate. Lots of female and male anarchists and POUM members charged with being Trotskyists, plus dissidents from their own ranks were jailed and indeed tortured by the Stalinists.[73] Rosario Sanchez Mora, having had one of her own homemade grenades go off in her hand, and having recovered, worked as postmistress on the front, which is to say she distributed mail to the soldiers as the bullets whistled around her ears. Later, she was captured and served years in the jails of the fascist regime, as did thousands of her comrades.[74] In most instances, those of them who were taken prisoner by the enemy during battle were brutally raped and then murdered. Some of them were lucky and were hauled off to prison; those who were even luckier regained their freedom after six, seven, or ten years. After which, it was not unusual for them to carry on with their work underground and perhaps to endure further arrests. In any event, it was only after decades had passed and Franco had died that they were able to embark upon a normal life, with a feeling of freedom and security.

"Fifí"
Fidela Fernández de Velasco Pérez

Running Fifí to ground was no easy thing to do. Her name cropped up in virtually every conversation, but nobody could supply us with her address. After we pressed them repeatedly, the reason was eventually admitted: Fifí was, in a way, an oddity. She was, not to put too fine a point on it, unduly mannish. It would soon become apparent that what made Fifí stand apart was the fact that, to this day, she shows a pride in having fought on the front lines: "And why would I have had any problems using a gun?" she asked me in the interview we were eventually to hold.[75] "There was a war on and we had to halt the fascists. I shot at anything that moved. The only thing is, "she added as a second thought, "that I would not have had it in me to kill a prisoner. Her equipment consisted of "a good rifle, the best I could get my hands on" and some homemade bombs, put together by her unit's *dinamitero*, and for a while that was none other than Rosario Sánchez Mora, nicknamed La Dinamitera. But that was in the middle of the war, by which time the militias had been converted into a regular army, and only a few women managed to stay on at the front. Fifí, whose given name is Fidela Fernández de Velasco Pérez, and La Dinamitera both belonged to this select few. Fifí really would have been the last person to put up with being sent back into the rearguard: "I was always this way," she says. "Always eager for a fight. Never had any interest in women's prattle."

Fifí was brought up in one of the poorer, traditionally working-class barrios of Madrid. From an early age, she was acutely aware of the injustices around her and also to the working class' resistance to those injustices. Her barrio had always had a revolutionary reputation. In the wake of the fascist victory, it was cordoned off from the other barrios by a wall of barracks. Fifí is the third born of four siblings, a stroppy girl very much aware of the precise differences between the sexes and unfairness within the family. Her father and brothers always got larger servings of food than her mother and sisters. Fifí asked her mother why this should be and was told that the boys needed more. "You have no idea how much I need," was her response, not that it did her any good. Naturally, Fifí got up to mischief in the barrio with her brothers, loitering around the barrio with them and even accompanying them as far as the river, strictly off limits for children: "When we got home, my father beat me, but did not even lay a finger on my brothers."

In the yard of the house where Fifí grew up there were two vehicles, one a van and the other a taxi belonging to one of the neighbors. Fifí used to wait until her father went out, then would slip furtively out into the yard and teach herself to drive. Later, when she felt that she was good enough, she would take the taxi for secret drives through the city: "Luckily, nobody ever caught me. Otherwise there would have been hell to pay!" she says, grinning at her youthful cheekiness.

But it was not long before her various pranks and joyrides were leaving her dissatisfied. She came to realize that her private, isolated rebelliousness was doing her no good. "I was on the lookout for something to invest my struggle with some meaning. I wanted to take on something concrete, the source of all these injustices." At the age of thirteen, Fifí entered the Communist Party's youth organization. "I felt that this was more to my liking." Her parents were not exactly keen on the idea, but they allowed her to go ahead because her father, himself a socialist, at least understood why his wilful daughter was becoming politicized. And, in spite of her tender years, she, like all the children of that working class barrio, made a telling contribution to the household income. Fifí worked as a dressmaker and she says that she liked the work. But now she spent her free time with her Party comrades, reading the socialist classics with them and learning how to use weapons, since military training was part and parcel of the training of a young Communist. The youth organization made no distinction between girls and boys on this score.

When the news broke of the fascist officers' military coup, Fifí didn't need to go looking for a weapon because she was fully armed and standing guard on the Party local: "We knew that something was in the offing and we did not trust the peace, so we were well prepared." Fifí was very clear about what she was going to do now: she was going to fight. At barely sixteen years of age, she went home to pick up her things and say good-bye to her parents. "Come on, give me a kiss, for I am off to the war. I have to go off to war," she told her parents. She never got the kisses. "They neither beat me nor raised their voices nor said a word to me. Not one word." They knew that they were not going to be able to rescue this girl and that there was no point in contradicting her.

Fifí was next sent up to the front lines, where her unit managed to beat the fascists back and even got hold of a cannon. And it was Fifí, no less, who brought the cannon into Madrid. Later, it was on towards Toledo then back again to the sierras around Madrid, where Fifí fought in the column which had Rosario Sánchez Mora as its *dinamitera*. She can still recall the details of how the bombs with which the heavy-and light-artillery militias stood up to the enemy were put together: "We took a few cans of condensed milk and filled them with broken glass, stones and nails and added the dynamite. The fuse stuck out the top and we had to be quick about throwing them because the cord was quite short." From time to time, the entire column would use condensed, rather than fresh milk so as to obtain the materials for bomb-making. The militias' rifles were of little service in battle, in contrast to the technical excellence of the enemy's equipment as he advanced with cannons and machine-guns; the only halfway effective weapons were these makeshift, homemade bombs. "We never had enough arms nor enough munitions," Fifí relates: the finest weapon in the armory of the republican units was their courage and the willingness with which their members fought, contrary to what was happening in the fascist army, where the troops had frequently been dragooned into service. On the front, Fifí was not merely in the front lines, but she also belonged to an assault team that was always deployed in the most dangerous positions. From time to time, she used the lorry to ferry out the wounded and the dead. At the age of twelve, she hadn't hesitated to take a borrowed taxi for a jaunt around the city, so why wouldn't she have taken a risk now with the lorry?

Life on the front was tough. Fifí slept in the mud, in the snow, on top of stones. Frequently she would not sleep at all but would crouch in the trenches, standing guard. Often there was nothing to eat, "in which case one just had to go hungry." And when there was food to be had, the men and women alike took turns doing the cooking. Fifí says: "No difference was made. Everybody did everything. And sometimes it would be my turn to peel the potatoes, albeit not very often." There is every likelihood that Fifí would have been none too keen on cookhouse duty. These days she lives mostly on fried eggs, bread, and sardines—which she shares with a stray cat. "They treated us like men in every respect," she says "and the fact is that we behaved like men too." Except when their femininity just had to be deferred to: "I always used to carry cotton wool in my pockets. And, whenever I could, I would disappear for a moment, change the cotton wool and toss it on to the fire or bury it, unseen, in hole. The worst thing was when I had to go to the toilet. Of course, there were no toilets: and, for the men, that was no problem. Whenever I couldn't go, I had to bide my time until the chance came for me to disappear for a moment."

To this day, there are rumors in Spain—even in Communist circles—to the effect that the women in the front lines were prostitutes. The blue overalls that were a suit of honor where the men were concerned, whereas, in the women's case, symbols of prostitution. Fifí says: "Yes, there were prostitutes, but primarily in the rearguard. They plied their trade there. But that had nothing to do with us, those of us who were fighters. And our male comrades knew that very well. None of them would have dared get too close to us. They did not see us as women. Nor would they have wanted to. Down in the trenches we were as filthy and lousy as they were, and we fought and lived the same way they did. To them, we were not women, but merely other blokes."

But, one day, after the disbandment of the militias, an officer of the regular army showed up at Fifí's unit and had the effrontery to slight her for being a woman. He said that she slept under the stars with the men. Fifí recalls: "It was not said to me but to the male comrades who passed it on to me. I went straight up to him and gave him such a punch on the snout that he fell to the ground." Not the sort of thing one does to an officer, especially if one is a woman. In fact, the recipient of the blow wanted to haul Fifí up before a court martial, but her comrades stepped in to warn him that, if he were to try anything of the sort, they would also report him for having slighted the honor of a female combatant—which is how things were left.

Fifí and her comrades-in-arms saw it as only natural that she should be able to carry on fighting in the ranks of the regularized army. She believes that whether a woman might stay on was dependent upon her performance. In any event, she was not the only one. "Furthermore," she insists, "what I learned at the front is that women are braver than men and tougher, with a higher threshold even for physical pain." Asked about the widespread view that women are not cut out for fighting, but are better suited to social tasks, Fifí's answer is very clear and to the point: "That's nonsense. I have nothing more to say." Full stop.

After a year and a half's service on the front, Fifí was wounded and, when she recovered, the Party put her in charge of setting up a convalescent home. For three solid months, she worked at this in a disciplined way like a good Communist, but she soon realized that this work was not for her and she told Party headquarters as much. The comrades were obliged to agree with her—and entrusted her with another task. They sent Fifí to the CIF (the Party's secret service) Communist intelligence service school. She passed all the examinations and, thereafter, started to work as an agent behind the enemy lines. She also had, once again, a mission at the front: fighting fascist agents. To this day, she will not go into the details of her work: "The first thing I learned was to keep my mouth shut, and I see no reason to do otherwise now."

Shortly before the war ended, the Casado Junta, a provisional government under the moderate socialist Casado, seized power in Madrid in order to surrender the city without any resistance to the fascists a little while later. But, prior to that, the Communists were persecuted and many of them were to be handed over as prisoners to Franco's victorious troops. Fifí too was arrested along with three female CIF comrades. Since the jails were by then filled to bursting, they locked them up in an old villa—which does not say much for the intelligence of their persecutors because these women were really crafty. "We made good our escape by sliding down a gutter-pipe," Fifí relates and adds, regretfully: "Unfortunately we had to leave our little tools behind." The women's tools turn out to be their revolvers and hand grenades.

After her escape, Fifí joined a flood of people fleeing towards Alicante where rumor had it that vessels from a number of European countries would put in to rescue the population from the fascist threat. Tens of thousands camped out on the beaches of Alicante, trembling as Franco's troops drew ever nearer. They all knew the fate that awaited prisoners. Only very rarely would the fascists kill somebody without having first cruelly torturing him, raping the women until their bodies were bleeding hunks of meat. People waited and waited, but the ships did not come. Instead, the fascists came and threw up a huge concentration camp on the beach. After the initial general confusion, they started to classify the prisoners: over here the civilians, over there the former frontline fighters, the anarchists and Communists on active service, etc. The latter, whose numbers included Fifí, were shipped to Madrid by train. Fifí knew what lay ahead of her, but she did not allow herself to be paralyzed by fear. She was only twenty years old, but she had seven years' experience as a militant under her belt. In a lightning-fast move, she switched trains halfway there—only to find herself in the lion's den again. The carriage was crammed with fascist soldiers bound for home—whereupon Fifí regaled them with a touching tale of how she had escaped from the Reds at the eleventh hour when they would have loved nothing better than to carve her up, she being a fascist nurse now searching for her regiment. She asked her beloved comrades if they could help her or at least take her with them as far as Madrid. The beloved comrades, who, in any event, had need of the services of a nurse, cordially invited her to accompany them. "And when we arrived," Fifí recalls, still surprised by the experience, "a lieutenant took me to one side and told me to take care, that your story won't work a second time, and he gave me twenty-five pesetas, which was a lot of money at that time."

At which point, Fifí made a serious mistake: she returned to her parents' house. "I had neither papers nor any contact with the Party, nor the foggiest notion of where else to turn." She was making a skirt for herself when the police raided. Her sister reacted quickly and passed herself off as Fifí. When they took her away, Fifí realized that she could not let things stand as they were: "My sister had a heart complaint, and anyway, I knew that torture was used in the jails." She went to the police station and gave herself up. So began, at the end of the civil war, phase two of her struggle. Fifí was taken to Ventas, the feared Madrid women's prison, built to hold 800 inmates, but now crammed with 11,000 of them, without adequate support or the most elementary sanitary arrangements. The only good thing Ventas had going for it was that, as Fifí says, "there were too many of us for them to torture us all." Fifí was one of the ones who evaded torture. However, the first few months after she was tried—and sentenced to death for her secret agent activities—were served in a number of prisons, on death row in each case. "We never knew when it might be our turn. Every day we thought that the following day they would be coming to fetch us." Fifí spent the bulk of her time incommunicado, and then, in Granada, she had a cell-mate. "She also had her gravely ill son with her. It was ghastly. She would always be saying: 'If only the boy might die before me!' The thought that they might take her away and that the child might be left alone and ailing and not knowing why his mother would not be coming back drove her to distraction." Luck was on their side: the boy died before the mother could be executed.

After spending months on end awaiting death day and night, Fifí was transferred back to Ventas and placed in a group cell, where she learned that her sentence had been commuted. A new life now began for her; the women formed a group and spent their days educating themselves and discussing politics. The leader of the group was Mathilde Landa who established a legal advice office in the prison and, having been a lawyer in civilian life, offered the women an information and advice service. "She was a very erudite woman," says an admiring Fifí, "having pursued two careers, of which the law was only one, and she was in charge of the Party, underground." Fifí joined her in starting to reorganize the Party inside Ventas prison.

Fifí was alive and working again for politics. But, whereas in the case of most of her female comrades—to the extent that conditions in an overcrowded prison allowed—such work brought them the agreeable feeling of belonging to a group, Fifí had to contend with something that officially does not exist. She was declared suspect of displaying a predisposition to strike up amorous relationships with other women. "The Party's morality was very inflexible," she relates. "Once it came to light that one of the female comrades was mixed up with a married male comrade, there was a move to expel her from the Party. Her, not him. And this when he had been separated from his wife for quite some time." Homosexuality was utterly taboo. Communists had to be free of that decadent bourgeois sickness. "But of course there were homosexuals in the Party, male and female," says Fifí. Whether she herself might be one, she does not say. Her notoriety is enough for her. "Sometimes I felt terribly lonely amid those thousands of women," she recalls of her time in Ventas prison, "and, whenever I came upon one who took my fancy, then of course we spent a lot of time in each other's company." But the Party's watchful eye was open. Fifí was formally instructed not to keep company with the same woman all the time during exercise period in the yard. Even today, her hackles rise. "Even if we had been in love, what were we going to do with 11,000 women looking on?"

She cannot forgive herself for the fact that she—albeit unintentionally—was capable of acts of cruelty. One of her secret service comrades had not managed to evade torture. Fifí: "An unbelievable amount of pus oozed from her vagina. They had tortured her until she was

Women in training before leaving for the front

pulverized." The woman was taken from her cell to the infirmary and there she managed to whisper into her ear: "Fifí, take care over what they want to extract from you." Fifí's horrified reaction was: "What did you tell them?" But she had misunderstood her meaning. "Later, her sister, who had also been arrested, came to see me and told me that she had told her: 'Tell Fifí I am dying for what she knows and haven't said anything.' She died, pained that I could have suspected her of having given me away because they tortured her, when, in reality, she had not uttered one word."

Eight years later, Fifí was pardoned: "They had to release us in dribs and drabs because the prisons were so overcrowded that they did not know what to do with so many people." Fifí knew very well what she had to do. What she did not know was how to go about it. In the absence of (forged) papers, with no contacts and no home, illegal work was out. Furthermore, she had not a single penny to her name. But Fifí managed to muddle through. She reestablished contact with the underground Party and got by for a time without papers, until she got hold of some forged ones and lived wherever she could, working wherever she could find work. In the 1950s, she was Spain's first and only female lorry driver. Two male comrades had set up a store dealing in cleaning materials (as a front) and Fifí handled the hauling side of things. "The war was tough, really tough," but cannot compare with what she had to endure as a female lorry driver. "The brutality, bestiality, humiliation, and insult that I endured then was worse than all the time I spent on the front." But Fifí is not one to complain or feel sorry for herself. Nor will she go into details of this brutality, at which we can only guess. What she will talk about are the relatively anodyne experiences that can be written off as anecdotal. For instance, one time she pulled up at a filling station and had scarcely climbed down from the lorry when the men who were there started to call out: "Lads, lads, come here and take a look. Spanish men aren't good enough now. Now they have women doing our jobs." There followed a cascade of obscenities—and they even came to blows. Another time, one of the customers to whom she was delivering goods asked her what she would think if women were driving taxis too, taking the work away from the men like Fifí was doing. Her response was—as it almost always was—short and blunt: "For a start, I don't know what man I'm taking the work away from. And, secondly, ever since the world began, it's been the men who have been taking the work away from the women."

Although engaged in underground work for the Communist Party, which was outlawed until the death of Franco in 1977, she was never arrested again. Shortly before the end of the dictatorship, she built herself a little house in the hills above Madrid, on the outskirts of a tiny village—with her own hands. The plot, a few square meters, was a gift from a cousin who reckoned that it was high time that Fifí retired. "The only thing I could not do was plastering," she tells us, "but I picked it up." Now, Fifí works as a bus driver, driving coaches connecting the sierra villages one with another and with Madrid. Once again, she is the first and only woman in that job.

Nor did she go into retirement when the Caudillo finally died and Spain celebrated the demise of fascism. The Party was made legal and the underground struggle ended. But the fascists in her village refused to admit defeat and tried to make la roja, Fifí, pay: "One day along comes a lad of fourteen, the son of one of them, and he tells me: 'I've been told to tell you that my father cannot sleep as long as you remain alive.'" His elders came along later. Every night a gang of drunks would rampage around Fifí's isolated house, shouting and singing fascist anthems and calling out: "Shoot Fifí!" Until the day their threat became a reality. They grabbed Fifí and dashed her head against the stone wall of her home until they thought she was dead. Fifí survived and, on leaving the hospital, reported the men. To this day, she suffers the after-effects: powerful headaches and blurred vision. Sometimes, she is suddenly rendered blind and has to walk very carefully to avoid falling. She lost the case: the men were released on appeal. Good reason for a celebration: The men wanted to celebrate their victory outside Fifí's house. Fifí was expecting this and greeted them wielding a broad kitchen knife. Once they had all mustered outside her door, she rushed out and charged into them. "They scampered like rabbits. Unfortunately, I failed to get my hands on any of them." That still rankles her today. But, since then, they have left her in peace. For now.

"Chico"
Julia Manzanal

"Everybody used to just call me Chico. Even though they knew very well that my name is Julia. But, because of my boyish appearance, the name stuck. To this day, there are people who call me that."[76] The elderly woman saying all this bears no resemblance at all to a boy. Her hair is worn carefully crimped, she is wearing a bright summer frock and, at first glance, she looks like a lovable granny, still youthful, whose grandchildren exist only in her head. On closer scrutiny, there is something in her bearing and in her eyes that, going by the prevailing gender roles, one can only describe as somewhat mannish. The first thing she shows me is her application for invalid benefits. The money is not the only thing she is interested in; her primary concern is to secure official recognition as a frontline fighter with the rank of political commissar. (Her application was granted in April 1988.) Julia went to the front at the age of seventeen, donning the khaki uniform and Thälmann cap, and binding her breasts to avoid their being noticed. Which is how the flirtatious cigarette girl, at whom the men used to whistle in the streets, turned into Chico. At seventeen, she was the sole support of her family: the work she did was illegal. The State's cigarette monopoly specifically banned what many Spanish women did in order to put food in the mouths of their families: buying tobacco and cigarette papers, and rolling cigarettes to be sold singly or in handfuls (bound with colored ribbons). Spanish men, from bank managers to workmen, subscribed to an out-and-out cult of these hand-rolled cigarettes which, Julia relates, were looked upon as something special and a touch erotic. Even workers with no money would scrape together their last céntimo until they could afford one every now and then. As did the odd rich man who reckoned that, by buying her tobacco, he might also succeed in buying the cigarette girl. Time and again, Julia had to listen to propositions that she always rejected; if there was no other choice, she became rude. In addition to such admirers, the police would not leave her in peace, so her trade, although lucrative, was very demanding. And part of her earnings had to be spent on dresses and shoes, because a cigarette girl had to look good and dress well, and had to look as if she had no need to work. This was hardly a chore to Julia because she loved to wear pretty dresses in the finest fabrics and genuine leather shoes.

Julia grew up in a working-class barrio, although she did come from a family of workers. Her mother had no money, but she educated her children "like princelings." And even though her princes had to work, they were not allowed to neglect their education. From a very early age, Julia learned to live alongside ambiguities. Her mother came from an aristocratic, but utterly impoverished family. Her father was an electrical technician, but he never played a role of any significance in Julia's life. Her parents divorced in 1931, when the republican government made it legal to do so. After that, her father never laid eyes on Julia again. Her mother worked as a dressmaker. Julia recalls: "She was a great woman, a fighter, but a top-notch fighter. And she was a fantastic dressmaker too. They used to call her 'hands of silver.'"

At the age of eleven, Julia left school to start work at a cement plant. Her mother insisted that she carry on with her studies after work, and she took shorthand and typing. Later, Julia made hats, before working as a dressmaker-embroiderer, turning her hand to anything that came along, because she had all but become the head of the family. At fourteen, she started to work for Standard Electrical where she made telephones on the assembly line. Meanwhile, she had already joined the Communist Youth association and the Socialist UGT union: "But, in those days, it was all something of a game to me and I wasn't really politicized." The game took a serious turn when the Standard Electrical and Telefónica workers went on strike. The strike ended for both firms once the employees' demands had been granted. "And then it turned out that what had been agreed to had no validity for us. We had thought that the two firms were one, but now they were acting as if they had nothing to do with each other." Julia and other female colleagues decided that they would not resign themselves to this. They became angry and thereby presented the management with the ultimate grounds for dismissing them. Julia had already come to their attention during the strike; together with other female employees, she had systematically beaten up the scabs.

After being sacked, Julia was unable to find work and, from that point on, she got by as an illegal cigarette vendor, and began to show a more serious interest in politics for a very straightforward and persuasive reason: "I had already had my run-in with capitalism and had learned to hate it." On the day of the military coup, July 18, 1936, she formally joined the Communist Party. Prior to that, she had thrown herself into reading the classics: Marx, Engels, Lenin, Stalin, but also some Bakunin and the writings of other anarchists. Years later, when they arrested her, the police uncovered piles and piles of anarchist publications in her apartment. Despite this, Julia plumped for the Communists. "I already knew the folk from the youth association and the union, and quite simply I identified with the Party." Once a Party member, her education became more concrete, and military training was added to theory. "I was very happy at the time." Her eyes were opened to a new world, a world where, for the first time, men did not run after her but showed her respect, a world where she could dress like a man and move around at liberty. Julia demonstrated an extraordinary talent and, following basic training, she received training in how to be a political commissar. They gave her a Mauser and she stood guard at the entrance to the Party local: but this was not enough for her and she asked the Party to give her a "real job," which they did. Julia Manzanal was appointed as political commissar to the Madrid municipal battalion and went off to the front. In addition to her rifle, they gave her a .38 Messerschmitt revolver, in which she still takes pride today.

Her work was varied. She had to keep soldiers briefed on developments on the front and on political developments, run literacy classes and political courses, spurring on the troops and seeing to it that there was no loss of morale during the quiet times when the men would be lounging around, louse-ridden in their trenches, with nothing to do but wait for the next onslaught. She saw to it that the men did not gamble away their pay, that their families received financial support, that the fighters were kept supplied, that there was always enough victuals, arms, and munitions. Julia took part in meetings of the political commissars from the various units and consultation meetings with the staff officers, and wrote up reports for the commands. She also participated in the fighting and did sentry duty, even though it was not, strictly speaking, within her remit, and on the odd occasion, she did some spying work. "Once we were so close to the enemy troops that we could hear what they were saying. It was rather amusing. 'Look what they served us up for dinner again today: beans and salad, like dogs.'"

It was Chico here and Chico there: Julia-Chico was everywhere. Sometimes she travelled to Madrid to collect her troops' gear personally. "The Mujeres Antifascistas supplied us with uniforms, blankets, thick socks. There was one really pretty young girl who developed a crush on me. She would stare at me with cow eyes every time I arrived to make a collection." Chico had no intention of letting the girl in on her secret. Julia brazenly flirted with the girl and—in addition to the personal pleasure, still apparent as she tells the story—she secured the best uniforms and the thickest blankets for her troops.

Her experiences as the person responsible for troop morale were less amusing. She hesitates for a long time before going into the following story, but makes up her mind to do so, because "it needs saying, if you want to know the truth." One day, a captain presented himself to her and said: "Commissar, there is something we have to tell you, but we are not sure how to put it, because you are a woman." Julia replied: "Just forget about my being a woman and spit it out." Whereupon, without further ado, they filled her in on the story: The food for the unit was shipped in on the back of a female mule: "And the men have been doing filthy things with the beast." It was Julia's duty as political commissar to put an end to this—which she did. "But it was hard. The very fact that it was a woman addressing them on this matter came as a shock to the men." Julia solved the problem by disposing of the female mule. "Now they were the mules and they had to carry the food themselves."

Julia was the only woman in her battalion and, in that entire sector of the front, the only woman with a military command. She insisted that the men show her respect, that they treat her like one of the lads and ignore the fact that she was a woman. She wasn't Julia; she was Chico. And, when you came right down to it, she was one of their superiors. In spite of everything, Julia was not able to avoid a few humiliating experiences. She travelled with an officer from a different battalion to attend a meeting in Madrid. On reaching the city, he invited her to go for a drink and, all of a sudden, blurted out to her: "Right, now you've shown that you can withstand anything. So now let's find some whores." Knees trembling, Julia queued up outside the brothel with the men. "These guys made me sick... But I was forever having to prove myself, and I reckoned that this, too, was something I would just have to put up with." Among those waiting, she came upon a few comrades who found the situation much to their amusement. "You must come up with us," they begged her. To which Julia replied: "If you'll treat me to a cigar and a newspaper, I'll go up." Julia managed to pull her cap down over her face, sat down at a small corner table, inhaled great mouthfuls of smoke, and pretended to be absorbed in the reading of the paper. She had not been sitting for long when one of the women said to her: "Hey, young lad, don't you want to chat or something?" Julia mumbled a refusal. Finally, her companions were ready. "By the time I got outside, never in my life have I feel so wretched." The following day, when she went along to the staff meeting, she told her superior officers of the incident. "They gave me a real dressing-down. They reckoned that I shouldn't have let things get so far, that I'd let myself be dragged down to the level of a common soldier." But that wasn't what had bothered her. She was more affected by the reproach, that what she had done had been misdirected heroics. Julia says: "That's exactly what it was. It was a sort of heroics, but utterly absurd. My only thought was for my own defense. I had always been under pressure to keep on proving myself." In point of fact, she was not, for all her claims, one of the lads. Women on the front always had to be twice as brave as their male counterparts, and twice as tough, and could not let themselves be shocked or surprised by anything. The Staff officers preferred charges against the colleague who had taken Julia to the brothel for disrespecting her rank. "That was a great relief to me; that they would not let it pass and sought to punish him. Later, I even intervened to make sure he did not lose his stripes."

Cognizant as she was of the ambivalence of her situation, she strove to avoid all ambiguous situations. She always wore her male clothing, though once, during furlough from the front, she put in an appearance at a dance wearing a dress and was later afraid her comrades, who were quick to see that their Chico was an attractive young woman, might thereafter see her in a different light. Like everybody else, Julia slept under a blanket or, if by chance there was one available, on a mattress. She frequently had to spend the day unable to answer calls of nature simply because she did not know where to go. She stuck it out and, by night, under cover of the darkness, would slip away to some corner, tree, or bush. Menstruation was the biggest problem. "All day long I was unable to change my tampon: sometimes, the dried blood caused ulcers on my thighs." But she never gave anything away, and none of the men could even have dreamed of the secret worries on their comrade's mind.

She stepped outside of her role just once and had to pay the price for it. She met up with her boyfriend, who, in his role as battalion envoy, showed up where Julia's troops were stationed: "And then it happened." Julia discovered that she was pregnant and knew that this could not be reconciled with life on the front. She managed to find a midwife who performed an abortion for her the following morning. By evening of that very same day, Julia was up and about again on the front. She managed to survive in spite of bleeding for forty consecutive days. None of those around her ever suspected a thing. She managed to sort the matter out for herself in silence and secrecy.

When the militias were disbanded and the women were withdrawn from the new regularized army, Julia was able to stay on with her battalion for a few months, but with no rank. Later, the Party pulled her out and sent her back into the rearguard. Julia was very unhappy about this but complied. They made her secretary of the Friends of the Soviet Union and, from time to time, she did some work with the Membership Secretariat and looked after propaganda issues. After Franco's victory, she carried on working for the now outlawed Communist Party right up until she was arrested. She returned to earning her living as a cigarette vendor—itself an illegal occupation. Julia would later recall with some amusement: "At the time I didn't know who I was more afraid of, the Civil Guard or the Treasury people."

A male neighbor turned her in and, when the police came knocking at her door, she did not have the time to dispose of the weapons that some friends had been hiding in her home. So Julia resorted to a few tricks: "I had to kick up quite a scene in order to throw them off the scent." Julia welcomed the policemen, offering them coffee before opening her cupboards for them and displaying great willingness to cooperate. In the end, she confessed to them: "Since you're going to find it anyway, I'd rather take you to it myself." And, implicating herself, she opened a secret drawer in the kitchen table which held piles of Communist propaganda material and anarchist magazines. Julia recalls: "And this satisfied them. Had they found the arms, my life would have been forfeited." Julia was committed to the Ventas women's prison and, on April 3, 1940, was sentenced to death for the crime of rebellion. After a few months, her sentence was commuted first to thirty years' close custody. Julia's daughter was just fourteen days old when they arrested her mother. When Julia had been obliged to quit the front, she had met up again with her boyfriend and became pregnant again. This time, she decided to keep the baby in spite of her difficult and dangerous living conditions. "I wanted the baby and I was very happy. And then I had to take her to prison with me. That was awful. They never tortured me; my torture was the child's presence. First, she caught fleas and, then, her entire body erupted in festering sores and, finally, she caught meningitis." Julia recalls most of the children in jail dying of meningitis. "Day and night she squealed and cried, and there wasn't a thing I could do to help her, not a thing. I would have preferred torture over that." The women begged the warders to fetch a doctor, only to be ignored. By the time of the child's death, she was barely ten and a half months old. A few years on, Julia was transferred to a prison in the Basque Country that was even worse than Ventas: "The dampness was terrible. We were constantly bedding down on wet mattresses." As a result of the dampness, Julia contracted severe paralysis of the legs, was left unable to walk, and had to stay two years in the infirmary, unable to move. As soon as she was able to walk again, they moved her to Barcelona and thence to Palma de Mallorca. Her odyssey through the prison system brought her back to the North, to Bilbao, until she finally arrived in Almeria, where she received her pardon.

When Julia got back home, she had to begin all over again from scratch. "They had impounded everything. My mother and brothers were all sharing one room. And there I was spreading out my blanket on the floor." Her boyfriend, the father of her child, had died in prison. Julia found work as a saleswoman for an insurance company, and, one day, she came across an old comrade with whom she had been on friendly terms before the war: "We were both greatly delighted to see each other again and we hugged like brother and sister." They chatted at some length and realized that each of them was alone. Why not become a couple if they got on so famously? They began to live together, Julia had another daughter, and eventually they married: "There was nothing else to be done. We sorely needed family assistance, but of course, that State benefit was available only to married couples." They both carried on working for the underground Party, but Julia's husband insisted that she take on only minor tasks involving relatively little risk: "I would have liked to do more, but he was very afraid on the girl's behalf. He would always say, 'Leave the more dangerous matters to me, because if they put you back in prison you'll lose this daughter as well.' And, in truth, they were keeping me under constant surveillance. In any event, I would not have been able to tackle anything of importance."

After the death of Franco, Julia grabbed her chance and threw herself enthusiastically into working for the Party and rose to become a member of the leadership council, before founding the pensioners' branch of her trade union. At its first congress, she was elected press and information secretary. And today? "To this day I am still active in the Party, although I have problems with the new policy. When we were underground, we were more radical and most resolute—only somebody who really embraced the cause in its entirety was a member. These days it has all changed. But I am still a part of the struggle, because when all is said and done, that is my life."

"La Dinamitera"
Rosario Sánchez Mora

There is even a poem written in her honor, to the heroic legend of the female dynamiter who sacrificed her right hand in the fight against fascism. Rosario Sánchez Mora, La Dinamitera, was the hardest to get to talk about her experiences as a front-line combatant during the civil war. When she finally relented, I was long gone from Spain, and Pilar Panes Casas, who took over the task of conducting the interview with her, had to make a solemn promise that she would not ask a single question relating to her private life.[77]

From a very early age, Rosario had close contact with politics. Her carpenter father was a member of the radical republican party Izquierda Republicana and, not content merely with having a political opinion, he made great show of it—this in the days when Spain was still under a dictatorship. Rosario was born in 1920 in a little village in the province

*A militia woman
on the Aragon front*

of Madrid. When she started school, her father required her and her sisters to wear (republican) tricolor ribbons in their hair. "But the school mistress would not let us into the school wearing those three colors. So we had to leave home wearing the tricolor ribbons, remove them en route and tie up our hair with white ribbons—making sure that neither of them got creased, or my mother would scold us. And go through the same process in reverse order on the way home."

At sixteen, Rosario went to Madrid to train as a seamstress. She had no money to pay for an apprenticeship, but she did not want to be a burden to anyone. Somebody had told her about the Aida Lafuente Cultural Center where she might learn a trade for free, as well as pick up a smattering of general education. The center consisted of a number of buildings owned by the Unified Socialist Youth, which was, in fact, an offshoot of the Communist Party. This did not bother Rosario because in her home village she had seen very plainly the meaning of poverty, but also that of solidarity and resistance. In spite of all this, she held rather aloof from politics. Learning a trade was of more interest to her than the discussions taking place between her colleagues. She relished the happy atmosphere among the female students and between them and the female and male teaching staff, and gradually she began to show an interest in the other matters that the staff would touch superficially upon during the classes in accounting and shorthand. When, eventually, somebody suggested that she join the Party, she readily agreed, though she still did not take a particularly prominent part in any of its activities. But when, two days after the fascist officers' coup, a band of comrades from the JSU burst into the class to ask for volunteers for the militias, Rosario had a rude awakening. She asked whether they were looking for girls as well and put her name on the list. The very next day, she was on her way to the front, unbeknownst to her parents, since "they would never have given me permission."

When she arrived in Buitrago de Lozoya, her sector of the front, this was the reception that greeted her: "Everybody off. Wait. Now we distribute the gear." The gear turned out to be a pair of overalls; a militant's cap; a plate; a knife, fork and spoon set; an ammunition pouch; munitions; and a carbine. Rosario did not quite know what to do with all this, never having handled a rifle before. The volunteers, who had yet to receive any military training, were posted along with the rest to the trenches and, once there, received a sort of crash course in weapons training. "It was explained to us how to load a carbine and how to take aim at a target. And then they went and told us that, in any case, we had to keep firing constantly to let the fascists know that they could expect fierce resistance from us. And the fact is that our carbines had a range of barely thirty meters. They were really old rifles." Rosario was right up in the front lines in a sector of crucial importance, where Madrid's supply of drinking water came from, and it had to be held at all costs. Rosario remembers: "It was really hell. There was shooting day and night and, of course, as a result, we learned very quickly how to fight."

The militia members, female and male, scarcely had time to sleep. They took turns while the fighting was going on, to snatch at least three hours' rest wrapped in blankets, with a rock for a pillow. "It is odd, but after a time you can sleep even in the midst of the most hellish racket of warfare. It was hard, but we managed." The worst thing for Rosario was standing on watch. Not because she was afraid to die, but because she was conscious of her responsibility towards the others: "You were afraid of failure, of maybe falling asleep, afraid that the war might be lost because of you, that the comrades might be attacked and murdered. It's hard to believe the lengths to which one's imagination can go in a couple of hours. In my case, there was the additional consideration that I was a woman, which made it all the more imperative that I not fail."

Rosario was not the only woman with her unit, and she recalls her female comrades with pride: "I have to tell you that we women militia members were very courageous. We were sixteen or seventeen years old at the time, and we completely forgot about our fear and we fought and egged on the others. Many of us perished." As Rosario sees it, the courage and tenacity of the women were not particularly surprising because she is convinced that "fear and cowardice have no sex." But, like everybody else, she realizes this is not the general opinion, which is why the militia women tried twice as hard as the men, never uttering a word of complaint, standing guard a few minutes longer than the men did, precious minutes stolen from the sleep they so urgently needed.

After two months of nonstop fighting, Rosario had a forty-eight-hour furlough that she used to visit home. "My pass was like that of any other soldier, an official document, stamped with the name of my company. I saw it as a genuine acknowledgment." When Rosario reached her home town, she was given a heroine's reception; her parents were cross with her, but proud of this extraordinary daughter of theirs, and her girlfriends marvelled at her militian's uniform. After this gratifying success, the sixteen-year-old returned to the hail of bullets on the battlefield. Now they transferred her to a flying column and, after a time, to the Dynamiters' Detail. This was a real distinction, since, as a rule, it was only men who were made dynamiters. Rosario learned how to manufacture bombs and how to throw them in a variety of attack formations: "Normally, we trained using only the dynamite cartridges. We would light the fuse, our fingers a couple of centimeters from the cartridge, so that we could feel the heat off the copper as we threw them." During training, Rosario was already putting bombs together for the troops. The fight must go on. The sensational news of her unit's boasting a woman bomb expert spread like wildfire. Rosario became la Dinamitera.

But then, in September 1936, she suffered her accident. There were holes in the roof of the granary where the bomb-making equipment was stored, it rained and some of the fuses got wet. Rosario was just learning how to mount an attack in close formation: "We were spread out diagonally in one line when I found myself way out to the far left. My arm brushed against the comrade on my right. We were lighting up, one after another, along the line. The fuse in my cartridge was alight but I could hear a noise like whistling. Somebody shouted, 'Throw!' but straight away somebody else called out, 'Don't throw!' I reacted like lightning. If I were to throw, the dynamite might hit my comrades in the eyes and make mincemeat of the ones alongside me. Which is why I turned around, but before I could dispose of it, it went off in my hand, blowing it to shreds." Rosario slumped to the ground and panic seized her comrades. Some scurried off in search of a doctor, while others stood around, dumbfounded by the thought that the accident happened because Rosario tried to protect them. She had just a single thought in her mind: "I could feel the pain and the gushing of the blood, and I was thinking: Above all else don't let me scream or pass out. The mere fact that I am a woman means that I have to make an effort to control myself."

News of Rosario's accident spread like wildfire and she received loads of visitors to the military hospital. "Even the philosopher Ortega y Gasset came to see me," relates a gratified Rosario, "and later he made a point of going to my parents' village to break the news to them himself."

But that was not the end of the war for Rosario. Far from it. "Obviously, with only one hand now, I could not stay on the front as a militia member, but the fight went on." As soon as she was discharged, she reported back to her unit to see how she might still be of service. She worked as a telephonist with her divisional staff in Madrid, but soon found that this was not a suitable occupation for la Dinamitera. At the start of 1937, she was appointed postmistress on the front and was issued with a pass enabling her to move freely throughout the entire theatre of military operations and a permit to carry a sidearm and rifle. Her new job threw her back into the thick of the war, something she welcomed: "Every day, on the stroke of eight, and not a minute later, which was very important, I would collect the classified mail. Then, with a driver and the paymaster of the front, after passing through all the checkpoints, off we would go to meet up with all the divisional postmen, hand over our sacks of correspondence, and pick up the letters from the troops. I also had to deliver correspondence in person to the staffs of the various brigades and commissariats, and some commissariats were located smack dab in the middle of the trenches. Furthermore, I looked after a number of sections personally. This I could only do on foot, because our vehicle could not venture so close to the firing line. During these outings, I sometimes had to dodge machine-gun bursts, take cover from crossfire, and bombs could be heard exploding nearby."

Rosario's post was one of considerable responsibility. The generals knew how important it was to troop morale for the soldiers to get letters from their families, and for their wages to be paid on time. But, since the highly disciplined, utterly trustworthy, and exceptionally courageous person in charge of the front's mail happened to be a woman, they made do with offering her a few words of praise. "Normally the job would have been filled by an officer of the rank of sergeant. I felt honored by the confidence that had been shown in me when they appointed me postmistress, but I wouldn't have had any objection to the promotion that never came my way." When her division was pulled back, she did another stint as a telephonist back at command headquarters: then she was asked by la Pasionaria if she might like to work for the Labor Commission, too. The commission was in charge of deploying women to fill the jobs left vacant by men, for, when the men were away on the front, all posts previously regarded as unsuited to women were filled by the "weaker" sex. No post would have been less well-suited to la Dinamitera.

When Casado's Junta seized power in Madrid, and mass arrests of Communists were made, it so happened that Rosario had heaps of compromising material at the command headquarters. She raced there to find a female comrade and a young boy standing guard and she asked them to help her destroy files, minutes, lists, receipts, and addresses. They gathered together all of the papers to be found there in the main building, carried them out into the yard and set them alight—thereby saving the lives of quite a few female and male comrades.

At literally the last moment, they scrambled aboard one of the lorries bound for Alicante. There, Rosario met up with tens of thousands of fugitives in the fascists' concentration camp. Like Fifí, Rosario was taken aside and brought to Madrid, being a well-known political activist. They sentenced her to thirty years in prison and, like most of the prisoners of war, she was released after a few years. She went off to live with a girlfriend and, to make ends meet, she turned to black marketeering. She tried working as a cigarette vendor like Julia Manzanal and eventually found work as a sales assistant in a tobacconist's, where she stayed up until retirement age.

She married back in 1937, but refuses to talk about this. When, in spite of this, Pilar Panes Casas ventured to ask her about her private life, Rosario flew into a rage and even threatened to throw her out of the house. But, in her anger, she said a lot more than she really meant to do and revealed how it must have wounded her to hear the frequent implication that the women on the front were prostitutes: "That's nonsense! On the front we were all militians, people of left-wing ideology and unbelievable ideals for which we were ready to die. I was sixteen when I went to the front. I went there a virgin and returned a virgin. All this is just fascist propaganda designed to insult and blacken the women! In the trenches the fascists used to call out to us: 'Cowards! Do you have to bring your womenfolk along because, by yourselves, you just can't hack it?'

She is also critical of her own male comrades. She cannot forget that she received no formal recognition of the very heavy, highly responsible work she performed and insists that, at the very least, there must be no repetition of this in the future: "We have to learn from experience. We women must learn not to serve in the army in the absence of regular conditions. We not only have to fight to secure the right to exercise the same responsibilities as men, but also to secure the same recognition."

Tito's Partisans

"The peasant girl has escaped."

1

The women in particular gazed, wide-eyed, at Marjetka. They were heartened by this young partisan who, in her Tito cap and rifle in hand, had joined with the others to storm the movie theater and overpower the SS men and soldiers inside. It was ten o'clock at night on April 3, 1943. Slovene partisans had stormed the theater in the little town of Mezica, in southern Carinthia, abruptly interrupting the Nazi propaganda film show. Two guerrillas had disconnected the projectors while the rest disarmed the troops in the audience, as their commander delivered a speech to the film-goers in the room, Slovenes, for the most part, listened with great satisfaction and applauded with gusto. It had been an act of daring simply to enter the town, render the *gendarmerie hors de combat* and get right down to propagandizing. And there was a ready audience for that propaganda. Some 90 percent of the Slovene population of Carinthia were in sympathy with the partisans, supporting them, feeding them, and hiding them in their homes.[78] People knew that the National Liberation Army included women; sometimes their own daughters took to the mountains and handled guns just like the men. There had been a radical alteration in values. This young woman, who had held the despised SS men at bay during the storming of the movie theater, was a heroine admired by the other women. Even the men had learned that, suddenly, there were women who had quit doing the dishes and switched to cleaning their machine-guns.

Upwards of 100,000 women were members of Tito's National Liberation Army. One in four of these perished in the course of the struggle, some 40,000 were wounded and 3,000 left incapacitated. 2,000 women served as officers and 91 won the highest distinction: the title of "People's Hero."[79] "I am proud to command an army in which so many women serve," Josip Broz Tito, chairman of the Communist Party of Yugoslavia and commander-in-chief of the National Liberation Army, had declared in his welcoming address to the national congress of the Antifascist Women's Front on December 6, 1942 in Bosanski-Petrovac.[80]

Tito's salutation was not simply some hollow phrase, but could be taken very seriously. The Communist Party of Yugoslavia had carried out a lot of propaganda among the female population, especially Tito's election to the chairmanship in 1937: and, compared with the other Communist parties of Europe, it had sketched out an exceptionally forward-looking women's program that was endorsed at the fifth national conference in 1940. That program called for equality of political rights for women, including active and passive entitlement to vote, and for equal pay for equal work, as well as targeting double standards in the social and legal treatment of rape, trafficking in women, prostitution, and other sexist forms of discrimination. This work quickly bore fruit as increasing numbers of women organized within the party or its women's organization. The Antifascist Women's Front, which was launched at the same time as the National Liberation Army, numbered two million active members by the end of the war.

In the 1930s, Yugoslavia was a poor agricultural country. Seventy-six percent of the population lived and worked in the countryside, and the working class accounted for only 11 percent of the population as a whole. Illiteracy rates were high and nearly three million women—or 68 percent of the women in Yugoslavia—could not read or write. In some areas of the country, the infant mortality rate was the highest in the world—only 1 percent of women were able to give birth with medical assistance, and there was no midwife in a thousand villages. Wages in Yugoslavia were among the lowest in Europe. In every occupation, from school teaching down to laboring, women earned less than men: the majority of female wage-earners were unskilled laborers sharing conditions of extreme poverty with their families. There was a quota for civil servants limiting the numbers of women employees: the Financial Law of 1934–35 banned married women from employment in the public service. In 1937, schoolmistresses' wages were cut by between 30 percent and 40 percent. The monarchist military dictatorship that ruled Yugoslavia from 1929 strenuously rejected female suffrage, which the preceding government had already put on to the back burner until some vague future date. The only concession made to the female population was religion.

But the power of the Church was becoming increasingly shaky, even in the most remote villages. The Communist Party, launched in 1919, had been banned back in 1921, after scoring considerable electoral success in 1920. In several large cities such as Belgrade and Zagreb, it had won a majority and taken one third of the seats overall. After the outlawing of the Party, the Communists stepped up their work in the rural districts, where their most important activists were the schoolmistresses who carried out propaganda among the parents of their pupils, particularly the mothers. In 1939, the Communist Party of Yugoslavia launched a far-ranging campaign in favor of voting rights for women, but by 1940 it realized that, although much of the female population was sympathetic to the Party and its demands and supported its work, only 6 percent of Party members were women. Consequently, on the eve of the fascist occupation, the Party drew up an almost feminist program for women and declared the struggle for women's rights to be one of the core points in its overall program.

Meanwhile, the reactionary military government was sympathetic to Nazi Germany and exported much of the country's farm produce to the Third Reich. This merely exacerbated the poverty in the population. There were hunger-driven revolts by women and young people in some cities, which quickly snuffed out by government gunfire. At the same time, the government passed laws discriminating against Jews, while the Nazis, as a reward for this, postponed their decision to expel the Slovene population from German Carinthia.[81] On March 25, 1941, the Yugoslav cabinet signed the Tripartite Pact—the alliance with Germany and fascist Italy—but, two days later, the country was convulsed by militant demonstrators chanting "War rather than this Pact!" and "Better dead than slaves!" The scale of the demonstrations left no doubt that the bulk of the Yugoslav population was not in sympathy with government policy. On April 6, 1941, German aircraft bombed Belgrade as the Wehrmacht and the fascist armies from Italy, Bulgaria, and Hungary invaded the country and carved it up into occupation zones. In Carinthia, the policy of Germanization was implemented, as thousands of Slovenes were expelled into Yugoslavia so German farmers might move onto their land and into their homes. The District Central Department for Nationality Affairs in Klagenfurt circulated the appropriate lists to the SS command posts.[82] Also in April 1941, within a few days of the invasion, the Communist Party of Yugoslavia set up its Military Committee, out of which the National Liberation Army would shortly emerge, and it called upon the demobilized soldiers not to surrender, but to hide their weapons. On July 4, 1941, the Party issued its summons to armed resistance, and shortly after that, an uprising erupted right across the country; forty cities and hundreds of towns in Serbia, Croatia, Bosnia, Herzegovina, and Slovenia were declared liberated zones. The headquarters of the military leadership were established in the liberated town of Uzice in Serbia. The popular uprising forced the Germans to leave behind a lot more occupation troops than anticipated, and to organize local fascist military formations, as well as build upon those already in existence, such as the Croatian Ustasha, the Chetniks in Serbia, and the Anti-Communist Militia in Slovenia.

Meanwhile, in the liberated territories, the National Liberation Army was being organized on the basis of partisan units. Women, who had not only been involved in the uprising from the outset, but had carried out important work, organized themselves under the aegis of the Antifascist Women's Front. Since most of the men had joined the army, Party work at every level was in the hands of the women, and such work was frequently riskier than direct participation in the armed conflict. Antifascist women's committees were formed inside both liberated and occupied territories. Liberation Army fighters went from village to village, city to city, to recruit new members and enlighten the women about their work. That work, in fact, was all-embracing, ranging from typically women's work to sabotage operations. The women knitted socks and sewed uniforms for the troops, prepared hideouts for Party members on the run, collected medicines, bandages, clothing and money, not to mention arms and munitions. They looked after the families of the arrested and organized prison escapes. They acted as couriers across the length and breadth of the country, bringing news, leaflets, outlawed reviews, attack orders, and deliveries of arms and explosives. The peasant women had to gather in the harvest unaided, not merely their own crops but those of their neighbors who happened to be in prison, on the run, or in the forests. Women printed up the underground newspapers and operated the radio stations. In Ljubljana, women transmitted the partisans' radio show from the city center. Women dug up the streets to hold up enemy tanks and mounted guard on the liberated villages. A March 1942 local bulletin from the Party committee in Grahovo declared: "It is nothing out of the ordinary for the young girls to mount guard and carry out patrols armed with rifles, hand grenades, and revolvers."[83] Members of the Antifascist Women's Front blew up telephone exchanges and power stations, and liquidated enemy officers. Thousands of women ended up in the fascist jails and concentration camps. Without the work they did, the partisans would scarcely have managed to survive, let alone fight with any success.

In the liberated territories, the National Liberation Army and Antifascist Women's Front carried out a comprehensive literacy campaign, which was of particular benefit to the female population, a solid two-thirds of whom could not read or write. Special schools were also set up to offer political education courses to women, as well as first-aid and basic general education classes: for many of these women, this was the first education they had ever experienced. In addition to the literacy drive, magazines for women were published, one or two per region, as well as the official publication of the Antifascist Women's Front, *Zena Danas* (Woman Today).

Many women joined the partisans directly as nurses, cooks, and doctors, as well as serving as armed fighters. According to official Yugoslav historiography, they had no problems being accepted, but, from statements from female former partisans, we may deduce that the recruitment of female fighters was organized along different lines from region to region.[84] The female and male partisans in the forests and hills were dependent upon the operation of the infrastructure in the villages and cities. They emerged from their hiding places to do their laundry in farmhouses, to seek treatment for their wounded, in search of food, or to forage. Peasant women kept the partisans briefed on enemy troop movements, and about gendarmes, spies, or agents. It was unremarkable for a man to become a partisan. On the one hand, because of prevailing gender roles, but also because they were in greater danger: men were dragooned into forced labor and, in Carinthia, Slovene men were also subject to the draft. Many of them deserted immediately or when they went on leave and there was no choice for them, but to take to the hills. In any event, the women were left behind and their illegal work in the open was crucial to the liberation struggle. So, it cannot be argued that women were recruited on their own merits. Female partisans from Slovenia argue that it was not until they were in imminent danger of being exposed, arrested, or deported that they joined the combat units. As long as they could manage it, they were obliged to carry out their tasks in the infrastructure.[85]

However, the National Liberation Army did include 100,000 female members. Not all of these were active fighters, but when the first partisan unit was launched in 1941, fifty from Belgrade joined as fighters. Nearly 6,000 women fought in the ranks of the Liberation Army in Macedonia. In some battalions of the Voivodina brigades, women accounted for a third of the membership, and as much as 20 percent of the membership of the youth combat brigades were girls, and, even in the Muslim community of Livno, sixty girls served with the 10th Herzegovina Brigade. Of the 175 fighters from Slovenia who were declared "People's Heroes," twenty-one were women, including the textile operator Pavle Mede Katarina, who was killed in January 1943 while leading the women's section of the Pohor Battalion.

The first women's combat unit had been set up on August 25, 1942; by September another two had been formed in quick succession. After their courage had been put to the test in their first armed engagements, women's units were set up nationwide. Military training lasted one month and women were appointed as commanders and political commissars. In the autumn of 1942, the spokesperson of the Croatian partisans announced: "There had been some doubts regarding the fighting abilities of our female comrades... On our way through Kordun, our second partisan fighting brigade, which includes a company of girls, fought in an engagement against highly motorized enemy infantry troops. In the course of the fighting, the young female partisans, along with their male comrades, mounted an intrepid attack against the enemy cavalry and, indeed, tanks."[86] By saying this, the frontline review was showing that it was perfectly obedient to the Party line. So, even though they were never quite implemented all the time and in all places, the principle was clear, as may be gathered from this excerpt from the official organ of the Communist Party of Yugoslavia's central committee, *Proleter*: "Many members of our Party still cling to the outmoded and unworthy view that women may not play their part in the struggle with a gun in their hands and that they have no business in a military barracks. These are the views of fifth columnists who seek to prevent women from playing an active part in the liberation struggle."[87]

At the December 6, 1942 national congress of the Antifascist Women's Front, Tito, himself, expressly reiterated the importance of women to the liberation struggle. "Comrades, the evidence is that women have carried most of the burden of that struggle, whether in the rearguard or on the front," he declared in his opening address to the congress. He added:

> The women of Yugoslavia, who have sacrificed so much in this struggle, who have stood so steadfastly in the front ranks of the national liberation front, are entitled to expect one thing today, tomorrow, and forever: that this struggle too must be productive for the women themselves, that no one can ever again deny them the fruits they have watered with their blood... Some people abroad [the reference here is to the conservative government-in-exile] seek to sustain the expectation that the old order will emerge triumphant again in Yugoslavia, with the women going back into the kitchen and having no more say. But, comrades, the women have withstood the test. They have demonstrated that not only do they have it in them to run the home, but they can also fight with arms and are capable of governing and of exercising power.[88]

Tough talking delivered with an aplomb that was not forthcoming from the lips of any other politician of this rank, from Paris to Vilna. Tito must have realized that not only certain forces outside the country, but also a good number of his own comrades were expecting that, after the war, the old order between the sexes would, more or less, prevail once more. But, for one thing, the women of the country had secured the right to vote and be elected for the first time in Yugoslavia's history. With the launching of the National Liberation Army in 1941, national liberation committees, a people's underground government, was also set up in the regions. Their deputies were elected in mass assemblies by open vote. As early as the first elections held in Slovenia, female deputies took one-third of the seats; elsewhere, they sometimes scored even higher and their numbers were growing constantly right up until the end of the war.

2

The Titoist partisans' liberation struggle soon spread into the Slovene territories in Austria. The Slovene population from Carinthia, which had relocated to Yugoslavia, fleeing persecution in post-Anschluss Austria, went home after the occupation of Yugoslavia and joined with the leaders of the Liberation Army in setting up partisan units in the bilingual part of Carinthia. In November 1942, Carinthia's first partisan unit came into existence: it was joined by Karel Prusnik-Gasper, shortly to become one of the main leaders of the Slovene resistance.[89] As early as August 1942, the Kranjc Battalion of the Yugoslav Liberation Army had been attacked near Robesch by an SS unit and had mounted a successful counterattack. News that the all-powerful SS organization had sustained an apparent defeat—the first ever within Reich territory—spread like wildfire. Perhaps the partisans' resistance was not an absurd dream after all? What if it was possible to defeat the Nazis? The spark of rebellion ignited the Slovene population. The first partisans to show up asking for food at one of the isolated farmsteads in the mountains were welcomed with open arms. And it was not uncommon for one of the farmers' sons to join them when they left. Simultaneously with the partisan groups, Liberation Front (Osvobodilna Fronta) committees belonging to the antifascist resistance's political organization (the equivalent of the national liberation committees inside Yugoslavia) were formed. The first underground Osvobodilna Fronta (OF) cell was set up in August 1942 in Lobning, near Eisenkappel: in eastern Carinthia alone, some 200 people, male and female, had joined the OF before autumn. The Eisenkappel area became a partisan center, a focal point for political activity. Men who had been drafted deserted and new leaflets were forever appearing, telecommunications posts were being attacked, bridges and rail links were being blown up. By the winter of 1942–43, the German authorities declared the area "hostile territory." The end of March 1943 saw the launching of the first Carinthian battalion, which mounted the raid on the movie theater in Mezica: now the partisans extended their theater of operations south and southeast of Carinthia. In late 1943 and throughout 1944, they scored great successes: the German army, the Wehrmacht, found itself obliged to station 10,000 troops in Carinthia, troops needed on the eastern front, and a constant reminder that there was another front inside Reich territory itself, a front that neither the all-powerful SS nor the Wehrmacht could keep in check. From the summer of 1944 onwards, the Slovene partisans, whose numbers had climbed to some 700, also had support from the Allies. At the same time, Slovene activists met with representatives from the Austrian resistance and, in November 1944, they launched a mixed Austrian Battalion that was incorporated into the National Liberation Army of Slovenia.

In the winter of 1944–45, the Germans launched a huge offensive against the partisans. They found themselves forced to occupy the Karawanken mountains in order to set up a line of defense against the Allies advancing through Italy, an undertaking frustrated by the actions of the Carinthian partisans and units of the National Liberation Army of Yugoslavia. The onslaught cost the lives of many female and male partisans, but the Germans were unable really to eradicate resistance. Shortly before the end of the war, unable to get the better of the partisans, they vented their fury on the civilian population. As late as April 25, 1945, just a fortnight before the liberation, the SS murdered eleven members of the Persman family in Koprein-Petzen, near Eisenkappel: from the grandparents down to the children, they were all slaughtered. On May 8, the partisans entered Klagenfurt alongside the British. The war was over.

Contrary to what happened in Yugoslavia, where the resistance had been organized right after the occupation, the Carinthian Slovenes launched their resistance relatively late. Except for a few young Communists who, after the failure of the February 1934 uprising, started to be persecuted and who, after the Anschluss, fled in the direction of Yugoslavia or went to ground, most of the population reacted rather passively, even after the Germans marched into Austria in 1938. For the most part, the Slovene population was made up of poor peasants living in small hamlets or isolated farmsteads. They were religious and non-political; an oppressed minority (although they made up the majority of the population in some parts of Carinthia) controlled by conservative clerical functionaries charged with maintaining order, keeping the peace, and preserving traditional customs and practices.

Ever since the Middle Ages, Slovenes had endured discrimination from the German-speaking population. After the bourgeois revolution of 1848, they were subjected to a policy of Germanization. The German-speaking bourgeoisie, who had a monopoly on trade and craft activity, industry, and the civil service regarded themselves as the policemen of the south and fought for a German Carinthia. When, in the wake of the armistice in 1918, frictions increased between Yugoslavia and the recently founded Austrian Republic over the matter of the Slovene territories in Carinthia, a Carinthian Fatherland Service (which, in 1924, changed its name to the Carinthian Fatherland Union) and defensive units were organized to resist incorporation into Yugoslavia. The 1920 plebiscite was a triumph for the Fatherland Union as Carinthia remained part of Austria and Slovenes had run up against a powerful and unscrupulous new impediment. By the late 1920s the Fatherland Union, under the chairmanship of Alois Maier-Kaibitsch, was agitating for German colonization in the bilingual territories and, through its land transfer agency, was selling land to interested Germans. After the National Socialist German Workers Party (NSDAP) was outlawed in Austria in 1934, the Fatherland Union solicitously made room in its ranks for these illegal Nazis and emerged as a trusted partner in the Eastern Marches. Following the Anschluss, the Fatherland Union not only disbanded itself, but was absorbed along with its entire apparatus into the NSDAP, and was able to carry on with its work with renewed strength. Maier-Kaibitsch was put in charge of Minority Affairs and was later made head of the District Department for Nationality Matters. The Slovenes' worst enemy now had carte blanche to determine their fate.

That fate was transference or, to put it another way, expulsion. There were plans to settle German-speaking Tyroleans and residents of the Kanal valley in Carinthia, whereas 50,000 Slovenes would be expelled in the direction of Yugoslavia and, above all, toward the territory between Kharkov and Rostov, in the lands occupied by the Soviet Union. Maier-Kaibitsch and his Fatherland Front pals had their lists all ready and waiting when the scheme was postponed, Berlin not wishing to alienate the Belgrade government unnecessarily. Within a few months of the invasion of Yugoslavia, the scheme was activated again. On August 25, 1941, Himmler signed an order for the forcible expulsion of the Slovene population from Carinthia. The operation was due to open with the expulsion of 200 families, supposed "enemies of the people and State." On April 14, 1942, the SS and police deported 186 families in cattle trucks to the Ebental concentration camp. The Slovene population's passivity concluded in violence: even those who had believed the promises that Hitler was going to wipe out the debts of the poor farmers, and that they were all going to receive food, awoke from their dreams. Since the first partisan groups surfaced at the same time as the first deportations were made, people had the chance to discover a useful outlet for their indignation, rather than sink into despair and resignation. Slovene partisan resistance in Carinthia had begun.

But in the wake of the liberation, defeat followed. The British, who had, in the closing months of the war, supported the partisans as allies and worked in conjunction with them, turned into persecutors as soon as they became an occupying force. Scarcely had the fight against national socialism been won than the struggle against Communism started. Participants in the liberation struggle, held in high esteem inside Yugoslavia, wound up behind bars in Austria in quite a few cases. The Carinthian Fatherland Front weathered zero hour with little difficulty and set about vilifying the partisans, labelling them as malefactors eager to deliver the country over to the Communist ogre Tito. It also persisted with its aim of working towards a German Carinthia. Many embittered ex-combatants simply took a back seat and said nothing. The official Austrian historiography makes no mention of the extraordinary contribution these women and men had made to the defeat of national socialist rule. When Tito fell out with the Soviet Union, they also fell out of favor with the Communists and were, at best, ignored. If any interest at all were shown in it, the history of Austrian resistance was depicted as monarchist, liberal, or conservative resistance, or else as the handiwork of the social democrats or Communist Party of Austria. Not a word was said of the Carinthian Slovenes' having turned a part of the Reich into enemy territory and or of their even having humbled the SS.

Female participation in the Austrian resistance from Vienna to Innsbruck was also similarly shrouded in obscurity. As late as 1983, in an article entitled "Women in the Austrian Resistance" Rita Thalmann, after examining the relevant bibliographic material, complained that the part played by women had been covered up completely. The only—the few—works on the subject (not cited in other works) have been written by women.[90] Thalmann looks to the—unpublished—dissertation by Inge Brauneis, which enumerates 300 verdicts handed down against women charged with having participated in the resistance (which is to say with having carried out acts as part of the organized resistance: these do not include sentences relating to isolated actions). Of these

300 women, 156 were Communists, 24 were socialists, 42 of them members of civilian associations, and 78 members of partisans groups. Inge Brauneis estimates that 18 percent of the women who belonged to partisan groups has taken an active part in the fighting.[91] But who these women were and what had induced them to make such a radical break with the role assigned them—until very recently, not a thing was known about this, even inside the resistance.

The year 1981 saw the publication, in German, of the memoirs of the Carinthian partisan commander, Karel Prusnik-Gasper—a work little known despite its importance, since, in Austria, with the exception of the Slovene population in Carinthia, nobody has any interest in the topic.[92] Prusnik-Gasper made several very respectful references to his female comrades, from Marjetka, who helped storm that movie theater in Mezica, to Zala, who was by his side when his partisan unit liberated Klagenfurt. Four years later, in 1985, came the first comprehensive acknowledgment in German (which is to say, non-Slovene acknowledgment) of the part played by Slovene women in the resistance.[93] The Viennese team of female authors Berger, Holzinger, Podgornik, and Trallori had interviewed women all over Austria who had engaged in antifascist activities. They also travelled out to Carinthia to speak with Slovene ex-partisan women. Lisbeth N. Trallori writes in her article, "The Unsung Resistance" that she found it extraordinarily hard to get these women to talk. They were reluctant because they feared that, when their histories became known, they would face further harassment or other reprisals from the authorities, or from the people around them. This attitude was especially pronounced in Carinthia where it is all too common knowledge that the Fatherland Union still carries on its political activities.[94]

When, in 1987, I visited Lobning, near Eisenkappel, to see Johanna Sadolsek, nicknamed Zala in her partisan days, for the purpose of conducting an interview with her, thanks to the groundwork laid by the Viennese team, I found things easier. However, I also had to overcome mistrust, the fruit of long and bitter experiences, until Zala showed any disposition to answer my queries with genuine openness.

3

How does a native-born peasant girl who has never had anything to do with politics end up a partisan?[95] What impels her to swap her rosary beads for a revolver? Virtually all of the Carinthian Slovene women who joined Tito's National Liberation Army were poor, had grown up in the direst poverty. They were familiar with hunger, toil, prayer, and little else. Zala never even had a pair of shoes to call her own. The only pair of women's shoes the family possessed had to be shared with her mother and grandmother. If one of them was going to Eisenkappel, the nearest town, the other two had to stay at home. Zala's clothes were always hand-me-downs. The farm that her mother worked with Zala's assistance was so deep in hock that they could not sell a hen without a creditor taking a cut. Zala's mother was unmarried, and her two children—Zala and a brother who left home to study in the seminary—had different fathers. This was a result, not of loose morals, but of the poverty and double standards that were the inevitable lot of the uneducated. Zala's mother had had only three years of schooling. Zala herself had six years of primary schooling during which she learned above all that the Slovenes were second-class people. Mira, the daughter of farm laborers, who later went on to serve as a radio technician with the partisans, was sent away after school, at the age of twelve, to keep house for some peasants. Things took an even worse turn when they sent her off to work as a maid in the home of some business people. There, in addition to doing the housework, she was expected to manhandle heavy planks in the saw-mill.[96] Zala used to help out on the farm, of course, during her school days. Her mother was a peasant who labored in the fields while her grandmother ran the house. She looked after the children, did the cooking and repeatedly mended their worn clothing.

In winter, it would be dark by the time Zala got home from school. The school was a long way away and lessons were not over until four o'clock in the afternoon. Like many others, Zala also walked through the snow in her stocking feet. From time to time, the teacher would take pity on them and dismiss them an hour ahead of time. But there was no compromise in the matter of language: the girls and boys were compelled to speak German at school. Since the Slovene children accounted for more than half of the class, they could not understand a word. During their first year, there was a school-mistress who also

Zala the partisan

spoke Slovene; later, children were fined ten pennies when they let slip a Slovene word.[97] Thus did politics determine life for these folk who themselves took no interest in politics. "Nobody there had any interest in politics, least of all the peasants. Every Sunday they would go to Mass and make their way home and start back to work. This was the daily routine. The only people of any importance were the priests."[98] In school, however, there was politicking: one of the teachers, later discovered to be a member of the outlawed NSDAP, gathered around him a select group of pupils who would later join the SS.

At seventeen, Zala had to get married. Her grandfather, the farm owner, had passed away and Zala's brother, the lawful heir, entered the priesthood, therefore renouncing his inheritance. This meant that only the women were left. One fine day, a peasant leader showed up from the city and they explained the position to him, whereupon he asked: "Right, let's see now. Who's going to be the farmer here?" Her brother demurred, so it was up to Zala. "I did not dare and did not know what to say, and my mother said: 'Right, she'll take over the farm.'" They all seemed to agree, but she had to marry soon "so as to have a man about the place." Zala found herself coming under pressure: "On a daily basis my mother, grandmother, and everybody would talk to me about getting married, but how could I get married just like that when I didn't even understand what marriage and all that meant? In those days we knew nothing...." So Zala married the nearest candidate, the son of a neighbor. "He was ten years older than me, and was good, I have to say, and progressive." Saying that he was good means that he worked hard on the farm and treated his wife humanely. Love was never mentioned. Michael Sadolsek, that being his name, was also intelligent, from what Zala says, and "progressive" actually signifies that he belonged to an underground Communist group.

Zala, highly intelligent herself, had her first contact with politics and learned to look upon Hitler's promises with a critical eye. In 1938, two years prior to Zala's wedding, Nazi Germany had annexed Austria and, in the ensuing propaganda onslaught, initially no distinction was made between German Carinthians and Carinthia's Slovene peasants. All of a sudden, it was announced that all debts were to be cancelled—an incalculable blessing for the small-holders, up to their necks in debt. Food was distributed; "there is enough for everyone," the impatient were lectured. It seemed as if an earthly paradise awaited Carinthia's needy population. Zala recalls that her dying grandfather was relieved to see that everything was on the way to being resolved. But, even as the food was being shared out, the first clouds appeared over the new paradise. Carinthia's Nazis failed to live up to their Reich colleagues' propaganda schemes and soon ceased making gifts to all and sundry. Jelka, another partisan-to-be, remembers: "Hitler's people were carrying out the distribution. Our gendarme was there to open and close the door, ushering people in one after another. When my turn came, and the door was opened for me, the mayor was inside along with a fanatical Hitler supporter...the gendarme grabbed me and shoved me outside into the queue of women outside... They had sent me an invitation to go there, but then they shoved me outside. They had already checked the register for the names of the people slated for transfer."[99]

In 1942, Zala witnessed the first forcible transfer: "That of the entire Stopac peasant family, a man and three women. 'Quick, quick,' they were told. They had to be ready within half an hour. Then it was all aboard the lorry and away they went." Zala also relates how they came looking for her and her family. In May 1941, she had given birth to her first child and, in the spring of 1942, her husband was drafted into the army. Zala managed the house and the farm on her own, with help from her mother, her grandmother, and some Polish and Ukrainian convicts assigned to them. Zala learned a little more about how the fascists treated folk. The convicts were not allowed either to eat or sleep in the house. The two laborers often had to leap up from the table and race for the stables, while the womenfolk of the family hurriedly hid their dishes, if the gendarmes dropped by on patrol to inspect the farm. Zala grew increasingly outraged by the inhuman treatment meted out to the Poles, by the transfers of Slovenes, and the round-ups of Communists. Two of those arrested finally returned, having been inmates in Dachau, to tell their neighbors "what Hitler is doing with the folk in the concentration camps." By which time, Zala had heard enough.

When rumors that there were partisans in the area ran through the village, her reaction was one of curiosity rather than fear, even though "Hitler had carried out a lot of propaganda, arguing that they were all bandits, murderers, and brutes addicted to killing people." What Hitler had overlooked was that one of these bandits might well be a neighbor's son. In spite of everything, Zala was not shocked until she saw her first partisans in the autumn of 1942: "We had finished the sowing behind the house, over yonder. Interestingly, when we saw them, they were armed and we were a bit afraid." There were ten or twelve of them, some in civilian dress, others in uniform. "They just ambled over to us and asked us if there were any German police around. And then they added, don't be afraid, we're from the Slovene Liberation Front and we have to drive out the fascists. You've seen how you are treated by them. You must help us beat Hitler." Zala was not afraid now, but she was thinking: "My God! Hitler is so powerful. He's never going to lose!" The partisans' response was that he would, and they told them all about their battles, the antifascist front, and the uprising in Yugoslavia. Then, they asked for Zala's help, saying that they had got lost and were looking for their battalion. Zala, nineteen years old at this time, took her first step into underground political work. She took the partisans to a neighbor, who she knew to have connections, and he brought the stragglers to a courier who escorted them to their unit. The first threads of a network had been woven together. What struck Zala as commonplace assistance, even though she realized that it was, in fact, forbidden, was punishable by the authorities as aiding and abetting malefactors and terrorists. Zala, who had just shown that she could be trusted, discovered that she was not the only one with links to the partisans. And she would shortly be hearing more from them.

It happened one Sunday after Mass. As Zala was leaving the church, a neighbor woman told her: "I've had a visit." Her conspiratorial tone suggested that it had not been a straightforward visit from a harmless relation. "They'll be coming to see you too," the woman told Zala as they walked together as far as the woman's home, where Zala was given further details. Shortly after that, Zala had her visit too. The visitor was Karel Prusnik-Gasper, and he had been commissioned to organize a branch of the Antifascist Women's Front in the Eisenkappel area. What he had to say was listened to very attentively. "We were young and, in a way, that is what prompted us," says Zala. Women who had been killing themselves toiling all day long as if it were the most natural thing in the world jumped at a mission that not only promised variety, but recognition too. They fully appreciated that it was risky, but their work would help "to drive Hitler out." That, too, was a factor, given their experiences of national socialism.

They were given posters, handbills, and placards to be distributed during at night, and sometimes in broad daylight: "Death to fascism," "Freedom for the peoples," they announced, as well as "German soldiers, Slovene soldiers, do not fight for Hitler!" Their homes were used for washing the partisans' laundry, for cooking for them, and food was carried out to them in their mountain hideouts. Zala cooked and her mother carried casseroles out into the forest. In Klagenfurt, the women bought up bandages and medicine in dribs and drabs, obtained from different pharmacies to avoid attracting attention. Sometimes, at night, the partisans would come down to the farm to sleep—especially if they were wounded. But, sometimes, there were also nocturnal visits from the gendarmes who meant to spend the night on the farms while out on patrol. If they had police visitors, the women would leave a prearranged signal somewhere close to the forest, a cross made of fallen branches. If the gendarmes were marauding in the area in the daylight, the women would hang a duster in the window. It may have looked like a curtain, but the partisans grasped its meaning. Propaganda material would be hidden in the stable or in the beehive, where even the SS did not dare venture when carrying out house searches.[100] Zala's husband was posted to the *chasseurs* barracks, and this furnished a splendid pretext for the hardest and most dangerous element of the work carried out by women: they wanted to persuade the Slovene soldiers to desert, and to recruit them for the partisans. The plan was worked out down to the smallest detail. To avert possible reprisals against families, they would pretend to have been press-ganged into it. The soldier, with his weapons, would be taken to the nearest partisan base. As soon as he was far enough away, his wife or mother would come running to the police station, crying and sobbing "They came and grabbed him and they took him away! What are we to do?" The ruse worked well, initially at any rate. But the women did their job so well that, increasingly, there were fewer and fewer Slovenes returning to the front after being on leave, and there were also many who had vanished directly from their barracks. This impelled the authorities to ban the soldiers from sleeping in the family home when they were on leave: they were to stay in Eisenkappel, with their wives, children and parents were required to travel into the city to see them. The whole area around Eisenkappel was declared "hostile territory."

The Germans' next move was to send special troops into the villages dressed as partisans. To this day, Zala is shocked at how slow she was to catch on: "They were marching through the village in broad daylight, wearing Tito caps!" But this matter was not just a source of amusement; the women were obliged to call once again upon their ingenuity. They had to get rid of these provocateurs, but could not directly poke fun at them: so what were they to do? When one of these bands billeted itself in the house of one of Zala's uncles—an old Communist—Zala and a female comrade from the Antifascist Women's Front scurried down to the police station in Eisenkappel and excitedly explained: "Partisans are in my uncle's house. They've been there all night and they're still there. We didn't dare do anything during the night, but now you must come right away and round them up!" "You did well to let us know," the gendarmes commended her, but they appeared to be in no hurry to apprehend the bandits.

But, already, the position of the female antifascists in villages near Eisenkappel was critical. In particular, the chair of the Women's Front, Zala herself, had been under suspicion for some time. Of course, she might vanish at any moment, but she remained in her post until the last moment. Because she knew that "the partisans did not want us women to join them, since we were a lot more useful to them at home, operating within the law." And she also knew what grave reprisals were hanging over her family if she were to openly throw in her lot with the partisans. If a woman like Zala was to abandon farm and family, there could be absolutely no doubt as to the reason. Not in her neighbors' minds, nor in the minds of the police.

On October 26, 1943, Zala's husband arrived in Eisenkappel on leave. Because of the recent ban, he was unable to go home to Lobning, but he was keen to see his son at all costs and persuaded Zala to let him come home with her. Under cover of the darkness, they crept inside. Zala had a bad feeling, fearing that the police might suddenly come knocking on the door. The following day, October 27, a sharp knock on the door was heard: "Open up!" Her mother did, and police officials flooded into the room. But they were not asking about Zala's husband who was standing in front of them, expecting to be hauled away. They took no notice of him; what they wanted to know was: "Where is the peasant woman?" Now Zala understood what was going on. Just to be on the safe side she put on a lot of clothes: woolen underwear, sturdy shoes, two sweaters. The police were taken aback but allowed her to proceed. Zala says: "I had always thought I would do things that way: if ever they captured me, I would try to escape. There were too many things I had done that they could charge me with." But, en route to Eisenkappel police station, no opportunity presented itself. Six Gestapo officials showed up to interrogate her. Zala played stupid and denied everything. The Gestapo men accused her of being the organizer, and they believed her to be *au fait* with all of the existing connections—as indeed she was. But Zala maintained that she knew no one, had no notion about anything, did not know what it was that they wanted from her. The interrogation dragged on for hours. There was one thing they were keen to know above all else: the whereabouts of the Leppen partisans' bunker. As it happened, Zala did not know this, so she found it easy to refuse to answer. But the police did not believe a word of it, and they forced her to come with them to seek out the bunker: she was bound and escorted by six Gestapo men and by seventy-six gendarmes who followed them into the night. Although her position seemed utterly hopeless, Zala had but one thought in her mind: "I have to get away." On and on they walked. Zala's escorts started to grow impatient. "Where's the bunker?" They pressed her again and again, and they threatened her: "You have no idea what we may end up doing to you. There's a fine surprise in store for you, if you don't show us where the bunker is!" Zala was only too well aware "what we may end up doing to you." She began to sob: "My hands, loosen my hands a bit. I can't go on any more. I've lost all feeling in my hands." When she sat down, crying and refusing to go any further, she finally got them to do what she wanted. As she walked along she tried to slip her hands out of the chains, twisting them, and she waited until they came to a very dark, overgrown spot in the woods. Then she abruptly dropped to the ground and rolled away to one side: "The peasant woman has escaped!" shouted one of the startled gendarmes as bullets and tracers started to whiz over her head. She bumped into a tree and passed out: when she came to, she thought: "Blessed Virgin, I'm dead now!" But in spite of the pains in her head she managed to struggle to her feet, blundering into some brambles, and on she ran, bleeding and scratched, until eventually she reached a small, sheltered copse where she waited for daylight to come. The next day, she came upon a team of woodcutters who gave some makeshift treatment to her injuries and fed her. Zala continued to flee as far as the farmstead of some peasant friends. When their daughters saw her approach, they were certain that they were looking at a ghost: "Holy Mother, Zala, but you must be dead. Surely they shot you?" they stammered, aghast. Eventually, they flung their arms around the spectre, once they realized it was the real flesh-and-blood Zala they had in front of them. The police had put out the story that the peasant woman Sadolsek had been shot dead while attempting to escape. There was no way that they could own up to the defeat implicit in a shackled woman' giving the slip to six Gestapo officers and seventy-six gendarmes.

The next day, Zala arrived at the partisan encampment behind the rocks at Breck. To begin a new life. Karel Prusnik-Gasper, the unit commander, has this to say of life in the encampment, in his memoirs:

> The partisan cannot afford the luxuries of fire, food, nor peace of mind. When we arrived, we first tackled the pine trees... Later we turned our attention to the frozen soil, digging out shelters. We worked hard from dawn until dark. Not until evening fell would Muri light the fire, and, by nearly eleven o'clock at night, the first food was ready, a sort of sour soup of potatoes and mutton, but with no bread of course. We set up our camp on top of the soil we had just excavated, under the open skies. After a few days,

the shelters dug in the ground were ready. They were bigger and better than the first ones, and we were even able to hold our political meetings "under shelter." We felt more at ease up there than down in the valley below. Nobody could eavesdrop on us and we could even sing. When the valleys were blanketed in thick snow, we lighted a fire during the daylight hours too and roasted potatoes... Worst of all was the infestation of lice... We used to wear the same clothes day and night, changing only very rarely. I only removed my shoes when I was changing my socks. And even then it was one at a time, not both at once.[101]

To his horror, Prusnik-Gasper discovered the first louse on Marjetka; it was crawling on her trousers. "'Marjetka,' I told her in disbelief, 'there's a louse!' Marjetka guffawed and said: 'Where you find rifles, there you find lice as well.'" Shortly after this, he himself felt a bite and wondered why. Marjetka blithely explained to him that it was simply due to his being lousy as well. "It seems that I was something of a spoilt brat towards Marjetka. 'First time anything like this has ever happened to me,' I told her. But the tiny partisan wrinkled her nose with contempt for this greenhorn soldier."[102]

At the start, Zala reckoned that she would not be able to stick it out. But then she grew used to the harshness of the partisan lifestyle: "We slept in the open air under the trees, even in winter. We used to break off some pine branches, lay them on the snow, and sleep on top of them. Come the dawn, we were stiff as boards, or else we had to get up during the night and move around to stop ourselves from freezing. And our feet and shoes were so stiff that we never took them off, except when we were changing or something like that, but, apart from that, we always slept in our clothes, clutching our guns, as we had to be ready at all times. We never knew when the enemy would be coming, nor from what direction."[103]

The burden was even heavier for the women who were also unable to change clothes when they had their period. Zala says: "This was very often critical. We had to wash in a stream. There were no compresses, so everything soaked into one's trousers and they stank. But, in the end, we put up with it. We had to." Organizing food was a complicated affair too. "Nearly always it came from those peasants who still had something left. But later on, things became very tough. Many of them had nothing left, some of them had been moved elsewhere so that only the wife was left behind, or two or three women who had not managed to bring in much of a harvest. And, every day, partisans would show up, one starving partisan and then another, also starving, so things were really hard for the householders, a lot harder than for the partisans."[104] Zala is very much aware of the problems faced by the women who had stayed behind to support the partisans, because she knows about them from firsthand experience. So the uncomfortable, demanding life of the women and men fighters living in the open, with their long forced marches from one sabotage operation to the next encampment, strikes her as easier than the dangers implicit in hard underground work carried out within the law.

Meanwhile, she had overcome her initial fears, and also her main concern about having to bed down surrounded by so many men: "Blessed Mother! I had thought, what's going to happen here! I won't bed down here, I told myself, and sleep alongside the men. I don't know how I'm going to manage." She was relieved to find that nothing untoward befell her: "I had no problems with them. They showed me respect at all times." She learned that partisans who carried out sexual abuse suffered death as a punishment. Only stable couples were allowed to engage in sexual relations, but even this was counselled against as contraception was hard to come by, and pregnancy spelled disaster. Many married couples were also serving in different units: when Zala's husband deserted and joined the partisans, she ran into him one time at a political meeting. Zala, Mira, and other women partisans, even today, underline the climate of comradeship that prevailed in their units. From what they say, no distinction was made between women and men and in the combat units per se, the men also took their turn at the cooking. The women played their part in all operations, regardless of the risks involved. "Frequently the women even set an example for the men," says Zala. As the Slovene population almost to a person was in sympathy with the partisans, they were occasionally able to indulge themselves and go on a spree: they would emerge from their hiding places and make for some peasant's house, or, more likely, some peasant woman's house, to which all of the neighbors had already been invited and they would hold a party: "We had music and dancing and a grand old time."[105]

When Zala reached the partisan encampment, she was given some basic military training, which, in her case, did not take too long because, like many mountain peasant women, she already knew how to shoot. She was assigned to a political unit, a team of six or seven specialists who travelled from village to village, from one partisan base to the next, giving political classes, carrying out propaganda, and recruiting new members to the Liberation Front and Antifascist Women's Front. Occasionally they might be caught up in a skirmish, have a brush with a patrol, or stumble into an ambush, in which case, they would defend themselves just like any combat unit. But, in the afternoons, when the others could snatch a little rest, Zala had to type up reports for the political leadership on the typewriter that never left her side. Once, when her team was surprised by the police—while having dinner at a farmstead—and had only just shot its way free, Zala absentmindedly left her typewriter behind. As soon as she realized her error she went back to collect it, even though the police had thrown a cordon around the whole area. Zala was by then the Antifascist Women's Front secretary for the entire Carinthia region, a position of some eminence, but one that involved a lot of extra work.

Women like Mira (who acted as a technician) supplied the material basis for Zala's political work. In underground shelters atop some mountain, under a rock, or hidden in a haystack, Mira would type up leaflets, illegal reviews, and reports for Radio London. Initially, the only way she had of reprinting the typed material was to run off countless carbon copies herself, an interminably wearying and laborious procedure. Later, the units in Carinthia were to find themselves a more professional technician from Yugoslavia, and Mira got a copying machine. In addition to this sort of work, she did sentry duty and took part in patrols, armed, of course, for her own protection and for the protection of the gear in her care. And—unlike Zala or Marjetka, the fighter—Mira also took her turn at the cooking.[106]

By Zala's reckoning, women accounted for about 20 percent of the personnel in the partisan units.[107] Some of them were full-time fighters, others political leaders like Zala, some were nurses, and others—especially the older women—worked in the kitchens, did the sewing, and looked after the cleaning in the shelter. But women also held high office, Zala stresses, and were military commanders or political commissars with big battalions—even though this was chiefly true in Yugoslavia. Zala takes pride in these women she got to know during her three months' training in Yugoslavia.

Early in July 1944, Zala began her journey to the Dolenska liberated territory. She trudged for eight days from base to base, from courier to courier, until she arrived at the military school. There, she took theoretical and practical classes with seventy-six trainees. The curriculum covered fascism, imperialism, capitalism, and communism, but also military tactics and weapons-handling. Furthermore, there was a dentist at her disposal, a huge relief to the fighters who were away in the mountains for months or years at a time.[108] Zala enjoyed the school, the classes, the discussions, and conversations with her female comrades. She passed the final examinations with commendation—she who had only had six years of primary schooling, and who had scarcely had the time to study because she'd had to help out by working around the farm. Later, she had to return to the front lines where conditions had, by the autumn of 1944, become tougher than ever.

The Allies' entry into Italy and the escalation of the partisan struggle in Carinthia created lots to keep the German army occupied. In the winter of 1944–45, it launched its big push against the Liberation Army. In spite of heavy casualties, the partisans managed to hold on to their most important positions and, by May 7, 1945, they were entering Eisenkappel.

On May 8, when they were en route to Klagenfurt, news broke of the German surrender.[109] Karel Prusnik-Gasper, in his memoirs, recounts: "We proceeded with caution all the same. My machine-gun and Zala's machine-pistol were kept trained on the adjacent forest throughout."[110] Rightly so. Some scattered Chetnik fascist troops and a few isolated units of Ukrainian and SS troops held out even after the surrender. Zala and Prusnik-Gasper, shortly before entering Klagenfurt, had to disarm a group of SS members who showed little inclination to surrender.[111]

Zala had come through the war with no major flesh wounds. Though, for two years, she had lived with the knowledge that "the last bullet is for me," since being taken alive by the enemy was a fate worse than death. Zala states all this casually and naturally, without any histrionics. The sensation has nothing to do with fear. The female and male combatants soon learned to come to some accommodation with their feelings. They lived from day to day, from operation to operation, the focus continually upon the next target—carrying out some sabotage operation—and upon the ultimate objective: "putting paid to Hitlerite fascism."[112]

> One thinks about nothing. No thoughts of home, just of what is in the offing... By then, I had overcome my fear. It left me cold, utterly cold. If there is a war on and you are continually in danger, you get used to it and it does not matter whether you are a woman or not. It makes no difference. Lots of times I felt impelled to reflect: if it should be my turn next, I have no complaint.[113]

But then Zala found out about the tragedy that had struck her home. In November 1943, one month after she had fled, the police had showed up at the farm. At the time, the family was hiding a partisan who had come to collect his clothes. The police saw this as further grounds for exacting an even harsher punishment for Zala's disappearance. They tossed incendiaries into the stable, which erupted into flames immediately. The partisan, who tried to escape, was shot in the back and died instantly. Then they turned to the livestock and loaded it aboard a truck. After the livestock, it was the people's turn. Zala's two aunts and cousins were taken to Auschwitz, only one of the aunts surviving. In the end, they allowed her grandmother and Zala's two-year-old son to escape, but they traced Zala's brother to his seminary and deported him to Dachau. Zala's mother managed to escape, fleeing into the mountains where she joined the partisans, and, right up until the end of the war, she worked tending the sick and cooking for her unit.[114] A courier brought this news to the officer commanding Zala's section, not daring to tell her directly. But she had caught a few snatches of his report and pressed him for the full story: "Whereupon he told me everything that had happened. I wandered off from the bunker for a few meters and wept... I had no idea how I was going to carry on, how anyone could endure all this."[115]

And the ghastly news kept coming. More farms were put to the torch, their inhabitants (from the oldest to the youngest) deported, shot, or thrown alive into the flames. The Russian fascist Cossacks behaved even more cruelly than the police or the German SS: "For instance, there was one woman in Ferlach who had been shot in the thigh and was thus unable to escape. This was when the war was nearly over, in February 1945. They cut off her breasts, these Cossacks serving with the SS, and, using a knife, they started to flay her little by little: there was blood everywhere, and then one of them took pity on her and finished her off with one stroke of the knife."[116] Other women were raped and then slowly tortured to death. "I did feel hatred then," says Zala, a hatred stronger than her indifference to the dangers all around her.[117] Yet there is no way that she would have been able to turn the tables and put a prisoner to death or even "torture somebody into talking. I couldn't do that now, nor could I have done it at the time."[118] But, knowing very well that there are others who are capable of such things, she always carried a hand grenade with her, just in case she found herself with no way out.

"The last bullet or bomb was for me," says Zala, as she recalls—with some amusement these days—a situation in which she reckoned that her time had come. Along with a male comrade, she had walked into a police ambush. Initially, they were both able to escape and take cover behind a boulder, but they knew, or imagined, that they were surrounded. "Whereupon I said to him, 'Now put a bullet into me or I'll do it for you.' He grabbed my pistol and said: 'We're not going to kill ourselves just yet!'" Luckily for her, because, after hours and hours of waiting behind that boulder—"we didn't even dare breathe"—they were able to scramble away unhurt. Her comrade, who had refused to take that final step, would spend years after the war telling just about anyone who was willing to listen: "I'm the only one who ever saw Zala tremble." Her granddaughter Maja Haderlap told me, after my interview with Zala, that her grandmother was really proud of this, that no one, apart from him, had ever seen her tremble.

Zala was accepted by her comrades as an equal, but the odd one reckoned that she was too hard for a woman, too mannish. A female fighter who trembled on a regular basis would have been despised and not taken seriously. One that never trembled made them uneasy. Following the liberation, when they all returned to their former existence—and to their former roles—there were some ex-comrades who thought it improper that Zala should defend her active part in the struggle and, indeed, take some pride in it. Other former women partisans slipped back into their womanly role and said that they had carried arms solely for their own protection, but had never fired them. Zala was not able to lie to herself this way. From time to time, this set her at odds with her own people and drew open hatred from one-time adversaries who had long since recovered their positions and honors, and who had no compunction about displaying their contempt for Slovenes and feelings of vindictiveness with regard to the onetime partisans, female or male. "The Germans' propaganda said that women became partisans just to get off with the men."

They were dubbed "red whores." Zala was insulted by the militant German patriots of Carinthia, even after the war. They called her a "killer" and a "partisan whore." During the war, a fascist neighbor, capitalizing upon the fact that Zala's husband was in the army, attempted to force himself upon her on two occasions. Both times she successfully fought him off. Once (this was before her flight), when she was troubled by acute tonsillitis, he spread the rumor that this was the result of whoring around with partisans—and he steadfastly refused to make any retraction when she came home officially as the victor, with him as the vanquished. In fact, the female and male partisans were only winners during the first three days of the liberation. The old Slovene-hating, reactionary patriotic order was restored in Carinthia with impressive speed. Even the British, who had until recently been allied with the Liberation Army, wasted little time in hunting down and jailing their former allies as Communists.

Zala returned from Klagenfurt to her home in Lobning deeply disappointed, to be confronted by a heap of rubble. Parts of the building had been consumed by the flames; the remainder was an uninhabitable ruin, the livestock gone, the fields ruined. She had no time to catch her breath, much less rest from the fatigues of the war. Zala and her husband had to set to work right away if they were to have at least a roof over their heads. Whereas the former Nazis (who largely clung to their fascist ideology) were taking up the better paid positions, Zala and many of her former comrades-in-arms, female and male, had absolutely nothing, and struggled through many more long years of bitter poverty. Not that Zala had fought with an eye to reward; she fought because she despised the fascists and also had hoped that, in the wake of the liberation, a new society might emerge in which social injustice would be no more. But she had never imagined that things could have turned out so differently. She had not reckoned upon the contempt and hatred with which she had to contend in the liberated Carinthia.

She, who had breezed through her courses in Yugoslavia, been all-Carinthia secretary of the Antifascist Women's Front, and held positions of political responsibility among the partisans, now had no time left for political activity. Her days were taken up by the work of rebuilding her farmhouse and, then, with the exacting work of peasant life. And she had another baby, a girl. Time passed and Zala grew old and weary and sometimes lost all will to live. She contemplated suicide when the bitterness came over her: "I haven't tasted anything of life. I married so young, then the war came, then I had to start all over again from zero."[119] For decades, nobody showed any interest in her past, in her struggle. Like all of the Slovenes in Carinthia, she learned to keep her own counsel. She did not talk about the war, much less about the part she played in it, because the only ones who asked questions were her past adversaries, and they were gathering ammunition for their campaign against the Slovenian population.

When, in the 1970s, young Slovene women and men studying in Klagenfurt or in Vienna started to take an interest in their compatriots' history for the first time, they would turn up with pencil and pad, only to be met with a refusal and distrust. "And why do you want to know this? There is no point, leave us be..." was the most common response to their questioning. Some of them, the most pig-headed ones who proved they were serious, eventually managed to break through the silence. Nowadays, there is a team of people, academics and students, contributors to the bilingual review *Kladivo*, working on research into the resistance of the Carinthian Slovenes. For the most part, they work without pay, with barely any official subsidy. It is to them alone that we are indebted if, finally, we have some insight into a chapter of Austrian history over which a veil of silence has been deliberately drawn. Just as well for the former partisans, female and male, who after fifty years of sneering, discrimination, and general lack of interest, are able to savor the sweet surprise of discovering that there are people eager to learn of their past and, indeed, who are proud of them. This very belated recognition may not be official, but it is no less sincere and enthusiastic for all that. "You youngsters are the first ever to come," Zala told me at the end of our interview, "but I am happy now that you have."

The Netherlands

"Never forget that you are human beings."

1

The boy and girl rode along the street, hand in hand. The man perched on the top of a ladder painting his house-front (and Lord only knows where he found the paint in the middle of war-time), stopped what he was doing for a moment to look them over. They did not appear to be particularly in love. The girl could be quite a looker if she would make a bit of an effort. The spectacles were particularly unflattering. And the young man did not look particularly sturdy. Then again, how could it be otherwise, when nobody had enough to eat, what with this accursed war. The man on the ladder turned away from the two cyclists. Across the street, he saw green-uniformed police on foot patrol. "Quickly, get out of here," he called out to the boy. "The Germans are coming!" The youth hesitated for a moment before the pair pedaled furiously away from the scene. For some time now, the Germans had been on the lookout for men between the ages of eighteen and thirty-five to send off to work somewhere in the Reich. In fact, that was the least that could befall this youth. His problem was, first, that he was carrying a large-caliber revolver, and, second, that he was not a boy at all. Those two facts would land him, not in some German factory, but in a German concentration camp. Or he might be walked out directly into the sand dunes for execution—after torture and interrogation, of course.

The fact is that the young man was a girl, and that girl—just like her companion—had for some time been on the Gestapo's wanted list. These two frantically-sought super-terrorists were classified as the most wanted. And their being on bicycles on this particular day was no accident: they were on their way to carry out an operation. Specifically, they were en route to assassinate an officer of the German security service. Not that this would be their first such operation, nor their last. And, while the police had thwarted them today, they were able to complete

Truus Oversteegen (Menger) and Hannie Schaft disguised as a couple

their mission successfully a few days later. The girl in the unflattering spectacles was Hannie Schaft, the much wanted "redheaded girl," who had been living outside the law since she turned twenty. The spectacle lenses were of plain glass and Hannie's hair had been dyed black. The lad was Truus Oversteegen, who had been active in the armed resistance to the German occupation since she was seventeen.[120]

In the Verzetsmuseum (Museum of the Resistance) in Amsterdam, there is a somewhat yellowing photograph of the couple. Truus is shown in an apprentice shoemaker's cap with the peak pulled down over her face and we can glimpse shirt and tie under her overcoat. Hannie is wearing a flowery scarf on her head with her dyed black hair tumbling out from underneath; her coat has a leather trim collar, and the overall impression, with the false spectacles, makes her look harmless and innocent. The pair are smiling at each other like lovers, but it is obvious from their expression that they are fighting to contain their laughter. A male student who, for a time, lived in the house used as a hideout by the two resistance fighters (and by Truus' sister, Freddie, the third member of the team) took this photograph with his ancient camera—breaching all of the rules of clandestinity. When Truus Oversteegen—Truus Menger these days, having married—showed me this photograph, she was torn between delight and afterthoughts of loathing. On the one hand, she was amused by it; on the other, "I was even wearing men's underwear to give myself a greater feeling of authenticity. It was awful. I put the fly to the rear, but that made it no better."

Some 25,000 female and male Netherlanders worked for the armed resistance against the German occupation. They knew that the vast bulk of the population was behind them and that they could count upon the passive resistance of hundreds of thousands who would harbor fugitives (Jews, men on the run from forced labor service in Germany, resistance fighters) and feed them and, if need be, act as go-betweens: distributing the underground press, transporting forged ration cards and documentation, handing out flyers, and sticking up posters. In the Netherlands, there were civil servants who supplied the resistance with blank identity cards and certificates, artists who refused to work for the controlled—*gleichgeschalter*—media, medical personnel who resigned en masse from their professional federation, now run by the occupying forces, university professors who publicly protested the dismissal of Jewish colleagues, students who went on strike over the "certificate of Aryanness" required of the universities, priests from both main churches who preached against the deportation of the Jews and instructed their parishioners to conceal persons in danger. [121]

The Netherlands also had the NSB, or National Socialist Movement, the only party not banned by the Germans, who had wholehearted and diligent assistants within its ranks. As in every country, there were sympathizers and collaborators, spies and traitors, but, here, the bulk of the population repudiated Nazism. By the age of six, girls and boys had been taught to keep their eyes open and stop playing if the police came into sight, because of the need to alert the "*onderduikers*" (the submerged), meaning the illegals, so that they might have time to disappear and retreat into their hiding places in the basements or lofts. Women played the main roles in this passive resistance (punishable by death, as was active resistance). They could venture out into the streets without fear, (unlike men old enough to work), they could ferry illegal material in their shopping baskets or in the baby's carriage, without attracting undue attention, and, in the early years of the war at any rate, they were not monitored as closely as the men.[122]

On May 10, 1940, the German army invaded the neutral kingdom of the Netherlands. On May 13, by which time defeat looked certain, Queen Wilhelmina fled to England, with the cabinet in tow. On May 14, the German air force, the Luftwaffe, bombed Rotterdam, almost a thousand people dying in the ruins of the devastated city. A few days later, Winkelmann, the Dutch commandant general, signed the surrender and German tanks rumbled into the capital. In Amsterdam alone, 150 people took their own lives on that May 15, most of them Jewish. The initial panic was followed by a lengthier period of deceptive tranquillity. The occupation forces strove to win over the population and Albert Seyss-Inquart (the erstwhile Austrian lawyer from Vienna), appointed by Hitler as "Reich commissar for the Netherlands," delivered a reassuring speech when he took up his office on May 29; the Germans had no intention of oppressing the country or its inhabitants, nor of imposing their own political doctrine. "The Führer's sole desire, we know, is peace and order for all persons of good will."

But good will was not shared by all. One month after the speech, the Dutch celebrated the birthday of Prince Bernhard as "Carnation Day." Many people followed the example set by the Queen's son-in-law and wore a carnation in their buttonhole. They hung out flags and mothers dressed their children in red, white, and blue (the colors of the national flag). Newborn children were now being christened Juliana, Wilhelmina, and Bernhard.[123] Even so, and in spite of such petty gestures of protest, a feeling of relief was in the air. The Nazis did not seem all that bad. Only the politically active, the ones who had harbored fugitives from Germany prior to the German invasion, realized that these misleading appearances could not be maintained for long. The Communist Party, banned within a month of the invasion, was organizing illegally. Those families who had harbored German Jews or political dissidents were obliged to acquire now crucial conspiratorial skills. Dutch Jews, unable to flee, started to look around for hiding-places.

On October 3, 1940, the occupation forces published a decree to the effect that civil servants had to submit a "certificate of Aryan-ness." On October 22, they ordered an inventory of all Jewish-owned businesses and companies: shortly after that, placards were installed in all public places and amenities (from swimming pools to park benches), bearing the inscription "No Jews" or "Prohibited to Jews." Jews were deprived of their bicycles, their goods and premises were impounded, they were expelled from the universities and banned from all municipal or state office. January 1941 saw the first violent attacks mounted by the NSB on the Jewish population. A month later, the police sealed off

Amsterdam's historic Jewish quarter. On February 22, the Jewish Sabbath, the first raid was carried out inside the Jewish quarter; 389 men were arrested and later transported to Buchenwald and Mauthausen. The raid was a reprisal: shortly before, a German patrol that had attacked the Jewish-owned Koko ice cream parlor had been driven off with a strong dose of ammonia gas.

Lots of the female and male workers living in Amsterdam's Jordaan quarter had to pass through the Jewish quarter on their way to work, and they witnessed for themselves the terror tactics that the Jewish population had to endure. Three days after that first raid, on February 25, 1941, the railway workers issued a strike call. The revolt started off in the tram service and municipal cleansing department at 4:30 AM, and, within seven hours, the whole of Amsterdam was in the throes of a general strike. In the foundries, the civil service, the banks and businesses, everywhere, work ground to a standstill. By 2:30 PM, the strike had spread to Haarlem and on to Velsen, Weesp, Hilversum, Utrecht, and Zannstrek. (Word did not reach other parts of the Netherlands in time.) This was a unique occurrence: a general strike that erupted completely under German occupation, the very first strike against the policy of anti-Jewish pogroms. Activists distributed leaflets with the watchwords: "Strike! Strike! Strike! Demand the immediate release of the Jews! Declare your solidarity with us! Take Jewish children into your homes!" The Germans reacted by declaring a state of emergency. Gestures calculated to woo the Dutch people ceased. The German police opened fire on the crowd of strikers and arrested hundreds of people; four of those arrested were sentenced to death and the rest had to serve lengthy terms of imprisonment, while the city authorities had to pay astronomical fines.

Now the resistance started to organize and the earliest illegal publications started to appear. With time, the number of illegal publications climbed to 600 different titles with a print-run of 10,000 copies. The Communist Party set up combat groups, and other small groups also determined to make the switch now from passive to armed resistance. Just one year after the Germans' entry, the Dutch economy was placed wholly in the service of the German war effort. The first people conscripted for forced labor service were the 140,000 unemployed Dutch; a year later, on March 6, 1942, all men aged between eighteen and thirty-five were obliged to perform forced labor in Dutch firms under the control of the forces of occupation or, increasingly, in Germany itself. Press gangs marauded through the streets rounding up all men of suitable age. Tens of thousands of Dutch dodged their obligation by dropping out of sight, and many of them, not content with hiding, joined the resistance. The Jews, who were the first to go to ground—on July 14, 1942, the first mass transport left Amsterdam-Schouwburg for the Westerbork holding camp, from which three trains left for Auschwitz and other death camps—were followed by non-Jewish Dutch who refused to render forced labor service. Over 25,000 Jews had managed to find themselves a hiding place, and now thousands more hiding places were needed, and there were ration books and false papers to be procured. For that very purpose, a Calvinist minister and the boss of the Kuipers-Rietberg company, known as Auntie Riek, launched the Landelijke Organizatie, or LO, which would soon boast upwards of 14,000 operatives of both sexes. The LO arranged addresses, identity cards, food, and clothing: its mainly female membership queued for hours on end to obtain the necessary food, stamps, and medicines. They moved material across the various districts of the city, and even across the country. If it was already hard for an innocent housewife, who had only to shop for her family, to be able to see to the upkeep of her *onderduikers*, the female messengers had to contend with embarrassing experiences as well as the dangers implicit in their work: it was not uncommon for a German trooper on a train or tram to try to flirt with one of these pretty girls. An underground messenger with a dozen phony identity documents and a parcel of illegal reviews in her bag could not afford to ignore him and thereby run the risk of provoking his wrath. She had to smile at him and exchange a few words—and thereby ensure chastisement and the utter contempt in her compatriots' eyes.[124]

Since there was too much work involved in tinkering with documents that were stolen or procured by other means, especially in view of the massive numbers required, the members of the resistance found themselves forced to get hold of blank forms by raiding the official agencies issuing such papers and ration books. They also had to set up well-appointed forgery workshops where expert hands (frequently artists and printers) could work without interruption—and to order. To handle this sort of work, which was beyond the capabilities of the regular members of the LO, the LKPs (Landelijke Knokploegen) were established—nationwide fighting teams specializing in holdups, forgery, and, later, in sabotage. Quite independently of the LO and the LKPs, there were tiny left-wing groups close to the Communist Party, which, since late 1941, had been carrying out armed operations: killing Gestapo and SD officers, high level collaborators, and traitors within their own camp. They blew up railway lines and telegraph posts and also managed to rescue some of their imprisoned female and male colleagues. One such group (made up predominantly of artists and students), mounted an attack on March 27, 1943 against the Census Office in Amsterdam, in the course of which, as intended, they burned many of the personal details of *onderduikers* and other resistance members. Another group, of which the feared trio, Truus and Freddie Oversteegen and Hannie Schaft were members, specialized in executions of SD officers and traitors. The general population's reaction to these operations varied, some being enthused by every effective blow struck against the forces of occupation, while others, by contrast, believed that all that these operations achieved was brutal reprisals. Later, entire houses were blown up and the inhabitants of streets where attacks took place were deported or shot. Although these armed groups did have women members, they usually only took part in laying the groundwork. Truus and Freddie Oversteegen and Hannie Schaft were an exception.[125]

When the general commanding the Wehrmacht, Christiaansen, pronounced on April 29, 1943 that all men with service in the Netherlands army and navy would retroactively be treated as prisoners of war, a general strike erupted across the country and, in some areas, dragged on until May 8. Farmers in Twente, in northern Holland, would persist for another two months in their refusal to supply the Germans with milk. The strike ended with 150 dead and triggered a fresh wave of brutal terror. But, in spite of all the repression, in spite of the treachery and the torture, the resistance groups carried on fighting and stepping up their work, and there was a steady influx of new recruits. The biggest organizations, alongside the LO and the LKPs, were the Communist Party (including the independent groups closest to it), the Orde Dienst (OD), which was further to the right, the independent and left-wing Raad van Verzet in het Koninkrijk Nederlanden (Kingdom of the Netherlands Resistance Council), and the National Comite van Verzet (National

Resistance Council), made up especially of intellectuals. From London, the government-in-exile coordinated support to the resistance through its British allies and broadcast daily to the occupied country through Radio Orange.

On September 5, 1944, the allied military forces reached the Dutch frontier and liberated part of the country, before coming to a halt at the great rivers. The Netherlands was split now into a southern, liberated territory and a northern zone still under occupation. That very day, the government-in-exile launched the Binnenlandse Strijdkrachten, or BS, under the command of Prince Bernhard. All of the armed resistance in the country was now supposed to acknowledge the primacy of this army, which they did (with a few exceptions, such as the Communist Party), although some leftist groups such as the Raad van Verzet showed little enthusiasm in doing so. From Great Britain, officers with no experience of the real conditions in the country were sent in to militarily overhaul the groups which had hitherto operated on an autonomous basis. At the same time, the new government started, even prior to liberation, to exclude and sidestep the Communists who were the most active participants in the resistance. This strategy was also not to the liking of many non-Communist comrades, female and male.

That autumn, the worst stage of the war began for the population of the part of the Netherlands still under occupation: the winter famine of 1944–45. The occupation forces stole all existing food stocks, impounded harvests, and cut off the power and the gas supplies. People felled whole forests in search of firewood for heat and, still, thousands froze to death and perished from hunger: in all, some 18,000 people lost their lives. The only food was a watery soup of kohlrabi and potato skins, and people swapped their last remaining garment for an egg or some bread. In the cities, the rumor that there were potatoes in a particular location triggered a massive pilgrimage of women and children who walked until their feet were raw, only to discover that the reports were untrue, or that everything had been given out by the time they got there. In February 1945, many of the female and male citizens of Amsterdam were surviving on 340 calories a day.[126] The hunger pangs were even worse for the *onderduiken* and the illegals, in the first instance, because they could not venture out in search of food and, in the latter, because they did not have the time to do so, since, in spite of the dire conditions, they were still working all-out for the liberation. Only the new officers, Truus Menger tells us, lived in surroundings of relative plenty. During her visits to headquarters, the famished female fighter marvelled at the rations she witnessed on the tables, at the cigarettes being smoked, and the amounts of cognac being sipped.[127]

The famine winter was followed by a spring of very severe repression. The occupiers stepped up the hunt for hidden Jews and other *onderduikers* and infiltrated many agents into the resistance groups, often successfully. Even in the final weeks and days before their defeat, the Germans were shooting resistance prisoners, female and male alike. Among them was Hannie Schaft, the "redheaded girl."

2

Haarlem, late 1941. A knock comes to the door of the Oversteegen family home. The mother opens up, but the caller asks to see her two daughters: Truus and Freddie, seventeen and fifteen years old respectively. He wishes to speak to them alone. "We're getting an underground army together," he says, after scrutinizing the girls. "Do you think you could help out? We want to fight like the Russian partisans do, with arms and acts of sabotage." If they do join this shadow army no one must know, not even their mother. Such is the discretion required of them. They both agree. They understand perfectly. "Could you take a life?" the man asks Truus. She is taken aback and cannot answer immediately. To put it simply, she does not know. Freddie answers for her: "I never have." Meanwhile, Truus had given it some thought: "If we're talking about a real fascist, somebody locking people up and torturing and killing them, then I suppose I could. But how does one know who really is one of them? Not all German soldiers are fascists." No, of course not, the mysterious visitor replies: their attacks would target only high-ranking officers, leaders, traitors. Why is he approaching them, the sisters wish to know. He says that he has heard of them in the Party, the rumor being that they are very brave and trustworthy. And, anyway, in the Soviet Union, the women and girls play their part in the partisan struggle as well. And women could move around more freely because the Germans, basically, could not conceive of a women doing such things. "And how are we to learn how to shoot and all that?" Truus asks. As soon as you give a definitive answer you will receive full training. Truus and Freddie give their answer: Yes.[128]

It was no coincidence that Frans, the *nom de guerre* of their com-mander-to-be, wanted to get an exact fix on the Oversteegen sisters. In spite of their extreme youth, they were already experienced clandestine fighters. For years, they had been hiding Jews and other victims of perse-cution from Germany, and, since the start of the occupation, they had been distributing the Communist Party's outlawed review *De Waarheid* (The Truth), daubing graffiti on shop fronts, and sticking up posters. Truus and Freddie had grown up from a very early age in a climate of political activism. Their mother was a Communist and, at the age of five, Truus had taken part in her first demonstration and heard the cat-call-ing from those observing from the sidewalk: "Those Reds should have been strung up from the lampposts." What are Reds? Truus would ask her mother. "We are, along with all the people walking with us," came the answer. Truus and Freddie's parents were divorced; the girls lived with their little brother and their mother on social assistance—which meant not just poverty, but lots of humiliating experiences as well. For instance, families receiving social assistance were entitled to only two blankets. So, every time there was an inspection visit, the girls had to hide the third blanket, switching it from bedroom to kitchen and back again, shifting it into whatever room the woman from the Department of Social Assistance was not poking around in. Once they even had their social assistance withheld because it was alleged that their mother had sub-tenants in the house. In fact, from 1933 onwards, there were often invited guests in the Oversteegen family home, but they not only paid no rent, but very frequently would have to share what little the family had. They were runaways from Hitler's Germany, steered towards the Oversteegen household by Red Aid, or poor Jewish families who had learned the address of this house, whose doors were always open, from circles associated with the Party. In the end, the Dutch government, under pressure from its powerful neighbor, declared such help illegal: now the fugitives had to find themselves sponsors. If they had none and were discovered, they were hauled away to a central refuge. It was at this point that Truus and Freddie finally learned the basic rules of conspiracy, for their mother had no intention of closing her door: how-ever, now her guests had to take care not to attract attention.

At the age of fourteen, Truus started work as a maid. She hated the job, especially of the supercilious tone in which she was ordered around. On her second day, the mistress asked her if she had emptied the chamber pot in the bedroom yet. Truus was outraged at this: it was going too far, but she did not dare risk losing her job. So, up she went to the next floor to collect the chamber pot. She was about to make her way downstairs again, when she realized that the master had followed her. It was obvious that he wanted something of her, so she went over to find out what. He put his hand between her legs and attempted to kiss her. Truus emptied the contents of the chamber pot over him, lost her job, and, with it, the additional revenue so sorely needed by the family. But her mother's reaction was levelheaded: "You were right. I would have done the same myself" was all she said when Truus explained why she had been dismissed.

Her mother was the moral example that left its mark on the lives of Truus and Freddie. Their mother taught them that not all Germans were Nazis, that Germany had also produced a Rosa Luxemburg and a Karl Liebknecht, that the people they were hiding were Germans too. This they ought never to forget. And there was one other thing that they should always bear in mind: "You must always help each other. Neither of you must abandon the other." Their mother explained the theory and the practice of fascism to them. Once (this was after the invasion), they had a Jewish family living with them, a woman with two small children, and some personal effects for the *onderduiken* arrived one day. These effects included the clothing of the husband, who had been captured by the Nazis, and the clothes were soaked with blood. His wife collapsed in a flood of tears, with the two children petrified at her side, white as corpses. "See," their mother told the girls, her eyes filling up with tears of anger and pity, "that's what fascism means." Truus and Freddie had learned the lesson. When they decided, in the wake of that visit from Frans, to join the armed resistance, they told their mother that they were about to embark on a dangerous undertaking about which they could not talk, not even with her. "I am not quite sure what it is that you are about to do," Mrs Oversteegen replied, but she offered them this precious precept, "but, whatever you do, never forget that you are human beings. You must never espouse the methods of your adversary and behave like fascists yourselves."

Before being accepted into the team, Truus and Freddie had to undergo a trial by fire. Frans paid them another call: "Tonight you must demonstrate whether you have courage and whether you are cut out for this sort of work." He arranged a rendezvous in the woods on the outskirts of Haarlem, but did not tell them exactly what would happen. Trembling from the cold and emotion, the two sisters walked stealthily through the wood, starting at every sound, and expecting to stumble upon a monster behind every tree trunk. But they stuck it out bravely until Frans showed up. When he asked them if they were afraid, they answered with a proud silence. After he had told them a little about the work of the resistance, he suddenly asked them the address of a specific person. Truus and Freddie knew the man and they knew his address too, and they could not bear the fellow. However, they bit their tongues rather than give details of his address, even to a comrade. Frans' request irked them, and they started to have doubts about his being cut out for conspiracy. In any event, they told him forcefully that they were not about to say one word on the matter. Whereupon he produced a pistol from his pocket: "The address, and be quick about it. You have walked into a trap." He identified himself as a Gestapo officer and flicked off the safety catch of the pistol. "Bastard!" screamed Truus, and, at the same time, Freddie jumped the man as Truus wrested the gun out of his hand. The two girls fought like lions, punching and biting and kicking, and missed hearing the desperately cursing Frans telling them that it had only been a test, to stop now, and let him be, that he was no Nazi. Nor did they stop when they realized what he was shouting. They were too angry for that. Finally, when he was lying on the ground, Truus held him there at gunpoint as Freddie stuck the boot in a few more times. Frans limped away with lips swollen, one eye blackened, and his face covered in scratches. The two sisters had passed the test better than he could have hoped.

It was now time for Truus and Freddie to learn how to use a pistol and revolver, how to strip them down, clean, load, and fire them. Freddie was the first to put her knowledge to practical use. Her mission was a difficult one, because she knew the man she was to kill. He was a comrade who had switched sides after being arrested. After he was released, the others quickly realized that everyone he greeted on the street was eventually being arrested. It was plain what was going on; there could be no doubt. Freddie was entrusted with the task and carried it out without mishap. When she returned, she could not catch her breath, she was crying and asking Truus over and over, "How could we do such things?" The two sisters talked through the night, plumbing every argument, every emotion. By dawn, they knew that what they were doing was right, no matter what.

Then it was Truus' turn. Her operation was perhaps even more difficult than Freddie's, for the traitor marked for execution was none other than a man with whom she had fallen in love. She wanted to make very sure, to check everything out for herself. There must not be as much as a shred of doubt left. Although she believed the comrades who assured her that they had checked the man out thoroughly and that there was no doubt that he had turned traitor, Truus had to convince herself. She went to a restaurant he frequented, and waited until he showed up. When he arrived, Truus withdrew on the pretence of using the toilet. In the cloakroom, she checked the pockets of his overcoat. She discovered a Walther, a pistol used only by the Germans. She continued her search and came upon some German documents: "I could not read what they said, but the rash of swastikas was enough for me." Truus arranged to meet up with him that evening, telling him that she had an important secret to confide in him. That night, when they met at the agreed rendezvous, she tackled him straight out: "I know you're working for the Germans." "Too bad for you," he replied, drawing his gun and cocking it. This was final proof for Truus. The Walther merely clicked, for Truus had emptied the chamber, just in case. Now she drew her own gun, took aim, fired, and did not miss.

The team within which Truus and Freddie worked was made up of five men, plus the two young girls. Later, when Hannie Schaft added to its strength, the three women set up a special commando unit within the group. There was an atmosphere of camaraderie, as several of the group had known one another from the old days, from the youth organization or the Party. The combat unit, while not formally belonging to the Communist Party, had close ties to it, and every one of the members was experienced in left-wing political activities. Operations were discussed in every detail. Most of the activists had a working-class background, except one of the men plus Hannie Schaft, who were students. Initially, this led to occasional friction, with the proletarians distrusting the bourgeoisie, and each side arguing about reliability and their misgivings about the others. But, as their work proceeded, they very soon came to learn about one another and then to trust each other. The animosity turned into wisecracks, with the two factions poking fun at each other, and at themselves.

All members of the group were leading a strictly underground existence. Truus and Freddie changed their lodgings frequently because it was too much of a risk to stay in one place too long. If they happened upon one another in the street, they could not afford the slightest indication that they knew each other, no matter how tempted they might be. Talking about operations was also strictly prohibited, although Truus and Freddie breached that rule. It was all but impossible for them to go out, take somebody's life, and then behave as if nothing had happened. Assassinations of officers from the SD proved less of a problem. The latter were out-and-out fascists, the enemy, the ones bringing endless suffering to so many. Anyway, they were outsiders, strangers. Truus and Freddie found it much harder to take the lives of people they knew. They knew that a traitor was as bad as a Nazi officer, because he was turning over his own people to these same killers and torturers. But they knew him. They had worked alongside him, maybe even taken a liking to him. After such operations, the two sisters would stay up all night just talking and talking, digesting the fact that they had taken the life of somebody with whom they had only recently been chatting and laughing. "One evening was particularly ghastly," Truus relates. "As ever, we were listening to Radio Moscow, and they broadcast a program in which a young female partisan talked about her struggle. She wept as she described how she had once shot at a German tank, how there had been a very young German soldier with a likable face and open expression, quaking with fear, and how he had died. She said that was when it came home to her that not all German soldiers were Nazis. But we couldn't afford the luxury of making such distinctions." Truus, who, right from the start, had modelled herself on the example of the Russian partisans and identified with those women who, often, were no older than she, was greatly impressed by Nadja's story. It also gave her encouragement. Didn't she have things a lot easier than Nadja? She didn't have to kill ordinary German soldiers; she only killed those truly responsible, the real Nazis who knew what they were doing, and those who cold-bloodedly delivered to them people who would then be put to the knife. These two young girls of fifteen and seventeen were incredibly disciplined. Discipline also meant carrying out operations that they themselves regarded as lunacy or found deeply repugnant, such as "Operation Slut." Frans, the commander whom Truus and Freddie had floored when they were being put to the test, had devised a special operation for the two sisters. Dressed as prostitutes, they were to lure a German officer into the woods, where he could be killed. "We didn't even have a clue as to what to wear," Truus relates. "So they sent us to the cinema." Not that that was of much assistance. "In such matters we were children, real children." The children were now issued with the appropriate get-up, make-up, and perfume. "I couldn't even stand the smell of myself!" Truus tells us. They were given ten florins—an incredible amount of money for them—and off they went to the place frequented by their SD officer and his colleagues. When Truus and Freddie got there, he had not yet arrived. They had to wait. At the next table, an ice cream sundae was served that, to the two girls, looked just like heaven on earth. They had never seen, much less tasted, anything in their lives to equal it. But now they had a fabulous sum of money—ten florins! They ordered an ice cream sundae. It tasted as good as it looked. Still the German had not shown up. Why not order a second sundae? No sooner said than done. While the pair enjoyed their unexpected stroke of good luck and devoured the ice cream, their make-up started to run and they quite forgot that they were prostitutes. In came the SD officer. He sat at a table near theirs, but did not so much as glance at them. Horrified, the sisters remembered what they were there to do, and they tried to appear louche. To no avail. All of the male customers ignored them completely. Only the waiter approached to tell them that it was closing time and they should settle up. Of course. How much? That would be thirteen florins. Truus explains: "I could have slid under the table, I was so embarrassed. I had to confess to him that we only had ten florins. It was awful. He threw us out of the premises in the most humiliating fashion. We went home in tears, in utter despair." The sisters' confidence in that particular superior was shattered forever.

Then, one day, Hannie showed up. Hannie Schaft was twenty years old, a student who had joined Raad van Verzet some time previously and collected money and food stamps for the underground—and still felt that there was something more that she could be doing. She was eager for "real," "armed" work, she would explain, if pressed. In the end, she would be accepted into an armed commando unit in which she was the sole female. Meanwhile, Truus and Freddie had to leave Haarlem, their native city, because it was becoming too dangerous for them to stay there. They moved to Enschede and, for cover, worked in a hospital whose female administrator was an underground activist.

It was at the beginning of 1943 that the governor accosted Truus at work: there was a young woman who wanted to see her, claiming that she was her best friend. "And," the governor added, "if you have serious business to discuss, you'd better go into my office." Truus looked inquisitively at this best friend of hers: "She was gorgeous. Wavy red hair and a very pretty face." However, the rules of conspiracy insisted that no one should be trusted. In her memoirs, *Toen Niet, Nu Niet, Nooit* (Not Then, Not Now, Not Ever), Truus explains: "I had one hand in the pocket of my nurse's uniform where I always carried my pistol. The girl facing me also kept a hand in her pocket, with the other in a clenched fist on her knee." If she was from the SD, it would all boil down to speed of reaction. "Frans sent me." "Who's that, Miss...?" "De Wit." "Right, Miss De Wit, could you explain yourself more plainly?" Silence. Their eyes locked. And suddenly they burst out laughing, both at once. By the time they regained their composure, each of them drew her pistol from her pocket and had to laugh again until tears ran down their faces.

The three women now formed a special team. Truus was in charge, Freddie the observation expert, and no action could be dangerous enough for Hannie. The trio were so successful that the Gestapo was soon hunting them as terrorists. Hannie dyed her hair black, Truus dressed up as a boy, and, for a while, they carried out their attacks posing as a couple. Freddie took on the task of gathering intelligence about the target: where he lived, what route he took to work, when and where he moved around free of surveillance, where he might be taken by surprise without being seen, the likely chances of a safe getaway. After Freddie had drawn up her plan of action, Truus and Hannie came on the scene. Freddie would loiter in the vicinity and cover their retreat. It nearly always worked. And, if there was the occasional mishap, Freddie had planned such a subtle escape route that all three could get to safety. Not that the trio of girls confined themselves to *attentats*. They also transported illegal publications, visited the families of detained female and male comrades, helped print up leaflets, and forged identity papers. They got by on ten florins a week, scarcely enough to put food on the table. They were given a separate cigarette allowance and a few extra ration stamps for the family in whose home they were hiding out. "We were always hungry," Truus says. "For breakfast we had our limbering up, a cup of tea or, rather, a cube of ersatz tea dissolved in water, and a slice of bread." Then, it was off to headquarters to see what assignment awaited them. All day long, they did not have a minute to themselves and, only when the evening drew on, could they relax a little. "We also laughed a lot," Truus recalls, "you cannot live and carry out such work for years without a laugh." Hannie taught Truus and Freddie English as well as German, because there was no telling when it might be useful, she told them; and, anyway, German was the language of Heinrich Heine. They told one another stories, true and invented, and dreamed of everything they wanted to do once the war was over at last.

Before joining Truus' group, Hannie had worked with Jan. Since the two groups were, for reasons of confidentiality, strictly separate, Hannie and Jan hardly saw each other anymore: this was hard, for the pair were in love. In fact, nobody must find out about their being lovers, because Jan was married, and moral standards were quite strict (as far as women went, at least). But Truus and Freddie soon discovered their secret. So they were none too surprised when Hannie, breaking all the rules, wanted to go on an operation with Jan. Their target was a high-ranking SD officer. Truus was fast asleep when Hannie suddenly turned up at the foot of her bed, rigid and out of breath. "They've captured Jan!" Hannie had been the first to fire a shot, then Jan. Hannie, as agreed, then sped away on her bicycle. But Jan had doubled back again to check that they had hit their target. The German opened fire at that point, and Jan was so seriously wounded as to render escape impossible. Hannie blamed herself for arrest, and then started planning how to free him from hospital. When she was forced to accept that there was nothing to be done, because a whole army of Gestapo personnel were guarding their unexpected captive, she lapsed into a state of complete petrification: "She neither ate nor slept nor wept nor spoke. She carried on like that and was like a living corpse. She would not allow anyone near her, not even Freddie and me."

Once again, it was Frans, the commander who had sent Freddie and Truus out on "Operation Slut," who proposed a patently kamikaze operation. They all turned him down—all three agreed that the plan was unrealistic. Then, Hannie got to her feet and said that she would do it, if necessary, on her own. Truus recalls: "When we left headquarters, I grabbed Hannie, put my pistol in her hand, and told her, 'If you want to commit suicide, you'd better take my gun just to be on the safe side.' She never flinched. Whereupon I shouted; 'You're no resistance fighter, you're not a fighter at all, nor a good Communist. You're just a little girl trying to look important!'" That hit home. Hannie finally collapsed in a heap. Truus brought her home, put her to bed, and let her cry until she fell asleep, exhausted: "The worst was over."

Truus, the young commander, always strong, always disciplined, always answerable for the others, was also not above an attack of weakness. At the time, she was terribly ashamed. Now, she can accept that it was just how things were. It happened in mid-operation: she was leaning against a wall, her pistol in her pocket with the safety catch off, ready to open fire, when all of a sudden she went to pieces. "I simply slid down the wall, and the last thing I saw was my sister's utterly bewildered expression." There was a dental surgery in the house across the street; some people who had seen Truus collapse insisted on taking her there. Freddie, who had quickly palmed Truus' gun, had no option but to go along with this. It was a gamble. The dentist gave Truus first aid and then opened a bottle of wine. "Drink this, little lady. I was keeping this bottle for liberation day, but today is occasion enough, eh?" Truus had to stay in bed for three days with a high fever. But, as soon as she felt more or less well, she set to work again.

In retaliation for the railroad strike of 1944, the Germans unleashed a wave of brutal repression. And then the hungry winter set in. The Germans were impounding foodstuffs by the ton, while the population went increasingly hungry and cold, and more and more arrests were made among the resistance. Truus' group had had to close up shop for a while for security reasons, but, when the arrests were so obviously soaring, it was self-evident that treachery was afoot. The security service had managed to penetrate some of the groups. Truus and her comrades decided that, all misgivings about security aside, the time had come to strike again. Freddie, their intelligence expert, spread her tentacles and soon came up with a certain security service officer who was behind all the arrests, and who was also implicated in the trade in foodstuffs. The problem was that it was all but impossible to get at him, as he rarely ventured into the street. However, Truus, Freddie, and Hannie made up their minds to have a go. A man who was exploiting hunger in the population, and who had also, through his agents, managed to put heaps of comrades to the sword—and would carry on doing so unless they stopped him in his tracks—was worth braving any danger for.

Freddie drew up her plan of action—they meant to attack him in his own home—the date was fixed, and Hannie and Truus prepared themselves. Truus was rather startled to watch as Hannie combed her hair neatly and donned her make-up. She lost patience and wanted to know what the point was: they weren't going to a dance. Hannie was aware of Truus' impatience: "Truus, darling," she jokingly retorted, "I am going to my death clean and tidy. And now, as for our SD friend, we'll show him the just desserts of a man-hunter." Off they went. On reaching his house, they spotted Freddie nearby, pretending to mount her bicycle. Everything was going well: the coast was clear. Hannie knocked and a woman answered the door. "It's about a food transport for Frisia," Hannie explained; the two harmless girls were admitted. From inside they could hear the fellow complaining: "Even when I'm off duty they can't leave me in peace!" Truus and Hannie drew their guns and burst into the room, opening fire as they did so. "Murderer!" screamed Truus as she emptied her gun. Within seconds they had gone back downstairs to their bicycles and were speeding from the scene. Freddie caught up with them after a few streets. "We did it," hissed a still panting Hannie, "One less bastard in the world!'

Their work went on. It was while taking part in a sabotage operation—the blowing up of a railway bridge—that Truus made the acquaintance of Pit, the group's explosives expert and her future husband. She learned how to use dynamite, how to construct a bomb, and how to place it on the tracks. The fight against the occupying forces was escalating daily. There was a mad rush forward and not a moment's respite, a moment to rest. In addition to her regular work, Truus also took charge of the rescue of Jewish children of both sexes. She almost always managed to find her charges a safe haven without mishap. She is still in touch with some of them who live in America or Israel today.

When the southern Netherlands was liberated in September 1944, the forces of occupation in the north stepped up their drive even more. Huge swathes of territory were combed and many Jews who had, until then, been staying relatively safely in the countryside were obliged, overnight, to look for fresh hiding-places. Truus was put in charge of smuggling a group of Jewish children into the liberated territory in the south. Dressed as a Red Cross nurse, and carrying the appropriate papers, she collected the twelve girls and boys from the platform in Amsterdam railway station and boarded a train. They crowded into the compartment

together. The youngest was three years old; the oldest, twelve. The terrified children stared into space, not daring to look at Truus, who was
trembling inwardly every bit as much as they were. Once the two "German
officers" (Amsterdam resistance members) handed the children over to
her, Truus had sole responsibility for them. Only the eldest child met
her gaze with eyes full of hatred and contempt. After a period of silence,
Truus could stand the game of hide-and-seek no longer. She explained
to the children who she really was and how she was going to bring them
to a safe place, but that they would have to play out this sham until they
got there. The little ones did not understand her, the older ones disbe-
lieved her. The oldest made no bones about his contempt for her. Truus
was feeling more wretched than ever. Suddenly, the compartment door
swung open and two armed German officers burst in. Truus jumped to
her feet and roared, "Heil Hitler!" She stood at attention and handed
over her papers. The officers scrutinized them, but they appeared to be
waiting for something more. "On your feet! Heil Hitler!" she barked at
the children, raising her right arm again. Obediently, the children stood
up. Their right arms shot up and they snapped, "Heil Hitler!" Only the
oldest one, white as a sheet and tight-lipped, remained seated by way of
a protest. "Would you be so kind?" Truus asked him peremptorily and,
when he still did not budge, she struck him a resounding slap. Tears
welled in the boy's eyes, but he stood up, arm out and said "Heil Hitler!"
Truus' legs almost went from under her. The Germans grinned smugly
and finally left the compartment. A weeping Truus tried to explain to
the boy why she'd had to do that. He turned his back to her, his cheek
still bright red. "God damn these Germans, I thought, and I felt really
bad, as I were in the wrong."

It was dark by the time they got there. Truus explained to the
children that they now had to go down to the river, where they would be
ferried across to the opposite bank by boat. The ground was mined and
the Germans patrolled the area with dogs, so the group had to make as
little noise as possible and could not stray from the path opened up by
Truus. "The children were fantastic," Truus writes in her memoirs, "neither crying nor coughing. They were unbelievably disciplined and brave."
They reached the river safe and sound, but now they had to wait for the
water to reach the right level. The children were starting to get nervous.
They were hungry and needed to go to the toilet, and the smallest of them
began to cry. Truus was on edge. The seconds seemed to drag by until

time seemed to be standing still. She told the children stories and this provided a little distraction, but not for long. The doyen of the group, who by now had realized that Truus had not been lying, helped her as best he could, taking charge of the older children, while Truus looked after the smaller ones. But, then, there was no choice. Truus realized that there was more risk in continuing to wait with the restless, crying children than in boarding the boat ahead of schedule. She shepherded them onboard and cast off. They had barely left the bank when flares appeared in the sky, lighting up the bank as if it was daylight. The Germans reached the bank with their dogs and were shooting. The oldest child stood up and shouted, "Come on then, shoot, you damned Krauts!" Bullets slammed into his slim frame. "Hit the dirt!" Truus shouted to him, but it was too late. The boat capsized and the children were plunged into the rushing current. Truus, barely able to keep her own head above water, tried desperately to help them, but the current was sweeping them away and there was nothing she could do. She sighted one hand sticking out of the water, grabbed hold of it, and wrestled with the young body to reach the bank. It was the youngest of the children, Rosa, and she was still alive. Truus ran around heedless of the mines, and had to crawl back through the gap in the barbed wire through which she had slipped earlier. She raced to the nearest house. "Had those people been pro-Nazi that would have been the end." But they were decent folk, who welcomed them in and hid them until they were able to continue more or less safely. "After the war I still had nightmares and dreams about being hunted down, although these have cleared up. To this day, I still dream about those children. That certainly won't ever leave me."

Not that this tragedy was the only one. Shortly before the war ended, Truus learned, through an underground courier, of the sad plight of a five-year-old Jewish child who had been in hiding, utterly alone, in a basement for the past eight months. Truus was horrified. She could understand the fear of the people hiding him, who did not dare have the boy in the house with them, but she could not countenance the boy remaining in the basement on his own. She sought her commander's permission to take the child to a new, safer and more humane hiding place in the home of a family in the countryside. But the child's parents heard what had happened, and insisted that the child be reunited with them. Truus was against this: three people in a single hiding place. That was almost always too many. But, in the end, she deferred to the desperate wishes of the parents and promised to deliver their son, Loetje. She rendezvoused with him, as agreed, very early one morning. Loetje was in a deserted square, lost and alone, beside a suitcase that was too big and heavy for him. As Truus writes in her memoirs: "This little five year old had to conduct himself like an adult. He gave me the password and I gave him the agreed response, although I could scarcely speak. I'll never forget those eyes. The eyes of a wise old man in a child's face. I never hated fascism as much as I did at that moment."

Truus tried to raise the lad's spirits and he laughed readily at her jokes. On they went, side by side, kilometer after kilometer. Then, Truus could stand it no more. She left her bicycle at the side of the road, knelt down, and took Loetje in her arms. They both cried themselves hoarse. After that they felt better. Truus told him that she was going to take him to his parents and Loetje's face lit up with delight. "Did you know that I had a friend down there in the basement?" No, Truus answered in surprise. The boy had been down there on his own all that time! "Yes, there was a little rat who would come every day and sit in my hand, honest!" Loetje was very proud of himself and Truus was very proud of Loetje. But they could not afford to stop for too long. They pressed on. At this time, the British were mounting regular bombing raids against the transportation of German troops by Dutch road and rail. Truus and Loetje were cycling parallel with a railway line. They heard a buzzing in the air; it got awfully loud, and was joined by another nondescript noise. Truus grabbed the boy and hurled herself with him to the ground. Too late. Loetje had been hit by a piece of shrapnel from a British bomb. He was dead, as were the other folk who had been making their way along the road. There were corpses and bicycles everywhere. Truus alone had emerged unscathed, by some miracle. Sick with grief, Truus had to tell Loetje's parents what had happened. "The father broke down completely and he hurled himself at me, shouting and punching me until his wife and some other people eventually managed to pull him off. I felt so guilty that I could not defend myself."

Ever since the resistance had been made subordinate to Prince Bernhard's military forces, Binnenlandse Strijdkrachten, the atmosphere among the fighting women and men had changed radically. New commanders had shown up, who did not behave like underground fighters but more like military officers. Operations were not discussed any more; they were merely ordered. While activists endured the hunger and cold, at headquarters they had fresh vegetables, meat, real coffee, and a range of alcoholic drinks on the table. Formally, the Party had disbanded Truus' group, but Truus, Freddie, and Hannie (and other comrades too) carried on. The Binnenlandse Strijdkrachten commanders now wanted to reduce and, if possible, erase the influence of the Communist Party, which accounted for a sizable portion of the armed resistance. But the trio of girls was, by then, a legend among the resistance figters, who were unwilling to give up on the prestige of being able to claim: We are working with Truus, Freddie and Hannie, who Berlin itself is in hot pursuit of. The three girls carried out the occasional assassination and participated in significant sabotage operations, but they were also used for operations that were somewhat more questionable. For instance, on several occasions they had to transport packages, even though mail was not within their remit. "But, being Communists, we were disciplined." They carried out their missions, but their misgivings grew. In the end, things appeared to Freddie to have gone too far. On one of the endless cycle trips—when they had to pedal their bikes while half-dead from the cold, hunger, and exhaustion, just to deliver some ominous package, running the constant gauntlet of German roadblocks—Freddie, the most outspoken of the threesome, suggested that they sneak a look at this merchandise for which they were risking their lives. They opened one of the packages (imagining them to contain weapons, papers, spying equipment, and the like) and found that it contained tobacco and gems. Truus remembers: "Hannie wept with fury. I screamed my lungs out: 'We're risking our necks for this!' This guy was trafficking in tobacco, gems, and other goods with his contact in The Hague, at our expense." When they insisted on an explanation, they were told that these things were needed for bribing SD officers. The trio did not believe a word of it and refused to carry on with missions of this sort. They trusted nobody and only felt comfortable with their old comrades. In such circles, the rumor was that some of the elegant gentlemen operating under the supervision of the British secret service were also working for the Germans. Truus muses: "Those were by no means easy times. This had nothing to do with our fight against fascism. For years, we had been risking our lives without hesitation, but now we thought twice about every operation, especially its real implications, and whether we were really going to do it." Sometimes, they did not even have to think about it. Sometimes, the situation was awfully clear. At the beginning of 1945, in the middle of the famine winter, Truus, Freddie, and Hannie had to present themselves at headquarters. This was a particularly important mission, they were told, an operation to free prisoners. This was exceptionally good news, the trio thought, and liberating prisoners was worth any risk. Their commanding officer seemed very gratified by their response, and he spelled out the plan to them: "From a friendly source, we know where the children of Seyss-Inquart go to school. You are to go to The Hague and check when the children leave home and when they get back from school. Then you will abduct the children." Truus was at a loss for words. It was Freddie who answered first: "Brilliant. Now we're using children too in this war! Count me out!" She stood up, furious, followed by Truus, who informed their superior, "She's quite right. I too refuse to open fire on children, if something goes wrong. You'll have to get somebody else." All three walked out. Hannie spoke for all three when she spelled out her position again: "We are not Nazis. Resistance fighters do not murder children."

Those were Hannie's last words, figuratively speaking. In March 1945, the three women prepared themselves for one of their last missions. They were to mount a grenade attack upon a collaborator's business. Truus and Freddie waited impatiently for Hannie, because she had always been punctual. Living outside the law, one cannot afford to not be punctual. The day before, March 26, Hannie had delivered a parcel of newly printed copies of *De Waarheid* to the distribution center, by bicycle. The Germans had stopped and searched her en route—and had discovered not just the newspapers but her pistol as well. After some hours under questioning, they realized just what an important capture they had made: this was the "redheaded girl." When Hannie failed to show, Truus and Freddie went to headquarters, where they found out about Hannie's arrested. But no one knew where she was being held. Truus forgot all the rules of conspiratorial activity and went from prison to prison, and even called at the German secret service headquarters. Eventually she discovered that Hannie was in the women's prison on Amsterdam's Amstelveense Straat. This was in April. In Amsterdam, quite accidentally, Truus bumped into Pit and some other comrades with whom she carried out a sabotage operation a few months later. She told them what had happened, and the men, without batting an eye, declared themselves ready to help free Hannie. Truus' spirits lifted again. She managed to get as far as the governess of the prison. The latter looked in a thick book, shook her head and told Truus: "She's not here any more." Truus knew what that meant.

Hannie Schaft was tortured for days on end. On April 17, they took her out to the sand dunes at Bloemendaal. The first shot merely grazed her. "I'm a better shot than you are!" Hannie shouted at her killers. They replied with a hail of gunfire. Hannie was twenty-three when she died.

The May sun was beating down with full strength, the trees were in blossom, and people were dancing delightedly through the streets. The *onderduiken* took their first stiff-legged steps of freedom. Truus paid a visit to Marie, an underground colleague who had been hiding Philine, a Jewish woman. Liberation Day found them sitting together, celebrating on the grass at Marie's house. Philine had lost her entire family to the gas chambers. Truus was thinking about Hannie, and about whether she, Freddie, and all the others would be able to turn back the clock and lead completely normal lives in future. Her happiness had a bitter aftertaste. But Truus still clung to some glimmer of hope. She travelled to Amsterdam and joined the throngs waiting outside the prison for the political inmates to be released. She was carrying a bunch of red tulips. But Hannie was not among the ashen figures passing through the gates.

The women and men fighters of the resistance were drawn up in a long line in the main square. The army was arrayed in front of them in their honor. Medals were awarded to those with the most meritorious records. Truus and Freddie were not among those decorated. Just as the ceremony was about to conclude, one of the commanders stepped forward and barked the order: "Eyes left!" The soldiers formed up facing to their left, where Truus and Freddie stood along with their underground comrades. Their merits were beyond dispute. But they had one grave failing: they were Communists. Truus was awarded decorations and orders from every conceivable country, from the United States to the Soviet Union, and a tree was planted in her honor on the Avenue of the Just in Jerusalem. "But neither I nor those like me have ever received one single medal from the Dutch government."

Instead, she was awarded a rather questionable task. She was to hunt down Nazis who were still in hiding, Nazis who would, presumably, have no hesitation opening fire if discovered. Not that Truus did this for long. When she married Pit Menger, her resistance colleague, she fell under the prohibition barring married women from working. She had to stay at home. Like Freddie. Freddie became a housewife and mother. "That was our tragedy, that all of a sudden, women like us were left with no option but to become housewives. It is hard to understand today, but in those days there was nothing that could be done."

There is only one thing from which Truus has never retreated right up until the present day: political activity. However, she feels that she could have done more. Since childhood, her dream had been to become a sculptress—she, the daughter of an ordinary working man and a mother who'd had to live on social assistance. It was an unlikely prospect for someone like her. But, secretly, she kept the dream alive. Her husband discovered that one of his old resistance colleagues taught sculpture at the recently launched Free Academy of Plastic Arts. Truus enrolled and made a reality of her dream. Today, she is an artist of international repute. In 1983, she won a competition called by the former Princess Beatrice for a monument to be erected to the resistance. In Haarlem, she erected a statue four meters high, the figure of a woman, in honor of Hannie Schaft and all the women in the armed resistance. In a park in south Amsterdam, there is a monument dedicated to the old Jewish market: a group of Jewish girls and boys with their arms around one another. Truus' traumatic experiences are mirrored in her art, and she cannot break free of them. When I visited her for her interview, there was a sculpture of a boat with children hanging over the sides in her studio. Dead children, obviously.

The cold war had a very harsh impact on Truus. Neighbors and even former friends of both sexes abruptly severed all relations with this incorrigible Communist. In 1952, the police banned a demonstration in Hannie Schaft's honor. The girls and boys who, in spite of this, carried on placing wreaths of flowers in the dunes where Hannie had been executed were arrested and brought to trial. Truus and Freddie were called as witnesses in the so-called Velser Case,, in which a number of high-ranking officers of the Binnenlandse Strijdkrachten stood trial for trafficking in gems and, even worse, for their activities as double agents—which Truus and her group had their suspicions about at the time, even though they never quite dared fully to believe it. Sordid matters came to light that the sensationalist press used to blacken the reputation of the resistance. The radiant image of liberators was besmirched by filthy stains. But the blame was heaped, not upon those dubious characters whose hands were dirty, but upon folk like Truus and Freddie, who had helped frustrate their designs. Two attempts were made on Truus' life. Once, a bomb was thrown at her house and, later, shots were fired at her while she was in her car. But Truus refused to be intimidated. She carried on working in her study and on the Party's behalf. She reared her children and, to this day, visits the schools to tell young people what things were like back then, when she was young and fought against the Nazis. And there is another dream that Truus has turned into a reality: she travelled to the Soviet Union and met up with Nadja, that young partisan girl who had spoken on a Radio Moscow program once about her scruples and restored Truus' spirits.

France

"I defended my honor as a Jewish woman."

There was quite a number of them. Initially they had wanted to set the prisoners free, but others had already seen to that. So a portion of the group decided to implement item two on the agenda: the destruction of a garage near the Parc de la Tête d'Or. But their luck ran out and the Germans stumbled upon them. With much effort, and by the skin of their teeth, they managed to escape. The team tried to disperse into the quarter without attracting attention. The flight of seventeen-year-old Dina Lipka, a fighter with the Lyon MOI's Carmagnole group brought her to a Pétainist Youth club. When she realized where she was, she rushed out, aghast, into a courtyard. Shots barred her entry. There was no way out now; she was caught in a trap. Two German motorcyclists entered the yard, looking high and low, and spotted Dina, who had taken cover as best she could behind a barrel. Dina let them come as close as she dared before drawing her revolver, taking aim and squeezing the trigger. "I wanted to grab their revolvers, but I didn't have time," she relates. "I jumped over a wall and, to this day, I do not know how I managed it." On the far side, she bumped into Anna, a comrade. The streets were swamped with Germans. The two young girls tried to look as innocent as possible. They came upon two bicycles and saw this as their chance. They stole the bicycles and pedaled as fast as they could in the direction of Villeurbanne. There, in the huge working class district on the outskirts of Lyon, open revolt had erupted. Anna and Dina had scarcely arrived before they were manning the barricades that their comrades had just erected, and, for five days, they fought a ferocious battle with the Germans.[129]

Since November 1942, Lyon had been the scene of intense anti-German activity. A handful of resistance fighters were creating more and more headaches for the Germans and their French auxiliaries. They blew up arms factories and supply depots, derailed troop trains, gunned down German officers and their French collaborators.[130] Behind these outrages was the French resistance's most militant and effective unit: the MOI-FTP (Main d'Oeuvre Immigrée-Franc Tireurs et Partisans), armed units of Communist Party-organized immigrant workers. From Paris to Lyon and from Marseilles to Nice, the MOI fought the German occupation. The militant women and men of the MOI were the first to embark upon armed resistance, and the last to receive any credit for their war record in postwar France.

In German-speaking countries, the MOI is practically unknown. But, in France, too, it is only a few years since the veil of oblivion—deliberate forgetting—has been lifted. For the MOI was not made up of authentic French people, but of foreigners, immigrant workers, most of them Jews.[131] These fighters carried a triple stigma: they were foreigners, they were Jews, and they were Communists. Theirs was a particularly difficult situation. Regarded as Communists and perpetrators of atrocities, they were regarded by the London-backed Gaullist resistance with little sympathy.

As immigrants (or the children of immigrants) and, thus, virtually always internationalists, they were at odds with the nationalist line peddled by the Comintern. The Communist Party of France, increasingly patriotic since it had allied itself with De Gaulle, had a hard time accepting the very un-French names of its most active fighters.[132] Moreover, Jews had no roots in the country: they were unassimilated and had no Great War medals to display. And, since they did not claim to be Zionists, they were not well-regarded by the bourgeois Jewish organizations either. They kept to themselves, to their relentless struggle against fascism, and to their steely determination to avenge murdered Jews. In official French histories, they receive no mention. Nor has Communist historiography anything to say about the MOI.[133] The resistance was the handiwork of the French, the authentic French, and not of some Polish Jew or Italian immigrant from who knows where.

Since the end of the First World War, France had been the destination for large numbers of immigrants fleeing to this traditional country of asylum, partly for political reasons, partly for economic. First came the Armenians, who managed to escape from the mass murder visited upon their people. In the 1920s, in came refugees fleeing from Mussolini's Italy, helping to swell the already large number of Italian immigrant workers. Next came the Polish Jews, who quit their country

following the great pogroms; and Hungarians fleeing from dictatorship; and Rumanians fleeing from fascism.[134] Most of these were simple
workers, and a smaller number were Hungarian students who came to
France to pursue their studies in the wake of quotas for Jewish students
that had been introduced in the universities of their homeland.[135] These
immigrants soon realized that they were unwelcome guests in France.
Among immigrants who were shamelessly exploited in factories and
endured the contempt of the native-born population, and over whose
heads hung the constant threat of expulsion by the authorities, there
was a sardonic adage: "*Liberté, Egalité, Carte d'Identité.*"[136] Used as cheap
labor, they were also shunned by the trade unions. Their offspring
were held up to ridicule for their strange-sounding names and their
faltering efforts with the French language. Their homes were damp,
dark, and wretched; the womenfolk had to work genuine miracles just
to put food on the table each day. And that food was always the same:
herring with potatoes.[137]

The only French organization looking after these immigrant workers was the Communist Party. In the 1920s and 1930s, it espoused a more
internationalist approach, did not look upon this mass of underrated
proletarians as foreigners, and reckoned, with good reason, that it might
be able to recruit a fair number of new members from among them. Many
of the political fugitives had previously been working actively in their
homelands on the Party's behalf, while others leapt at the chance of membership in a structured group that held out the prospect of campaigning
for their own rights. The MOI, or Immigrant Labor, was launched and
organized along linguistic lines. In left-wing French circles, the acronym
MOI was translated as "Mouvement Ouvrier International" (International
Workers' Movement).[138] Paris soon boasted a Rumanian, an Armenian,
and an Italian branch, as well as the largest, most populous Jewish branch,
whose members were drawn from a miscellany of nations, but who could
nevertheless communicate readily with one another in Yiddish.[139] Most
of these were Polish Jews: in 1939 a total of 160,000 immigrant Jews were
living in France, and over half came from Poland. The Jewish branch of
the MOI in Paris launched its own youth organization, a Jewish trade
union, a cultural association, a sports club, and its own Red Aid section.
They published a newspaper in Yiddish, the *Naije Presse*, which was read
by more than just group members.[140] Immigrants' children grew up in the
working class Jewish quarters of Belleville, Nation, and the Marais; many

of them were members of the sports club and later fought in the ranks of the FTP-MOI (the FTP, Francs-Tireurs et Partisans, being the Communist armed resistance organization). [141]

When the Communist Party was outlawed in 1939, the MOI was also officially dissolved, but continued to exist beneath the surface. In a way, its members found illegality easier than French Communists did. Many immigrants had already been living pretty much illegally in France anyway.[142] After the German invasion, part of the MOI concentrated on the organization of civil resistance, procuring accommodation, hiding-places, and forged papers, and publishing newspapers and leaflets. Others prepared for armed struggle through the OS (Organization Spéciale—Special Organization).[143] However, during the first months of the German occupation, those members in greatest danger, and most disposed to do whatever it took to fight back, were not able to do so in the manner they preferred. The pact signed between Hitler and Stalin prescribed a policy of passivity that paralysed the Communist Party of France, and consequently the MOI, although its Jewish members at least were very clear from the outset about what to expect from this nonaggression pact.[144] Those were certainly the toughest times, not just for Jewish Communists, but also for many other Party members unable to turn a blind eye to the fact that their female and male comrades were being persecuted and tortured in Germany and German-occupied nations—while the Comintern said not one word about the matter. The Spaniards, female and male, and the International Brigade members, who had been interned in camps after the defeat of the Spanish Republic before escaping to France, now found themselves with hands tied in occupied Paris. But they hoped to be able to resume their fight against their powerful adversary. On May 8, 1941, the first breakthrough came: the daily newspaper *L'Humanité* carried an appeal on its front page: "French [people], fight for national liberation!"[145] A month earlier, the first MOI members had already been organizing themselves underground. When, in the wake of the German army's invasion of the Soviet Union, the Communist Party of France called for armed resistance, the immigrants' organization was ready for action. The earliest armed operations started in Paris in August 1941: railway lines were blown up, premises frequented by German offices were attacked, and German servicemen executed. That same month, the Vichy government passed an emergency law against offences perpetrated in the name of Communist or anarchist motives.[146] In September 1941, De Gaulle in London officially recognized the Communist Party, but, in a radio broadcast, also strenuously condemned the attacks on German officers.[147]

A French police antiterrorist unit, the BS (Brigades Spéciales) was set up alongside the German SD and Gestapo to hunt down resistance fighters. Late in 1941, the small and comparatively poorly organized groups that had launched the struggle against the German invaders had all but been dismantled, their members jailed or executed.[148]

In March 1942, the Communist Party revamped the armed resistance through the FTPF (Francs-Tireurs et Partisans Français). The FTP-MOI, subdivided into five combat groups, was made an autonomous group under the FTPF umbrella. The majority of the membership was Jewish, plus Rumanians, Czechs, a number of Germans, Italians, Armenians, and Spaniards. Many of the youngest Jewish members were drawn from YASK, the Jewish sports club, and the FTP-MOI personnel styled themselves the "sportsmen."[149] Older fighters like Sophie Swarc, who had already served time in Poland for being a Communist, or Yanina Sochaczewska, who found herself obliged to flee Paris in order to escape her pursuers,[150] were now joined by the youngsters of the second generation, who had grown up in the midst of poverty, but with a sense of identity derived from living in quarters like Belleville or Nation as the "round-up generation."[151] On July 16, 1942, the German occupiers arrested 13,000 Jewish women, men, and children, and held them in the Vélodrome d'Hiver, before shipping them, after a stopover in a French camp, to the camps in Poland.[152] The girls and boys who evaded this roundup, but whose parents and siblings were transported to their deaths, had a single thought in mind: Vengeance!

The authorities in charge of the occupying forces passed their first anti-Jewish decrees in October 1940, in close concert with the Vichy government—cooperation that would become a regular feature from then on. All Jews had to register with police stations. Only a few, generally immigrants from fascist countries, defied this order.[153] In the spring of 1941, the collaborationist government set up its Jewish Commissariat-General, which, a short time later, launched the Union Générale des Israélites de France, equivalent to the Jewish councils of occupied eastern Europe.[154] In May 1941, all foreign Jews were required to report to a specific location, bringing clothing and food for at least two days. Five thousand complied and were shipped to the death camps.[155] When, on August 20, 1941, the French gendarmerie carried out a huge roundup in the XIth arrondissement (Belleville), a further 5,000 Jews were deported to Poland via Drancy.[156] In March of the next year, the exclusion of the Jewish population from public life was completed: they were barred from entering any restaurant, cinema, or public amenity, and banned from being on the streets after eight o'clock. In June 1942, the wearing of yellow stars was introduced and, a month later, there was the Vel d'Hiv roundup. On November 11, 1942, when southern France came under occupation, the thousands who had escaped to the unoccupied zone lost all prospect of salvation.[157]

Women were active members of the MOI from the day it was launched. The Polish Jews, especially, had been active fighters when they arrived in Paris, and, among the Italians and Germans, the women from the International Brigades were tried and tested antifascists. Following the German invasion, a number of these women took charge of political and victualling tasks, organizing an effective infrastructure, and then smuggled batches of Jewish children out of the country.[158] Other female members of the MOI and the girls who joined them in the wake of one of the roundups, joined the FTP, which amounted to the armed wing of the MOI.

At the start of the war, French women were practically without rights. They could not vote, nor were they even entitled to a passport of their own. Before they could accept paid employment, their husbands' permission was required. In 1936, only one in three women worked (according to the official figures).[159] The women from the MOI, who were not normally French, were in even worse straits than the female citizens of the Republic. Not only were they not entitled to vote, but they did not even have any rights of residence. If they worked outside the home, it was almost always illegally, in small garment sweatshops, and for scandalously poor pay.[160] But, unlike authentic Frenchwomen, many of them took an interest in politics, or were actively involved in them. Nearly all of the women members of the MOI came from left-wing backgrounds. The few women who resorted to armed resistance without having any political background were the exceptions.[161] Women's participation in the resistance was quite high. In his book *La Résistance organizée des Juifs*, Jacques Ravine recounts that forty-one of the sixty-nine people arrested in Paris in the summer of 1943 as resistance fighters were women.[162] The overall percentage would have been somewhat smaller. In the list of fallen resistance fighters given in David Diamant's book *Les Juifs dans la Résistance 1940–44*, 110 of the 725 names were women's names—14 percent of the total.[163]

Prior to the appearance of those two books in the 1970s, the resistance was regarded as a wholly male affair. Even in underground resistance publications, with few exceptions, there is no specific reference made to women.[164] In the histories in the wake of the liberation, women go unmentioned, as does the MOI. They received no decorations or citations of honor—in addition to many men, a mere six women were awarded the title of "chevalier de la libération."[165] Not until the 1975 symposium of the Union des Femmes Françaises at the Sorbonne did female historians and witnesses from the time make the first public references to the theme of women in the resistance.[166] Three years later, Ania Francos' book came out under the telling title of *Il était des femmes dans la Résistance* (There were women in the Resistance).[167]

The MOI fighting groups in Paris raised a female unit of their own that looked after the transportation of arms and bombs, as well as the surveillance of likely targets. Every group had a female courier passing on intelligence and instructions from headquarters to the activists, organizing meetings, and passing on news. From September 1942 on, the MOI even had a female partisan unit of its own, made up wholly of women and carrying out sabotage and assassinations.[168] In his *Diary of a Jewish Partisan*, Abraham Lissner explains how two women from this group were arrested right after one operation as they emerged from the Porte d'Orléans metro station carrying explosives. Unfortunately, he does not give their names. The third member of the team, Hania Mansfeld, nicknamed Hélène Kro, was later arrested at her home. As the police were searching her apartment, she jumped out of the window and died. Her two female comrades were deported, never to return.[169]

When a commando from the FTP-MOI attacked the German barracks in the Rue Vaugirard on November 15, 1942, the operation also involved two women who had previously transported the bombs for the mission. On February 3, 1943, six female and male partisans from the MOI attacked the German anti-aircraft defenses and military barracks near the Quai d'Orsay: again it was women who had procured the arms and munitions. The unit's dump was six kilometers from the target location and the women had ferried all of the gear the whole way on foot: this was an almost inevitable precautionary measure, for public transport was under continual surveillance.[170] Two young, innocent-looking girls with heavy shopping baskets had more chance of evading notice.

Most of the MOI activists were ordinary militants whose names have never come to light. Often, even the members of a group did not know the names of their colleagues, since they used *noms de guerre*. The essential point was to maintain the group's clandestine character. The less each member knew, the less the torturers might extract. The names of a few women are known: Olga Bancic, for instance, who fought with the FTP-MOI in Paris, was beheaded in Stuttgart on May 10, 1944, on her thirty-second birthday. Or Annette Richtiger, known as Anka. She had lost both parents when they were deported to a death camp and, a short while later, her husband and comrade-in-arms, Jean, was captured while fighting the Germans. She herself held out almost to the end. In June 1944, she was transporting her unit's machine-gun, an item of incalculable value in that the MOI never had enough weapons, let alone heavy weapons. When Anka reached Douai station, she found herself in the middle of an air raid, and was forced to make a snap decision: to flee the area with everyone else or stick it out and hold on to her precious gun. She stayed put and, thus, perished at the age of twenty-four during an Allied air raid.[171]

Among the women fighters in the south of France, Rywka Frid enjoyed a certain celebrity. Rywka Frid, alias Gisèle Mermet, alias Odette, alias Rosine was born in Tuszin, Poland in 1923, and changed her name to Grynvogel when she married. In December 1942, she had joined the resistance in Lyon: first, as a courier, she had carried information and documents and, later, arms and munitions, until she was sent to Grenoble to help set up an armed resistance unit in May 1943. In July, she was appointed emissary of the MOI's general interregional headquarters in Marseilles. It was her task to keep lines of communication open between various units and headquarters, and to distribute gear stolen from the dumps of the Italian occupation forces in Grenoble to the commandos in the Alpes Maritimes region.[172] Rywka also participated in a number of *attentats*, her most spectacular feat being the bomb that blew up the officers' casino in Nice, a bomb that she planted along with Alfred Woznik, known as Max. Max disguised himself as a German army officer and "Odette" was his elegant lady friend. They entered the well-lit salon of the casino and sat at one of the tiny marble tables. Max sipped absentmindedly at his coffee while his companion buried her nose in some fashion magazines. She had left her purse on the empty chair beside her, so as to feign forgetfully leaving it behind when they left the room. Once the premises had filled up, the elegant couple drifted slowly towards the exit. The bomb exploded a short time later.[173]

By the time Marseilles was liberated, Rywka was utterly alone and she eventually retreated into civilian life in September 1944. Her entire family and her husband had been murdered in the death camps, her brother having been captured by the Germans while on active service for the MOI. She was the sole survivor.[174]

There were also women among the FTP-MOI's technicians. Boria and Hadassa Lerner, Bessarabian Jews, made bombs for the resistance in a pokey little room in Paris' Latin Quarter. They were both arrested. What became of Hadassa is not known. Boria, we know for certain, was executed on October 1, 1943.[175] Taibké Klescelski, who made hand grenades, mines, and bombs in Saint-Rémy-les-Chevreuse, died when some explosive material new to her went off as she was taking it for examination in the resistance laboratory.[176]

Some women even rose to join the political (but rarely to the military) leadership of the MOI. Paulette Rappaport-Gruda, for example, who already had a record of political activity in Poland, took over, from Adam Rayski, leadership of the UJRE (Union des Juifs pour la Résistance et l'Entraide—Jewish Union for Resistance and Mutual Aid) in the southern zone, when Rayski was obliged to step down because he was too well-known. Mina Puterflam joined the MOI leadership, southern zone, in the summer of 1943; the Italian Communist Estella Noce-Longo was also a member. Thérèse Tenenbaum was the political boss of the eastern departments. When Wolf Boczow, the commander of the leading MOI combat groups in Paris, was arrested by police, his wife, Henriette Towarsky, filled his shoes until she was also arrested and later deported.[177] In the autumn of 1942, Annie Kriegel joined the leadership of the UIJ (Union des Jeunesses Juives—Union of Young Jewish Females), the youth wing of the MOI, and later held the position of technical chief in the three-person leadership of her fighting unit. Finally, Catherine Varlin joined the leadership of the FTP-MOI 35th

Rywka Frid

Brigade in Toulouse and was later elected to the leadership of all the FTP personnel in the region.[178]

However, it is believed that it was a woman who betrayed the MOI combat groups in Paris. After the disintegration of the initial small groups and the launching of the FTP, MOI activists embarked upon increasingly hazardous operations. In March 1943, the backlash came; twenty-four fighters were rounded up, almost simultaneously. But the groups carried on. In his *Diary of a Jewish Partisan*, Abraham Lissner has this to say of the period between April and May 1943: "Those were certainly our peak months of activity. The underground bulletin read like dispatches from the front: Four high-ranking German officers executed. Sixteen German military units attacked with grenades in a variety of locations in Paris. Five garages burned. Nine hotels destroyed. In all, thirty-four sabotage operations, of which fifteen were carried out by Jewish partisans."[179]

When all of its leadership and many of its militants were arrested in June and July of 1943, the FTP-MOI found itself obliged to reorganize. There were already suspicions that there was a traitor, or several traitors, at work. However, not only did they carry on, but they even stepped up the fighting. A team was set up under Wolf Boczow, specializing in derailment of troop trains, and a second unit, under the command of Marcel Rayman and Manouchian, carried out assassinations in the city.[180] On July 28, a bomb destroyed the car of General Von Schaumburg, the Greater Paris district commander; on September 28,

MOI members executed Dr Julius von Ritter, the man in charge of drafting French people for forced labor.[181] The year 1943 was an important year for MOI fighters for other reasons too: the Red Army had won the battle for Stalingrad and the underground press was reporting an uprising in the Warsaw ghetto—which was stimulating and encouraging news for Jewish activists, as well as an incentive to get involved.

In November the BS (Special Brigades) launched their great offensive. For some months, the French antiterrorist unit and the Gestapo had been keeping surveillance on MOI members and had gradually been able to map their network. With the help of traitors (today, suspicions focus specifically upon a man and a woman, both of whom survived the war), they managed to trace the organization's structures.[182] Surveillance on some isolated members led them to others, until they had virtually the entire membership of the FTP-MOI within their grasp. Then, on November 13, they swooped in and were gratified to discover that, among the detainees, were "fifty-eight Jews of varying nationalities, twenty-nine foreigners, and twenty-one French Aryans."[183] The Nazis were elated: these terrorists were virtually all Jewish and foreign scum.

A propaganda machine cranked into action: the French now had to be shown who was bringing the awful reprisals down upon them, who was to blame for the heavy hand used by the occupation forces, which had been otherwise so peaceable and civilized. Millions of copies of the famous red poster, the *Affiche Rouge*, were copied and posted all over the country.[184] "Liberators?" was the question asked in large letters at the top; and below this was an answer to that rhetorical question: "Liberation from the army of terrorists." Between the two was a photograph of ten men regarded as awful super-terrorists—seven of the ten were Jews. Under the photographs, in accordance with their pursuers' racist criteria, they were exposed, in order of arrest as: Grzywacz, Polish Jew; Elek, Hungarian Jew; Wajsbrod, Polish Jew; Witchitz, Hungarian Jew; Fingerweig, Polish Jew; Boczow, Hungarian Jew; Rayman, Polish Jew; Fontanot, Italian Communist; Alfonso, Spanish Red; Manouchian, Armenian, leader of the gang.

In 1985, French television broadcast the film *Des terroristes à la retraite* (Terrorists in Retirement), made with the assistance of surviving members of the MOI. It sparked off a furious debate and thereby helped publicize the MOI, habitually denied a voice until then. The press, as well as the former resistance fighters, female and male, were intrigued by the "*Affiche Rouge* Affair." The film's director, Mosco, expressed his suspicion that the Communist Party may have handed over its own most active, though not authentically French, groups to the Germans. Some former MOI fighters endorsed his suspicions; others vehemently denied it. The Communist Party strove in vain to prevent French television from broadcasting the film. The fact is that the fighters of the MOI, long before the big waves of arrests, had known that their pursuers were on their trail and that they were in grave danger. Adam Rayski, who refutes Mosco's thesis, reports that in May 1943 the MOI had asked the Party leadership if they might stand down for a time. The answer was no: "Communist cadres cannot stand down." Rayski says: "As disciplined Communists, we abided by our orders."[185] But, in his reply to an article in *Le Monde* by Stéphane Courtois, he also says that the MOI would not have been able to stand down: the Jewish quarters of Paris were home to them, their normal, everyday surroundings "our natural theater of operations."[186] Anyway, the resistance simply had to maintain a presence in Paris, the capital.

What cannot be denied is that the newspaper *L'Humanité* devoted a mere fifteen lines to the execution of twenty-three MOI fighters from what was termed (by the Germans) the Manouchian gang, on February 11, 1944, and printed not one word about the group from March 1943 until February 1951.[187] Later, there was the occasional mention, very much in passing, and Manouchian was the only person mentioned by name.

Back in 1942, De Gaulle sent Jean Moulin to France to unify the various resistance groups in the unoccupied zone, as well as to overhaul the structures of the CNR, the National Resistance Council. De Gaulle's strategic thinking was not based on direct action, but on making preparations for X-Day, when the Allies would invade.[188] The Communist Party plainly opted, right from the start, for immediate armed resistance, but in the course of the negotiations—at Moscow's behest—it reached an agreement with De Gaulle. Finally, in November 1943, when the armed MOI was decimated in Paris, the Communist Party succeeded in foisting itself upon the De Gaulle government in Algiers as a partner.[189] Thus, the Party was pressured from two sides to espouse a strictly nationalist line: by the western allies through De Gaulle, and by the Comintern or, indeed, after that was disbanded in May 1943, by the leadership of the Soviet party.

But, in the eyes of the Communist Party of France and its allies, its most active cadres were something of an embarrassment. They bore names like Bancic and Grzywacz, described themselves as internationalists and to make matters worse, were suspected of being trigger-happy. The suspicion that the Communist Party may have been keen to be rid of these awkward cadres is, to say the least, understandable.

Dina and Henri Krischer and Jacquot Szmulewicz, MOI activists in Lyon, themselves marked by bitter experiences with the Party and its policy of silence, nevertheless, deny such suspicions. They find it inconceivable that the Communist leadership could knowingly have allowed MOI members to be captured by the Germans or delivered up to them.[190] Those times were not exactly the best suited to thinking things through with a level head, argue still other ex-members. Those female and male fighters were poorly equipped, some of their forged documents were disastrous, and the rules of underground life frequently prevented the free flow of information. There are hundreds of reasons to be gone through in order to explain why the FTP-MOI was dismantled before we settle on the darkest scenario.[191] It looks as if a clear answer will never be found to this question of historical truth.

2

The smashing of the FTP-MOI in Paris did not spell the end for the organization and its struggle. Resistance continued in the south where, belatedly following the German invasion of the hitherto unoccupied zone, armed MOI units were set up: Carmagnole in Lyon, Marat in Marseilles, Borzeck in Nice, the 35th Brigade in Toulouse, and, later, Liberté in Grenoble.[192] Credit for the struggles of these groups (particularly Carmagnole and Liberté) not being consigned completely and utterly to oblivion, is primarily due to Dina and Henri Krisch and Herbert Herz. The Krischers, who live in Nancy, set up an archive in Geneva, working busily and painstakingly with the assistance of Herbert Herz. There, they have been gathering an almost complete catalogue of the activities of Carmagnole and Liberté. They publish journals on the group's history, try to organize exhibitions, and strive to ensure that, in the most salient locations at any rate, plaques are erected to the memory of those who perished in the fight against fascism.

Mina Kugler during the war

In Dina Krischer's home in Nancy there is a yellow star pinned to the wall of her study. This is the Jewish star that Dina had to sew onto her overcoat when attending high school in Niort. Along with some other classmates, she set up a self-defense group, but her parents opted instead to flee to Lyon, to the as-yet unoccupied zone. When the Germans invaded Lyon too, Dina's parents retreated into a hiding place with their children. After a while, Dina switched to another sort of illegal existence: she became a member of the armed resistance and the Carmagnole group.[193] And she was by no means alone in this: The Carmagnole group in Lyon included twenty-six women activists.[194]

Prior to the war, comparatively few Jews lived in Lyon. There were between 3,000 and 4,000 in the city proper, 2,000 in the Villeurbanne suburb and between 150 and 200 in Saint-Fons. Most of them were well-established, assimilated Jews from Alsace and Lorraine, who had quit those provinces for nationalistic reasons when they were annexed by the Germans in the war of 1870. A further influx of Alsatian Jews arrived when the German Third Reich recaptured Alsace. They were joined by thousands of families from the occupied zone of France. In 1942, the chief rabbi claimed that some 700,000 Jews were living in the entire Lyon area.[195] As early as 1941, the city had a Jewish Communist group made up of former MOI militants from Paris.

The first Carmagnole nucleus was organized in June 1942, under the auspices of the MOI leadership in the southern zone. All MOI armed groups in the region had joined the MOI units of the FTP and were under the control of the FTPF high command, the Communist Party's combat organization. Each command level (regional and supra-regional) was under the control of a leadership troika made up of a military chief, a technician, and a political chief. The fighters, female and male, were organized into teams of three people, then groups of three teams, and finally into sections each containing three groups, companies, and battalions. Shortly after the German invasion, in November 1942, Carmagnole was established as an FTP-MOI fighting unit in Lyon. At the beginning of 1943, part of the group (especially compromised members, or those who had been identified by the Germans) moved to Grenoble, where they launched the Liberté unit.[196] Collaboration between the two groups was very close right up until the end. They shared and swapped intelligence, logistics, and cadres.[197] There was a very high proportion of Jewish fighters in both groups, 65 percent in the case of Carmagnole.[198] The remaining members were Italians, ex-members of the International Brigades from the Spanish civil war (including two women, Mina Kugler and Hélène Jacquinot), plus some Spanish women and men.

A fair number of the Carmagnole members came from Paris; they were youngsters from the roundup generation which, to some extent, had not yet been involved in the armed struggle in Paris, but who had distributed leaflets and illegal publications and served their apprentice-ship in the underground. An exception to the mainly working-class membership was the Transylvanian Jews studying at the Chemistry Faculty of the University of Lyon (or at the Technical University in Grenoble).[199] To these were added the Polish Jews working in the mines at St.-Pierre-la-Palud, near the city, who, although not Carmagnole members, kept the group supplied with pilfered explosives.[200]

Dina Krischer and Jeanine Sontag, the products of bourgeois homes, were quite atypical of the group. Henri Krischers' parents came from Galicia (the part of Poland annexed by the Austro-Hungarian Empire). They had emigrated to Dortmund, where Henri's father worked as a coal hauler, and where Henri himself was born. When his father died of tuberculosis, Henri's mother joined a group of Polish Jews evading military service, and eventually wound up in Nancy, where Henri grew up an outcast, one of the despised community of Polish Jews. His mother was a dressmaker, and the man who she subsequently married, and who acted as a father to Henri, earned his living loading bags of cement. Nancy's Jewish population was like the one in Lyon, well-established and assimilated, and it kept a scornful distance from the Jewish immigrants from eastern Europe. But, with the passage of time, the latter built a world of their own. Henri's mother struck up a friendship with a woman who was not only intelligent and politically well-informed, but who was an emancipated woman to boot. With her girlfriends, she discussed fascism and the brown menace (a reference to the color of the Nazi uniforms) to the emerging rights of women in Germany. Henri listened and learned. His mother learned to read and write Yiddish and was eventually appointed chairwoman of the Union of Jewish Women in Nancy. Henri joined the Jewish sports club. His mother sent her little prince, her only child, to a high school where he had a chance to experience and discover for himself what class distinction is all about. He was the only one from a working-class background; the others had no scruples about openly reminding him of the fact, but this merely added to his profile in the sports club. He was politicized there as much as at home. Many of the sporting types would subsequently throw in their lot with the armed resistance. Henri Krischer wound up in the Lyon Carmagnole.[201]

Carmagnole was organized on the basis of eight member groups, each one led by the usual troika of chiefs (military, technical, and political). The entire unit would number some thirty or thirty-five fighters—less than forty at any rate. They led a completely clandestine existence, in apartments open to all, with forged papers and whatever (little) money they received from the Party. Arms, ration cards and even cigarettes, they had to secure for themselves. They had to turn their backs on their families and could not tell them where they were staying, much less what they were doing. Many of them found this the toughest rule. Especially in Jewish families where the ties of affection were very close: family member helped one another contend with poverty, contempt, and persecution; supported one another; the children loved their parents and, from a very early age, understood that they were answerable for the family's fate.[202] When Dina Lipka (or, after her marriage, Dina Krischer) realized that her parents were starting to run out of money, she was just seventeen years old. She explained to her parents that she had found a job and an apartment, which is why she wanted to leave home and stop being a burden on them. In actual fact, she had neither.[203]

In Carmagnole's early days, the fighters' logistical support ranged from poor to disastrous. They did not have enough weapons or apartments, and some of their papers would not pass even the most cursory examination. Many of them died in the attempt to procure arms.[204] Unlike other resistance groups in the south, the MOI partisans got no support from the British allies in terms of equipment or intelligence.[205]

Nevertheless, they embarked upon the task. On November 10, 1942, one day prior to the German entry into the city, they sabotaged the tram depot. On November 11, as the German army marched in, a grenade was thrown at a column of German vehicles, albeit unsuccessfully.[206] Once the group had finally been set up, Carmagnole's relentless fight against the forces of occupation began. Initially, female and male partisans organized actions in Lyon once or twice a week. Later, things changed to intervals of two or three days, and, in the final months, there might be several actions per day.

On February 10, 1943, a Germain artillery train was burned. On February 25, another German vehicle depot was blown up. On February 27, a bomb was dropped into the middle of a Wehrmacht unit. At half past midnight on March 5, two transformers were destroyed and another was rendered inoperative two and a half hours later. This was followed by bombs in factories working for the occupation forces, a blaze in the Wehrmacht petrol tanks, rails loosened in order to derail trains, and armed attacks on cafés frequented by German officers. On April 25, 1943, Carmagnole fighters began their operations at 7:25 AM with a bomb in a garage that did work for the Germans. At 9:55 PM, they attacked the Masséna hotel, killing two and wounding seven. The Germans responded by imposing a 9:00 PM curfew, shutting down cinemas and theaters, and banning sporting events. But Carmagnole refused to be cowed and, within five days, was marking the first of May after its own fashion.

On May 18, the prefecture in Lyon announced that an anonymous panel of Lyon citizens had posted a 100,000 franc reward for information leading to the arrest of the perpetrators of the April 25 outrage. Three days later, Carmagnole attacked German officers in the Café Morel. During their operations against the rail network and their attacks within the city, activists had to take ever increasing risks by attacking vehicles transporting money and administrative offices. They were in need of funds, ration books, and forms for forged documentation. They attacked German soldiers to strip them of their weapons. On the morning of July 20, 1943, a proclamation from the prefect's office informed these desperately sought terrorists that the curfew had been moved forward to 8:00 PM, and that the price placed on their heads could still be claimed. A few hours later, at 11:15 AM, they attacked a group of German soldiers. Shortly after that, they were the ones having to defend themselves against a German attack, but they managed to get away unharmed.

On October 24, in broad daylight and in the open streets, they took on a Gestapo unit that had arrested three of their comrades. Two Gestapo officers were killed in the encounter and the activists successfully made off with a machine-gun and a pistol. On November 8, 1943, a Carmagnole commando stormed a factory making radio telegraphy and radio transmission equipment. The material damage wrought was enormous. That same afternoon a partisan squad attacked the Royal Cinema, frequented by members of the occupying forces, as well as an officers' party: the toll was a dozen dead, including three high-ranking officers. In November 1943 alone, Carmagnole groups carried out sixteen *attentats*.

On January 28, 1944, they were out on the streets distributing bread coupons and leaflets to the populace. The number and impact of their operations increased throughout 1944. They were carrying out two or three *attentats* almost every day. After the allied landings in Provence on August 15, 1944, the women and men of Carmagnole marshalled all their resources again—liberation was in sight and they had to do what they could to expedite it. MOI fighters did not wait for the allies to get there: they had already taken matters into their own hands, but now, with pooled resources, their final objective was just around the corner. Carmagnole was now fighting openly inside the city, handing out ration books in the marketplaces, killing traitors, continually severing rail links, and blowing up one arms plant after another. In July, Carmagnole commandos executed five Gestapo agents. Pursued relentlessly, they did everything in their power to drive the enemy out of the country.

On learning that the resistance had liberated Paris, they resolved that the city of Lyon, too, must be liberated before the arrival of the allies. Following the allied landings in Provence, Carmagnole, which had hitherto operated solely in an urban guerrilla capacity, organized a *maquis*—a base in the countryside to which the compromised or the wounded could retreat, and from which they might also launch strikes. In this *maquis*, out in La Croix du Ban, there were at least five women fighters. The possibility of retreat now held out the opportunity to plan operations designed to free captives.

On August 24, forty activists came together to mount a large-scale operation. They exchanged gunfire with a German unit and open fighting erupted in which several Germans perished, but nearly all of the activists managed to escape. Carmagnole's retreat turned into a victory procession towards Villeurbanne. When they reached Lyon's working-class quarter, the residents applauded them from their windows, took to the streets, and mingled with the female and male partisans. They blocked the streets, threw up barricades, stormed the city hall, and disarmed the police. Villeurbanne had risen in revolt. The Germans were soon on the scene and entire days of fighting ensued. Now, events moved quickly, one after another. On August 25, the Carmagnole unit from the La Croix du Ban *maquis* occupied Craponne. Three Carmagnole companies, bolstered by other groups, marched into Venissieux, Montplaisir, and Montchat and erected barricades. On August 28, the Carmagnole *maquisards* occupied Sainte Consorce. On August 31, FTPF patrols were monitoring the Route Nationale. Finally, on September 2, after losing many of their comrades in the recent fighting, the Carmagnole fighters, together with other Communist resistance groups, units from the Gaullist FFI (Forces Françaises Intérieures—French Forces of the Interior), and American troops, took Lyon.

Jeanine Sontag did not live to see the liberation. On August 20, 1944, she was shot by a German firing squad.[207] Jeanine Sontag had been born in Switzerland in 1925: her parents, well-to-do Polish Jews, settled in Strasbourg. Jeanine grew up a sheltered daughter from a good family, pampered by her mother and adored by her father. She was not conscious of being a Jew until Strasbourg was occupied by the Germans. Her parents fled to the unoccupied zone. Jeanine attended high school and went on to study law. This young woman with no political background, who had never sampled the degradation of hunger and emigration, and whose family had never known what it was like to be deported, suddenly broke with her former existence and joined the resistance. Being bourgeois, she first approached the Gaullist underground. She worked with a propaganda and training unit, acting as a courier, transporting and distributing reviews and leaflets. But

Jeanine Sontag,
only weeks before her death

this was not enough for her. She wanted to do more. In the spring of 1944, at the age of nineteen, she made contact with Carmagnole and made it plain what she was after: she wanted to fight for real, with a gun in her hand.

Like all applicants, she first had to write up a *curriculum vitae*, and that very nearly was her undoing. As Henri Krischer remembers it: "She wrote that she had been with the Gaullists. Whereupon some dim-witted Stalinists said: she is a spy and just wants to find out what we are doing. There was even talk about whether she would have to be killed. Eventually an Italian comrade saved her by mentioning that she was Jewish. That settled it." Not quite completely, however, because some comrades could not quite set aside their distrust. Jeanine struck them as too bourgeois; she liked to dress stylishly and talk passionately about literature and, from time to time, made fun of their inflexible discipline. They argued that she was a touch imprudent and seemed incapable of abiding by the rules of clandestine life, and was therefore a danger to the entire group. Others, like Henri Krischer, appreciated those very qualities in her: "She was well educated, and one talked to her of literature and all that. This was unusual in our groups. We used to talk about politics and various theories. But talk about Rimbaud? That, one did not come across very often." Jeanine was truly enchanting, adds an upbeat Henri, an excellent fighting woman.

When Jeanine, known as Jeannette, joined Carmagnole, the unit was going through its most intense and most dangerous period. Jean-

Illustrated poster commemorating
Jeanine Sontag and the Saint-Genis-Laval massacre

nette took part in robberies of arms depots and, like all the rest, carried twenty-five kilos of explosives in her knapsack all the way back to the city. She also was involved in the setting up of a patrol to execute German officers, plant bombs in factories, or derail trains. She won herself a reputation as a courageous, utterly disciplined comrade with a capacity for endurance.

At noon on July 3, 1944, Jeannette's group entered the Gambetta garage, carrying explosives and incendiary materials. The workers were outside enjoying their midday break, but the activists failed to realize that the garage owner was still in his office. He called the police, and a special unit cordoned off the building, leaving them with but one option: to clamber on to an adjoining roof across a narrow plank. The men, Henri Krischer recounts, had leather shoes that they had stolen from some labor service warehouses. But the Carmagnole women, because of the constant money shortage, had to make do with crude wooden shoes. Henri Krischer continues: "Jeannette had damaged her feet with those shoes and had huge ulcers all over them." She lost her balance and fell.

Simone Motta in the 1950s when she was in the army

A male comrade still tried to assist her, but she had injured one of her legs and could not stand. She handed him her pistol and told him: "Get away!" The others managed to escape, but Jeannette was arrested by the Gestapo, who had arrived as backup for the French special unit. To this day, Henri Krischer feels the despair of this story, although he himself was not involved in the affair. "But what could they have done?" he says, in defense of his comrades. "With an injured companion, we could not have hidden anywhere. The French would not have let us through their door, and no one would have sheltered two resistance fighters after this sort of an operation. And, had a comrade stayed behind with her, the Germans would have had yet another prisoner."

The Gestapo tortured Jeanine Sontag in Montluc prison for seventeen days. They burned her breasts with cigarettes. They scalded her legs until she could not walk. They left her without food for six days, with only dirty water to drink. They beat her again and again, until she lost consciousness. Jeanine uttered not so much as one word. Finally, on August 20, ten days before the liberation, she was taken away to a quarry to be shot.

Mafalda Motta, known as Simone, did live to see the liberation. Simone came from a family of Italian antifascist workers who had settled in Grenoble. Every one of them, from the mother to the youngest child, was active in the resistance. "Simone was extraordinary, in the political field as well as on the sports field," Henri Krischer relates. "She was a cyclist and in those days a woman cyclist was something of a sensation."

After the Liberation in September 1944: Simone, Jacqueline, and Silvie
(standing) in the center of the group

In 1939, Simone settled in Albertville on her own. She did ironing for a living and worked for the Communist Party. Right after the Germans invaded, she began to play an active part in the resistance. First, she distributed leaflets and newspapers, but soon she was transporting more unsettling items—explosives that she ferried from the La Mure mines to the groups operating in Dauphiné and Savoy. At the start of 1943, she dropped out of her lawful existence and prepared for the life of a full-time fighter.[208] When she joined Liberté in Grenoble that year and then Carmagnole in Lyon, she was thirty and already an experienced activist. She took part in all of the unit's *attentats* and holdups, and finished up in charge of three Carmagnole groups.

"She was a Communist through and through," says Henri Krischer, "but was never into politics: she was a fighter, an activist. And," he adds, "she behaved like a man."[209] Not just in battle, but in fact. It would later come to light that Simone preferred women. "We took that for granted at least," Henri Krischer explains, and Dina agrees. "But," she says, "That was of no matter. Our private lives were of no significance."[210] Dina was on lots of operations with her friend Jacqueline and Simone, and she

Nelly Waysmann-Villevielle

relished the chance to work with the two women. Simone, who everybody described as being something of a tomboy, was also quite able to present herself as an attractive girl should the situation require it. Hand in hand, she and a male comrade would stop outside the gates of a factory and coax the doorman into letting them inside: she and her "husband" were looking for work. Scarcely had he opened the gates than the loving young couple would draw their pistols and, with other comrades lurking a short distance away, attack the factory.[211]

During the Villeurbanne uprising, Simone held the Germans at bay with hand grenades. Come the liberation of Pusignan, when her commander was seriously wounded, she assumed command. In the liberation of Lyon, she headed a battalion of her very own and, a short time later, she joined the regular army with the rank of second lieutenant.[212]

In addition to Simone Motta, other women fought in the Liberté ranks. Out of the list of thirty-eight active MOI partisans in Grenoble, ten were women.[213] One was Nelly Waysmann (Villevieille). She came from a family of working class Polish Jews and had joined the Communist Youth while still very young, before finally winding up, at the start of 1944, with the Liberté resistance fighters. First, Herbert Heinz recalls, she acted as courier, moving arms and munitions. Later she learned how to make bombs herself. From then on, she spent entire days and nights in the group's arms dump, unable to venture out into the street for a long time. The stench of explosive materials had permeated her hair and clothing."And the stink was so offensive that it would have given her away immediately," says Herbert Herz.[214]

Liberté was the only armed resistance group in Grenoble.[215] Its operations were no less intense or effective than Carmagnole's. On May 1, 1943, Grenoble was still under Italian occupation. Liberté opened its struggle with an attack on the Grenoble-Chambéry railway line. In September 1943, after the Italians had pulled out, Grenoble was occupied by the Germans. As early as September 5, Liberté scored a spectacular coup, when it managed to plant a bomb in a factory making lorries for the Todt organization, causing material damage to the tune of 15 million francs. Destruction of steel plants became Liberté's speciality, although it also attacked vehicle depots, hut enclosures, and cafés and hotels frequented by the Germans. On August 19, 1944, Liberté launched the final push for liberation. They began by taking over post offices, the radio station, and the Grenoble railway station, and concluded on September 4, 1944 with a bloody engagement against retreating German troops who inflicted the last of Liberté's fatalities.

3

By the time the Lipka family reached Lyon, it had already been through a veritable odyssey that had taken it from Russia and Poland as far as Germany and, thence, to northern France, from there into the west, until they eventually arrived in the south of the country. That odyssey had begun when they fled anti-Semitism in tsarist Russia and finished in a hideout in the occupied city of Lyon, amid fears of being discovered and deported to a camp in Poland.[216]

"My grandmother was a highly intelligent woman," Dina recounts proudly. Her mother's widowed mother—with a host of youngsters to feed—had become a purveyor for the Tsar's army (in Russian Poland) and was a woman who knew her own mind. For instance, she did not want her future son-in-law, whose health was already weak from having had typhus, to perform long years of military service, as Jews were required to do in the Tsar's empire. She bought him out and, knowing that there was no guarantee of security for Jews—that contracts and receipts issued to them were ultimately not worth the paper they were written on—she sent the young couple out of the country. This is how Dina's parents wound up in Coblenz, where her father set up a bank and where the first of his children, a boy and a girl, were born. But, then, her father's brother arrived from America and urged the young family to move there. He cautioned them about the dangers of inflation, was distrustful of the Germans, and managed to convince Dina's father. But, at the time, immigration quotas for America had been filled, and the Lipka family had first to go to France to apply for their papers. After this brief diversion, they would be able to board a ship for the promised land. They went to Sedan near the border with Belgium, living on their savings and waiting for their visas to come through. Their money was petering out and there was no sign of the visas, so Dina's father decided to stay in France. That was in 1925, the year Dina was born.

Her father worked in heavy industry, working hard and saving, and he was eventually able to set up his own iron-monger's business. "Things were going well for us," Dina says. "We were relatively well off." The Lipkas obtained French nationality and dreams of America receded. Family members joined them from Poland and the Soviet Union. Dina was brought up by her maternal grandmother, since her mother worked in the shop. Her grandmother spoke Yiddish to the children, her father Russian, her mother Polish, and Dina and her siblings learned German as well. When she started school at the age of six, just about the only language Dina did not know was French. When the headmistress expressed surprise at this, Dina's father soothed her by saying: "Give her three months and she'll be speaking French better than you."

Dina could easily have picked up the language of the country playing with other children, but that was out of the question. "My father was very strict. We girls were not allowed to set foot outside the house. I was even taken to school and collected later." Dina's parents were religious, but open-minded at the same time. "There were two facets to our existence. We prepared our food in accordance with Jewish ritual, observed the Sabbath and other feast days, but we led a very modern existence." The very same father who kept his daughters indoors at all times and forced them to rise at six o' clock in the morning to tidy up the house before going to school, also told them: "The most important thing for a woman is her independence. You must learn a good trade so that you won't be dependent on anybody." Naturally, the girls attended high school and went on to university. But it was equally natural that they had to lend a hand with the housework and keep to religious observance. Every Thursday the Hebrew teacher visited the house.

Dina Krischer (Silvie) at age nineteen

Dina wanted to be an archaeologist: "At high school we had a teacher who had a real passion for the ancient world, and his enthusiasm was so contagious that I could not conceive of studying anything else." That was in Niort. The population of Sedan—including the Lipka family—had been evacuated to this little town north of Bordeaux at the outbreak of the war. Dina was living in Niort when the Germans invaded, and it was there that she was forced to sew a yellow star on to her clothing. In Niort, she witnessed the first roundups and, along with some Jewish high school chums, she set up a self-defense group. Her parents started to make fresh plans to emigrate, but then decided to move to Lyon in the (as yet) unoccupied zone, where they had relations. But the Germans were hot on their heels. Within a few months of their flight southwards, the German army marched into Lyon. After everything that the family had gone through under the German occupation, Dina's father thought it best to go into hiding. He took his children out of school, found a hiding place, and bought them all forged papers. One of Dina's mother's sisters, Aunt Maria, who was only a few years older than Dina, was sent into the countryside with the youngest family members and the children of those who had already been deported. She managed to save all the children, but she herself was taken to Auschwitz. Dina recalls: "She was really pretty and young, just twenty-four years old. They picked her out for brothel service. She was forced into that for two and a half years. When Auschwitz was liberated, she committed suicide."

The Lipkas now went by the name of Charpentier. Dina was seventeen and did not like this new life, missed school, and, at home, could only help out her mother and read: "We read a lot in those days and chatted about politics and how to link up with the resistance." But for the young Lipkas, this was difficult. They were not members of any political group and, thus, had no connections. Despite this, Dina and her older brother were utterly determined: "We were keen to fight against the occupation, against collaborators, keen to do something. We had to do something. There had to be a way." Her brother was the first to find it, but he never breathed a word to Dina. He simply left home and disappeared without trace. Later, Dina discovered that he had joined a Jewish organization, the Jewish Combat Groups, which operated independently, but were close to the Communist Party of France.

Dina could now see how their money was slowly running out. Her mother had already sold off all her jewelry, because living outside the law is a very expensive business. Forged papers alone had cost them the earth. Dina made up her mind to strike out on her own so that she would no longer be a burden upon her parents—and maybe, just maybe, she might stumble upon one of the tortuous paths leading to organized underground work: "I was already aware of the existence of such people. They were wanted, and, because of what they were doing, the population was banned from going out at night. Everyone in Lyon knew that there were people fighting." Dina told her parents that she had found herself a job and lodgings. In actuality, she did not even know where she was going to spend the night. Her father gave her some money, then she packed her case and left: "There was a museum with a garden area. I meant to hide out and spend my first night there." She sat down on a bench and waited for darkness to fall. Sitting on another bench was a young girl who had not noticed Dina because she was crying. Dina engaged her in conversation, hopeful that she might perhaps know of somewhere she could spend the night. "It had dawned on me that she was Jewish."

The girl's name was Lydia and they had just taken her parents away. She herself had escaped the Germans because she had happened to be on her way to the bakery for bread at the time. They had locked up the apartment and sealed the door, and now Lydia did not know where to turn. Dina suggested that she go home, reckoning that "they certainly won't be back tonight." The next day they set about looking for lodgings and came up with a tiny room, with no wash-basin or bathroom, and no hot water. But it was a room, when all was said and done—and a room that they could still afford. Later, all of their money ran out; they went hungry. Lydia remembered that she had some relatives living out in the county, and decided to call upon them to ask for food and money.

"That day," Dina recounts, "I was lying in bed lost in thought when all of a sudden I heard some music. I was convinced that it could only have been coming from upstairs." Upstairs, which is to say in the apartment above her own, some queer folk were living. That, at any rate, was something Dina had realized already. They had a room even worse than hers and its sole window opened on to the stairs. They were young and there was no way of knowing which of them actually lived there and which did not. And, furthermore, "these folk were Jews. Of that much I was sure." Dina decided to pop upstairs. Maybe they would let her have something to eat.

There was a huddle of men and one women deep in discussion in the room. When Dina came in, a deathly silence suddenly descended. One of the men noticed that the girl was famished and offered her some food. Dina accepted a little food, but instead of leaving she stayed in the middle of the room, staring all around her. "There was a certain ambience," she explains. The others did not seem exactly overjoyed at the presence of this intruder. But Dina knew her own mind and she said: "Listen, if you're resistance, let me work with you. I've been looking desperately for people like you." Those she was addressing did not dare so much as breathe. Jacquot Szmulewicz, the official tenant of the room stammered, "No, no, good heavens, no way!" To which Dina replied, "Right, then just pay no attention to me."

Jacquot Szmulewicz later told me: "I still break out in a cold sweat when I think back to it." The very fact of their being all together in one clandestine hideout, making noise, flew in the face of all the rules of conspiratorial activity. But for a neighbor to blow their cover was a disaster. There was only one factor mitigating this horror: the neighbor was a Jew. A Jewish woman with a French name and no yellow star. Which meant that she was living outside the law.

Dina managed to convince Jacquot and the others. They asked her to write them a detailed *curriculum vitae* and, in the end, they put her in touch with the *maquis*. There, Dina learned how to use a gun and the basic rules of underground life, and she found out about the various options open to her as an activist—from courier work to surveillance work. But Dina could see only one option: "I told them that I wanted to fight just like a man." Her instructors agreed, and the new recruit returned to the city. From then until the liberation, she threw herself into one operation after another.

They gave her new documentation—she was now known as Silvie and looking for fresh lodgings. When her parents found out that she had joined the resistance, her mother called on her at her new lodgings and begged her to come home. She cried and was desperately frightened. Dina explained the reasons for doing this, how she had been on the lookout for this path for years and could not, and did not want to, back out now. "Eventually she understood. She wasn't angry with me, just scared. As she left, she said to me, 'There's only one thing I want, to see you come back alive.'"

Living outside the law with the resistance was tough. Dina relates: "When you get home after a nighttime operation, after the curfew has begun, you give your clothes a quick wash and go to bed for two or, at most, three hours. At noon, there was the daily meeting to attend. We used always to meet up at noon, for one thing, because that was when the workers got out of the factories, so we wouldn't be noticed in the crowds; and, for another thing, so that we might get some sleep at least. You had to arrive at twelve o'clock on the dot and not one minute after twelve. That was when arms and materials would be distributed, and then off you went with your group to carry out the next operation."

There was not even the time to feel lonely. Members of the various groups were not supposed to meet privately (although they did anyway), and every one of them had to lead a solitary existence, unless they were involved in a specific operation. This lonely existence was book-ended by what few hours' sleep they could snatch each day. "We were always on the go." Nor did they have the time to queue in the shops. They used ration books snatched in holdups as a sort of *baksheesh* currency. They would offer the baker or the butcher more coupons than required so that they would not have to wait their turn. In the intervals between operations proper, they raided distribution offices and cash deliveries and, if need be, a tobacconist's shop. The loot would be taken to headquarters for distribution to the different groups. It never even occurred to them that they might set something aside for themselves. The upshot was that "we were always hungry: sometimes we couldn't talk of anything but food." Once a month, Dina, like the rest, went out to the *maquis* for a little rest, a square meal, and to catch up on her sleep. Such holidays lasted exactly twenty-four hours and not one minute longer.

Dina was in the group under Jacquot's command and, there, she struck up a friendship with Jacqueline, a comrade-in-arms. "We were very fond of each other," she relates. "Jacqueline was a marvellous woman and an excellent fighter. We were very good friends and were always delighted to be able to go on an operation together." From time to time, they worked in a threesome: Dina Lipka, Jacqueline Bloch, and Simone Motta.

Dina tells of one of Jacqueline's typically heroic operations. It was one of the many nocturnal operations. A rail line was to be sabotaged at several points, which is why the group was bigger than usual. As ever, everyone travelled on his or her own, or in twos, taking the tram to the end of line and walking the rest of the way, until they had left the city precincts behind them. This had to be done before ten o'clock, because that was when the curfew, imposed as a result of Carmagnole activities, came into force. The group would wait in the woods to make sure the coast was clear, and then walk the ten to fifteen kilometers to the target location. There, they split up. The first group stood guard a little up ahead, a second group guarded their rear, while a third group loosened the rails with a tool specially made for the purpose. Dina's task was to shuttle between one group and another to check what was happening or if things were going awry.

On this particular night, shots suddenly rang out: Germans! Dina explains: "It really was odd. The Germans were as startled to see us as we were to see them, and, caught up in our fear, we both dived for the same ditch." Jacqueline threw a hand grenade and, in the ensuing gunfire, there were wounded on both sides. Jacqueline was hit in the thigh by a bullet, but, instead of cutting and running, she raced fifteen kilometers to tip off the comrades waiting in the city for the operation to finish. They promptly stole a lorry and set off to pick up the others. Jacqueline, with a bullet in her thigh, went with them because only she knew the exact location. The rescue operation was a success and, on the way back to the city, they encountered some German trucks, which were also on their way to pick up the wounded. "That was another fine shock for us, but then we started to sing gaily, as if we were youngsters

*Jacqueline Bloch Schynckmann
during the Liberation*

out on an excursion. Not until it was all over and we were all safe and sound did Jacqueline look to her wound."

Dina and Jacqueline were also participants in the riskiest operations, the so-called patrols: "There were eight of us. Two in front, two behind them, and, in between, two on each side of the street. When a German officer showed up, the flanking pairs were to open fire on him and make off with his weapons." Henri Krischer says that, as far as he was concerned, this was the worst mission and he would secretly be praying: "Don't even think of approaching on my side!" Dina agrees, but she stipulates: "Naturally, I was afraid too. We all were, all the time. But shooting as such... My aim was to liquidate as many of them as I could. The fewer that were left, the better. I hated them. I was filled with hatred for the Germans and, more so, the collaborators." Forty years after the war's end, Dina told a congress on Jewish resistance in France: "I defended my honor as a Jewish women and avenged our own."

Even though she could not have dreamed of the scale of the slaughter of Jews as carried out by the Germans—who, as Henri says, "made an industry out of extermination"—she knew that all her relations in Poland and the Soviet Union had vanished, that all of those deported from France would not be coming back alive. Dina was fighting as a Jew more than anything else. She had not joined the MOI because it was a Communist organization, but because "I could see that it was a real fighting movement and meant business." As for the Party, she had her reservations: "Class struggle, sure. I could understand that. I agree with that completely. But I am not the sort to obey readily, and I cannot submit to a party line and say, sure, amen to something that goes against my grain. There were so many who were forever saying yes and swallowed everything just because they did not want to lose their position in the Party, or because they were too cowardly to express their criticism. A political movement has to exist to struggle for an objective, for an ideal, and not just so that a few people can hold some petty office in it. I had grand, pure ideals and would have given my life for them. But I could not keep my mouth shut, and was not one to resign myself to things. That went against my grain. Everyone has to know what he is doing and take responsibility for it. Because he believes in it, not just because the Party so ordains."

Dina fought right to the end, until Lyon was liberated. When all the members of the armed units were incorporated into the regular army, Dina received an NCO appointment: "We went to a barracks. They suggested to us that we go out to Indochina. We women had to offer ourselves as volunteer nursing auxiliaries." Dina found the prospect unattractive and she quit the army. Her parents had survived the war in their hideaway, so Dina went back to living with them and began to look for work. She soon found a good job with an import-export firm, but her father decided to go back to Sedan and took it for granted that Dina would be coming with them. After all those months of independence and such heavy responsibilities, after living the life of an underground fighter, the female warrior reverted to being a daughter—a dutiful daughter, even though she did not like it.

For Dina Lipka, life in the wake of the liberation and peace bought at the price of bitter struggle, meant hard work and complete isolation. Her parents reopened their business. Dina worked fourteen hours a day for the firm. She was far away from her female and male comrades, and there was no one in Sedan with whom she could talk about her experiences or her more recent past. Although there were resisters in Sedan too, "there was no comparison with everything that the MOI had done," says Dina. "There may be an element of vanity in this, but our operations, our struggle was unique and without parallel. So I preferred to say nothing about it." After the war officially ended in May 1945, the wait for returning deportees began. Dina travelled to Paris, to the Hotel Lutetia, the arrival point for all returnees. Of her entire family, only one uncle and a female cousin survived. A woman

*Poster showing
the women of the
Carmagnole-Liberté
group*

survivor of Auschwitz told her of her Aunt Maria's suicide. Her family had vanished in a puff of smoke, like millions of others.

Dina married the son of one of her father's partners. Now she worked for her husband's firm, looked after the house, and had two children, a boy and a girl. "I had no time for reflection," she says. "We had a huge house that I had to look after, and I had two children and my work." She never gave up her job because "a woman must always have her independence." She stuck this way of life for twenty-four years. Then her daughter was killed in an accident. Shortly before that, Dina's mother died, and, shortly afterwards, her husband closed up the firm and disappeared for good with the proceeds. Dina returned to the parental home and now works for her sister, who has taken over the business. "And, then, along came the invitation to the twenty-fifth anniversary of our group. I was on my own. My son was working away from home, and I made up my mind to attend the celebration."

For the first time since the war, Dina saw her former colleagues, female and male, from the Carmagnole and Liberté groups. The celebrations lasted five days, which Dina thought wonderful, though her delight was not quite complete. In the interim, members of the group had fallen out with one another, some refusing to speak to others, and some had even failed to show up. The erstwhile MOI fighters had had all sorts of experiences since the war. Many had returned to Poland and then, in view of the growing anti-Semitism, returned to France, disillusioned. Some had severed all connections with the Party, and others could neither understand nor accept that. Others had conformed to the Party's nationalistic line and taken on French names, and this defied the understanding and acceptance of those less disposed to renege on their Jewishness.

In spite of it all, Dina was happy and enjoyed those few days, when, for the first time, she was able to speak freely and openly again about her past, and meet up again with her close friends from those days. Among them was Henri Krischer, or *l'amiral* (Admiral) as he was known to his comrades. He had also been married, and the pair grew closer. "We all know how these things happen," chuckles Henri. "I loved her, and she loved me." They married, and Dina moved to Nancy to live with Henri. A short time later, they started up their Carmagnole and Liberté archive to document the MOI resistance in southern France and help rescue it from oblivion and silence. This undertaking brings them into continual contact with old comrades—and through the project, the importance of which is acknowledged by all, few differences of opinion have been laid to rest.

Only Jacqueline, her best friend and comrade in the days of struggle, remained out of contact. "I telephoned her after I finally traced her number in Paris," Dina recounts sadly, "but she just said, 'I'll call you,' and hung up right away." That was four years ago. "She has turned her back on it all and has no wish to see anyone from our group." Dina suddenly seems very weary. I ask her if she has Jacqueline's address. "No," says Dina, before she perks up again. "But I'm going to get hold of it. Then I'll go see her and that's that. Yes, that's what I'm going to do.

Jewish Resistance in Eastern Europe

Like sheep to the slaughter?

Everybody knows that there was an uprising in the Warsaw ghetto, yet the pictures that moved the world only show victims. A boy at the head of a bunch of captives with hands in the air. A child broken by the violence of the victors. Along with photographs of the piles of clothing, the skeletons, and the death camp crematoria, that photograph became a symbol for the fate of the Jewish population in eastern Europe. Symbols of unprecedented butchery, and of an allegedly passive and submissive stance on the victims' part. They let themselves be taken "like sheep to the slaughter," it is said: those who offer a different view were few in number.

And those who asked why the people who did not actually put up a fight failed to defend themselves are also few in number. If we look at the unbelievable difficulties that organizers of Jewish resistance had to overcome, we can find the answer to that question—if we take into consideration the isolation in which the ghetto dwellers were kept, the hostility from the bulk of the non-Jewish population, the almost complete absence of assistance from the non-Jewish resistance, and the tricks and guile that the Germans used to mislead the ghetto dwellers about what fate awaited them.

In spite of all of which armed underground organizations grew up in forty ghettos in eastern Europe: in central and western Poland alone (which the occupation authorities described as the *Generalgouvernement*), twenty-eight Jewish partisan units were formed, and there were another thirteen mixed units in which female and male escapees from the ghettos served. In eastern Poland, Lithuania, and the western part of the Soviet Union, some 15,000 female and male partisans saw action, partly in groups of their own and partly in conjunction with Soviet guerrillas.[217]

When the uprising began in April 1943, the Zydowska Orga-
nizacija Bojowa (ZOB), the Warsaw ghetto's fighting organization,
could count upon 800 active, trained fighters of both sexes. One of the
founders of the ZOB, and a member of its leadership, was a woman
called Zivia Lubetkin, twenty-nine years old, who, even before the
war, had been one of the leaders of the left-wing Zionist movement.
When the Germans entered Soviet-occupied Poland, she fled, only to
make her way back later, in order to organize resistance in the Warsaw
ghetto.[218] The Warsaw ghetto uprising proper (following the armed
revolt in January 1943) started on April 19, 1943 and, as an organized
phenomenon, lasted well into May. Even so, in the summer of 1943,
the German authorities were still reporting clashes with armed ghetto
residents hiding out in the rubble of an area razed to the ground by
fire.[219]

The earliest incitement to an armed uprising was drafted in Vilna.
On January 1, 1942, members of the youth group of the left-wing Zionist
organization, Hashomer Hatzair (Young Guard), came together to discuss a text written by Aba Kovner, the man who would go on to become
the leader of the Vilna ghetto resistance and the partisan campaign:
"Don't allow them to drive you like sheep to the slaughter! Young Jews,
put no trust in your deceivers!... Don't allow yourselves to be misled by
the dreams of those blinded by despair. Those who were deported from
the ghetto will never return, for all Gestapo trails lead to Ponar. And
Ponar spells death. [The SS and the Gestapo shot down tens of thousands of Vilna Jews in a wood near Ponar]... Don't allow them to drive
you like sheep to the slaughter! True, we are weak and have none to help
us. But our only dignified response to the enemy must be: Resistance!
Brethren, better to die as free fighters than survive on the clemency of
the murderers. Resist unto the last breath you ever breathe!"[220] Although
this summons was addressed only to the brethren, it was meant for the
sisters too. Women like Vitka Kempner, who carried out the first act
of sabotage in Lithuania, played an important part in the resistance in
Vilna. In September 1943, the Farejnikte Partizaner Organizazie (FPO)
revolted against the big extermination drive mounted by the Germans.
Female and male fighters, who had escaped from the ghetto after the
revolt was crushed, sought refuge with partisans in the surrounding
forests and, from there, launched one of the most effective units of
the partisan resistance in eastern Europe. Their songs, such as *"Sog nit*

kejnmol, as du gejst dem letztn Weg" (You Never Can Tell When You'll Be Making That Final Journey) and "*Stil, di nocht iz ojgesternt*" (Silence, the Night Sky Had Filled with Stars) are still being sung today, and remind us that women played an active part in this fight.

At the end of February 1943, a session of the executive committee of the Zionist youth organization in Bialystok resolved to organize armed resistance. Some of the female and male resisters were to set up partisan bands in the surrounding forests, while others would lay the groundwork for resistance inside the ghetto. When on August 16, 1943, the Germans attempted to uproot the entire ghetto they met with ferocious resistance. Fighters strove to tear down the wall to allow as many people as possible to flee to the forests. While some of them successfully guided the mass exodus, a group of young women held the enemy at bay in close-quarter fighting, and even succeeded in forcing them to give ground for a while. One of the central figures in the Bialystok resistance was Chayke Grossman, who managed to make it to the forests where she fought as a partisan until the end of the war.[221]

In Krakow, members of the Akiva Zionist organization, along with the Communists and the left-wing Zionists of Hashomer Hatzair, launched the United Resistance Movement, a fully-fledged urban guerrilla operation that did not confine its actions to the ghetto. The underground organization in Krakow, which had numerous women members—including Gusta Drenger, whose diary from those days would later be published—carried out attacks on Wehrmacht supply trains, and cafés frequented by German officers, and warehouses storing important material for the war effort. One of the declared aims of these urban guerrillas was to show that "Krakow is not a German city, where Frank can do whatever takes his fancy."[222] [Governor-General Hans Frank lived in Krakow.]

Minsk was the sole ghetto in the western part of the Soviet Union (east of the 1939 borders): in every other city in this territory, the German occupiers murdered or deported the entire Jewish population. The Minsk ghetto had to serve as a labor camp catering to Wehrmacht needs.[223] But here, too, the occupiers were unable to impose their rule of terror without suffering heavy losses. A young Jewish woman named Halina Mazanik assassinated the commissar-general for Belarus, Wilhelm Kube, in his own home in Minsk. The ghetto resistance, which

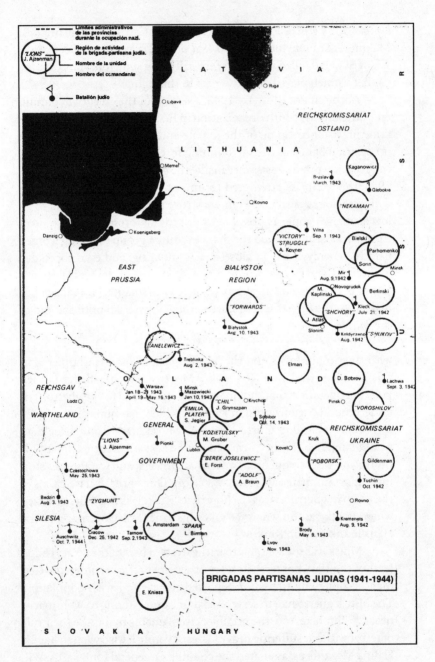

Map showing the locations of Jewish Partisan Brigades, 1941–1944

had resolved from the outset that the only sensible course was to set up a partisan unit in the vicinity (on the basis of the rationale that "ghetto means death"), devoted itself to smuggling people out of the ghetto to the forests. Women held posts of importance, inside the ghetto and among the partisans alike. Dora Berson, who had spent months smuggling folk out of the ghetto and escorting them into the forests, was the founder of the 11th Minsk Partisan Brigade in the Rudensk area.[224]

2

Under what circumstances did the Jewish resistance organize and these struggles take place? The strongest underground organization in Poland was the Polish Union of Rebels, an adjunct of the government-in-exile in London; it would later change its name to Armia Krajowa (Home Army). Its commander, up until mid-1943, was Stefan Rowecki. Leadership of the Polish resistance in Poland itself was in the hands of the "government delegate" appointed by the cabinet-in-exile in London, with the endorsement of the political headquarters in Warsaw, the PKP, which purported to represent the majority of the Polish population.[225] In charge of the political leadership was General Sikorski of the Workers' National Party, an old Christian democratic party with a rather weak left wing, of which Sikorski himself was a member. It also had a strong and profoundly anti-Semitic right wing, one of whose members was Stanislaw Jankowski, who Sikorski appointed government delegate in March 1943.

The PKP was an amalgam of four parties—the Peasant Party, the National Party, Sikorski's Workers' National Party, and the Socialist Party. The bulk of this coalition was of a pronounced anti-Semitic hue. Thus, some leaders of the Peasant Party had been members of Piast, a right-wing group implicated in the 1920 pogroms. Also, a few key officials of the Workers' National Party were former members of General Hallers' army, which had been behind the 1919-1920 pogroms. The right wing of the PKP was represented, above all, by the ONR (Radical Nationalist Camp), an openly fascistic organization of fanatical anti-Semites. One of the ONR groups, the Plough and Sword organization, is even described in a formal introduction to the history of the Armia Krajowa as a group "of which the Gestapo took over the leadership."

In February 1942, the National Union of Rebels was renamed the Armia Krajowa (AK). The AK leadership under Rowecki was made up mainly of right-wing prewar officers and ONR personnel. When, in the wake of Rowecki's arrest in the summer of 1943, leadership of the AK passed to General Bór-Komorowski, the ultra-rightist elements tightened their grip once and for all. The National Party, which had its own armed wing, the 70,000-strong NOW or National Military Organization, decided in November 1942 to place NOW under the authority of the Armia Krajowa. Many of NOW's units bridled at this decision and launched the National-Socialist Union (NSZ), which became the shock troops of one of the ONR fascist groups. In October 1942, the NSZ embarked upon its "Special Operation No 1," which created an international furor. In part, this operation consisted of the massacre in Borów, a village in the Krasnik area, where a unit of the Gwardia Ludowa (the Communist Party of Poland's People's Guard) was based. On August 9, 1943, NSZ troops murdered twenty-six members of the Gwardia Ludowa and four peasants, hacking off their heads with axes and dismembering their corpses. The Gwardia Ludowa managed to get a report on the massacre through to Moscow, and Stalin himself subsequently briefed the British and American allies on the matter at the Teheran talks. The scandal prompted the British allies of the Polish government-in-exile to demand an explanation from General Bór-Komorowski, who, until that point, had refused to condemn the massacre. But this did not prevent Bor-Komorowski from continuing his flirtation with the NSZ. In the end, he absorbed it into the Armia Krajowa in March 1944.

The years 1940 and 1941 saw the Polish General Staff and the Armed Resistance Union in London proceed with work on the first General Uprising Plan. That plan emphatically ruled out partisan activity, as well as other forms of armed resistance, as a weapon in the struggle against the German occupation. "Active struggle against the Germans in Poland," should not, the plan suggested, begin until "the burden of military defeats, hunger, and weariness eventually bring the German people to the point of collapse, and break down the discipline of a demoralized German army driven to desperation by the unlikeliness of victory, with troops starting to desert and withdraw to their own country along with their families... Not until such time as both these symptoms of German collapse are present simultaneously will the requisite conditions be in place for an uprising on our part."[226]

Thus, the official Polish resistance, backed by its British and American allies with money and all sorts of military and logistical backup, renounced the armed struggle in occupied Poland. This renunciation meant not only that they would await the advent of more favorable circumstances, but also that they were refusing to help other groups prepared to fight actively against the enemy prior to any German collapse. Furthermore, one segment of the Armia Krajowa specialized in breaking up and wiping out Jewish and Communist partisan units.

The decisions in the second General Uprising Plan, drafted in 1942 after crucial changes in the German army's circumstances following its invasion of the Soviet Union, did not, in essence, differ from the first plan, except that a rider was added: "The uprising could begin earlier, provided that there is sufficient active armed assistance from without." What this amounted to was a call for direct intervention by the western allies. Those who devised this plan made no bones about the implications of this wait-and-see, passive policy of resistance: an armed uprising or an escalation of partisan activity would only benefit the Red Army, and, as a result, would be prejudicial to the interests of the Polish people.

The main characteristics of the official Polish resistance and its military wing, the Armia Krajowa, were consequently an anti-Semitism that ranged from the virulent to the active, a resolute anti-Communism, and a repudiation of armed resistance (until such time as the Germans might collapse).

In August 1943, three months after the final extinction of the Warsaw ghetto uprising, General Bór-Komorowski made public his "Paper on the Anti-Gang Struggle." In so doing, he adopted the terminology employed by the national socialists, who described partisan groups primarily as gangs. Armed gangs made up of Jews and fugitive Soviet prisoners of war were supposedly—from what Bór-Komorowski claimed in his declaration—engaged in terrorizing the inhabitants of Polish cities and villages: "Men and women alike—and Jews above all—are involved in such attacks. Such disgraceful actions of immoral individuals are largely responsible for the complete ruination of many citizens, who are already suffering from four years of ongoing struggle against the enemy." The Armia Krajowa commander deplored the fact that the Germans, to whom the population had looked for assistance, were not intervening with sufficient vigor. As a result, and "for the protection of the innocent population" and "with the agreement of the government's delegate [he had allegedly] issued instructions to my commanders to resort to the use of arms in the event of looting or if subversive elements show themselves... I have likewise ordered my commanders to ensure cooperation of the local population with the government delegate's structures, so as to establish early warning arrangements and local self-defense organizations."[227]

This meant that the official, government-controlled Polish resistance was not only throwing its weight behind the population's anti-Semitic—and all-too-often murderous—behavior towards the female and male fighters fleeing from the ghetto, but that the Armia Krajowa, instead of taking on the German occupiers, was to engage the Jewish and Communist partisans in battle. On this count, it is also interesting to note that Bór-Komorowski and Stroop (the man who crushed the Warsaw ghetto) alike remarked upon the high proportion of Jewish women implicated in the armed struggle. Both the Nazis and their anti-Semitic Polish opponents looked with some annoyance upon the blatant rebuttal of two of their most cherished prejudices—about Jews' not being able to fight and women not being fighters.

The only Polish underground groups to give any support to the ghetto fighters (with the exception of a segment of the Polish boy scouts and a few individuals or tiny units from the official underground) were the Communists and a handful of minuscule leftist groups. The Communist Party of Poland, a quarter of whose militants were Jewish, was disbanded by the Comintern in 1938, at Stalin's behest. In January 1942, it reappeared as the Polish Workers' Party, or PPR. It still had a sizable proportion of Jewish members and, after the murder of its first general secretary, Marceli Nowotki, it was run for a year by the Warsaw Jew, Pawel Finder, until he was picked up by the Gestapo in November 1943. His successor as general secretary after that would be Gomulka.

The PPR's armed wing, the Gwardia Ludowa (People's Guard), which became the Armia Ludowa (People's Army) in 1944, became the chief ally of Jewish ghetto fighters and partisans of both sexes.

The official Polish resistance had justified the wait-and-see tactics of its General Uprising Plan by arguing that armed operations would merely attract reprisals from the Germans against the civilian populace.

Trybuna Chlopska, one of the Communists' underground newspapers, would counter this argument thus:

> If that be the case, why is it that, in Warsaw, where there have thus far been no partisan actions, hundreds are being rounded up in the streets on a daily basis and summarily murdered by the Gestapo? Or perhaps Auschwitz, Treblinka, the murder of almost the entire Jewish population, or the deportation of Poles for use as slave labor in Germany— where they are mistreated on a daily basis—are the results of partisan activities? Of course they aren't![228]

The Communists' underground newspapers adopted a categorical stance against the anti-Semitic line of broad swathes of the Polish population. In October, the second issue of *Przelom* stated:

> As a consequence of centuries of work by reactionary and anti-social forces, part of Polish society at present looks upon the murder of the Jewish population as something that does not affect them. In addition: there have been cases of active collaboration with these murders and comment to the effect that a foreign body in the Polish organism was being eliminated at last. There can be no doubt but that [our] reactionary nationalist sectors have managed to inoculate Polish society against many Nazi crimes. But the time has come when it must be stated plainly and bluntly that the murder of the Jewish population means that a part of the Polish populace is being exterminated, and the loss is not measurable in numerical terms alone.[229]

A few months later, in February 1943, the PPR's Krakow regional committee published an explicit appeal in favor of support for the Jewish population. After bluntly condemning all who, "hyena-like, rejoice in the misfortunes of fellow human beings, robbing the Jews even of their last remaining belongings and blackmailing the ones that managed to escape the clutches of the butchers," the Krakow Communists' statement continued:

> Already the Jews have rebelled in many locations in a desperate tussle with the Germans. Making them freedom fighters. The numbers of Jewish refugees and partisans will

continue to grow. We have an obligation to help them. We have to reflect that, if they can look to us for moral support, instead of meeting with rejection and indifference, they will find it all the easier to muster the courage to flee and to confront the occupation. Consequently, we must create a climate of friendship, compassion, and of helping hands... Harbor the fugitive Jew if he should ask your help! Do what you can to help the Jew escape from the clutches of the fascists and warn him when danger approaches. Rescue the Jewish children, roaming through the forests and the fields, from death by starvation. Hang the labels of traitors and friends of Hitler—with whom our nation will be settling accounts in the future—on all who collaborate with the murderers, who help them capture Jews, who steal from Jews, or who deliver them up to the Germans!... Let us remember and state it loud and clear: An anti-Semite is Hitler's ally, and a Jew is our ally in the struggle against Hitler![230]

However, the Communist Party of Poland, the PPR, and its military wing, the Gwardia Ludowa, were not a mass movement, since they had scarcely any arms, their regular lines of communication with the Soviet Union broke down for long stretches of time, and they had to be constantly on the alert against the possibility of arrests and murders. Many of the Communists had a two-fold threat hanging over them, as Communists and Jews. Theirs was an alliance of weaklings. But whatever they lacked in terms of arms, logistical support, and support among the population, they made up for in determination and commitment. The women and men of the Jewish resistance not only had to grapple with rejection and, indeed, persecution at the hands of part of the official Polish resistance, but a whole host of seemingly insurmountable difficulties as well.

3

The ghettos were relatively cut off from one another and from the Aryan parts of their respective cities. Leaving the ghetto was prohibited: only the work battalions employed in workshops beyond the walls could pass through the ghetto gates each morning and evening, and then only under close surveillance. On October 10, 1940, Governor Fischer issued a special edict affecting Warsaw, to the effect that "a Jew leaving the assigned residential quarter without good reason is to be punished by death." And the same fate awaited any Pole found "knowingly harboring or otherwise abetting" a Jew.[231] As early as November 8 that year, a security police court meeting in summary session passed the death sentence upon the first two Jews who breached the ban.[232] Meaning that anyone carrying out tasks such as gathering news and spreading it from ghetto to ghetto, establishing and maintaining contacts with non-Jewish comrades or friends, and, at a later date, organizing the supply of arms risked death the moment they set out on their mission, the moment they ventured outside this walled prison. It was primarily the women who carried out these dangerous tasks and, as a result, they shouldered the burden of functions crucial to the struggle of the Jewish underground organizations. In the absence of news, contacts, and arms, all resistance was doomed to failure right from the outset. Without the work of the ghettos' female messengers, there would have been no uprisings in Warsaw, Vilna, Bialystok, or the other cities.

Not just anybody could do this work, for the difficulties started the moment one set foot outside the ghetto and multiplied greatly as the mission proceeded. The essential prerequisite for pulling off this sort of work successfully was to look as Aryan as possible. Anyone looking Jewish was doomed the moment they stepped beyond the ghetto. Vladka Meed, a member of the Bund and of the ZOB, the Warsaw Jews' fighting organization, explains in her memoir, *On Both Sides of the Wall*, just how delicate the matter of outward appearance could be. A head scarf could cover up many things, one could wear a crucifix, and hair could be dyed "...but how was anyone to hide that underlying melancholy, that hunted look? Our non-Jewish friends were forever telling us: 'Your eyes are a give-away. Try to look livelier and happier and you won't attract so much attention.' But those eyes were still watching, still peering into shadows, casting a quick glance over the shoulder... Those eyes, stalked by the fear of betrayal, stalked us and gave us away. Aryan-looking Jews were forever asking their Aryan friends: 'How come we can always be picked out. Do we perhaps look less than perfectly Aryan?'"[233]

Language was another problem. Lots of Polish Jews spoke only Yiddish, and even those who spoke Polish were betrayed by their accents.

Anyone living in the Aryan part of the city, or coming and going all the time, also had to become conversant with Polish Catholic practices, had to know how to conduct themselves in church, had to know the prayers, feast days, the responses and stock phrases. And, even then, not everyone who spoke perfect Polish, was blonde and blue-eyed, could control the look in her eyes, and could go around all day mouthing Hail Marys could escape the notice of the *smalcowniks*, the Poles who had made a specialty of extorting Jews. Anyone denouncing a Jew to the Germans received a per capita reward; but, for the *smalcowniks*, this was not enough. Once they had run a Jew to ground, they followed him or her to their hiding place. Then, they began to extract the very last possession from their victims, by threatening to report them to the Germans. Once the extortionist could be sure that his victim had nothing left to give up, he then went to the Germans, handed over the address, and claimed his per capita bounty. Such Polish collaborators were feared even more than the Germans, who were easier to shake off. The occupying forces had a certain mental picture of what a Jew should be: if one didn't fit that picture, there was every chance of evading arrest. However, these Poles knew how to pick out their Jews. In her memoirs, Vladka Meed writes, "Seemingly, there was something about us that was unmistakably Jewish, something that a Polish eye could readily pick out at first glance, especially the eagle eye of a Polish policeman and, above all, the trained eye of the *smalcowniks*."[234]

The women survivors interviewed by Marie Syrkin also always mention this matter. German soldiers and police went around with the idea in their heads that Jews looked like the caricatures in *Der Stürmer*. It was beyond them to imagine that a young woman who embodied their ideal Gretchen might be a member of that despised race. Reyna, a courier from the Warsaw ghetto, reports that she had passed through several streets infested with German checkpoints without mishap, only to be spotted by a Polish woman, who promptly shrieked, "Jew! Jew!" Reyna, who knew that she herself looked perfectly Aryan, turned to the woman and said to her in menacing tones, "Call me a Jew again and I'll see to it that you get your just desserts." Some Gestapo personnel came over. Reyna turned to them and complained about "insulting remarks" from the woman. The Gestapo men checked Reyna's (well-forged) papers and laughed at the absurd suggestion that this girl could actually be a Jew. Reyna came out of this particular incident well.[235]

In such situations, survival hinged upon the quality of one's forged papers. Yet, whereas the Germans customarily contented themselves with running a critical eye over the identity papers, that was frequently not enough for the Polish police. They insisted on hearing about family details, information about the district where one was supposedly living, or about one's alleged birthplace. The slightest question about the answers could prove fatal. Men were arrested very often just to check if they were circumcised. That was one problem the women did not have to face at any rate, and yet another reason why they were chosen for courier duty. Generally speaking, it was easier for women to disguise themselves. By donning a head scarf, they might pass as Polish peasants, and they could walk through the streets carrying heavy bags without attracting too much attention. It was easier for them to bribe officials with a smile and, besides all that, both the Germans and the Polish police regarded women as less suspect and dangerous than men, who were, in any case, frequently arrested in the middle of the street and dispatched to forced labor service in Germany.

Such young women resisters provided the earliest intelligence about the situation in the other ghettos, brought the first reports of the mass murders in Vilna to Warsaw, ferried the reports from Warsaw to Bialystok and from there to other cities. They crossed through Poland, Lithuania, and Belarus with the first calls to armed struggle; and, later, they procured arms and smuggled gear into the ghetto for the making of bombs and Molotov cocktails. They were also the first resistance members to pay with their lives for their activities. Sofia Satorska, the first female Communist fighter killed in the Warsaw ghetto, a female liaison with the Communist Party of Poland, was murdered in 1940 by the Gestapo. Lena Kozibrodzka, the emissary of the left-wing Zionist groups in the Warsaw ghetto, was the first of their members to be arrested by the Germans—they killed her in Auschwitz. So far as is known, none of these women betrayed their comrades of either sex, not even under the most awful torture.

Every mission was a journey into the unknown, a tempting of fate—and, while there were difficulties attendant upon operating on both sides of the wall in just one city, travelling around the country was much more perilous. Jews were banned from using public transport, the trains were monitored, and the stations kept under surveillance. Emissaries very often had to pass through a half a dozen checkpoints on their way from one city to another. Standing before their pursuers with pistols and explosives hidden in their shopping baskets and a forged passport in their hands, they would toss them a smile, engage them in small talk and banter like harmless Polish peasant girls. Having overcome that hurdle, though not without a moment of two of flirtation, there was still the return leg back to the ghetto, which officially they had never left. Crossing the perimeter wall or slipping through a gap in the barbed wire, they might be caught at any moment. If, on their way back home, they tried to take cover by slipping into the ranks of a labor battalion, the Polish police or German guards might well take a little more care with the head count than usual, screening everyone, or picking just her out for screening. Emanuel Ringelblum, historian of the Warsaw ghetto, expressly singles out the important part played by these women on behalf of the resistance.

> It would take the pen of a great writer to do justice to these heroic girls, Chayke and Frumke... They brave death on a daily basis... They travelled from town to town, reaching out to places hitherto untouched by any envoy or Jewish organization... How many times did they look death in the eye? How many times were they stopped and searched?... The history of Jewish womanhood is a glorious chapter in the story of the Jewish people in this war. And Chayke's and Frumke's occupy the front page of that story.[236]

Despite the indefatigable efforts of these female couriers, it was not until later that knowledge of the scale of the mass murders reached the ghettos. The systematic extermination of the Jewish population in eastern Europe began with the entry of German troops into the Soviet Union.[237] Prior to that, in Poland, the occupiers had advocated for the notion of ghettoization. All the Jewish inhabitants of a town would be packed into a single district and crammed into houses filled to the bursting point, in unbearably unhygienic conditions, with no fuel for heat and startlingly inadequate food rations. To this was added forced labor in the workshops inside and outside the ghetto, work that lasted twelve hours and, occasionally, nineteen hours per day. The elderly, the weak, and the poor who did not have the money to buy what they needed on the black market, soon succumbed to these conditions. By June 1942, 100,000 people in the Warsaw ghetto had starved, frozen, been worked to death, or had succumbed to the epidemics that were continually erupting. Women who succeeded in getting hold of something to eat wrapped their bags in barbed-wire to deter the thieving hands of the impoverished children shuffling aimlessly through the streets.[238]

It was in 1942 that the facts regarding the mass exterminations started to filter through, but few people took the reports seriously. They were too ghastly, too farfetched to be true. In February 1943, three men who had miraculously escaped being gassed in Chelmno, briefed the Warsaw ghetto authorities on the gassing of 80,000 Polish Jews and several hundred gypsies from Besarabia in November and December 1941. They were greeted with undisguised skepticism, recalls Marek Edelmann, one of the leaders of the uprising.[239] Back in January 1941, the sisters Sarah and Roza Silber from Vilna had turned up to alert people in Warsaw to the massacres in Lithuania and Belarus.[240] But it was some time before this intelligence was to filter through *and* be believed. Even when the left-wing groups started to organize armed resistance in some ghettos shortly after Poland was occupied, on the basis that fascism had to be resisted as the number one enemy of mankind, resistance in the ghettos proper—for a number of quite understandable reasons—failed to embrace the notion of armed uprising until it became plain that the Germans really did have plans to annihilate the entire Polish people.[241] This was at a time when the first deportation trains had pulled out for the death camps and shortly before the big extermination operations had been set in motion.

4

Plainly, it was not enough to just intend to resist the butchers by force of arms. Anyone wishing to use a weapon had first to get hold of one. But getting weapons was the hardest problem for the Jews of Poland and Lithuania. The Armia Krajowa refused to give up any of its well-stocked arsenal. In December 1942, the Warsaw unit of the AK handed over a dozen handguns and a handful of ammunition to the ghetto resistance. Some of the guns were in such a deteriorated condition that they proved unusable. In January 1943, the AK commander sent London a telegram addressed to his superior, Sikorski: "Now, when it is already too late, Jews from a variety of small Communist groups are turning up, wanting arms from us, as if we had heaps of them. As a token, I gave them a couple of pistols. I am not at all sure that they are going to use them. I am reluctant to give them more since, as you know, we are short ourselves."[242] Rowecki was not being truthful on this score. According to his own figures, the Armia Krajowa's Warsaw detachment then had 135 heavy machine-guns, 190 light machine-guns, 6,045 rifles, 1,070 pistols and revolvers, 7,651 hand grenades, and 7 small anti-tank grenade-launchers.[243]

Given that they were not going to get anything from this source, in spite of their repeated pleas, the Jewish fighters, female and male alike, had to find weapons by other means. Some were secured through pilfering German weapons dumps. Some were bought from smugglers in the ghetto and arms dealers in the Aryan part of town. Even so, prices reflected the desperate situation: a handgun plus ammunition clip cost a Jew somewhere between 10,000 and 20,000 zloty. Purchased on behalf of the AK, the same weapon went for just 3,000 zloty. Rifles, much better suited than handguns to street-fighting, were priced almost beyond the reach of Jews: the asking price was 25,000 zloty.[244] It was not unusual for weapons hurriedly delivered and hidden away, and thus not examined prior to purchase, to prove unserviceable upon closer examination. Even so, if such extortionate prices were to be paid—for often defective merchandise at that—the money had first to be raised. That, too, turned out to be enormously complicated. The bulk of the ghetto population could not even feed itself, and only a few of those with any assets left were in sympathy with the resistance. Those few readily gave their money. Others were forced to give money—at gunpoint, if necessary. Occasionally, resisters also raided the ghetto bank where the Jewish Council's funds, and those of the smugglers and black-marketeers, were kept, pending the Germans' "taking charge of them."[245] Every one of these fund-raising operations, in turn, carried numerous dangers. In the case of a bank robbery or robbery of a private individual, such risks were obvious, but there were also risks for the inoffensive collector of donations, who had to identify herself as a resistance member in order to ask the ghetto's wealthier residents for money, thereby running the risk of being denounced. This explains the arrests of couriers who smuggled such hard come-by arms into the ghetto, like Regina Justman, who was arrested by the Germans while carrying nine revolvers and five hand grenades issued to her by the communist Gwardia Ludowa. For all their efforts, the rebels never managed to arm themselves adequately.

5

In addition to all these technical and logistical difficulties, there were also internal problems that proved tougher on the Jewish female and male fighters, since they brought them into confrontation, not with the Germans or Polish anti-Semites or collaborators, but with their own people. The underground organizations did not emerge spontaneously at the instigation of the ghetto inhabitants; they were the creations of political groups whose arguments on behalf of armed struggle were not always enthusiastically welcomed by their companions in wretchedness. In essence, there were three groups that instigated and organized resistance in the ghettos and steered it towards uprising: The left-wing Zionist youth movement, the Bund, and the Communist Party, or rather, its ghetto cells.

Members of the Communist Party of Poland, which had been disbanded by the Comintern, had carried on with their work in loose organizations such as Sickle and Hammer, the Union for Liberation Struggle, Spartakus (insofar as they had not succumbed to mopping up operations, or been delivered by Stalin to the Gestapo) and, in January 1942, they reorganized as the PPR, the communist Polish Workers' Party.

The Bund was set up by Jewish members of the Russian Social Democratic Party and, from the moment it broke away from the latter, it operated as an autonomous organization within the social democratic orbit. It became one of the largest and most active socialist groupings under the tsarist empire (in the Russian portion of Poland, that is), and was the biggest organization among the Jewish workers in Russia and Poland, female or male.[246] The Bund put out several widely-selling reviews—in Yiddish, the Bund's agitational language. Toward the end of the nineteenth century, acute differences of opinion arose inside the Social Democratic Party. In particular, the group around the review *Iskra*, which Lenin edited, was opposed, in principle, to autonomous organizations for Jews. On the second day of the June 1903 congress of the Russian Social Democrats, the Bund quit the party en masse. In the arguments between Bolsheviks and Mensheviks, the Bund sided with the Mensheviks and, from 1912 onwards, was an autonomous section of the Menshevik Party. Following the success of the revolution, this ensured that it was banned, and that its leaders were persecuted by the Bolshevik Party.[247]

After 1918, the Bund in Poland carried on playing a primary role as the representative of Jewish workers of both sexes, and as a self-defense organization countering the pogroms of the 1920s and 1930s. In the last elections before the German invasion, in 1938, it stood out as the party taking most Jewish votes.[248] From the outset, the Bund regarded itself as part of the workers' movement in Russia and Poland and campaigned for socialism in those countries—a socialism that would also bring liberation to the Jews, along with absolute equality of rights and partnership in the collective working life of a society devoid of class or racial differences. The Zionist policy of emigration and establishment of a Jewish State in Palestine was vehemently rejected by the Bund.[249] Even after the German occupiers had driven the Jews into ghettos, the Bund carried on looking upon itself as a part of the Polish workers' movement and attempted to keep up its contacts with the PPS (the Polish Socialist Party).

Among the Zionist parties and groupings, those on the left played a leading part in the formation of the ghetto underground and partisan struggle. Even when the revisionists (the right-wing Zionists) also launched combat units (especially the Betar youth organization), they never matched the success of the left-wing Zionists (except in Warsaw) or, above all, their youth organization. During the 1905 revolution, three proletarian-Zionist factions surfaced, the most significant being the Jewish Workers' Social Democratic Party or Poale Zion. Borochov, the leading ideologue of Poale Zion, argued that the Jewish people was entitled to a territory of its own, where it might constitute itself along class lines in order to prosecute the class struggle under normal conditions, and thereby arrive at its own Jewish socialist State.[250] One fraction of the party busied itself expressly marrying Communism and Zionism. This led, in 1919, to Poale Zion's splitting into a right wing and a left wing: the left wing applied for admission to the Third International (Comintern), but was rebuffed.

A comparatively independent role was played by the left-wing Zionist youth organization Hehalutz (Pioneer). Its girl and boy members were prepared in rural kibbutzim and urban collectives for life in a socialist Eretz Israel. They organized along quite autonomous lines and were fairly independent of the hierarchies of the Zionist organizations. Three of the youth organizations would play primary roles in the Jewish resistance under the German occupation: the Marxist Hashomer Hatzair, the moderately leftist Dror (Freedom) and the moderately liberal Akiva which took the initiative in armed struggle, particularly in Krakow.

The invasion of Poland by German troops also created panic and disarray among the Jewish parties and factions. Many of their known leaders fled to that part of the country seized by the Soviets, attempted to get away to Palestine, or went to ground. As well-known personalities, they were at more risk than most and had reason to be afraid of immediate arrest.[251] The youngsters who spearheaded the youth organization also retreated into Soviet-held Poland, but, unlike their older comrades, they decided to make their way back into the danger zone. They would have found it easier to escape, since they were young, fit, and independent; had connections with their comrades in Palestine; and, out of all the refuge-seekers, they stood the best chances of emigrating. Even so, they threw away all these advantages in order to rejoin the threatened Jewish masses in the territory under German occupation. Among them was twenty-five-year-old Zivia Lubetkin, co-founder of the Halutz and, later, one of the leading instigators of the Warsaw ghetto uprising.[252] The decision to return to certain Hell was not an easy one for these young women and men. Marie Syrkin tells the story of Hanka, who lived as a member of the Halutz group in Lemberg, which had not yet been occupied by the Germans. Her group decided to dispatch one of their number to Warsaw: their task fell upon Hanka, who had always stood out as an especially courageous and reliable comrade. In order to get across the border separating the two zones, Hanka had to swim across a half-frozen lake by night. As she slipped into the icy waters, her nerve failed her and she turned back. Nobody took her to task for this, but Hanka could not forgive herself. Two days later, she vanished from Lemberg. The next they had of her, she was in Warsaw.[253]

Until the Germans marched in, the Halutz groups had given a wide berth to political activity among the diaspora Jews and concentrated their efforts mainly on emigrating to Palestine. In the light of the new circumstances, they changed their outlook and, step by step, these young folk were taking up social and political responsibilities inside the ghettos.[254] They marshalled their militants, made some new recruits, and organized themselves into cells which came together on a regular basis to discuss the situation and tackle practical tasks. They set up collective kitchens, secret libraries, illegal schools, and even university courses; they looked after the starving children roaming around the ghetto and published a number of illegal reviews. Initially, these reviews were primarily intended for the movement's members and were written in the appropriate jargon, dealing with ideological discussions and disagreements inside the groups. However, they were soon to change their tune, and the youth movement's underground press started to target the apolitical, unorganized ghetto population as well, and switched from being the group bulletin to an important news source for the whole Jewish population.[255] The isolated ghetto inhabitants, cut off from all contact with the outside world, were able to learn about developments in other cities, read foreign radio bulletins on the progress of the war at the front, learn how to construe the Germans' decrees and actions, and—eventually—that there were folk in the ghetto ready to stand up to the occupiers.

As they grew through such activities, the Halutz groups were turning into conspiratorial associations capable of vouching for and relying upon their members. Against this backdrop of relatively safe conspiracy, they held their first discussions about the rationale and potential for armed resistance—a seemingly nonsensical notion, given the superiority of the enemy and their own isolation and the almost utter absence of external support. None of these youngsters had the relevant experience. Hardly any of them had done military service or had any inkling of military tactics. These young women and men, between sixteen and twenty-five, knew weapons only in the form of book illustrations. Their people's centuries-old anti-militarist traditions had also left its mark on them. "Jews do not know how to fight," the Poles and Germans were agreed. "We are men of letters, not men-at-arms," their own elders would retort.[256] The youngsters reviewed their history, harking back to the wars against the Philistines, the campaign of the Masada besieged who had refused to surrender, and they also looked to the traditions of revolutionary Russia where Jews had been well represented in the ranks of Social Revolutionaries and Bolsheviks alike. After all, Trotsky, founder of the Red Army, was a Jew. With what few weapons they could get hold of, these youngsters began to train—girls and boys alike. They had grown up together, lived and worked alongside one another on the rural collectives and in the city communes, and they were not about to differentiate between the sexes now when it came to handling of pistols and revolvers.

6

Once these youngsters had reached an agreement with one another, they had to win over their elders, the old party militants, to their notion of armed resistance. This turned out to be one of the biggest problems in organizing of the ghetto underground. The elders were as dubious about active opposition as everybody else. They could not forget their prewar experiences, their disagreements and frictions. Bund and Zionist officials were not disposed to work in concert with Communists—both organizations had been banned and persecuted by the Soviet government. The Communists were dubious about the Bund because it had fought alongside the Mensheviks, and about the Zionists on the grounds of their separatism.

The Bund held the Zionists in contempt as petit bourgeois elements seeking to drive a wedge between the Jewish workers and the broader workers' movement, and the Zionists fought the Bund because it was against the establishment of a Jewish State. But, on one point, the Bund and the Zionists were in agreement—their repudiation of the "young hotheads "who were ready to work with the Communists and who, it seemed, were now threatening to help provoke even greater reprisals from the Germans than those already suffered. [257] The killers ought not to be furnished with any pretext for still more massacres, the cautious politicians scolded the youngsters of the Hehalutz movement. Those ghettos that did good work were respected by the Germans, preached the official authorities from the Jewish Council—which had been put in place by the Germans. "This is not the first difficult trial to which our people has been subjected," was the soothing reassurance from the religious leaders. Not that all of these arguments left the young hotheads cold. They had respect for their elders and naturally placed some value in their reasoning. In his autobiographical notes, Emanuel Ringelblum, one of the younger elders, who later went over to the advocates of armed struggle, writes of twenty-four-year-old Mordecai Anielewicz, leader of the Warsaw ghetto uprising: "Anielewicz and the youngsters from Hashomer Hatzair and the workers' organizations placed gave too much weight to the opinion of the adults, those conciliators and calculators, who used to measure and weigh everything and would come up with all sorts of ready-made arguments."[258]

The argument that carried the greatest weight was the one regarding collective reprisals. For every resistance operation, innocents were immediately executed, and every political attack was followed by a German terrorist strike against the populace. If those pursuing an active resistance member failed to catch him, they would go off and look instead for his wife, her husband, their children or parents, and often, the neighbors in the house where the woman or man in question lived. The left-wing Zionist youth groups and the Communists held that the Germans needed no such excuses, that the utter annihilation of the Jewish people had already been decided upon, and that only two options remained: to live like slaves for a few days more—just as long as the butchers' mercy lasted—and then finish up in the gas chambers anyway, or to die with dignity. Such arguments ate up a lot of time—time that was vital for organizing resistance as effectively as possible. For example, in Bialystok, it was only on the eve of the uprising that an agreement was thrashed out between the different movements.[259]

7

Once the groups and parties had come to some agreement with one another and had banded together into one fighting organization, they still had to win over the populace to their cause. This, though, was one of the biggest and most tragic problems with which the resistance was forced to grapple. In many cities, such as Vilna or Bialystok, the fighters did not persuade the ghetto residents of the advisability of an uprising until the last moment. Warsaw, where the revolt turned into a popular uprising, with the entire population taking part, was the exception rather than the rule. The demoralized, the famished, and the terrorized hovered between hopes of surviving by some miracle and fatalistic acceptance of death's embrace. They were too tired, too exhausted by the continual harassment, the hiding, the daily wrangling over a crust of bread, the murderous toil in the workshops, to be able to contemplate rebellion. Or they clung desperately to the promises held out by the Germans and their accomplices, the claims that their labor was needed, whether in the ghetto or in the work camps deportees were being shipped to in the east. Many people gladly boarded the transports that were leaving because they sensed that this would hasten their death, and because they no longer saw any sense in a life made up solely of fear and wretchedness, loneliness and mourning for loved ones whose deaths had preceded their own when they had been transported into the unknown. Or, perhaps, it was also because they saw those supposed work camps as their sole chance of survival. Those who did not enlist as volunteers were conscripted, and anyone failing to report to the "embarkation point" at the prescribed hour was hunted down and, if found, shot. The Germans, keen to implement the *Endlösung* (Final Solution) as smoothly as possible, were forever devising new tricks and lies with which to deceive such folk. Even when the ghetto inhabitants clearly understood that those who had been taken away—the old, the sick, the orphaned children, the women, the unemployed—had not been transferred, but had been killed in burial pits they dug themselves in Ponar, or in the gas chambers of Chelmno and Treblinka, the killers still explained to factory workers served with their deportation orders that this was merely a transfer to another work site. Also, when the occupiers discovered that unrest was starting up in the ghetto, they mobilized a disinformation system specifically tailored to the city in question, expressly designed to sow confusion or to keep the rebels on tenterhooks regarding the precise timing of the scheduled liquidation. For instance, the Jewish fighting organization in Czenstochow discovered that the Germans meant to destroy the ghetto completely on the morning of June 25, 1943. The fighters, female and male, took up their positions and remained on the alert. On the afternoon of June 24, the news filtered through that it was all a false alarm. Resistance members returned their weapons to their dumps and went home or reported for work. One hour later, the Germans attacked the ghetto.[260]

The strategy of demoralization, pauperization, and disinformation eventually proved successful in many towns, but not against the resistance. Even in the most hopeless circumstances, when the time for an uprising came, the fighting organizations took up arms. Even the outwitted resisters of Czenstochow managed to regroup after their initial surprise and do what they could to hinder the efforts of the criminals. However, the insurgents were frequently out on a limb. The populace they sought to rescue from certain death, who they urged to use the uprising to escape from the ghetto, to escape deportation, or, at the very least, to take a few of the enemy to the grave with them, failed to play along. Aba Kovner, leader of the uprising in Vilna, reports that the thousands who had mustered at the embarkation point to be shipped off cast pitying looks at the fighters.[261]

In her memoirs, Chayke Grossman, one of the female organizers of the revolt in Bialystok, describes the tragedy of the despair in the ghetto during the mass slaughter on the morning of the uprising:

> Eight o'clock in the morning. Our couriers spread through the ghetto urging people to retreat into their hideouts, explaining to them and beseeching them: "Jews! Do not go willingly. This is no transport to Lublin. The Germans are lying, as always. Any transport leaving the ghetto spells death in the gas chambers. Hide yourselves. Fight with anything that comes to hand." Our comrades scuttled from group to group, beseeching and begging. But the river of people continued on its way through the streets. It was as if a quick death were easier than any prolongation of a life of torment. Living in a hole, in a crack in the wall, between the sewage drains, in Hell... Was this somehow regarded as a curse compared to a speedy death? Had we, perhaps, not grasped the desperation in the lives of parents who were obliged to watch their children go hungry, waste away, and die? A life without hope. What was such an existence worth? Maybe that was the reason the masses were scurrying towards death's embrace that morning... In vain, our comrades posted themselves along the approach routes. In vain did they block three bridges over the muddy Bialka. In vain did they try to herd the Jews back to their homes. They refused to heed us, and turned a deaf ear to our appeals.[262]

8

With the organizing of Jewish resistance still in the initial stages, controversy erupted over the best form of struggle. This was to break out repeatedly, fuelled by the notion that there was no indication that the ghetto population would join any uprising. The question facing the female and male fighters in the ghetto was: Should there be an uprising in the ghetto, or should they set up partisan units? Their answer to that question hinged upon a number of factors: Was there a forest close to the city? To what extent was the non-Jewish population (without whom any partisan unit would have a hard time surviving) friendly or hostile? Were there Soviet partisan units already out there which they might join, or from which they could at least expect support? In the cases of Lithuania and Belarus, the topography fit the bill, for there were extensive forests and swamps offering good concealment. From late 1942 or early 1943 onwards, there were also Soviet partisans operating in the area and, at the very least, they had the essential logistics and armaments, as well as contacts with the Red Army. Warsaw and other cities in central Poland boasted neither large, unpopulated forested areas nor large partisan units. Only a few isolated Gwardia Ludowa groups had established small—ill-equipped—bases constantly exposed to the risk of being turned in by the local population, or of coming under attack from Polish fascists or, indeed, from Armia Krajowa regulars. Whether because of its anti-Semitism or anti-Communist traditions, or out of fear of brutal reprisals by the Germans, or a mixture of both, the non-Jewish population took an extremely hostile view of partisans. Only in Minsk was the situation different: the Russian peasants backed the partisans—either out of conviction or from fear of reprisals by the Red Army, which was steadily approaching. Forests hindered the entry of German anti-partisan units, and the guerrillas already in operation were well-organized. Given these conditions, it proved feasible for the ghetto inhabitants to be smuggled out in dribs and drabs and escorted into the forests to set up combat units. The Minsk resistance promptly concluded, therefore, that there was no point to struggle inside the ghetto. In Warsaw, the ZOB also came fairly quickly to a decision on the ghetto-or-partisans controversy and pushed for an uprising inside the ghetto. Elsewhere, it took a long time before any decision could be reached.

Advocates of ghetto uprising reasoned that only a tiny fraction of the inhabitants would be able to slip away to the forests. There would be no way of getting large groups of people out of the ghetto without attracting attention. The old, the weak, and the children could never survive a long winter out in the open. Nor would a large group of Jews be able to subsist outside of the ghetto since, not only could they expect no material support from the population, but, indeed, could expect to be betrayed or subjected to pogroms. Furthermore, it was common knowledge that the existing partisan units were not taking anybody in unless they brought their weapon with them. And where could they hope to get weapons for the whole of the ghetto population, or even for those ready to escort them? To cap it all, if the young and the able-bodied, those capable of fighting, were to leave for the forests, that would leave the ghetto utterly defenseless, able to be wiped out without a fight at all.

To which the advocates of partisan struggle retorted that there was absolutely no sense in sacrificing oneself in a doomed struggle. It was not merely a matter of dying with dignity, but of fighting the enemy in the most effective manner. However, big sabotage operations, attentats, and direct attacks upon the Germans would only be feasible against the backdrop of a partisan campaign. The quicker the Germans could be expelled through concerted action by the partisans and the Red Army, the greater the number of Jews likely to survive.

In the end, these schools of thought resolved upon a dual strategy in most cities: the fighting organization would lead the uprising within the ghetto, but had to establish contact immediately with the partisans in the vicinity and set up small bases, to which any who survived the uprising might retreat in order to carry on the fight. Even the most enthusiastic supporters of guerrilla activity, advocated this strategy, since they were also not ready to leave their unfortunate ghetto companions to their own devices and deliver the defenseless population to the Germans.[263]

And so it was that these young women and men in isolated ghettos in Poland, Lithuania, and Belarus stood against a superior enemy—armed only with a handful of pistols, a couple of rifles, Molotov cocktails and homemade bombs made out of bottles, with acid-filled light bulbs, knives, axes, and bare hands—ready to inflict the heaviest losses they could upon the instruments of the Final Solution, and to perish with dignity instead of letting themselves be driven like sheep to the slaughter.

Warsaw

"Look, Hans, a woman firing a gun!'

Something like 400,000 Jews lived in Warsaw, according to the official figures prior to the entry of German troops.[264] Warsaw was a traditionally rebellious city, a workers' movement city, a city filled with Jewish life, and, along with Vilna, a fulcrum of Jewish politics in Poland. Whereas Vilna was regarded as the Israel of the diaspora, Warsaw was the heartland of the world's *intelligenzija*, distinguished by a climate of revolution that had peaked fleetingly in 1905. Now, in the wake of the Polish army's capitulation, a flood of refugees was bearing down on the capital, seeking shelter in the traditionally Jewish quarter, occupied chiefly by the Jewish proletariat, the poor, and the deprived. Ludwig Fischer, governor of the Warsaw district, approved an "Extra-ordinary Decree on the Establishing of a Ghetto in Warsaw" on October 2, 1940.[265] This meant that some 450,000 people were penned behind a wall six kilometers long and two meters high, with additional deterrence in the form of broken glass, barbed wire, and gates that were under strict surveillance.[266] With the passage of time, the Germans repeatedly whittled away at the ground it occupied. The number of inhabitants was swelled by the constant influx of refugees and displaced persons to some 500,000 by April 1941.[267] Whereas, previously, people in the quarter's working class districts had been living, on average, seven to a house, now there were thirteen in each. Thousands had no option but to live on the streets and in makeshift flop houses.[268] Time and again, the main streets and their offshoots would be cleared, and the residents would have a few days to leave their homes and come up with somewhere else to live. Now that they had concentrated their victims in the one location, leaving them wide open to attack, the Nazi authorities could start their work. Their aim? To "make Warsaw Jew-free." The tactics employed in stage one consisted of starving them to death. Governor Ludwig Fischer made no bones about his intentions: "The Jews are to perish of hunger and misery, and a memorial graveyard will be all that remains of the Jewish question."[269] This was to be achieved by two stratagems: radical curtailment of opportunities to work, and thereby of earning one's keep, and an equally radical curtailment of the food supply. In August 1941, the Bund review *Za Nasza i Wasza Wolnosz* (For Our Freedom and Yours) reported that, as of June 30, 1941, only 27,000 of the ghetto's 550,000 inhabitants had jobs.[270] To these must be added the small traders, the illegal workers, the people who could only find casual employment, as well as the smugglers, black marketeers, and organized crooks like the feared Gancwajch gang. Sixty percent of ghetto inhabitants had no income. 130,000 survived on the watery soup offered in the people's canteens, and upwards of two-thirds of the ghetto population went hungry.[271] The ghetto streets were plagued by gangs of skinny children trying to steal a crust of bread, or to come by one however they could. There were even instances of cannibalism. Emanuel Ringelblum recounts in his ghetto history how, at No. 13 Krochmalna Street, a desperate woman had eaten part of her child's corpse.[272]

The killers left nothing to chance. Calorie intake was precisely regulated according to race: Germans were allocated 2,310 calories a day, Poles 634, and Jews 184—and prices were fixed in inverse proportion.[273] Under these conditions, the first to die were the poor, the workers of both sexes, since in many of the workshops the Germans would use only workers who came with their own machines and work tools. The lucky ones who nevertheless managed to find work in the brush factories, tailors' workshops, and other textile firms were frequently female.[274] They toiled from eight in the morning until seven in the evening for poverty wages, from which further deductions were made for the two bowls of watery soup they had every day, and for social security contributions, which went straight into the pockets of the German authorities. Hunger, harassment, and infinite weariness turned these women's lives into a daily torment: "They are people [mostly women] who work seated in darkened corners and dank holes, on stools and benches, stooped over tables and machines, in the most horrific conditions. They sew dresses and garments, blouses and caps, mattresses and quilted bedspreads, and make toys, dolls, gold and silver foil, fly-paper, combs, safety-pins, press studs, slippers, sackcloth, and brushes. In the brush workshops, bristles are trimmed and the prickly wire fixed by hand. The fingers of the women and children are forever bleeding, covered in festering scratches. Their backs are stooped and their eyes surrounded by dark rings due to overwork... These are modern galley slaves who work for food alone, and the workers get only laughable leftovers to eat.[275] And piece-rates do not even allow them the time to eat, so the women have to wolf down the soup and work at the same time."

Epidemics spread through the ghetto: Exanthematic typhus, intestinal typhus, and paratyphus quickly wrought havoc among people already weak from hunger, cold, and exhaustion. The ghetto's self-help organizations did what they could to mitigate the problem, but they lacked the wherewithal, and the conditions of hygiene were disastrous. The upshot of this policy of starving and impoverishing the Jews to death would soon pay dividends for its promoters: By June 1942, 100,000 ghetto inhabitants, primarily refugees and workers, had perished.[276] Governor Ludwig Fischer was also satisfied with the results. At a meeting at headquarters, SS Brigadeführer Wiegand, the SS and police commander of the Warsaw district, pointed out yet another advantage of this starvation policy: it would put all thoughts of rebellion out of the heads of the Jews.[277] In this, however, he was proven wrong.

In January 1942, the sisters Sarah and Roza Zilber arrived from Vilna to report the massacres in Lithuania. They brought with them the FPO's (United Partisans' Organization, the Jewish resistance in Vilna) call for an armed uprising in the ghetto. They were followed by emissaries from Bialystok, bringing news of the systematic slaughter. They managed to arrange interviews with leading lights from the most important parties, but met with distrust and incredulity: this might well be happening in the central areas of the Soviet Union, but not in central Poland, much less in Warsaw, where there was no way of killing half a million people without the news getting out to the civilized world. In February came the first reports by eyewitnesses to the gassings in Chelmno, but few believed them either. Even though the Germans were continually lying, Governor-General Frank's promises that, come what may, the ghettos in Warsaw, Radom, and Krakow would be retained seemed a lot more likely at that point.[278]

The young Pioneers from the Hehalutz movement, the Bund youth, and the ghetto Communists, however, realized that these seemingly unbelievable accounts were the ghastly truth, and that something must be done to counter it. Other political organizations also started to search for contacts in the outside world. The Bund tried to rebuild and revive its relationship with the Polish Socialists; right-wing Zionists established connections with the PLAN, a radical Polish patriotic group. The revisionists had already launched a combat unit of their own at the start of 1942, the ZZW (Jewish Military Union). It would later play an active part in the uprising, but it did not amalgamate with the ZOB, the Jewish fighting organization that laid the groundwork for—and led—the uprising.[279] At the same time, the inhabitants of several streets organized themselves into autonomous residents' committees independent of the Jewish Council's official committees. They looked after the preservation and protection of their members and would subsequently become the incubator for the wildcat resistance.[280]

In March 1942, leaders of the left-wing Zionists (among them, Zivia Lubetkin) and the Communist Party met to discuss the prospects and format of concerted resistance. The upshot of this meeting was the launching, in May, of the Antifascist Bloc, which included the Hashomer Hatzair and Dror youth organizations, the Jewish Workers Party, (the left and right wings of) Poale Zion, and the PPR Communist Party. The Bund declined to join the Antifascist Bloc, but its youth wing fielded fighting groups of its own.[281]

At this point, a start was made on the explicit and systematic organization of armed struggle. Five Antifascist Bloc members made up each group, and each group trained in the use of explosives and acids, and received training in first aid. Only one of the instructors, May Szmid of the PPR, had had any military experience.[282] As a result the future fighters, female and male, had to acquire the necessary expertise by themselves—which explains why, in this particular case, the men had no edge over their female comrades. For the first time ever, these women and men felt a gun in their hands and learned how to use it, one and all, while discussing the best tactics for street-fighting, attack, and withdrawal. Even so, the women who, in their capacity as emissaries, had already shouldered the initial and most dangerous tasks involved in underground work, had barely any representation among the resistance leadership. The commander of the Antifascist Bloc was Mordecai Anielewicz from Hashomer Hatzair, and his team was made up exclusively of men.[283] Women, as Emanuel Ringelblum pointed out, were about to write the most glorious page in the history of Jewish resistance, but they were largely excluded from high-level decision-making—with some exceptions like Niuta Tejtelbojm (Wanda) and Zivia Lubetkin in Warsaw, Vitka Kempner in Vilna, Chayke Grossman in Bialystok, and Gola Mirer in Krakow.

On July 22, 1942, SS Sturmbannführer Hermann Hoefle informed the president of the Jewish Council, Czerniakow, that all "unproductive" Jews in the ghetto were to be transported to the east. The next day, white placards throughout the ghetto announced that, with the exception of those employed in German firms, members of the Jewish Council and Jewish police, everyone was to muster at the "embarkation point" for deportation eastward. That very day, the Jewish police (operating under the watchful eye of the Germans) herded 2,000 prisoners and 4,000 beggars and vagabonds onto lorries that pulled out immediately.[284] Each day, after that, thousands of people were shipped to the gas chambers in Treblinka, until this initial murder operation was wound up on September 12, 1942. Only 60,000 of the 500,000 female and male inhabitants of the Warsaw ghetto were left alive. The official Nazi census figures stood at 35,639, because they did not take account of the male and female illegals who had managed to go to ground and escape the roundups.[285] Only a few days before the operation started, representatives from virtually every political organization met to discuss the situation. "Resistance is futile," a few of them argued, "for we have scarcely any weapons, and there are too few of us." The Hashomer Hatzair and Communist representatives, on the other hand, retorted: "Even if these deportations do not spell the final destruction of the ghetto, we know that the refugees and those shipped to Warsaw have already starved to death by now. And, even if the deportees have indeed been taken to work camps, certain death awaits some 75 percent of them. So it is better to die with dignity, rather than like cornered animals. There is no other option. All we can do is fight. Even if we are only in a position to put up a symbolic fight, that will still be better than passive acceptance of slaughter... There is no alternative. Come what may, extermination awaits us. Let us slap the world's impassive face with this desperate action, protesting its indifference toward the Nazis' crimes against hundreds of thousands of Polish Jews!"[286]

That meeting failed to reach any agreement, but the advocates of armed struggle started to cast around for support from abroad. Their urgent, plaintive appeals to the official Polish resistance to support the ghetto with weapons, however, were ignored or emphatically rejected. Those few reluctant to stand idly by as Warsaw's Jews were annihilated did not have the wherewithal themselves and could offer only very limited assistance. One of the few attempts to help was mounted at the instigation of two women: Zofia Kossak-Szczucka, the chairwoman of a small Catholic organization and well-known writer of historical novels, and Wanda Krahelska-Filipowiczowa, a veteran of the Polish socialist movement. In the end, both were sent to a concentration camp for showing solidarity with the ghetto.[287] The well-armed Armia Krajowa plainly and simply refused any assistance, while a special agency of the official Polish resistance movement, Antyk (Anti-Communist Agency), blatantly welcomed the Nazis' extermination policy. In the summer of 1942, even as lorry-loads of deportees were leaving the city day after day, Antyk declared in an official communiqué: "Whether we like it or not, we are under attack from Communism. The Germans' extermination of Europe's Jews, which will be the outcome of the war between Jews and Germans, represents, as we see it, an undoubtedly laudable development, in that it will undermine Communism's explosive power after the German collapse, or even earlier."[288] Against this backdrop, the ghetto resistance was on its own and uprising became impossible.

Survivors of the annihilation operation were distributed through three work camps, each of them walled: the central ghetto (which the Germans called the "remaining" ghetto), the brushwork, and workshop areas (which the occupiers called the "productive ghetto"), where the manufacturers Toebbens, Schultz, Röhrlich, and Schilling had their plants.[289] The inhabitants of each of these areas were forbidden to speak to the inhabitants of the others. By now, the work in the workshops was straightforward forced labor, daily food rations consisted of a plateful of soup and a crust of bread, and working hours lasted between twelve and nineteen hours each day. The official pay rate of three zloty a day was handed over directly to the Jewish Council by the manufacturers and forwarded by the Council to the SS, who thereby raked in 100,000 zloty per day.[290] Vladka Meed, who was herself one of the conscript laborers for Toebbens, describes her labor vassalage in her memoirs:

> Half dead from malnutrition and pain, and under constant harassment, some female workers were no longer able to meet their work quota and collapsed over their machines. This would happen several times a day. The others had to take over her work in order to meet the quotas. The sewing machines would be clattering nonstop. With heavy head, dry tongue, and burning eyes, all that we could see were the green trousers of a soldier and the

needle—up ten centimeters, down ten centimeters—we stitched and stitched as the consignments mounted up, one after another... Our universe consisted of consignment after consignment. Impatiently, we looked forward to nightfall when, after wolfing down the plateful of soup that made up our daily ration, we might at last collapse into bed and close our eyes. If only we hadn't had to wake up the next day and return to this chaos! But there were days when we were even denied our yearned-for night's rest. The German's insatiable appetite for the greater and greater production sometimes required that we work for up to thirty hours on end."[291]

The overseer patrolled the workshop armed with a whip: if he spotted a woman asleep at her machine, she would be lashed awake. The female workers discovered a hiding place in one of the warehouses, where they could take turns laying their heads down, half an hour each. But even that retreat was discovered:

With a devilish "Aha!" he threw himself upon his defenseless victim and beat her mercilessly: the crack of the whip silenced the whimpers of his victim. Foam flew from his mouth as if he were a rabid dog... Such was life for us during the "quiet" times between one selection and another.[292]

The atmosphere inside the ghetto had altered greatly since the big extermination drive. Whoever was left alive had, in most instances, lost an entire family. There was scarcely anyone left in the ghetto but the elderly and the children, and the numbers of women had also shrunk out of all proportion. Whereas, at the beginning of 1942, there had been 134 women to every 100 men, the ratio now was 70 to 100.[293] By this point, officially registered children made up only 2 or 3 percent of the overall population.[294] Women and young men were the only ones left capable of work and eligible for slave labor. Then there were those living illegally in basements and garrets and amid the debris of the no man's land between the three ghettos. Had we fought back, these people now told themselves, our parents, our children, our loved ones would still be alive, or we would have faced death together and at least taken a couple of Germans with us. "People swore to themselves," Emanuel

Ringelblum recounts, "that the Germans would not flush them out of there again at no cost. We may die, but these atrocious trespassers will pay with their blood for our deaths. We need not worry about our survival, since each and every one of us carries his death warrant in his pocket already. We would do better to worry about how to die with dignity, how to go down fighting." By that time, this attitude was no longer confined to the organized fighters of both sexes. "The spark," recalls Vladka Meed, "started to fly, slowly and falteringly to start with, but gathering pace over time."[295]

On August 25, 1942, Israel Kanal, a member of the Zionist Akiva group, opened fire on the head of the Jewish police, Szerynski, wounding him in the shoulder.[296] This was the first terrorist attack in the ghetto and was widely welcomed. There was scarcely anyone who was hated more than this collaborator who, together with his men, had taken charge of the task of deportation, and whose every act had won the approval of the Germans. In late October 1942, the groups that had launched the Antifascist Bloc came together for a conference at which they decided to set up the Jewish fighting organization, the ZOB. The Bund threw its weight behind it. Mordecai Anielewicz from Hashomer Hatzair was elected commander, and the leadership included representatives from all the participating groups and parties (Poale Zion, the Communists, the Bund, the Hehalutz youth); the sole woman (confirmed) on the ZOB leadership was Zivia Lubetkin.[297] ZOB coordination teams were set up in every single workshop and standing representatives to the outside world were elected—responsible for the procurement of arms and hiding places and for relations with the official Polish resistance in the Aryan section of the city. Each of these teams was made up of six members, organized at workshop level. Alongside the ZOB, there was still the right-wing Zionists' ZZW which retained its autonomy, although coordinating operations with the ZOB.[298]

The ZOB resolved to launch its activities immediately: its first operations were directed against traitors and collaborators inside the ghetto. One woman was involved in the first two attacks. On October 23,1942, three Hashomer Hatzair members—Elijah Rózanski, Mordecai Grower, and Emilia Landau—executed Szerynski's lieutenant, Jacob Lejkin. Emilia Landau, daughter of the manufacturer Aleksander Landau, himself a patron of the left-wing Zionists, was one of the busiest ZOB fighters, and played a very important part in the January uprising.

On November 29, David Szulman, Ber Brojdo, and Sarah Granatsztejn (all three members of Dror) carried out—successfully—an attempt upon the life of the Jewish Council's Economic Department director, Israel First. David Szulman finished off First, the middle man between the Jewish Council and the Gestapo.[299]

The most important task, however, was still arms procurement. The ZOB had a couple of revolvers, but the weapons that Regina Justman had secured from the Gwardia Ludowa to struggle into the ghetto had fallen into the hands of the Gestapo, along with their female carrier. The PPR and the Gwardia Ludowa carried on with the efforts begun by Niuta Tejtelbojm, one of the main activists of the Warsaw resistance, to assemble pistols, revolvers, and hand grenades. Since firearms were so hard to come by, ZOB fighters started to make their own bombs and Molotov cocktails. Vladka Meed, who was involved in preparing the first bottle bombs, recalls: "Michal showed up in my basement in Gornoszlonska Street, with a chemistry book under his arm. 'Come on, I've something to tell you.' He read me a passage that spoke of potassium carbonate, hydrochloric acid, potassium cyanide, sugar, and petroleum. The chemical formulae made my head spin. 'It might be worth a try,' Michal decided. 'But what about the necessary equipment?' I asked. 'We'll try mixing the chemicals in ordinary everyday bottles,' he replied excitedly. 'I'm sure they'd do the job.'"[300] The pair set the wheels in motion to procure the necessary equipment, a difficult undertaking, since each component could only be procured in small quantities in well scattered shops. But the effort was well worth it: even the very first test produced an impressive explosion. However, it proved impossible to carry on with these trials in risky hideouts in the Aryan sector. Vladka Meed reported back to the ZOB and started to smuggle equipment into the ghetto, where a constant stream of bottle bombs was being churned out from various workshops.[301] Shortly afterwards, the Gwardia Ludowa handed over a recipe for the manufacture of Molotov cocktails, for which the same procedures were followed.[302]

The German occupiers' plan to leave Warsaw Jew-free had not yet been accomplished. The 60,000 people still left in the ghetto also had to be disposed of, according to Himmler (a view shared by Hitler). But the logically consistent supporters of the *Endlösung* ran into opposition from powerful industrial and Wehrmacht forces reluctant to let go of a certain number of Jewish slave laborers. Divisional General Schindler, the Wehrmacht inspector-general, and Max Frauendorfer, head of the Labor Department under Governor-General Frank, argued against Himmler's plans—with backing from Frank himself—contending that complete extermination of the Jews, especially of the 100,000 irreplaceable skilled Jewish workers, would have a negative impact upon war production.[303] Himmler was not disposed to give in on this. He visited the ghetto workshops and discovered that the entrepreneurs ensconced—Toebbens, Schilling and the like—were primarily interested in production to line their own pockets. And he could appeal to the accords of the Wannsee Conference, knowing that he would be wholly in agreement with the views of the supreme leader. As a result, the SS Reichsführer ordered the final destruction of the Warsaw ghetto, to be completed before February 15, 1943.[304] Although the ZOB was not aware of the exact date of the imminent annihilation operation, an armed action was scheduled for January 22—six months after the first major operation. It printed an appeal to the ghetto population and posted it up on all house fronts and workshops.

> Come January 22, six months will have passed since the transports out of Warsaw started. We all have vivid memories of the ghastly days when 30,000 of our brothers and sisters were deported and murdered in bestial fashion, in the Treblinka death camp. Six months of living in fear's vice-like grip, never knowing what the morrow would bring us, have passed... Today we have to realize that Hitler's executioners have only let us live because they seek to exploit our labor to the last remaining drop of our sweat and blood, right up until we breathe our last.[305]

The ZOB, by this point, had upwards of fifty fighting units of twenty to thirty members each. Out of these 1,250 female and male fighters, only a fraction were equipped with firearms: most had to make do with bottle bombs, light-bulbs filled with sulfuric acid, homemade hand grenades, and Molotov cocktails.[306] The few who did have a handgun or rifle knew that they had to make every bullet count, since ammunition was every bit as scarce as the guns themselves. Most fighters were still living within the law, going to work and sleeping in regular accommodations. Only five groups were already leading an underground existence, which is to say, only five were ready and waiting to take up arms at a moment's notice.

But the Germans succeeded in catching the resistance off guard. On January 18, four days ahead of the resistance operation scheduled by the ZOB, they entered the ghetto. Only the five outlaw groups were capable of an immediate response. But the invaders had not even considered that. When the lorry-loads of gendarmes, Latvian and Lithuanian auxiliary troops, and Polish police travelling down Gesia Street drew level with the Ostdeutschen Baustelle (East German Construction) workshops, ZOB activist Emilia Landau—who had already attempted to assassinate the ghetto's police chief—threw the first hand grenade, and hit her target. Several Germans were killed, but Emilia Landau herself was killed too.[307] The signal for attack was given, and the intruders found themselves surrounded by a hail of bullets and Molotov cocktails. Panic set in and frightened cries of "The Jews are shooting!" could be heard.[308] The Germans and their auxiliaries were forced to retreat twenty minutes later. When they returned, they brought lorries loaded with hand grenades, some armored cars, field artillery pieces, and machine-guns. Even so, the fighting persisted. The ZOB had spontaneously switched tactics from open attack to guerrilla warfare. Its fighters of both sexes threw up barricades inside the houses, waited for the assailants to enter, and then attacked them on all sides. In this way, they managed to seize much needed weapons from their dead enemies. But the organized ZOB units were not all that they had to contend with. Entire housing blocks, coordinated by their own block committees, took part in the defensive fighting. The fighting dragged on for four days, from January 18–21.[309] The Germans had suffered their first defeat at the hands of Jewish cowards, who were supposedly incapable of fighting. The shock left a deep impression.

Although the man in charge of the operation, SS Oberführer Dr Ferdinand von Sammern-Frankenegg, commander of the Warsaw district SS and police, managed to wipe out some 1,000 Jews and to deport a further 5,500, he had fallen far short of his target—the destruction of the entire ghetto.[310] At this point, Himmler suggested to SS Obergruppenführer Krüger, the head of security with the Generalgouvernement, that a barbed-wire-surrounded concentration camp be established, that all plants and personnel be confined therein—with the next step being the camp's destruction. But Krüger, chastened by the experience of the

January uprising, rejected the establishment of a camp, and set to work to remove the machinery from the ghetto, one by one, and began to use psychology in an attempt to deport the people. The German entrepreneurs with interests inside the ghetto reassured their workers that this was merely relocation to a new work-site, and tried to persuade them to make their way to the transports voluntarily.[311] However, this approach, which had worked elsewhere, failed in Warsaw. The ghetto dwellers were not falling for that trick again. The spark of revolt was already winging its way through the air, and the entire populace was making ready for the last act of the great drama: armed uprising and resistance.

The ZOB had weathered heavy losses: four out of five of its fighters had been captured or killed.[312] It prepared hurriedly to reorganize itself, but now—after the experiences of January—in proper underground style. After that its active militants led a barrack-style existence, and every hideout was simultaneously an arms and explosive dump. Day and night, watch patrols monitored accesses to the ghetto and adjacent streets. The Jewish fighting organization was ready to strike at a moment's notice.[313] Meanwhile, the ghetto residents turned their districts into outright fortresses. On the pretext of building shelters against air raids, the ghetto inhabitants created a perfect system of bunkers and routes through the sewers that not only linked homes with one another, but also led to the Aryan part of town. Come the uprising, the Warsaw ghetto was already a twin city: under the homes and streets was a sprawling labyrinth of hideouts and secret passages. Children used the sewer system to smuggle arms and food into the ghetto: later, this system would facilitate the flight of hunted fighters.[314] The civilians, which is to say, the women and men not organized in the resistance, procured weapons for themselves, arming themselves with knives, acid, and petroleum. ZOB representatives were now organizing openly in the workshops. In the brushworks, ZOB activist Sara Zagiel delivered an address that set out the fighting organization's aims: For a start, there had to be no repetition of what happened during the first big extermination drive in July of the previous year; secondly, the ghetto had to join in the overall struggle against fascism; thirdly, following the uprising, they had to seek a haven in the forests for as many people as possible, to carry on the struggle alongside the partisans. Even so, she made it clear that the uprising was doomed from the outset, that all thought of victory could be discounted.[315] "In spite of it all [that reality]" was the motto. Everybody took it for their own. Yitzhak Zuckermann, a resistance member, describes the new climate in the ghetto: "On the day that the Jewish purse-maker voluntarily, and expecting no recompense, stitched a pistol holster for the fighter; on the day the Jewish baker, blithely and free of charge, offered a crust of bread to the fighter; on that day we knew that we were among our own. The survivor community had turned into a community of fighters."[316] Between January and the beginning of April, Emanuel Ringelblum scribbled:

> We have seen how the psychological principle that an utterly cowed slave cannot offer any resistance was borne out. It appears, though, that the Jews are recovering somewhat from the harsh blows dealt them, that to some extent, they are successfully shrugging off the vexation caused by their ghastly experiences, and are wondering whether peaceable acceptance of slaughter adds to, rather than diminishes, their misfortune. No matter whom you speak with, you hear the same cry of pain: We should never have allowed the deportations! We should have taken to the streets, burning everything and tearing down the walls and fleeing beyond them. True, the Germans would have taken their revenge and we would have perished in our thousands, but never 300,000 of us. Now, we are ashamed of ourselves, having disgraced ourselves in our own eyes, and in the eyes of the whole world. Our wisdom did us no good. The time has come for us to fight back, to put up resistance.[317]

Vladka Meed recalls her visits to the ghetto a few days prior to the uprising. A childhood girlfriend, who she happened upon, knew that Vladka had something to do with the resistance: "'Wait a moment,' she said, meaning to delay me, then whispered in my ear: 'Could you tell me where I could get a gun?' Such was the mood in the ghetto: go to ground, resist deportation, and defend oneself at all costs."[318]

Vladka Meed and her female and male comrades from the Aryan sector of the city were working more feverishly than ever. There were connections to be made with the partisans, hideouts to be prepared for the fugitives, and still, above all, arms, arms, and more arms to be procured. Right up to the last minute, Vladka Meed was split between the ghetto and the Aryan sector, slipping through the wall, from one side to the other, pockets bulging with explosives, then slipping back across for further errands. ZOB emissaries approached activists outside the walls and urged them to supply more arms, more accommodations, and to do the impossible. Inside the ZOB bunkers in the ghetto, bombs and hand grenades were being churned out nonstop, and the billeted resisters were on continual alert. As far as combat assignments went, no difference was made between female and male fighters. The women were on a war footing just like the men, women were out on street patrol duty, women were liaising between all of the groups, women were filling bottles with explosive materials, making hand grenades and Molotov cocktails. But this was not all that fell to the female members of the fighting organization: They also had their household obligations to meet. Unlike virtually all other tasks, these were not shared between the sexes. Political and military leadership was a men's thing, the cooking a women's thing. Emanuel Ringelblum mentions a visit to an underground billet: "It was a two room apartment with kitchen at 32 Swietojerska Street. Three floors below was the factory police guard post. Ten people, ready for anything, stayed at the ZOB flat day and night. Weapons were stored there too. The activists could not leave the premises and provisions were brought in for them. One entered the place via the lofts of neighboring houses: the door was opened only to an agreed-upon coded knock. Three female fighters living in the apartment prepared the meals and carried out various dangerous missions and orders from the ZOB. The discipline and order were exemplary."[319]

The rebel leadership had split itself into four district commands, one for each sector of the ghetto. One looked after the central ghetto, another the brushworks area, another the workshops district (the "productive ghetto"), and the ZZW (the fighting organization of the right-wing Zionists) took charge of the area around Muranowski Square. In all, the ZOB and the ZZW had a total of about 2,000 active fighters, female and male. By this point, the ZOB embraced all of the leftist and moderate parties and groups—Hashomer Hatzair, Dror, the Bund, the Communists (PPR), the left and right wings of Poale Zion, Gordonia, Haonar Hatzioni, and Akiva.[320] Those selected to represent these groups and parties within the ZOB were men. However, some ZOB combat units were commanded by women.

Himmler was not disposed to wait much longer. His Führer's (fiftieth) birthday was approaching and he wanted to present him with the gift of a Jew-free Warsaw. In addition, the Germans tended to launch their surprise attacks on significant feast days, reckoning that their victims would feel safe on such dates. That year, in 1943, the Holy Week and Pesach (Passover) holidays fell together. Moreover, they both fell in the Führer's birthday week. The date fixed for the final destruction of the ghetto was Monday, April 19. After the disaster in January, Krüger was none too confident of Sammern-Frankenegg's ability to carry off the ghetto operation. A proven specialist in anti-guerrilla techniques was brought in—SS Brigadeführer Jürgen Stroop, who happened to be posted in Lwow at the time.[321] Stroop was an old battler, a co-founder of the NSDAP in Lippe, and, during the war, he had earned a reputation for himself in operations against the partisan movements in the Ukraine. Later, he would take charge of training special units for terror operations in the Caucasus. To Krüger, he seemed the right man to finish off the Warsaw ghetto.

On the night of April 18–19, 1943, the Germans ringed the ghetto with machine-guns and a dense cordon of Polish police. ZOB lookouts sounded the alert at 2:15 AM and, within fifteen minutes, the combat units were in position.[322] The assault began at five in the morning. Against little more than 2,000 resisters and a poorly armed populace, they mobilized an armored battalion, a Waffen SS cavalry division, two artillery divisions, a division of Wehrmacht sappers, a team of security police, Polish police, a battalion from the SS training school in Trawniki, some Ukrainian and Latvian auxiliary troops, and the fire brigade.[323] Against a couple of hundred handguns, a couple of rifles and machine-guns, against hand grenades and Molotov cocktails, the executive arm of the Final Solution deployed tanks, machine-guns, virtually unlimited numbers of machine-pistols, and unlimited supplies of ammunition, flame-throwers, gas grenades, and, later on, even mortars.[324] The well-equipped and trained attackers were led by a decorated general. The female and male ghetto fighters, hardly any of them older than twenty-five, were led by twenty-four-year-old Mordecai Anielewicz, who, up until very recently, like his colleagues, had never seen weapons except in illustrations.

When the invaders' first division reached the junction of Nalewski and Gesia Streets, they were greeted by a hail of gunfire. Terrified troopers fled, leaving behind a trail of weapons in their wake and these were hurriedly gathered up by the ghetto fighters, who then scurried back to their positions.[325] It was the same story at the intersection of Zamenhof and Mila Streets. The SS men and Ukrainian auxiliaries dove for whatever cover remained and retreated from the ghetto in disarray. At 7:30 AM, Sammern-Frankenegg scurried to the Hotel Bristol to report to Stroop: "It's all over in the ghetto. We've had to withdraw and can't get back in —and we have heaps of dead and wounded."[326]

At which point, Stroop took over. At noon, he entered the ghetto with 5,000 men, complete with light and heavy artillery.[327] The fighting now was concentrated around the warehouses of the Goods Registry and the hospital in Gesia Street. When the fighting women and men of the ZOB had no option but to withdraw, they burned the Goods Registry, where the SS had been storing possessions stolen from Jews or produced by Jewish slave labor. SS men then attacked the hospital, tossing the patients and nurses into the flames, smashing the heads of newborns infants against the walls, and slashing open the birth canals of expectant mothers.[328] On the afternoon of this first day, they ran into ZZW units in Muranowski Square and, shortly after, had their first sighting of wildcat groups from the general populace. That night, Stroop opted to pull out and assess his losses.

On day two, the Germans and their auxiliaries tried to attack the brushworks area. They ran up against such frenzied resistance that, in the end, they sent in envoys waving white handkerchiefs at the fighters to sue for a fifteen-minute truce: a historic development. The ZOB personnel refused to be taken in, and the attackers had further surprises ahead. "Look, Hans, a woman firing a gun!" called out one horrified soldier—and she was not the only woman creating work for the dumbfounded hero.[329] One person, watching the fighting from inside the Aryan sector, noted in his diary: "In an exchange of gunfire between SS men sheltering in the doorways of homes adjoining the ghetto and the Jews posted on the ghetto walls, the Jew in charge of the machine-gun dropped—having been struck by a bullet. At that very instant, the woman at his side grabbed the machine-gun, trained it on the Germans again, and carried on firing at them."[330] A Jewish eyewitness would later recount: "Our people fought as best they could... I watched the women's calm expressions. There was no sign of tears nor of fear. They appeared ready to die with dignity."[331] Given that the Germans could not gain the upper hand in the fighting, they used flame-throwers to scorch the earth of the brushworks area; ZOB fighters of both sexes were forced to retreat through the sea of flames. But they would not give up. Until April 22, they carried on fighting the enemy from the houses and the open streets. Whoever could not fall back meant to take as many of the enemy with them as they could manage. The painter Franciszka Rubinlicht, monitoring the fighting from her hiding place, noted what was happening: "Every young man, every young woman is dying like a hero today. Just now, a sixteen-year-old girl tied a bunch of hand grenades—the so-called bottle bombs—to her belt, soaked her hair in petrol, set herself alight, and threw herself on top of a passing tank. As luck would have it, she succeeded, managing to destroy the tank, killing herself along with the crew of the tank."[332] In his April 21 dispatches, Stroop noted: "For the first time it has been verified that the Halutzeh movement's women's organization is involved [sic]."[333] (Bernard Mark corrects Stroop here: the Hehalutz had no women's branch, but it did boast an outstandingly high number of women fighters.) These "Halutzeh girls," as they were habitually described thereafter, were to pursue him right into prison, where he would frequently talk to his cell-mate about them. He even went as far as to issue a special ordinance, under which captured women were to be painstakingly searched because, it seems, they were wont to be carrying weapons hidden in their knickers.[334] In the end, he eventually ordered that no female prisoners should be taken; instead, they should be shot immediately, given that, on repeated occasions, they contrived to detonate a hand grenade at the last minute, blowing up themselves and whoever was about to capture them.[335]

On day four of the fighting, the Germans decided to set the ghetto alight. Using flame-throwers, they set entire rows of houses ablaze, expecting the desperate inhabitants to jump out of the windows, so that they might shoot them down in mid-flight. A gratified Stroop wrote in his April 22 dispatches: "The Jews licked by the flames were jumping from the windows en masse, in entire family groups, or trying to climb down knotted sheets. Steps had been taken...to ensure that these...could be liquidated immediately."[336]

The fighting ghetto could expect no help from outside. The Armia Krajowa did, once, mount an attack outside the ghetto walls: A group of Pioneers, who had, on several occasions, passed arms through to the ghetto fighters carried out that attack, but it was primarily the Gwardia Ludowa that made efforts to assist the fighters from without. One of the few successful attacks was led by Niuta Tejtelbojm. On April 20, her Gwardia Ludowa unit knocked out a German machine-gun emplacement installed outside the ghetto walls.[337] At the same time, crowds of onlookers were filling the streets bordering on the ghetto and passing comments on developments, comments that were quite often favorable to the Germans.[338]

The fighting then switched to the bunkers. The assailants were obliged to change tactics. Given that they could rarely get inside a ZOB bunker except with taking heavy losses, they now switched to punching holes in the fortified walls in order to pump in poison gas or flood the bunker.[339] The strongest ZOB bunkers during this phase were located in Leszno Street. The Hersz Kawe combat unit, holding a bunker at No. 74 Leszno Street, was commanded by a woman named Roza Rozenfeld, who carried on fighting until she was literally neck-deep in water. When the SS saw that their time had come, they shot Roza Rozenfeld dead and, along with her, the young fighter Halinka Rochman who tried to shield Roza with her own body. Another four women—Zocha Brzezinska, Tosia Zebularz, Sara Klejman, and Chawa Brander—perished in these clashes.[340] Meanwhile, some combat groups found themselves forced to flee through the sewer system. Towards the end of May, the survivors from one position in Leszno Street were evacuated, but they could not all be spirited away immediately through the corpse-strewn sewers. Regina Fuden and Lea Korn, who had already successfully evacuated some of their female and male comrades, returned to the blazing ghetto to bring out the remainder as well.[341] However, the Germans had, in the interim, stumbled upon the route their victims were using to give them the slip. They proceeded to cordon off the manhole covers in the Aryan sector, waiting for somebody to emerge, or filled them in, or simply dropped poison gas grenades into the sewers, condemning the would-be escapers to a slow and horrible death.[342]

A bunker at 30 Franziszka Street withstood three days of intense gunfire, from May 1–3. When the Germans made up their minds to attack, ZOB fighter Debora Baran replied with a hand grenade, followed by a hail of bullets and more grenades. The attackers were forced repeatedly to withdraw. In the end, there was hand-to-hand fighting with several ZOB women, who put up ferocious resistance using their hand grenades. The victors failed to take any of the women alive.[343] As late as May 6, Leszno Street was still holding out. The rebels' last remaining positions there did not fall until May 7. One male survivor was later to recount: "Before we were able to break through the stone wall separating us from the underground passage [on the Aryan side], we found ourselves surrounded by the Germans. We made no reply to their demands that we leave the bunker. Then they used poison gas... It was plain to us that the game was up... The first to succumb to the poison gas was fighter Ita Heymann, who happened to be on guard at the entrance at that point. She was the first to commit herself. She drew her pistol, and kept her last remaining bullet for herself. When we crouched over her we could still hear her dying words: 'I don't want to be a burden to anybody, but I don't want to fall into their hands either.' Within moments the Germans were inside the bunker."[344] One of the unit's female commanders managed to shoot her way through the line of Germans and vanish into the nearby ruins.[345]

On May 8, the attackers stumbled upon the ZOB leadership's bunker at 18 Mila Street. They surrounded the bunker on every side and opened fire, drawing a prompt return fire. When, eventually, they also resorted to poison gas grenades, the female and male fighters within—including Anielewicz and his wife, Mira Furcher—argued for suicide rather than dying of asphyxiation. All too late, they discovered an emergency exit, and only a handful of them, including ZOB activists Tosia Altman and Zivia Lubetkin, managed to escape. By the time Stroop finally showed up at the bunker to reassure himself of his victory over the uprising's leadership, he was to discover that: "The people whom I would have loved to interrogate were all dead."[346]

Resistance headquarters had now been knocked out, but the fighting continued. In the last stages of the uprising, it was primarily the wildcat groups, the people from the ruins, who denied Stroop his final victory. An eyewitness would later describe these "ghostly figures" forever popping up from the ghetto's smoking, razed ruins to attack German patrols: "Out of the basements glided phantasmagorical apparitions...dressed in tatters and clutching a gun... In one lean-to, there were a couple of pots resting on some bricks, over which some filthy, unkempt women were cooking some food. The children were clamoring like animals for their share."[347] On May 22, Goebbels scribbled in his diary: "The battle for the Warsaw ghetto goes on. The Jews continue to

Women members of the
Warsaw ghetto resistance

resist."[348] Even in June, the Jews were still holding out. In the last attacks in Bonifraterska Street, fighter Janka Gontarska fell. Another group of youngsters was holding out in Kurza Street. When they swooped upon a detachment of German soldiers, they were wiped out by the latter. Among the dead were two girls.[349] Not until July 1943, a good ten weeks after the April 19 incursion into the ghetto, was SS Brigadeführer Stroop able to consider his mission accomplished.

The surviving female and male ghetto fighters joined the partisans; many made their way back to the city during the 1944 Warsaw uprising to participate in the fighting then as well. Zivia Lubetkin, one of them, sets out the pointed dilemma the Jewish fighters faced in taking part in the Polish uprising:

> The Polish government in London believed that the intelligent thing to do was to launch the uprising just when the Germans were retreating, but before the Red Army had entered the city. Thus, the hated foe from the east would be confronted with an irreversible *fait accompli*.

The city would have been liberated by the independent Polish army and government... We were as well-aware of the political nature of this uprising as the leaders of the PPR and the Armia Ludowa (as the military wing of the Communist PPR, the Gwardia Ludowa, had come to be described), but we resolved to play a part in it nonetheless... As we saw it, the uprising, for all its political implications, was still a fight against the Germans.[350]

The ZOB group gathered in its Leszno Street headquarters and made contact with the Armia Krajowa command. The surviving female and male ghetto fighters' offer to take part in the Polish uprising was greeted with less than enthusiasm. The ZOB envoys were turned away. Even so, they had discovered in the interim that the Armia Ludowa was mustering in the old city of Warsaw. Old contacts from the ghetto uprising days were reestablished, and the Armia Ludowa personnel welcomed the ZOB personnel with open arms. Zivia Lubetkin recalls:

> They were decent people with real fighting spirit. They were of the opinion that, since only a couple dozen Jewish fighters had survived the ghetto uprising, it would not be right for them to lose their lives now. They considered it a moral duty that we stay alive. Therefore, they wanted to post us to sectors where there was no direct danger of death. We, of course, refused to agree to these conditions. We had not thrown in our lot with the Polish uprising to make a good impression, but rather to fight.[351]

For an entire month, the old city was in the hands of the Gwardia Ludowa. Then the rebels were forced to stage a withdrawal: they had learned from the ghetto's experience and organized their retreat through the sewer network. This was the second battlefield the Jewish fighters had left by that route. After the Armia Ludowa surrendered, its activists went underground and passed themselves off as civilians, an option that was not open to the ZOB members, since anti-Semitism was still prevalent in broad swathes of the population, and the Germans continued tracking down the few, scattered Jewish survivors. In the end, Zivia Lubetkin and Mark Edelman managed to hide along with their group in a house half-destroyed by bombs, down beside the Vistula. After a month, their comrades found out that they were still alive and that the

Germans were on the brink of uncovering their hideout. Whereupon they staged a rescue operation that hinged upon a ruse: disguised as Red Cross members, they made it clear that they would have to return to the city—which the Germans had just evacuated—in order to collect typhus patients. The idea behind this operation came from Ida Margolis, a Bund contact and ZOB member in the Aryan sector of Warsaw. Along with the doctor Inka Schweiger, they orchestrated this daring coup, and pulled it off successfully; the entire band of ZOB women and men in hiding was rescued.[352] On January 17, 1945, this handful of survivors of the ghetto uprising watched as the first Soviet tanks rolled into Warsaw. They lived to see the liberation, for which they had been fighting for two and a half long years, with very contradictory feelings: delight that the terror was now over and the Germans gone, and inconsolable grief for the countless dead.

Vilna

"Liza calling."

Lithuania was regarded as the spiritual home of the eastern Jews. Roughly half a million Jews lived in the multi-ethnic state and made up its largest ethnic minority.[353] The heart of Jewish Lithuania was Vilna, which had not been absorbed into the then independent republic until 1939, thanks to a clause in the Hitler-Stalin pact.[354] Vilna was the home of the YIVO Institute, a unique archive on the history and culture of the eastern European Jews, which would later be misused as a complementary source in the Nazi Rosenberg's race theory. Vilna was the home of the political elite of the left-wing Zionist youth movement, given that it was the only city from which Polish (and Lithuanian) Jews might legally emigrate to Palestine.[355] A whole series of legendary leaders of the future Jewish resistance were in the city when the Germans marched in: among them were the future commanders of the armed resistance in Bialystok, Tamara Sznajderman and her husband Mordecai Tenenbojm-Tamarof, and Chayke Grossman.[356] So it was scarcely surprising that the notion of armed Jewish resistance should have emanated from Vilna and been spread from there into Poland, Belarus, and other ghettos inside Lithuania itself. And there was almost no other city where women played such an important role inside the ghetto and in the partisan units as in Vilna.

In 1940, the Red Army occupied Lithuania, and Vilna also fell under Soviet control. However, the sympathies of large segments of the population lay with the Germans; the state president and other high-ranking government officials fled to Germany.[357] Hatred of Russians had been increasing over time. The little country had been annexed on a number of occasions by Russia since tsarist times. The Bolshevik government also unhesitatingly turned it into a soviet republic.[358] Given that there was also a long tradition of anti-Semitism in Lithuania, there had been a series of anti-Jewish outbreaks during the state's brief period of independence, with Jews often being suspected of sympathizing with the soviet state.

Such suspicions had been wholly confirmed in 1939, when, given the choice of falling into the hands of the Germans or the Red Army, the Jewish population plainly opted for the latter.[359] When the Red Army actually invaded Lithuania in June 1940, and Lithuania fell under the sway of soviet legislation as a result, life naturally altered for the Jewish population, or, rather, for the Zionist community. Whereas Jewish wage-earners benefited from the socialization of the economy, a segment of the Jewish middle class lost its livelihood. All parties other than the Communist Party were outlawed, as was the non-Communist press. Private schools and libraries were nationalized. Yiddish remained the language of education, but Hebrew and religion lessons were prohibited. Zionist groups and parties were driven underground, as was the leftist Hehalutz Zionist movement. A single kibbutz belonging to the Marxist Hashomer Hatzair was able to survive within the law by being recognized as a kolkhoz.[360] Even so, this was the lesser of two evils, and when the Red Army found itself obliged to retreat in the face of the onslaught from German troops, an avalanche of Jewish refugees went with it.

On June 26, 1941, the Wehrmacht occupied Vilna: the SS and the SD also entered the city and embarked immediately upon their work. Together with Lithuanian volunteers, known to their victims as "hunters," they murdered 20,000 young men during the first week of the occupation. They were especially interested in the political and spiritual leaders of the Vilna Jews.[361] Between June and October 1942, the SS and its Lithuanian confederates butchered nearly half of the almost 80,000 Lithuanian Jews. The roughly 40,000 still alive by September were penned into two ghettos.[362] So-called "Ghetto No. 2" was set up in the medieval Jewish quarter, whose few narrow streets had been densely populated by three or four thousand people since the fifteenth and sixteenth centuries. The new masters now crammed 11,000 into this area, most of them old and infirm. The other 29,000 were taken off to "Ghetto No. 1," the new nineteenth-century Jewish quarter, which was slightly larger.[363]

Scarcely had the ghetto walls been erected than the massacres recommenced. For openers, the nonproductive elements within in Ghetto No. 2 were liquidated, and the ghetto broken up. But, in Ghetto No. 1, there were also daily selections until, by the end of that year, only 15,000 Jews were left alive in Vilna. Whereas, during the first weeks of occupation, the Germans had concentrated on exterminating the menfolk, they now started to catch up on their backlog of women.[364]

These mass murders did not occur, as they did in most other cities, in faraway death factories, but rather at the city gates: in Ponar, an ancient retreat. In the Ponar forests, the Red Army had excavated huge ditches to camouflage their tanks. From early on in the occupation, thousands upon thousands of Jews from Vilna were ferried out to these ditches, where they were ordered to stand by the edge and gunned down.[365] The Germans appointed Jacob Gens, a Revisionist (a member of the conservative Zionist organization, Betar) as the ghetto chief, and he made himself a name as the cruelest, most unscrupulous of all the collaborating officials in the Jewish Councils of Poland and Lithuania.[366] The occupation authorities' first attempt to set up a Jewish Council to their liking had failed. The left-wing Zionists had refused from the outset to appoint delegates to the Jewish Council; and the acknowledged leader of Vilna's Jews, the "father of the Lithuanian Jerusalem," eighty-six-year-old Jacob Wygodzki, a liberal Zionist, had also rejected it.[367] In the end, a Jewish Council was formed, its members, for the most part, from the enlightened middle classes, with the odd Bund official among them as well. The Nazis, less than convinced by this alliance, murdered the entire line-up even before the ghetto was established, and eventually found ideal confederates in Jacob Gens, who they made chief of the Jewish police, and the team he gathered around him. Gens made a name for himself as a staunch champion of the motto "work to survive," and he successfully enforced this tried and trusted tactic on behalf of his German masters. Right up until the final moment, he distracted the ghetto population with the belief that those who had survived until now would still be needed: they had to demonstrate, however, that they were skilled and tireless workers. Selections were carried out by Gens in person; here again we come up against an enthusiastic agent of the Nazi ideology: the law of selection made it possible to sacrifice the weaklings to get the strong.

When resistance began to form in Vilna, the ghetto population comprised mainly of young women and men who did slave labor inside and outside the ghetto, and who had the constant threat of selection hanging over their heads. Only those with certificates, which is to say, work papers, were entitled to live, and the certificate system was forever being changed. At first, work passes were valid for the particular laborer, whether female or male, plus their spouse and two children under sixteen. Unmarried certificate-holders would claim someone without papers as their husband or wife, and couples who had only one child or were childless would claim other people's children as their own. But, in the end, the right to life became valid only for named certificate owners. Anyone not working was marked down for certain death.[368] Activists from the ghetto's left-wing Zionist youth movement and Communist cell understood better than their female and male colleagues elsewhere, that the fate of the Jews in eastern Europe was not deportation to labor camps but extermination. Before anybody discovered what was going on inside Chelmno and Treblinka, the residents of Vilna had Ponar as proof of the Germans' true intentions. Members of the Communist Party, Hashomer Hatzair, Dror, or the left-wing Zionist organizations of Hehalutz, who had survived the earlier massacres, met in the ghetto to discuss the situation. Some Hashomer Hatzair women and men had found shelter in a convent: the mother superior of the Kolonja Wilenska Dominican convent, Anna Borkowska, kept the group hidden. That was where the idea of armed resistance was incubated: and it was from there that the idea of unifying all antifascist forces in the ghetto emerged.[369] Inside the ghetto, a group had grown up around Joseph Glazman, from Betar, and this group spread the watchword of "No going quietly to the slaughter!"[370] The "Convent Group" decided to make its way back into the ghetto and, a short time later, on New Year's Eve 1941, a crucial meeting was held: 150 members of the Hehalutz movement debated a summons to armed struggle that had been drafted by Aba Kovner. It was immediately endorsed and printed: "See to it that we do not go like sheep to the slaughter!... The only reply to our murderers is: armed uprising!... Better to fall as free fighters than live on the mercy of the murderers."[371] In addition to the Zionists, a Communist cell had been set up inside the ghetto, under the leadership of two men, Itzhak Witenberg and Berl Szeresznievski, and two women, Chenia Borowska and Sonia Madaysker. Sonia Madaysker (who was, like Chenia Borowska, a crucial activist throughout in the Lithuanian resistance) was twenty-eight years old. She had already served several years in prison and, despite her youth, was a fighter well-versed in underground politics.[372]

On June 23, 1942, all of the underground groups existing in the ghetto came together and launched the Farejnikte Partizaner Organizazie, or FPO. It included Zionists from the left and right, plus Communists and Bund members, a coalition unimaginable, or hard to imagine being achieved, in other cities. The Communist Itzhak Witenberg was picked to command the FPO because he was the one with the best contacts with the Communist resistance—the Jewish resistance's sole ally—outside the ghetto. There was an unusual number of women among the founders of the FPO, including the left-wing Zionists Roza Korczak, Tamara Sznajderman, Chayke Grossman, and Vitka Kempner, as well as the Communists Chania Borowska and Sonia Madaysker.[373] The FPO was initially organized into teams of three, with members of the same organization working together. Some months later, these groups expanded to five, with each member being drawn, insofar as possible, from different political organizations.[374]

But the FPO activists—with few exceptions—had no military experience: like their female and male comrades from Warsaw, Bialystok, and Krakow, they also had to teach themselves how to handle guns and explosives. In Vilna, it was not as hard to procure arms as it was in, say, Warsaw. The Germans had set up huge arsenals and repair workshops in Borbiszki, an outlying district, where they stored captured firearms and had them sorted out by Jewish slave laborers. Among those workers, there were FPO members who, at the risk of their lives, smuggled revolvers, rifles, machine-guns (in parts), and hand grenades into the ghetto.[375] In addition, the FPO tried to procure arms from the Armia Krajowa, but, like all the other Jewish resisters, it was also rebuffed by the superbly equipped army of the official Polish resistance. The Communists alone let the Jewish resistance have some of their tiny arsenal of weapons; however, they actually had so few that, for a time, they were receiving material assistance from the FPO.[376]

The FPO set to work the moment it was launched. A wave of sabotage brought the arms industry in Vilna grinding to a halt as FPO members among the slave workers of both sexes destroyed whole depots of machinery. At the same time, others churned out substandard equipment and defective spares. These were not discovered right away, but were uncovered at the front, by which time they had served their purpose—when a machine-gun suddenly jammed, when ammunition would not fit, or when a gun backfired.[377] Simultaneously, the FPO sent out a series of dispatches and emissaries to brief the ghettos in other cities on the Ponar massacres, and to spread the idea of armed resistance. Towards the end of January 1942, Chayke Grossman set off for Warsaw and Bialystok. She had been authorized by the Vilna and Warsaw Communists to bring the Bialystok Communists into a united front of all antifascist ghetto forces, and to commission them to organize armed resistance. The FPO had charged her to win the left-wing Zionists in Warsaw over to the cause of armed uprising, and also to raise money for the Vilna underground. She failed to completely persuade the Warsaw people of the necessity of fighting, but she did get the money she sought, and returned to Vilna with it in March 1942.[378] In the interim, the sisters Sara and Roza Zilber had been on tour, carrying out a number of difficult missions. They too made the journey to Warsaw, meeting with greater success than Chayke Grossman. They failed to convince the Jewish ghetto authorities, but their reports on the massacres did succeed in arousing the interest of the left-wing Zionist youth movement. When they were getting ready for the return trip to Vilna, they were arrested in the railway station, locked up in the Pawiak, Warsaw's political prison, and shot some months later. This was an irreparable loss to the FPO, for it meant a months-long interruption of communications between Vilna and Warsaw, and made it impossible to coordinate the two cities' resistance for a long time.[379] Chayke Grossman left Vilna in April 1942 to organize armed resistance in Bialystok.[380]

Around this time, the FPO established its first contacts with the Soviet partisans who had begun to set up a small base near Vilna. Argument about the correct strategy—ghetto uprising or guerrilla struggle—had split the resistance in Vilna. The young activists from all political groupings had stubbornly argued against the FPO leadership that any resistance in the ghetto was pointless, and that only the struggle in the forests had any prospect of meaningful impact. They rallied around Yekhiel Szejnboim from the Dror youth group, and, in the spring of 1942, they set up an organization of their own—the Yekhiel Group, some 1000 women and men. They made their own contacts with the Soviet partisans and laid the groundwork for a Jewish partisan unit in the surrounding forests.[381] The Soviet partisans were very keen on boosting their numbers with fighters belonging to the ghetto resistance: they, too, were against an uprising within the ghetto walls, and repeatedly sent envoys into the city to deliver their proposals and offers to the FPO. In April 1942, the commander of the Soviet partisan movement in Lithuania, Albertas Kunigenas (Alksnis) and the Jewish resistance leadership agreed to incorporate the FPO into the Lithuanian partisan movement as an autonomous branch operating in the ghetto, to keep in regular contact with the partisans through political commissar Margis, and to join these immediately after the ghetto uprising. Local command of the overall Lithuanian movement was exercised by the Vilna City Parties' Committee, to which Itzhak Witenberg, Berl Szerszniewski, and Chania Borowska were elected as committee members and voting representatives of the FPO. Sonia Madaysker was appointed to head the Komsomol (Union of Soviet Youth) inside and outside the ghetto.[382]

The Pole Irene Adamowicz took over the task of reestablishing contacts with Warsaw and other cities in Poland and Lithuania, contacts interrupted by the arrest and murder of the Zilber sisters, and by Chayke Grossman's departure for Bialystok. She travelled the length and breadth of the country, delivering messages, money, and arms, while peddling the idea of an armed uprising. Her greatest success came in the Kovno ghetto, where she met for two days with the leaders of the Zionist parties and the Hehalutz movement, who set to work building an armed underground organization right after she left.[383] In Vilna, the FPO had its first big sabotage operation in July 1942, the first mounted in the whole of Lithuania. Nineteen-year-old Vitka Kempner, a Hashomer Hatzair member and FPO activist, dyed her hair an even lighter blond, left the ghetto by mingling with a work brigade, removed the yellow star from her clothing, and took to the road. Her mission was, for a start, to come up with a suitable location where an FPO commando unit might mine the Vilna-Polotsk rail line, used by German troop trains en route to the eastern front. On account of the occupiers' ruthless reprisals, no suspicion must fall on the ghetto and, as a result, the location in question had to be sufficiently removed from the city and so situated that the saboteurs might place their mines unobserved. Within three days, Vitka had found the right location. Meanwhile, the mines were manufactured inside the ghetto. On the night of July 8, Vitka Kempner and two of her comrades-in-arms set off for Wilejka (Novaya Vilnia), some sixty kilometers southeast of Vilna. As one of the men stood guard, Vitka and her companion positioned the explosives. They made their way back to the ghetto without incident and waited with the remainder of the group in on the operation. The explosion was enormous and its impact considerable: a German troop transport and munitions train had detonated the mine, sending part of the train up in the air, derailing the rest of the carriages, and killing at least 200 soldiers. Peasants in the vicinity collected the weapons scattered around and later delivered some of them to an FPO partisan unit.[384]

One of the activists, who the FPO managed to plant as a secretary to the ghetto police, discovered that, in October 1942, the Jewish population of Oshmyany, a small Lithuanian town not far from Vilna, was to be liquidated. This mission had been entrusted to Jacob Gens and his team, at the instigation of the Germans. She reported the matter to the FPO, which then sent out a female emissary to alert the residents of Oshmyany. This task was entrusted to Liza Magun. Disguised as an Aryan, she slipped into the little town and briefed the Jewish population on what was in store for it. They refused to believe her.[385] Liza Magun had been born in Vilna. She was a twenty-two-year-old Hashomer Hatzair member and FPO activist. In February 1943, she was arrested and murdered in Vilna by the Gestapo.[386] When, a month later, the FPO drafted its combat orders, it picked "Liza calling" as the code and password to launch the military mobilization that started the uprising.[387]

Even as Liza Magun was making her way to Oshmyany, two women were setting out on an even more dangerous mission. The FPO no longer wanted to limit its contacts with the partisans to those made through political commissar Margis, as prescribed. The plan was a daring one, since, in order to reach the Soviet sector of the front, a lengthy journey across German-occupied territory was required. Then they had to somehow pass through the German front line positions. This task was entrusted to Sonia Madaysker and Cesia Rosenberg. They set out in early October 1942, dressed as Polish women and carrying forged Aryan papers. Twice they were stopped and twice they sailed through this difficulty to resume their journey, in spite of this evil omen. In the end, they were caught by the Gestapo, who did not, however, recognize them as Jews. Since their forged papers identified them as residents of Vilna, the Gestapo officers brought their captives back to Vilna, by train, under armed escort. The pair managed to escape a third time at the station. They had not accomplished their mission, but they had returned safe and sound to the ghetto.[388]

Inside the ghetto, the situation was deteriorating daily. The inhabitants were forever on the lookout for a certificate or a hiding place, worn down by inhuman slave labor, and terrified of the next selection. Even the hospital gynecological department was obliged to operate outside of the law. On February 5, 1942, the Germans made public a decree forbidding Jews from reproducing. Nonetheless, women kept having babies that they had to bring into the world in hidden recess of the hospital, where they would hide out until done breast-feeding. Some of these children were successfully boarded with families in the Aryan sector, while others were later registered with false birth-dates. The rest were deported in the next selection.[389]

In March 1943, the FPO published its combat orders, which also spelled out its binding practical political program: the number one objective of the Farejnikten Partizaner Organizazie was an armed uprising inside the ghetto that would facilitate a mass break-out and defend the lives and honor of the Jewish population. The FPO would then, and only then, throw in its lot with the partisan movement in the forests in order to carry on the struggle from there.[390] Shortly afterwards, on May 8, 1943, in the utmost secrecy, the city's Underground Committee was set up. It was joined by the three Communist groups operating in Vilna: the Lithuanian one, the minority Polish one, and the ghetto Communists. FPO members Itzhak Witenberg and Sonia Madaysker were also members of the Underground Committee, but in a personal capacity: the FPO, per se, knew nothing of the Committee's existence.[391] Events gathered pace after that. At the end of July 1943, the German security services arrested two Underground Committee members. Under torture, one of them confessed to keeping in contact with the Jewish Communist Itzhak Witenberg in the ghetto. On July 8, Kittel, the chief of the Security Police, turned up in the ghetto and issued an ultimatum: either they gave up Witenberg, or the ghetto would be wiped out. The FPO was confronted by an insoluble dilemma: through his activities on the Underground Committee, Witenberg had set the Germans on the trail of the ghetto resistance. The FPO was ready to defend itself by force of arms, but that would have meant a definitive uprising in the ghetto, and the population was not so disposed. Gens had finally drummed it into the heads of the ghetto residents that they had to choose between Witenberg and themselves, successfully ensuring that the residents themselves who hunted down the quarry and his colleagues. The resistance seemed to them like nonsense, madness: handing over the resistance leader looked like their only salvation. The FPO had to decide between abandoning its leader or preparing to embark upon a fight with its own people. His closest comrades, Aba Kovner, Sonia Madaysker, and Joseph Glazman called on Witenberg in his hiding place to let him in on the organization's decision: he was to give himself up. Following lengthy discussion, Itzhak Witenberg gave way and went off voluntarily to face death. The Gestapo tortured him over several days before murdering him. After the liberation, in the torture cell at the Gestapo headquarters in Vilna, Witenbeg's final words were discovered scrawled in blood on the wall: "Avenge yourselves! Itsik Witenberg, July 16, 1943."[392]

The tragedy of the "Witenberg case" forced the FPO to acknowledge that it had been mistaken in its assessment of the situation in the ghetto. It had refused to join the partisans because it had not wanted to leave the ghetto population defenseless, seeking instead to steer it towards rebellion. Many would perish in that struggle, but many would be spared as well—more than just the organized fighters of both sexes at any rate—and might flee to the forests. Now it had been brought home to them that the population was resolutely opposed to an uprising, and more inclined to attack the rebels than join them. Gens' poison had done its work. There had to be a strategic and tactical rethinking and contacts with the partisans intensified. Joseph Glazman, whose underground activities were known to his erstwhile Betar colleague Gens, had to quit the ghetto immediately. He took with him a group of twenty-four activists and made for the forests. The group, styling itself the "Leon Group"—after Witenberg's nom de guerre—was caught in a skirmish with a German patrol, and, in the end, only thirteen of them made it to the Narocz forest, ninety kilometers from Vilna, where they established a Jewish partisan base.[393] Security Chief Kittel knew that resistance members were escaping from the ghetto, and he threatened to escalate the reprisals: as immediate revenge for Glazman's escape, he had thirty-two men shot, and announced that, in future, he would have the family of the individual concerned executed or, should there be no family, his fellow tenants. The labor brigades were strictly organized into teams of ten: if there was one person missing from the team when they returned, the remaining nine would be shot.[394] Some factions in the FPO now tended to side with the view of Yekhiel Szejnboim, and prepared for an exodus to the forests, but, because of Kittel's threats, it was only possible to get small groups out of the ghetto.[395] And the resisters had still not quite given up on the idea of an uprising. When the Jewish woman Communist Gessia Glezer (Albina) arrived in Vilna, on Moscow's instructions, to negotiate their final incorporation into the partisan organization, along with the FPO leadership, the ghetto fighters refused.[396] No doubt, yet another reason for the refusal was the new policy line being pushed by Moscow. The specifically Jewish resistance was to dissolve and amalgamate with the local resistance: the keynote was national rather than ethnic organization.[397] The FPO, though, had always based itself on the idea of fighting as an autonomous Jewish unit, even within the framework of the partisan movement. On September 1, 1943, German and Estonian units surrounded the ghetto and prevented the slave laborers working on the outside from gaining entry. Inside the walls, the hunting down of the ghetto inhabitants began: the German occupation authorities had ordered the deportation of 3,000 men and 2,000 women to the work camps in Estonia. The FPO command realized that the moment of truth had come and circulated the watchword "Liza calling."[398] The first combat battalion assembled in Spitzalna Street. The second battalion was surrounded by the Germans before it could get to its arms dumps. The fighters of both sexes then decided to muster all available personnel in Straszuna Street, under the command of Yekhiel Szejnboim. The only arms they had were revolvers and hand grenades: the machine-gun for which they had sent would not reach them in time. In the middle of the afternoon, a German detachment crossed Straszuna Street and a megaphone was used to summon the residents to come out of their hiding places. The FPO commandos opened fire and the Germans replied with automatic weapons. Yekhiel Szejnboim was the first one cut down, mortally wounded. Roza Korczak, a twenty-two-year-old Hashomer Hatzair militant, took command and held the position until the attackers blew up the building.[399] She managed to escape with her life and joined the partisans. She would later write of the cul-de-sac in which the FPO found itself that September 1: "All our plans, our expectations, our calls vanished into thin air... No hope remained now, except that the battle about to be joined by a handful of fighters might turn into a mass uprising... Should it erupt, the rebellion would be just an isolated action with no hope of opening the gates to a mass escape."[400] The fighting in Straszuna Street bore that out, and induced the FPO to decide once and for all to retreat to the forests and throw in its lot with the partisans.[401]

Three envoys from partisan commanders Markov and Yurgis (S. Zimanas) showed up in the ghetto on September 7 and declared themselves ready to take in the resisters, on the condition—of course—that they bring along their own arms and their own doctors, of which the guerrillas were in sore need. The Lithuanian partisan movement was, at that point, divided into two zones: the north, in the forests bordering the river Narocz, was under Markov's command, and the south, in the Rudniki forests, was under Yurgis' command. In batches, the FPO activists quit the ghetto, bound for Narocz. While the last batch was making ready to flee, orders came from Yurgis that they should join his unit in the Rudniki forest. Again, the women and men of the Jewish resistance faced a difficult decision. Even though the forests at Rudniki were much closer, the fact was that the bulk of their comrades were already up in Narocz, or headed there. Splitting their already decimated numbers seriously jeopardized the prospects of an autonomous Jewish partisan unit.[402] But time was of the essence and the group placed itself at Yurgis' disposal. Vitka Kempner and Zelda Treger, a twenty-four-year-old Hashomer Hatzair member, organized the escape. They made contact with Sonia Madaysker in the Aryan sector of the city and drew up a hastily devised, but well thought out, plan.[403] On September 23, at nine o'clock in the morning, Kittel attacked the ghetto with his troops, bent upon its final destruction. The remaining 200 FPO fighters scurried for the sewers. Roza Korczak describes their odyssey: "The tunnel was pitch black. The flickering light of a lantern lighted our path, and off we set. My shoulders brushed against the sides of the drains and I could not move my hand... I had one overriding thought in mind: my gun must not get wet and I had to make sure not to fall behind. All of a sudden, the drain opened into a tunnel just a half a meter in height. I squeezed through. The filthy water reached my shoulders... The caravan stopped. The news filtered through that somebody had passed out halfway and was blocking the way... I had lost all sense of time... All of a sudden came the whispered order: Prepare to surface."[404]

The group had set out at noon: by seven that evening, with darkness falling, they had arrived. The manhole cover was thrown back and the exhausted fighters surfaced in a street in the Aryan sector of Vilna. Sonia Madaysker and her team were there to greet them and escorted them to the hiding places prepared around the city. They split up into two groups, one under the command of Aba Kovner, the other under the command of Chania Borowska, and made for the Rudniki forests. They arrived at the end of September.[405]

The Vilna ghetto's sick, infirm, and old were promptly murdered in Ponar; most of the women and children were deported to Majdanek; the remainder went to the labor camps in Estonia and Latvia.[406]

Bialystok

"Where are you going, Chaikele?"

Even though the city of Bialystok was Polish (at the start of the Second World War it was in the part of Poland under Soviet occupation), its Jewish inhabitants regarded themselves as being, by character and tradition, bound to Lithuanian Judaism, and a fair number of them took Vilna—the "Jerusalem of the diaspora"—as their point of reference.[407] On June 27, 1941, the German army invaded Bialystok under escort from the 316th SS Police Battalion, which, two hours later, would carry out its first massacre of the Jewish population. They herded all the men they could catch in the Jewish quarter's narrow streets into the main synagogue, boarded up the entrance, and set the building on fire. The flames ended the lives of a thousand men and youths, and a further thousand were gunned down in the streets. During July, the German occupiers murdered another five thousand Bialystok Jews in Pietrasza, half a kilometer outside of the city. On July 26, the order came for all Jews to move inside the ghetto over the next five days: 65,000 people were packed into an area of twenty streets. Leaving the ghetto was prohibited upon pain of death.[408]

The occupiers turned the Bialystok ghetto into one huge prison where living conditions were ghastly: it would remain this way until February of the following year. Bialystok, the second largest textile center of prewar Poland, was to end up as one of the Wehrmacht's main supply centers: the Jewish population accounted for most of the skilled work force, female and male, and, as a result, was spared extermination for a time. Its labor power proved, initially, indispensable. The Jewish Council cooperating with the Germans in Bialystok found it even easier than other ghettos did to win the population over to its "whoever works, survives" ideology.[409]

The first people to consider ways and means of resistance in Bialystok, as in so many other ghettos in Poland and Lithuania, were the young Pioneers of the left-wing Zionists in Hashomer Hatzair, and the Communists. The Communist cell in the ghetto allied itself with the remaining Communist groups in the city, forming the Bialystok Antifascist Bloc. The young women and men from Hashomer Hatzair, over time, found their thoughts about underground struggle bolstered by the emissaries from the Vilna FPO. At the beginning of 1942, Edek Boraks and Chayke Grossman from the Vilna Hashomer Hatzair showed up in the ghetto, contacted both groups, and handed over the FPO summons to armed struggle. Chayke Grossman had also been chosen by the Warsaw Communists to build a unified underground organization based on the Bialystok Communists and in conjunction with the rest of the groups. Her efforts bore fruit: by March, the Unified Antifascist Bloc was in place: it embraced not just Hashomer Hatzair and the Communists, but also the left wing of the Bund and, above all, its youth organization Zukunft (Future).[410] The Bund's right wing joined with the moderate left-wing Zionist Dror youth organization to form the so-called Second Bloc.[411]

Following the destruction of the rural ghettos in the vicinity of Bialystok, the Unified Antifascist Bloc resolved, in November 1942, to arm itself. At this point, the debate that had occurred in every eastern European ghetto, and which had led to different decisions, erupted: Which made more sense and would have more impact? Fighting in the ghetto or fighting in the forest? The opponents of guerrilla struggle contended that it was sheer cowardice to leave the population defenseless and powerless to fight—only the young and the able-bodied could opt to brave the dangers of living and fighting in the forests. And, besides, the prospects for success in the forest were not much better than in the ghetto, in that two essential preconditions were missing: thorough knowledge of the terrain and backing from other partisans or the populace. The strongest, most influential opposition to the partisan option came from the communist Chayke Mendelson and from the subsequent leader of the uprising, Mordecai Tenenbojm, who had arrived from Vilna and joined the Antifascist Bloc, despite being a member of the Dror organization.

The most vigorous champion of partisan struggle was Judith Nowogródzska, an old, well-respected Warsaw Communist. She regarded a ghetto uprising as plain suicide. Even though she knew that, on account of her age and her heart problems, she herself would be doomed to remain behind in the city, she used all of her powers of persuasion to at least save the young people and get them out to the forests.

The strongest faction in the controversy was made up of supporters of the third way, led by the Communists Rebecca Wojskowska (who later went on to become a political commissar with the Bialystok Forois (Forwards) guerrilla battalion) and Joseph Kawe. The third way advocated an uprising inside the ghetto, followed by a mass break-out in order to save as many of the residents as possible. At the same time, they would launch a partisan unit capable of welcoming the fugitives and carrying on the struggle. This was the option that eventually was carried, in spite of dogged opposition from Judith Nowogródzska. She drew her own conclusions from this, quitting the Unified Antifascist Bloc and launching an organization of her own, known as the "Judith Group" and recruiting mainly from young people of every political hue.[412] The "Judith Group," recruited its membership from among juvenile delinquents: it may well be the only instance of a successful alliance between politically organized resistance and members of the sub-proletariat, who would normally have been shunned by the organized left as questionable elements.

The controversy about ghetto struggle or forest fighting had not yet concluded when German troops marched into the ghetto on February 5, 1943, to mount their first large-scale extermination operation. The Unified Antifascist Bloc hurriedly drew up a battle plan. It would, however, never be put into practice, since all lines of communication had broken down and the resisters didn't have enough weapons. The three-person groups set up by the Bloc had to fight as best they could, armed with sulfuric acid, axes, knives, iron bars, and a couple of hand grenades. Since every one of these tiny groups was fighting on its own and in isolation, virtually nothing is known of their activities. What little eyewitness evidence has come down to us certainly has to do mainly with women. There was Frida Fiel, for instance, who tossed a hand grenade at a batch of Germans and was instantly mowed down by gunfire. But her grenade went off. Or there was the group of fighters led by Rachel Rozensztejn, Sarah Rozenblat, and Hela Manela, which, from a house in Chmielna Street, bombarded the Germans with bottles filled with sulphuric acid. Every one of these resisters perished, except for Sarah Rozenblat (who had left her son with a neighbor woman at the eleventh hour, in order to take part in the fighting) who managed to escape.[413] The extermination drive lasted from February 5 to 12, but the task could not be achieved as quickly and slickly as the invaders

Chayke Grossman's forged papers in the name of Halina Woronowicz

had thought. They also encountered resistance from the unorganized population: some 20,000 people had retreated into hiding places that, when discovered, they often defended with hatchets and iron bars. By the end of the week's hunt, the Germans had executed 2,000 people and transported a further 5,000 to Treblinka and 3,000 to Auschwitz. Before leaving the ghetto on the night of February 11, the Unified Antifascist Bloc gave a summary trial to known traitors and collaborators. Some were given a beating, others were killed.[414]

In March, a mixed-sex group of fighters left the ghetto to join the Forois partisan unit.[415] The two undergrounds discussed the February operation, the difficulties and errors surrounding it, and concluded that the uncoordinated operation of the two blocs was the main weakness. In May, they amalgamated and founded the Antifascist Struggle Bloc, with Hashomer Hatzair, Dror, Hanoar Hatzioni, Betar, the Bund, and the Communists as members. With some 500 fighters organized into five-strong teams, the Antifascist Struggle Bloc set up three units, one for each sector of the ghetto.[416]

Disunity had not been the resistance's only telling weakness— there had also been the dearth of weaponry. Every effort was now made to procure arms and explosives. Mordecai Tenenbojm, together with the Communist Daniel Moskowicz, the commander of the Struggle Bloc, turned to the political leadership of the official Polish resistance in Bialystok to ask for support. The Civil Resistance Directory responded to this request thus: "What is your position vis à vis the Soviet Union?."[417] Tenenbojm's written response to this read: "Dear Sirs, this is not the time to get embroiled in political 'negotiations.'... 200 grenades and a couple of dozen revolvers will certainly not have a decisive impact upon the rebirth of Poland, but may well determine the final days of Poland's second largest ghetto." In order to hammer home the urgency of his request, Tenenbojm added: "A conscientious Pole may serve his country by other means: he can wait for the day when the government of the Republic gives the order (to act). We cannot wait. For us, any day may be the day we are taken away for execution. We have to act immediately."[418]

His efforts were in vain. The Jewish resisters continued to rely upon themselves in the quest for arms. They had support from a couple of members of the Communists' Bialystok Antifascist Committee, and even from a couple of German antifascist soldiers, two Polish engineers, and some fugitive Soviet prisoners of war. Anything else, the fighters had to procure for themselves through raids on German arsenals, barracks, and repair shops. Once, they raided some Gestapo premises and made off with thirty rifles. Some young women working in a former Polish barracks stole a complete machine-gun and, having stripped it down, smuggled it back to the ghetto in installments. But the most daring operation was, of course, the one mounted by Chayke Grossman, Bronia Winicka, Malka Rózycka, and Hanna Rud. Three of these women managed to buy a machine-gun from a Pole living in the countryside, some distance from the city. That left only the question of its transportation. Bronia Winicka had the brilliant idea of telling her German boss that there was a chance that she could get hold of some beef. In return for the loan of his car, he could keep half. This is how four ghetto Jews delivered a machine-gun to its destination—a machine-gun destined for use against Germans, transported in a German's car. However, for all their efforts, the Antifascist Struggle Bloc proved incapable of procuring even somewhat adequate weaponry. Half the weapons went straight to the Forois partisans, ensuring that the fighting units, whether inside the ghetto or out in the forests, had too few.[419]

In June 1943, Himmler decided that the Bialystok ghetto should be destroyed once and for all. To avoid a repetition of the resistance offered by the underground during the February sweep and, above all, in the light of the Warsaw ghetto uprising, those in charge of the Final Solution entrusted SS Gruppenführer Odilo Globocnik with this mission.[420] Globocnik arrived in Bialystok, bringing with him a German police regiment and two Ukrainian battalions, specialists in counter-guerrilla warfare. On the night of August 15–16, Globocnik surrounded the ghetto with a triple cordon made up of local police units and gendarmes. His plan was to then move in himself with his 3,000 SS men, the Ukrainians, and the Wehrmacht regulars, as well as aerial support. By 2:00 AM, the cordon was in place around the ghetto. Activists from the Jewish Struggle Bloc, having just finished a crisis meeting where a battle plan had been drawn up to head off the German incursion at the gates, were just going to sleep when their lookouts raised the alarm.[421] Chayke Grossman, who had taken part in the meeting, describes the moment in her account, *The Days of the Uprising*:

> Gedeliahu...came into my room. It was about two o'clock in the morning. "Quickly, get up and get dressed," he said. "A German SS unit has arrived via the Yourovetska Street gate and right now are posting guards outside all the workshops."... All our plans undone: for instance, the plan to take the Germans by surprise before they could surround the ghetto, and to attack them the moment they walked through the gates—all of this was now impossible... We knew that our time to die had come.[422]

The leadership gathered again, made the requisite amendments to their battle plan, and summoned their fighters to be given their instructions and issued weapons. Three hundred of the fighters were issued with firearms and hand grenades: the other two hundred—primarily women—had to make do with Molotov cocktails, homemade bombs, knives, and axes.[423] Chayke Grossman recalls: "The girls raised a stink. They wanted to play their part in the armed attack. No one, not the men, nor the women, wanted to back down. But somebody was going to have to do so."[424] It was the women...or, at any rate, the women who were "mere" fighters, not outstanding activists like Chayke Grossman, Sarah Rozenblat, and Judith Nowogródszka. At four o'clock in the morning, the Germans posted their proclamation on the walls: everyone was to report for removal. Shortly after that, young girls from the

*Chayke Grossman
today*

orphanage pasted over the German posters with the summons of the Struggle Bloc:

> Five million European Jews have already been murdered by Hitler and his executioners. Only one tenth of the Polish Jews remains. Upwards of three million Polish Jews were tortured to death in Chelmno and Belzec, Auschwitz and Treblinka, Sobibor and the other death camps. You need to know that all the deported Jews have ended up dead. Do not believe the Gestapo propaganda about letters allegedly written by deportees. It is nothing more than a brazen lie. The path of the deportees leads to the gigantic crematoria and common graves in the depths of the Polish forests. We are all under sentence of death now. We have nothing to lose!... Don't let them drive us like sheep to the slaughter! Even though we may be too weak to defend our lives, we

have strength enough to defend our Jewish honor and our human dignity... Do not go willingly to death! Fight for your life until you breathe your last!... Or are you, perhaps, to hide in the slums as your nearest and dearest are taken off to be murdered? Or are you going to sell your wives, your children, your parents, your very souls for a couple of extra weeks of slave labor?[425]

However, the ghetto population turned a blind eye to the desperate summons and flooded towards the muster point. Chayke Grossman recalls:

Our scouts returned with harrowing news. Floods of people were making for Jorowiecka Street... Our comrades went from group to group, asking them, pleading with them. But the flow of people continued on its way through the streets... It seemed as if a speedy death would be easier than dragging out a life of torment... Like sleepwalkers they joined the flock... They refused to heed us... The position was very grave. We had to come to some decision immediately. But what? Should we stick to our old plan, even though the main motivation behind our struggle, defending the masses, had, in fact, evaporated?... Or should we commit an honorable suicide? Or should we alter our plans?[426]

To be truthful, the leaders of the Struggle Bloc had no intention of abandoning their plan: they clung to the hope that, even if it was at the very last minute, the populace would leap at the chance of a mass escape. Changes to the plan were needed because Globocnik, having learned from the Warsaw experience, had made mincemeat out of the Struggle Bloc's idea. The ghetto was divided into two districts by the Bialka river: one comprised of sturdy stone buildings, tailor-made for hit-and-run operations; the other, of small wooden shacks and huts. In between the two were huge meadows, open ground. Globocnik drove the crowds along the river, obliging the resistance to fight on open ground that afforded scarcely any cover.[427] The resisters were abruptly ordered across the river: obstructed by the crowds, they closed laboriously on their objective, leaving family and friends in their wake and on their way to their deaths. Chayke Grossman came across her own mother:

For a moment, I was tempted to ignore her and carry on my way. I was afraid of myself... But I could not help myself. I hadn't enough strength to walk past her wrinkled face, crumpled with age, and not gaze upon her grey head. I was ashamed to see her abandoned and alone. I was startled by my own weakness and felt like a deserter. But when I saw her, alone, the heart was torn out of me. I turned to face her. "Chaikele, where are you going?" I couldn't answer. I kissed her dried lips and her cropped hair and ran, ran far away. I never set eyes on her again.[428]

Somebody gave the signal to attack. A band of young women under the command of Milka Datner, Basia Kaczalska, Khaya Biala, and Fania (it has not been possible to verify her full name) set the factories and workshops alight. Simultaneously, a team of fighters mounted a machine-gun and rifle attack on Germans in Smolna Street and forced them to retreat. Meanwhile, the group around Milka Datner launched an attack on the palisade and tried to set it on fire so the crowds passing down Smolna Street on their way to the muster point could escape more easily.[429] Chayke Grossman recalls:

We understood that we were all going to die. We knew that the assault team forcing a hole in the palisade were going to be sitting ducks for the hellish enemy fire, and that, at best, only a handful would survive. But the crowds were behind us. We had to break through the cordon if they were to be able to escape. At that point, there were almost 20,000 of us Jews gathered there... Even if hundreds perished, several thousands could get away.[430]

When fighters of both sexes made the palisade the main focus of attack, Chayke Grossman was among them: "The palisade was right in front of us. Firing non-stop, we forced a way through. But our gunfire was not returned. Where was the enemy? We reached the palisade and started to file through." On the far side a machine-gun unit was lying in wait for the assault team.

The whole world began to quake... Then we heard gunfire, a hail of gunfire, and the comrades at the front tumbled, wounded, to the ground... We had to fall back and wound up in the gardens in Nowogrodzka Street...

We were in open ground with a clear line of sight to the enemy... A cannon spat fire...and the shrapnel whistled past above our heads. We hurled ourselves at their positions, but were forced to retreat again. I was firing non-stop. I tumbled to the ground, picked myself up again, and walked towards the palisade. I turned back again when a hail of bullets forced us to fall back... My feet were bleeding and I was covered in mud.[431]

By the time the fighting in Smolna Street ended, one team—the one that included Chayke Grossman—had managed to withdraw into the ghetto. Another group, made up of sixty fighters and unarmed civilians, had succeeded in escaping, but thirty-seven of them were gunned down in the process and only twenty-three reached the safety of the forests.[432]

While the fighting was going on around the palisade, Globocnik entered the ghetto. He was travelling in an armored car, flanked by three scout cars. His troops were led by an SS man standing upright on the first lorry—rather foolhardily—in an arrogant pose, brandishing a whip. Not that he got too far like that. When the detachment reached the Jewish Council building on Jurowiecka Street, Dora—a young woman from Warsaw—shot him off the lorry. She did not survive her daring attack.[433] But the Germans, who kept shooting in all directions as they went, would face further attacks. Resisters had taken up positions in three houses on the street, and they held up the column's advance. Renia Wiernik, an old Communist known as "the mother of the partisans," was the last survivor of a gunfight at No. 26. She waited until the Germans entered the premises before using her last hand grenade to blow up the butchers along with herself. After the column moved off again, it ran into a second group of resisters and, finally, at the end of Jurowiecka Street encountered ferocious resistance from Judith Nowogródszka's strong fighting unit, which was made up of sixty girls and boys. The Germans moved their scout cars up as they turned into Ciepla Street, but that did not do them much good either: they were greeted by a hail of grenades and homemade bombs from which even their armor did not emerge unscathed. The Ciepla Street defenders were primarily women and girls led by Sarah Rozenblat. Eighteen-year-old Frida Rybalowska managed to capture a machine-gun during the fighting, turning it around and directing fire on the attackers. The Germans opted to call in aerial support, and planes bombed the resisters' positions, killing many of them.[434] It was around two o'clock in the afternoon when they managed to encircle the surviving fighters of both sexes in the area around Smola, Nowogródzka, and Ciepla Streets.[435] Chayke Grossman recounts the final battle for the ghetto:

> The terrain in front of us was strewn with corpses. The fighting grew fiercer...the sun had climbed higher now and was beating down on our skin... Our numbers were continually dwindling and, gradually, our ammunition was running out. All of a sudden the entrance to Fabritzna Street, which had always been sealed off, burst noisily open and a tank loomed, making for Ciepla Street. It stopped suddenly. It seemed as if it had been struck by a petrol bomb. Now other tanks drew up and faced us: a couple of hundred fighters, the vanguard of an oppressed people, a bloodied nation. Ha! Ha! Ha! The laughter of death echoed through the streets and gardens: this was the battleground of the weak. Some people from the crowd joined us—everyday, ordinary folk, neither organized nor armed. One woman called out to the crowd: Come on, then! What are you waiting for? Get them!... Not many joined us, but the very fact of their arrival was very heartening. Once again, we would try to force a passage through the armed German cordon to force an escape route for the crowds assembled in Jurowiecka Street and waiting with bated breath, so close at hand and yet so far from us. The drone of a plane was heard overhead. It flew very low, circled over us a couple of times, and vanished again. Had it come simply to intimidate us? No, here it was coming back again, starting to open fire on us... Two columns of SS men approached us down Jurowiecka and Smolna Streets... They surrounded us with a wall of flame... Our ammunition ran out... The masses were not about to follow us. We would not be escorting them out to the forests, nor even into the final battle. We had killed Germans. We had fought and built a bridge with our own bodies: but the masses declined to cross it... The front line

was coming closer all the time and we were now virtually surrounded. But no! The order now came to hurl ourselves at the troop columns and through them, to link up with our units in Grodna Street. A single machine-gun covered our withdrawal... I jumped and started to run like a woman possessed... The revolver in my grasp was no longer of any use to me now. My overcoat was in tatters... From head to foot, I was covered in blood and grime. My throat burned, my heart pounded.[436]

Chayke Grossman tried to make it to Grodna Street, but in vain. When she could see that the battle was finally lost, she was overcome by doubts and despair. "Where were all the fighters I had seen alive just a short while ago, during the final minutes of fighting? Where were my loved ones? Without them, life held no meaning. I was the only one there, in the midst of the crowd waiting to be transported. All of a sudden, it came to me. What if I were to leave with them?"[437] She did not. She withdrew inside herself. What had been the point of fighting if she was now obliged to deliver herself up to the murderers? She told herself: "All your life you have been active in the resistance. You fought against the deportations and said: There they go, like sheep to the slaughter. Day after day, night after night, you swore to yourself and the rest: They must not catch us!"[438]

The following day, at the muster point, the Germans murdered parents who refused to be separated from their children. After that a thousand children were taken to Theresienstadt, from there, to Auschwitz, straight to the gas chambers.[439] On the night of August 19, Judith Nowogródszka suffered a heart attack. Even so, with the help of her fellow fighters, she tried to pass through the German lines with her group. Within a short time she was dead, having fallen in the ghetto uprising that she had so vehemently opposed right from the outset.[440] The Ciepla Street and Nowogrodszka Street resisters managed to hold out until August 20. And so ended the battle to defend the ghetto. Some of the fighters, female and male alike, were taken alive by the Germans. This happened to Sonia Szmit from Hashomer Hatzair, the last commander of the Bialystok resistance's Antifascist Struggle Bloc. But she was disinclined to surrender. Far from it. The Germans captured her and had her hemmed in, along with other survivors not yet deported, in a concentration camp hurriedly improvised inside the ghetto precincts. She encouraged her comrades-in-arms to dig a tunnel, and successfully supervised their escape. They made it to the forests, but, once there, many perished in a German ambush. Sonia Szmit was killed in the gun-battle.[441]

At this time, there was another group of resisters on a train bound for Treblinka, but they also had no inclination to give up. They forced a hole in the side of their cattlewagon: Wolf Wolkowski, one of the Antifascist Struggle Bloc leaders, shouted, "Jump, comrades!" thereby giving the signal for a mass break-out. Many escaped successfully and reached the Forois partisans' forest encampment. They included four Bloc fighters, three men and one young woman.[442] Chayke Grossman also managed to slip out of the ghetto and join the partisans. She currently lives in Israel.

Krakow

"Fear not. I'm not going to cry!"

Krakow, Poland's ancient capital, held one of the oldest Jewish communities in the country. There were 60,000 Jews living there when the Second World War erupted. By the end of 1939, their numbers had been swollen to something in excess of a quarter of a million as Jews from Austria, Polish Saxony, and the Warthe district were deported there.[443] Generalgouverneur Hans Frank turned the historic city into his residence, the capital of the Generalgouvernement of Poland, and straightaway stated that he could not countenance the presence of non-Aryans around him: Krakow had to be made Jew-free. On April 18, 1940, Stadhauptmann Schmidt decreed that all Jews had to quit the city before August 15. The Jewish population could not have complied with this decree even it wanted to, because where could they go? In September, 35,000 of them were forcibly deported. In November, Frank entrusted the final resolution of the problem to Obersturmbannführer Rudolf Pavl. A first step towards this objective was the concentration of the entire Jewish population inside a so-called "Jewish residential district." In March 1941, a walled ghetto was constructed in Podgórze, a Krakow suburb, with the usual ban upon Jews stirring outside the ghetto without special permission. In June 1941, "Operation Reinhardt" was set in motion: it involved transporting thousands of the ghetto's population to the death camp at Belzec, or being killed on the spot.[444]

The first resistance cell was set up at the end of that year. Krakow's Jewish community had a pronounced middle-class tradition and was greatly under the sway of the Agudat Israel party. The left had a rather weak toehold: the most influential Zionist youth organization was Akiva, a group that married the liberal ideals of the 19th century with a romantic, collectivist ethic of kibbutz life. In Krakow, the Akiva leaders were Adolf Liebeskind, Shimon Drenger, and his wife Gusta Dawidsohn-Drenger, known as Justyna. While in prison, Gusta Drenger wrote a war journal that managed to survive and that, these days, represents an important source for any study of the Krakow resistance. Given their social and political background, it looked as if the Akiva leadership might find it easier than the leftist groups and parties to seek out allies in the official Polish resistance circles under the direction of the government-in-exile in London. After they discovered that Jews could expect no help of any sort from the Armia Krajowa, they started to put out feelers in other directions.[445]

At pretty much the same time that Akiva turned itself into an underground organization, a second group formed inside the ghetto during the early months of 1942. Comprised mainly of Communists and members of the Marxist-influenced left-wing Zionist Pioneer group, Hashomer Hatzair, it was also debating the practicalities and prospects of a Jewish resistance and, by the summer of 1942, had set to work on it. In August, the group derailed a German transport train: since they did not have access to explosives, the saboteurs had loosened the bolts holding the track in position. That same month, together with some Akiva members, they raided the German Optima plant, stealing uniforms, winter clothing, and boots. Between August and September, Liebeskind and his Akiva group, as well as the Communist, left-wing Zionist group led by Heshik Bauminger (of Hashomer Hatzair), killed several gendarmes and SS men and also captured a number of weapons.[446]

Simultaneously, Akiva launched the first attempt to establish a partisan base in the surrounding forests. A partisan army along the lines of Tito's was Drenger's dream. As she saw it, the Yugoslav people's uprising was the initial spark due to light a fuse throughout the whole of Europe. Tito's partisans could not tilt the balance on their own, so it was a matter of creating a partisan army in every European country, so that their efforts might then be united and fascism successfully overthrown. "Everything is in our hands," Gusta Drenger writes in her journal, quoting her husband. "If all the oppressed people will lend a hand, how tremendous our prospects of success would be!"[447] However, the attempt to act upon this notion fell through. The little group, which had made a beginning by setting up a support base in the Rzeszow area, fell victim to animosity from the rural population, its own lack of experience, ignorance of the geographical situation, and, finally, treachery. The Akiva leaders had to change tack and confine their struggles to the city precincts.[448] On October 28, 1942, SS troops, Lithuanian and Ukrainian units, and Polish police surrounded the ghetto.

Six thousand inhabitants, mostly children and the elderly, were seized and transported to the Belzec death camp, while others were shot down right there.[449] The ghetto's two resistance groups thereupon decided to amalgamate. Gola Mirer had opened the first talks with the leaders of both organizations as early as the previous September. Mirer was a tried and tested Communist veteran who would play an important part in the Krakow resistance. In 1933, she was sentenced to fifteen years in prison, but successfully escaped and, since then, had been living underground. On the back of the October roundup, the groups speeded up their negotiations and, in the end, wound up launching the ZOB, the unified Jewish fighting organization that, by the end of that year, had some 300 members.[450] Following the shock of October 28, lots of young women and men had joined them. "Now they are free," wrote Drenger in her journal, "their last remaining ties to everyday existence now destroyed. Those who had previously hesitated about leaving a younger brother, only sister, or their parents, now, in the wake of the action, felt suddenly free."[451] Their parents or younger siblings had perished, gassed in Belzec.

The struggle, the ZOB determined, had to be waged within the city. The establishment of a support base for partisans had proved a dead-end: Generalgouverneur Frank and his henchmen had to be taught what it was like to be afraid, right where they lived. The ZOB organized along urban guerrilla lines: operations would take place, not inside the ghetto, but in the middle of Krakow, under the very noses of the Nazi bosses. Hashomer Hatzair and the Communists set up support networks in Krakow's Nowy Pradnik working-class quarter: Akiva was all for operations outside the ghetto, with the ghetto as a place to retreat to once an action had been carried out.[452]

As elsewhere, the main problem at that point was getting weapons. The Krakow ZOB also started by making overtures to the Armia Krajowa, whose local command was operating in an area even larger than the Warsaw command. However, the army of the Polish resistance loyal to the government could not spare a single gun for the Jewish fighting organization. In spite of being well-equipped, the Krakow command of the Armia Krajowa was not disposed to seriously engage the occupiers. Anyway, in addition to the stipulations of the government-in-exile's "Uprising Plan," the inactivity of the Krakow AK was explicable in terms of two further special considerations. For one thing, there were

sizable SS detachments present in the capital of the Generalgouvernement; for another, the government-in-exile in London was afraid that
the least provocation might prompt the Germans to level the historic
city. Add to this the broadly anti-Semitic line of the Polish resistance
that, in Warsaw as well as in other cities, refused to lend its backing
to the Jewish fighters.[453] The Gwardia Ludowa had scarcely enough
weapons to meet its own needs, but gave some to the ZOB, along with
the addresses of female and male comrades in Warsaw who might have
access to more. This dangerous mission was entrusted to Akiva's Hela
Schipper, who could pass for an Aryan and was issued with superbly
forged papers: but, even so, there were enormous risks involved in the
trip. In her journal, Gusta Drenger sets out almost insurmountable
difficulties faced by the resistance's female emissaries: and by anyone
venturing to leave the ghetto:

> How glib it was to say, "Run away from the deporta-
> tions!" How was one to get across the barbed wire under the
> watchful eyes of the police? You only needed a policeman to
> catch sight of your white and blue arm-band to be gunned
> down. [Jews in eastern Europe had to wear blue and white
> arm-bands.] You could remove the arm-band, of course,
> but if any passerby happened to spot you, he would hand
> you over immediately to the police. Even if you hid in the
> darkest of doorways in order to make this crucial change,
> somebody would assuredly have seen you go in as a Jew and
> come out as...what, in fact? And, even if you managed to dis-
> card the telltale sign, you were still yourself. Still a Jew with
> no arm-band. And one's Jewishness was betrayed by every
> faltering movement, every uncertain step, the rounded back
> that seemed to be carrying the full weight of slavery. One
> was betrayed by one's eyes, the eyes of a cornered animal,
> or by one's whole aspect, marked with the imprint of the
> ghetto... Thus, by the time he made it to the station, a Jew
> had already come through a whole host of battles... A Jew
> needed all the sangfroid in the world just to walk proudly,
> with head erect, through the station, to coolly return the
> police's probing looks, and, finally, to climb into the train
> carriage as if this were something he did day in and day
> out. [Jews were banned from travelling on the railways.] It

was inside the train that the common folk came into their own. There was no way of eluding these folk's inquisitive glances... By holding his nerves steady throughout, the Jew might conceal his identity, but he could not help overhearing the chit-chat of his fellow passengers, which made his blood boil. What were they talking about? They were talking about the Jews. Saying that, at long last, the Jews had had their comeuppance... And there he sat in his corner of the carriage, someone not yet over the grief of having lost his nearest and dearest, someone who could not afford to let a single facial muscle twitch.[454]

Hela Schipper made it to Warsaw safe and sound, and, on the return trip to Krakow, she brought two Brownings under her overcoat and three pistols with ammunition in her bag. She made this trip several more times, always loaded down with arms, until she fell into the hands of the Germans.[455] With the revolvers and pistols from Warsaw, plus the arms stolen from the Germans or obtained through robberies, the ZOB combat units had gathered enough weaponry to embark upon more ambitious operations. Between September and December 1942, they mounted a total of ten *attentats* and spectacular acts of sabotage, ranging from attacks on the Krakow-Bochnia rail lines, through attacks on SS officers, to arson of goods warehouses belonging to the Todt organization.[456]

Encouraged by these successes, the ZOB planned a concerted operation for Christmas. The experienced ZOB fighters Yitzhak Zuckerman and Eve Fulman arrived from Warsaw to help their Krakow colleagues, female and male, in their preparations. The final plan of attack, devised jointly by the ZOB leaders and the Communist Gwardia Ludowa, was put to the activists on December 17: at seven o'clock on the evening of December 22 the Cyganerja, Esplanada, and Zakopianka cafeterias, where German officials and officers were wont to spend their evenings, were to be attacked with hand grenades and homemade bombs. Simultaneously, other combat units would attack the officers' mess at the National Museum building and the Scala cinema favored by off-duty German soldiers. There were also parallel plans to torch several Wehrmacht and SS garages, to destroy the motor launches used by gendarmerie patrols on the Vistula, and to gun down any uniformed

German who might cross their path. This plan was in large part implemented: it came as a tremendous shock to the occupiers, as well as to
the inactive Armia Krajowa. Krakow, Hans Frank's capital, had ceased
to be a peaceful haven for the German masters. The Jewish resistance's
dreams of demonstrating that Krakow was not a place where Frank
could stroll at his leisure had become a reality. The tremors in Krakow
were felt even in Berlin. Although wholly preoccupied by the battle for
Stalingrad, Hitler insisted that Himmler explain how it could possibly
be that Jews could attack German officers and government officials in
the capital of the Generalgouvernement.[457]

The Gestapo's honor was now at stake. Tracking down the urban
guerrillas in Krakow turned into a witch-hunt: a number of traitors
made themselves available as bloodhounds. Between the end of December 1942 and the start of January 1943, virtually the entire ZOB
collapsed as its members were rounded up or killed in clashes with their
pursuers, like Hannah Spitzer and Hannah Sternlicht. Eve Fulman and
Eve Liebeskind (whose husband, Adolph, was shot dead while being
arrested) were captured alive by their pursuers. Eve Liebeskind's sister,
Mira, who had helped build the fighting organization in the Radom
ghetto and been involved in the Christmas operation in Krakow, was
shot following brutal torture. Shimon Drenger too had been picked up:
Gusta Drenger managed to escape, but gave herself up to the police—
she wanted to share her husband's fate.[458] As to her reasons for such a
romantic and suicidal act, one can only speculate. It may be that Gusta
Drenger, left on her own, after the entire group had been arrested or
killed, succumbed to a moment of desperation and fatalism. There is
an extract in her journal suggestive of this:

> To tell the truth, we are all weary of life. We cannot
> endure the panic much longer, and sometimes there is an
> unspoken yearning for the end to come quickly. The spirit
> of revolt has still not taken root [among the ghetto popula-
> tion] and nobody is willing to fight the enemy. Is that any
> surprise? Only someone who had not spent three years liv-
> ing with a burden of cruelty, humiliation, and deprivation
> could be surprised... I sometimes think that every trace of
> our people is to fade from the face of the earth, that our
> every memory is to be expunged. Nothing that we love and
> value will remain. By all that I hold sacred, my only wish is

for death. I have no wish to go on living. I do not want to carry on living in our ruins.[459]

Gusta Drenger was taken to Helclów prison, where she shared a cell with her comrades-in-arms, Gola Mirer, Shoshana Jolles, Genia Maltzer, and her own sister-in-law, Celia Drenger. There, in Cell No. 15, Gusta Drenger would write *Justyna's Journal*: she hid the loose pages in the stove, from which they were smuggled out by Jewish work brigades from the men's prison, and passed on to other trustworthy persons.[460] Why didn't these young women and men resign themselves to their fate? Why did they give themselves over to a hopeless fight against an all-powerful enemy? Gusta Drenger provides an answer in *Justyna's Journal* that also holds true for her comrades-in-arms in Warsaw, Minsk, Vilna, and Bialystok: "How could we not have done so? History would never have forgiven us that sin. What could have stopped us from doing the only thing left to anyone with any self-respect?... It is all the same whatever happens. We are doomed in any case. Let us leave behind the memory of deeds that, some day, might induce someone to look back on us with respect."[461]

Gusta Drenger's spirit of rebellion had bounced back. She started to think about escaping. The men also had already made plans to escape when the transport came to ferry them to be shot in Plaszów. On March 19, twenty women were taken away for deportation to Auschwitz, or for shooting in Plaszów: they included Celia, Gusta Drenger's sixteen-year-old sister-in-law, who bade her farewell with these words: "Fear not. I'm not going to cry." The thirty remaining women were removed from their cells a short while later and taken to the reinforced basement from which they would leave for Plaszów. It was here that they hatched their escape plan, put into effect on April 29. In two ranks, the women were marched from Helclów prison to the men's prison in Montelupich, where the trucks were waiting for them. Turning into the street outside the prison, Gusta Drenger and Gola Mirer jumped their guards. Some of their female comrades rushed to help them, while the rest scattered in all directions, as planned. Gola Mirer, Rose Jolles, and the running women were cut down by bursts of machine-gun fire: only Gusta Drenger, Genia Maltzer, and another two women escaped with their lives.[462] Gusta Drenger attempted to make contact with other Akiva survivors, finally rejoined her husband, and, shortly afterwards, met up with her sister-in-law Margot Drenger, who brought the two fugitives to a prepared hiding place near Wisnicz. Both were injured, shot in the leg, but they had little time for convalescing and they wanted to carry on fighting. After the liberation, Margot Drenger wrote: "There is every likelihood that they could have survived the war, but, a short time later, they returned to their partisan activities. They published a bulletin, organized operations, and transported arms from Krakow to Warsaw. It was on one such mission that they were caught. The precise circumstances and date of their arrest and murder are not known."[463] Later, it proved possible to establish the date at least: Gusta was arrested first on November 8, 1943, and Shimon Drenger shortly afterwards.[464]

While the surviving ZOB members were in prison planning their escape, the destruction of the Krakow ghetto was begun. On March 13, Untersturmführer Leopold Goeth set about carrying out his mission. Thousands of people were taken off to Plaszów to be shot, thousands more were deported to Auschwitz, and still further thousands were murdered on the spot. The remainder of the ghetto population—the ones fit to work—were sent to Plaszów labor camp. That camp was hell on earth. Those who endured the torments there envied those who had merely been taken to Plaszów to be shot. Goeth, an Austrian from Vienna, member of the outlawed NSDAP since 1930 and of the SS since 1932, having served in the Waffen-SS since 1940, had already proved his efficiency at extermination in Treblinka, Sobibor, and Belzec. In the Plaszów slave labor camp, he enforced a regimen so brutal that the inmates were comparatively relieved when, in January, it was redesignated as a concentration camp under regulation SS administration. Not that this redesignation meant that Goeth was immediately replaced. On May 2, 1944, he had all of the inmates line up, naked, for selection procedure. 1,400 were destined to die, gassed in Auschwitz; they included all of the children. When they were taken away in trucks, he forced their mothers to sit on the ground along the edge of the highway and watch as he howled the song "Mama, Buy Me a Little Pony," which was then all the rage in Germany.[465]

Those female ZOB fighters who managed to evade arrest and murder, joined the partisans in the forests of Wisnicz Novy. Hillel Wodzislawski, one of the Akiva leaders, had organized a partisan unit—following the big wave of arrests—that kept the German occupiers rather busy between April and September 1943: during that time they managed to derail a total of eleven trains on the Krakow-Lvov network.[466] Their successes brought the partisans into conflict, not merely with the Germans, but also with the Polish Armia Krajowa which—obeying instructions from London—was strictly opposed to any armed activity. When a ZOB partisan detachment was on its way to take punitive action against a Polish peasant who had betrayed one its support bases, there was an armed skirmish. After that, the local Armia Krajowa groups hunted down the Jewish partisans. They held out until the summer of 1944, after which the few survivors fled via Slovakia to Hungary, where they joined the Jewish resistance in Budapest.[467]

Minsk

"Fritz won't take me alive!"

When German troops crossed the borders of the Soviet Union on July 22, 1941, they brought in their wake the so-called intervention units, whose special commission was to liquidate Soviet officials, Communist Party leaders, and all Jews.[468] Progress by the Wehrmacht was accompanied by unbelievable carnage among the civilian population. In the conquered Soviet territories, the occupation authorities did not even try to build ghettos: Jewish inhabitants were slaughtered immediately. The only exception was Minsk, the capital of Belarus and, at the same time, the city with the biggest Jewish population in White Russia. Following the first brutal massacre, Minsk's Jewish population was kept penned inside two ghettos, one of which—as in Vilna—was quickly shut down.[469] In 1939, 80,000 to 90,000 Jews were living in the city, accounting for over a third of its population.[470] Right after entering Minsk on June 28, the Germans ordered registration of all males aged between fourteen and forty-five. The death penalty awaited all who failed to report. Some 40,000 showed up and were taken to an area near Drozdy, where they had to endure five days without food and water, beneath the glare of powerful searchlights, and surrounded by machine-guns. On the fifth day, the non-Jewish prisoners were released (temporarily). (The numbers of people murdered by the German occupiers up to the liberation in July 1944 came to 700,000 in all.) At the same time, the occupation authorities ordered all Jewish intellectuals, including those older than forty-five, to hand themselves over. Many did so, thinking that they would be spared on account of their being intellectuals. A short time later, the band of Jewish prisoners held in Drozdy, plus those added to them, were taken to a nearby forest and mown down with machine-guns.[471] The city's surviving Jews were penned in the two ghettos. There, behind the walls and the barbed wire, the murders continued. Every night, gangs of German thugs would burst into a number of homes, setting them alight and raping the women. In the big roundups on

August 14, 25, and 31 the occupiers dragged thousands more women and men out of the ghetto with them.[472]

By the end of July 1941, the underground movement was up and running inside the ghetto. In many respects it was an exceptional phenomenon—compared with ghettos elsewhere in Poland and Lithuania. The Minsk resistance wasted no time forging an alliance between different political tendencies. Soviet Jews regarded themselves as part of the Soviet resistance and immediately set to organizing along those lines. Contrary to the situation everywhere else in eastern Europe, the Jewish Council and Jewish police also carried out agitational work in Minsk, not as collaborators and confederates of the German authorities, but as the elected representatives of the Jewish population. The president of the Minsk Jewish Council, Elye Mushkin, was himself an active resistance member. In addition, the Jews of Minsk did not have to contend with an environment as hostile as their unfortunate female and male colleagues in Poland and Lithuania. Their relations with the Belarussian population were, in part, more friendly, and there had even been a degree of intermarriage between the two population groups (unthinkable in Polish Belarus). This led to more than one Russian woman following her husband, even into the ghetto. Consequently the Minsk resistance did not have to combat and overcome opposition from the Jewish Council, nor was it utterly isolated and in jeopardy from the non-Jewish population. Both these advantages helped speed the formation of an armed defense force, and fostered the decision to unite with the partisans instead of staking everything on an uprising within the ghetto. "The ghetto spells death," was the watchword spread by the Minsk underground organization following a crucial meeting in August 1941.[473] It decided right away to procure arms, since "a rifle was a passport to the forest," and to smuggle the inhabitants out of the city ghetto and into the nearby forests in batches.[474] Some of these would join the existing partisan units already, and the rest would establish Jewish bases proper. Given that the Minsk resistance's strategy consisted of rescuing as many ghetto inhabitants as possible, special family encampments had to be set up, support bases for partisans where both armed fighters and the unarmed population might survive in safety. Workers in the Germans' arms dumps and armaments plants stole rifles, revolvers, and ammunition, and smuggled these into the ghetto. Young women were especially important in this task.[475] Thanks to their dexterity, a large stock of arms was built up inside the ghetto: the women emptied entire arms dumps, which did not, of course, go unnoticed. By the autumn of 1941, at the latest, the Germans were aware that what appeared to be a quite strong resistance had taken shape in the ghetto.

One October morning in 1941, three gallows appeared in the city square. Two men were hanged from them and, in between, a young woman: all three wore placards around their necks stating that they had fought against the German masters.[476] One month later, on the 24th anniversary of the October Revolution, German troops encircled the ghetto. They forced 12,000 people to go inside a goods warehouse and left them there all day, packed together so tightly that small children smothered to death in their mothers' arms. The next day, the men were shot in Tuchinka. The women and children endured a slow death in gas trucks.[477] Before long, Isai Pavlovich Kazinets, known as Slavek, made contact with the ghetto resistance leaders, and informed them that there were four other underground organizations in the city. Following the meeting between Slavek and Hersh Smoliar, leader of the ghetto group, all five groups amalgamated into one resistance organization under Slavek's leadership. From the outset, they looked upon themselves as the city wing of the partisan movement: one of their most important aims was to get as many Jews as they could out of the ghetto and into the forests.[478]

The massacres continued. When another 5,000 people were murdered in Tuchinka, the ghetto survivors armed themselves with knives, scissors, and anything else that came to hand. They made it plain that they were ready to defend themselves, and that it would be better to die right away than to submit docilely to deportation and massacre. The Mink ghetto population—to the extent that it was aware of the underground and its plans—was agreed upon fighting its way to the forests: like the population of Warsaw, it closed ranks around the active resistance.[479]

Nevertheless, there were difficulties implementing this plan. The partisans would only take people who were armed and fit for service, as well as doctors. The establishment of family camps to cater for the civilian population was becoming increasingly urgent: too many had died already, and there did not appear to be any end in sight to the butchery. In December 1941, news arrived that commander Bystrow was prepared to take in large parties of Jewish partisans. Immediately, several women and men took to the road and, in the Rudensk area, they set up a machine-gun unit of their own, which became one of the most active and effective partisan units in Belarus, and was subsequently incorporated into the Stalin Brigade.[480]

On March 2, 1942, the ghetto celebrated the feast of Purim. Wilhelm Kube, the commissar-general for Belarus, one of the most notorious butchers in the occupied Soviet territories, decided to mark the feast day with a massacre. On March 1, he instructed the Jewish Council to dig a huge trench in Ratomskaya Street. Then he insisted that 5,000 people be handed over to him. The Jewish Council refused. At ten o'clock on the morning of March 2, SS troopers and Ukrainian units stormed into the ghetto shooting indiscriminately at anyone on the streets. They seized some children and brought them to the trench. Their next target was the orphanage: they forced all of the children out and marched them to Ratomskaya Street, where Kube was waiting for them in his limousine. (Some reports have it that Eichmann was in the vehicle as well.) The SS men proceeded to push the children into the trench, tossed quicklime over them and buried them alive. At the height of their panic, Kube stepped out of his car and started to toss candies to the children who screamed and cried as they asphyxiated. Kube's heroic act during the Purim massacre was the crucial factor in the partisan movement commanders' decision that he had to be executed.[481]

In the grip of despair, the ghetto resistance strove to move the evacuation of the population forward. Even as the young girl fighter Mina Liss, the ghetto's envoy, was negotiating with the partisans over setting up a family camp, the Germans were arresting Niunka Markovitz, the chief organizer of operations to procure arms and then smuggle them out to the forests. The Gestapo stepped up its hunt for the organized underground and also managed to catch Mina Liss on her way back to the ghetto. In spite of awful torture, she did not disclose a single name, which is why her captors opted for random shootings.[482] Anyone not already dead by this point owed his life to the fact that industry and the Wehrmacht needed slave labor. They were worked until they dropped, and disposed of at their first mistake. At the "October" plant for instance, young women were employed—especially former medical students. One day, they arrived ten minutes late for work: they were all taken to the city center and shot.[483] In Minsk, too, the continued existence of the ghetto could be chalked up to the usual friction between the supporters of the Final Solution, on one side, and industry and the Wehrmacht on the other. The Wehrmacht refused to give up the labor power of highly skilled Jewish workers. They lobbied Himmler, initially with support from Kube, who, as the colonial master of Belarus, had an interest of his own in the unpaid labor of his Jewish slaves.[484] However, Kube had a change of heart when he realized that his female and male slaves were working towards their own liberation and, thus, toward a German defeat. On July 31, 1942, he forwarded a report, "Anti-Partisan Struggle and Jewish Activism in the White Ruthenia General District," to his immediate superior, the Ostland (the eastern territories) Reich commander, gauleiter Heinrich Lohse. "In all engagements thus far with partisans in White Ruthenia, it has been found that Jews...are the mainstay of the partisan movement," the report read.[485] It went on to add that, in view of this major threat to the German administration, dealing with the Jews of White Ruthenia was a political priority. There was the danger that the Jewish population might lend its support to the partisans, which was why he reckoned that the wisest course was to eliminate all Jews from White Ruthenia. Notwithstanding this, he ran up against the requirements of the Wehrmacht in its capacity as an employer of Jews, requirements that would probably escalate. In any event, Kube would be grateful if they would refrain from shipping Jews from the Reich into Minsk, at least until the partisan threat could be dealt with. The Jews were an enemy of Germany, and they represented a threat that might prove costlier than any services they might render as a labor force.[486]

In any event, Kube had managed to arrest and murder some of the most important resistance members: the underground had to be reorganized. The ghetto was split into two zones, one under the command of S. Kazdan, the other under Celia Madaysker, the sister of Sonia Madaysker (one of the leaders of the Vilna resistance).[487] Sabotage operations were stepped up. Workers destroyed some of the uniforms being turned out from a former Soviet factory, the remainder being carried off by partisans. In other firms, female and male workers wrecked machine rooms or stitched uniforms and boots in such a way as to render them unserviceable. Three women—Rosa Liphiskaya, Celia Butbinik, and Katya Zirlin—assisted by an eleven-year-old boy, managed to smuggle an entire arsenal out to the forests.[488] A group of ghetto inhabitants also set up a new partisan unit near Koidanovo: over the following months it grew to a brigade of 15,000 female and male fighters. Breina Kreinowitz was elected liaison, her mission was to get people out of the ghetto to Koidanovo. As soon as she had delivered her group to the base—complete with arms, clothing, and sometimes even a radio transmitter—it was back to the ghetto to pick up the next batch.[489]

A large-scale German attack on the forests around Minsk forced the Jewish units to give ground, and contact with the ghetto broke down. Emma Radova, who was in charge of the liaison service, reached the ghetto and promised assistance for the city resistance, but the ghetto leaders turned her down: the only real assistance would re-established contacts with the partisans, and speedy evacuation of the remaining population to the forests. On their own initiative, they sent out couriers—Herschel Smolar, Sonia Levin, and Dora Berson—in three directions. Berson would go on to launch the 11th Minsk Brigade in the Rudensk area a short while later, but, even then, kept returning to the ghetto to pick up new groups, until she was neutralized in an armed clash with German police.[490]

In July 1943, the partisans who had passed a death sentence on Kube at a field court martial made their first attempt on his life. They ambushed a convoy of high-ranking German officers and killed a number of them, but Kube was not among them. Subsequent attempts also failed, until David Kemach, head of the partisans' intelligence department, took the matter in hand. He discovered that Kube liked to have young women as his household staff in his private residence. The staff Kube had at home was painstakingly screened by the Gestapo, but Kemach nevertheless managed to plant a couple of young partisan girls among them. Maria Borisovna Osipowa, an officer from Kemach's department, decided which of the women was best suited and most likely to carry out this difficult mission reliably. On a number of occasions she met surreptitiously with Halina Mazanik, who worked in Kube's home as a maid. Eventually, Osipowa asked her if she would take on this mission. Halina accepted without hesitation. A short time later, she made her way to the forest to pick up explosives, which she hid in a basket of eggs, before she made her way back to the city with her girlfriend and comrade-in-arms Maria Graievska. There, a resistance member took charge of the gear. On September 20, 1943, Maria Borisovna Osipowa handed the bomb to Halina Mazanik. Halina proceeded to Kube's home as usual and, as ever, the sentries on duty wanted to search her. "Look," she told them, "I have a silk handkerchief and a bottle of perfume here for Kube's wife. Tomorrow I can fetch you a similar handkerchief for your wife." With a smile on her lips, she entered Kube's home and made straight for his bedroom, where she positioned the bomb with a fuse timed to detonate at midnight. As she was coming back downstairs, she bumped into Kube's wife who spotted her edginess and asked her what was going on. "Nothing," Halina replied. "It's just that I have an awful toothache. Could I slip out to the dentist?" Kube's wife gave her permission, just this once, on the condition that she get back as quickly as possible. But Halina Mazanik had no intention of coming back. That same day, she was taken back out to the forest. Her family had been taken out a little while earlier, so that they too would be in a safe place. At the stroke of midnight, the bomb under Kube's bed exploded, ending the life of one of the occupation regime's most sadistic killers. Halina Mazanik carried on fighting alongside the partisans, and survived as a highly esteemed veteran in Minsk. It was not until years after the war that it came to light that she, who everybody had thought of as Russian, was in fact Jewish.[491] Since the Kube assassination had been planned and carried out in the utmost secrecy, other partisan bands had no knowledge of it. At the same time, that very same night, they carried out a great bomb attack. This team, from the Kutuzov unit, included two men and two women—Celia Klebanova and Vitka Rudovich. The bombing on the night of September 20 was their third successful operation: the first two had been the derailing of a train loaded with tanks and blowing up a military transport train.[492]

Meanwhile, they had also managed to establish a family camp under the supervision of Simon Zorin. The commander of the Budiuni partisans, Semion Goczenko, whom Minsk Jews had freed from a prisoner of war camp, proved his gratitude by allowing Zorin to establish a camp in his territory for civilian ghetto refugees. In almost no time, there were 600 people living in this camp. Some of these set up the Parchomenko combat unit; most, as members of what was known as the 106th Zorin Division, made themselves useful by looking after the active female and male partisans, sewing their uniforms, making them shoes, and tending to the wounded. The family camp had its own laundry, bakery, and medical services. The children took care of special tasks: it was up to them to guide the remaining ghetto inhabitants out to the camp. Twelve-year-old Sima Perston stood out as the bravest and most tireless of them all. Back in the ghetto she'd had to watch the killing of her mother and little brother, and now she volunteered for the most dangerous missions. Before setting off, she would listen attentively to her instructions and rehearse them word for word. Then, she would stuff a pistol into the pocket of the overcoat she had made for herself and soothe her superiors with the words: "Don't worry, Fritz won't take me alive!" Off she would go. Sometimes, she found it impossible to gain access to the ghetto: in which case, she would hide in a bomb-wrecked house outside the barbed wire that ringed the ghetto and wait there, enduring the hunger and the cold, until night fell. She would then slip into the ghetto with the first work detail to happen along, and set to work. After the ghetto was liquidated, Sima participated in military operations as the youngest fighter. In the summer of 1944, she marched at the head of the partisan army as it entered liberated Minsk.[493]

The evacuations were called off at the end of October 1943, because the partisans had found themselves caught in attacks by German special units. As soon as the aggressors fled, Celia Klebanova returned to the ghetto to collect further batches. All in vain. The Minsk ghetto had been destroyed on October 21: the female envoy found herself confronted by smoking ruins.[494] On the day of the final massacre, twenty-six inhabitants had managed to find a hiding place and survived the slaughter. Half a year later, by June 1944, only thirteen of them were still alive: the children had slipped into comas and the adults were also on the verge of starving to death. Musya, a young Aryan-looking girl, decided to take a gamble. She emerged from her hiding place and went off into the city in search of food. Quite by accident, she bumped into Anna Dvach, a former work-mate, who promptly took her home with her, fed her, and guided her back to the ghetto with a parcel of food. Thanks to her assistance, the final thirteen ghetto inhabitants survived in their hiding place until the Red Army entered the city on July 3.[495] A total of 10,000 Minsk Jews survived murder and deportation by seeking the safety of the forests, more than in any other city in German-occupied eastern Europe. Half of these survivors died in action as partisan fighters, and 5,000 survived to see the liberation.[496]

With the Partisans

"Hush, the night is filled with stars and the
frost is burning brightly."

Rachel, from the small eastern Polish town of Kletsk, (her surname has never been established) was just sixteen years old when her parents were murdered by the Germans in October 1941. Nine months later, in July 1942, the occupiers torched the Kletsk ghetto. A few inhabitants managed to force a hole in the palisade and escaped. Rachel and her sister also squeezed through the narrow gap, but only Rachel made it through: her sister was killed by a German bullet. Rachel ran and ran until she reached the forest, wandered from village to village and, finally, when she could go no further, sought lodging for the night in a farmhouse. The peasant woman gave her a friendly reception, fed her, and even invited her to stay.

But Rachel's only desire was to reach the partisans. The following day, she crossed the Soviet border and came upon a gang of farm laborers. One of them, an elderly man, took her home with him. Overnight, she was able to catch up on lost sleep, but next night her host explained that the Germans had threatened to take reprisals: anybody harboring Jews was to be shot immediately. He showed her the trail into the forest and, once again, Rachel found herself wandering on her own through the moonlight, terrified of every sound. She walked and walked until she came to an isolated house. She knocked on the door, was invited to enter but the householder did not strike her as very trustworthy. However, Rachel was too exhausted to go on walking. "What are we to do?" she asked him. "Give me up to the Germans, if you want." But the man had no such intention—initially, at any rate: "You're too pretty to be given up to the Germans," he replied. Rachel snapped, punched him, and ran outside. When she reckoned she was safe, she sat down to catch her breath, but heard more footsteps. The chase was on again. Somebody called out "Rachel," and she thought that her time had come. However, her pursuer turned out to be a friend from town who was also looking for the partisans. They decided to continue on their way together. Then they heard shooting. The Germans! Crying with exhaustion, Rachel and her friend crawled toward a haystack, where they waited for twenty-four hours, hidden under the straw, scarcely daring to breathe. After nightfall the next day, they dragged themselves out and found themselves faced with a gang of armed men. They had the look of partisans about them, and indeed that they were. They had to spend another day in their hiding place. The group would send a messenger to come and fetch them. But, instead of a messenger, a German gendarme arrived. "You! Out!" he shouted at them. He demanded their papers, threatening them at rifle-point. Rachel was the first to emerge and identify herself. His checks completed, the gendarme ordered them to come with him. They followed him, deeper and deeper into the dense forest, and he ended up delivering his two prisoners to the camp of the Soviet partisan leader Kapusta. He divested himself of his German uniform and donned his partisan uniform. Kapusta himself turned up to look them both over for himself. His first question was: "Why didn't you bring weapons? We can't harbor you unless you have arms." Having reached her destination after such an odyssey, it never occurred to Rachel, even for an instant, to give up now. She managed to convince Kapusta. They were allowed to stay, but in the next attack, they would have to get hold of the requisite arms for themselves.[497]

When the German cordoned off the ghetto on September 23, 1943, Vitka Kempner realized that all escape routes had been closed for the last FPO group in Vilna, still hiding out in the ghetto. But they would have to get out somehow. With Zelda Treger and Sonia Madaysker, she drafted a plan to escape through the sewer system. It worked: Vitka Kempner, Roza Korczak, and their female colleagues were escorted to safe hideouts in the Aryan sector of the city. But this complicated and dangerous journey was only beginning: their goal was the partisans in the Rudniki forests.

The group split up. Fifty women and men, including Chenia Borowska and Aba Kovner, waited in the basement of the Pushkin Palace for the messenger to come. Vitka Kempner, Zelda Treger, and Sonia Madaysker liaised between the various hideouts, keeping them supplied with food and fresh clothing, and keeping the partisans up to date. However, instead of the promised guide, a courier arrived from the urban guerrillas with the message that they would have to make their own way there: several guides had been picked up and killed by the Germans on the way into the city. The female and male FPO fighters stole their way through the darkened streets in twos and threes. It was after midnight when they met up outside the city and set off together. After twenty-four hours of trudging, they arrived at their destination: the support base of the Soviet partisans led by Commander Jurgis in the Rudniki forests. They were expected. They had arms with them, so there was no problem. The women were also incorporated into the combat units without a hitch: Vitka Kempner joined a group specializing in sabotage, Chenia Borowska became a battalion political commissar, and Zelda Teger was soon on her way back to the city to pick up surviving ghetto inhabitants.[498]

Two routes led to the partisans. Most Jews escaping from the ghettos and labor camps had no option but to follow the trail to the forests. Neither organized politically nor armed, all they had was their lives and nothing more. Many of them were not necessarily looking to fight: their number one priority was a chance of survival. Most of them failed. They blundered into German checkpoints or peasants who betrayed them to the Germans. Or they were murdered by anti-Semitic Polish civilians or by elite units from the Armia Krajowa. Or they strayed into swamps and died of hunger and cold. Occasionally, they even managed to find the partisans, but were turned away because they did not have the look of partisans and had brought no arms with them; or because their ranks included women and children, who the partisans were reluctant to let jeopardize their vital mobility; or because they were Jews, and the Soviet partisans included quite a few anti-Semites at decision-making levels.

The story was frequently the same with the armed groups from the ghetto resistance. They did not all enjoy such well-organized connections to Soviet commanders as the Vilna and Minsk resisters. Sometimes, they were simply stripped of their weapons and handed over, defenseless, to German mopping-up troops. Up until the end of 1943, the partisan movement in Poland and Lithuania, and even in certain parts of the Soviet Union, was nothing but a meaningless agglomeration of people, including petty criminals, looters, and ultra-right-wing anti-Semites. The situation was not clarified until some purposeful detachments arrived on the scene from the unoccupied territories of the Soviet Union, bringing substantial arms and equipment, and giving the movement an overhaul. But, for most Jews, that was already too late. By the end of 1943, all of the ghettos had been destroyed and many of the survivors had been murdered as they blundered through the forests.[499]

The CPSU Central Committee had issued a call to partisan warfare against the German invader as far back as July 18, 1941. But it was left at this for a long time, since, after Stalin's internal purges, barely enough experienced officers were left to staff the Red Army proper, let alone to staff the guerrilla war. May 30, 1942 saw the establishment of a general council for partisan warfare, under Stalin's supreme command. By that time there were already 10,000 pretty much wildcat partisans operating in the occupied Soviet territories, and these were now to be reorganized along military lines. The smallest independent unit was the detachment Otryad made up of between fifty and one hundred fighters of both sexes, and divided into sections and companies. Later, the detachments would be thrown together into brigades, and the latter, finally, into brigade groups. The big brigade groups in strategically important territories would make up divisions. However, experience showed that operating in smaller-scale units was a lot easier and more effective.[500]

The most important objective of partisan warfare was to draw as much of the German army as possible into counter-guerrilla operations, thereby weakening the front. In the latter half of 1943, the German army found itself compelled to pull 10 percent of its forces back from the eastern front for deployment against the partisans, who had become a serious menace to the occupation forces and their supply lines. Irregulars would attack German patrols, barracks, and arms dumps, sabotaging the power supply, capturing food and clothing shipments, and, above all, severing rail links. Frequently, German troop trains loaded with soldiers and munitions would run into mines and be blown up, or would find themselves derailed by tracks torn up by partisans.[501]

Partisan life, though, was not all attacks, raids, and sabotage. Day-to-day life was wearisome and no less dangerous than military activity. There were few guerrilla bases able to remain unmolested in one location: most camps had to be dismantled, removed, and reassembled after a short time. They marched for days at a time into swampy areas, far from forests that German troops had invaded, away from whatever region had become unsafe. Encampments consisted of small camouflaged huts, foxholes, and caves. In less secure areas, fighters had to sleep out in the open, during the summer months at any rate, so that they could move out immediately, without leaving behind any tell-tale evidence. In the swamp areas, the mosquitoes were a plague even worse than the lice. In winter, cold was a constant companion, since the smoke from a fire could have given them away. Women and men alike slept in their clothes, and it was rare for anyone to have a change of clothing. Daily food rations had to be procured, at grave risk, from the peasants in the local villages. If not offered willingly, food would be commandeered. If that was not possible, or if the peasants, as was frequently the case, had nothing even for themselves, they just had to go hungry. Any foraging operation was a wearisome chore, given that the targeted village had to lie far from the encampment, in order to throw potential pursuers off the scent. In winter, everything became even more complicated, since there was no avoiding tracks in the freshly fallen snow.[502]

Only the bigger brigades stationed in comparatively safer swamp areas could afford the luxury of setting up family camps: The survival of smaller units, operating in the more accessible forests near the big Polish cities hinged upon having unrestricted mobility.

However, family camps were the only hope of survival for fugitive and weaponless ghetto inhabitants. Jewish resisters persistently urged their Soviet allies to allow such camps, but were rarely successful in their pleas. Even where the topography allowed, commanders refused to be burdened with the civilian population. The demands of guerrilla tactics were not the only rationale behind this: there was also the matter of political considerations. Partisan groups and whole Red Army detachments alike were organized on the basis of nationality: Lithuanian units under the command of Lithuanian officers should fight in Lithuania, Ukrainian ones in the Ukraine, Polish-Belarussian ones in Polish Belarus, and so on. The Jews, with no territory of their own, and scattered through every one of these regions, were absorbed into the unit corresponding with their home regions. With only a few exceptions, their pleas to form ethic units of their own were turned down.[503]

Added to this, much of the population, from Lithuania to the Ukraine, was traditionally anti-Semitic, and the Soviet leadership was afraid that the numerous Jewish partisans of both sexes might create difficulties for the partisan movement as a whole. From a purely tactical viewpoint, such considerations were, of course, correct. Many peasants refused to supply food to Jews and, even worse, saw nothing wrong in reporting partisan groups with identifiably Jewish members to the Germans or local collaborationist police. Yet those very same peasants were ready to support the Soviet partisans, after Stalingrad at the latest, not so much out of sympathy as because they saw them as the victors-to-be. True, the presence of Jews in substantial numbers might generate dangers and hostility. Then again, the partisans themselves, and some of their officers, were not free of anti-Semitic sentiments and prejudices—so much so that, on occasion, the lives of Jewish fighters were in jeopardy from their own comrades. Not until the end of 1943 was there any improvement in the position of Jewish survivors among the partisan movement, when, as part of a structural overhaul, clear and specific orders were laid down regarding any hint of anti-Jewish conduct, and political commissars were dispatched from Moscow to protect Jewish rights.[504] In some places in Belarus, the Ukraine, and Lithuania, family camps were set up to accommodate the fugitive civilian population. Women with small children to look after, or who for some other reason were debarred from taking part in actual fighting, lived in these camps with the children and the elderly, under the protection of a small armed unit, and they saw to it that food and clothing were made available for the female and male fighters, they made shoes and uniforms, repaired weapons, and tended to the sick. They also saw to it that social life was as organized as possible, took care to create a climate of warmth and a homely atmosphere. Survivors speak of outright parties, nights of singing and poetry reading, joke-telling, and even the staging of plays.[505]

Whether the women arriving in a partisan camp were armed or unarmed, active ghetto fighters or plain civilians, they were told they could go to a family camp, or, if there was none, that they could work in the camp kitchens. It was not unusual for them to be stripped of their revolver—which they had risked their lives stealing from some German arms dump and smuggled back into the ghetto—on the grounds that women simply knew nothing about fighting, and the men were short of weapons. Thus, some women were required to perform the kitchen duties, their rightful role, before they could join an armed unit. Even the most active female fighters were not spared such sexist exploitation. Returning from some perilous operation, where they might well have blown up a train, attacked a gendarmerie post, or raided a munitions dump, they were still expected to make the meals and, if possible, darn the socks of their comrades-in-arms. Only in the larger guerrilla bases were housewifely duties clearly shared between special kitchen, clothing, and sewing details made up of women and men alike, sparing the women and men on active service from such chores.[506]

In spite of severe sanctions, there were also instances of rape, and many women found themselves obliged to take a trusted male comrade as their husband, sharing a bed with him in order to avoid molestation.[507] Sometimes, commanders and other high-ranking officers took a woman from their unit as a lover, whether she liked it or not—they even awarded women to other officers on their staff.[508] The bibliographical record (which I have been able to consult) tackles such problems only in passing, if at all. The surviving women fighters most likely to record their experiences, in written or oral form, were also the least likely to have something like this happen to them. No one would have dared allocate a Vitka Kempner, a Chenia Borowska, or a Chayke Grossman to anyone. These celebrated, tried, and tested resistance fighters never saw the inside of a field kitchen. They were just another man along on military operations, if not the actual leaders in charge. But there is one thing that they had to share with their less celebrated sisters: women had to try twice as hard. Rushka (it has not been possible to establish her surname), interviewed by Marie Syrkin during her research into surviving Jewish fighting women in Palestine, tells us that each individual woman felt answerable for her entire sex.[509] Each of them had to demonstrate continually that, as fighters, women were every bit as competent and dependable as men. None of them could afford the luxury of weakness or mistakes, since that would have had implications for all women.

Rushka recounts how, en route to a sabotage operation, she fell into a pond. This was in the middle of winter, and her waterlogged clothing froze to her skin. Her comrades urged her to turn back, dry off, and stay under cover, but Rushka refused. With her clothing turned into an icy carapace, she carried out the operation, placing explosives on the rail tracks and returning to camp. And she was not, by a long shot, the only one to act that way. Women were continually volunteering for the most difficult operations, uttering not one word when wounded, and barely any pausing for breath or rest between one operation and the next. In a speech delivered to a group of women workers in Tel Aviv, Rushka praised the performance of her former female comrades-in-arms:

> If, harking back, I start to consider the work we carried out, from the very first to the very last hour, my thoughts must always fly to the young women, many of them close friends with whom I had grown up, and with whom I shared this time fraught with dangers... I cannot think of a single aspect of our work that does not call to mind some young comrade. Let me tell you something about them. Above all, there is one thing I want you to know: these were not exceptional women. They were not especially educated women with special qualities. They were girls who had grown up working and, in that fashion, had gained in maturity, until they could live up to higher demands. Not one of them was exceptional. They all were. We were able to see how people excelled by carrying out their demanding and dangerous duties day after day. And it was precisely this that was most difficult: the fact that the work had to be done afresh day in and day out. That takes more courage than an act of heroism that lasts only a couple of minutes. Those young women were called upon daily to show their heroism and that is just what they did.[510]

The Germans were aware that there were women—Jewish women especially—fighting with the partisans. They would soon try to capitalize on this startling fact. V.A. Andreyev, who commanded a partisan unit in the Bryansk forests, recounts the story of Irena, a young woman of uncommon valor and zeal.[511] She had shown up at his unit one day, admitted to being Jewish, and asked to be taken on. She was put through the usual tests and came through with flying colors. The final test was to gun down a Wehrmacht commander. She had no problem getting hold of a gun: off she went, shooting the German from behind. The next day, the partisans learned that the commander was still alive. Irena had shot the wrong man—a subordinate officer who resembled his superior in build and appearance, and who had seemingly been planted, as a double, for protection. "Don't worry, it's one fascist less in any case," her comrades soothed the upset Irena. "The important thing is that got back alive." Partisan commander Andreyev says of the young girl fighter: "She was an important asset to our troops... She cleaned and ironed the men's clothes, did their laundry, sewed, and darned. She systematically and painstakingly learned how to handle all sorts of weapons, and missed no opportunity to participate in military operations. Thanks to her contacts in Vigonichi [a nearby town] she even managed to lay hands on ten rifles, several pistols, and flares in various colors for the battalion. Only once did she misstep. We were sitting around the fire. She was toying with some flares, when a green one caught fire and exploded over the camp, just as an unidentified aircraft was flying over the forest."[512]

But it wasn't a mistake at all. It was intentional. Irena was a German spy, and her cover would be blown, quite by accident, a short time later. Shalom Cholawski recounts a similar case. A young woman who claimed that her name was Marusya, and who passed herself off as a Soviet prisoner of war who had escaped from Minsk, presented herself to the partisans in Nesvizh. She, too, was accepted into their ranks. She gave herself away when she accepted a mission to procure arms, and returned with nothing less than a complete machine-gun that she simply could not have transported unaided. Irena and Marusya were not the only spies, posing either as Jewish or Russian women, that the German secret services planted among the partisans—which became yet another obstacle for women who were genuine. Women who came along later were treated with diffidence, as any one of them could be an enemy agent.[513]

The history of the Jewish partisan women remains largely unwritten. Only a few such women are known by name, but we do not know much about them. One of them was Zenia Eichenbaum, from Pultusk. She was fourteen years old when she fled to Slonim to escape the Germans. No sooner had the first partisan unit been set up in the forests around Volchi Nory than Zenia Eichenbaum joined it, working as a nurse to start with. She was part of 51 Group, a Jewish unit from the Shchors detachment, under the command of Fyodorovich, himself a Jew—which explains why he gave his approval to an all-Jewish unit. When she turned seventeen, Zenia refused to carry on acting as a nurse, wanting instead to become a fighter. As early as August 1942, she took part in the Kosovo attack, when 51 Group earned its reputation as one of the most successful units in the Belarus partisan movement. Fyodorovich had discovered that roughly 500 Jews still alive in Kosovo were scheduled for elimination on August 3. On August 2, along with his female and male fighters, he swooped down on the town to attack the German garrison, winning the battle and destroying the barracks. Three hundred of the Jewish inhabitants left with the partisans. The 200 who remained behind in the town were butchered the following day when the Germans recaptured it. 51 Group also earned a reputation as a special unit displaying exceptional dexterity and courage in sabotage operations against railway lines. One of its best and most indefatigable saboteurs was Zenia Eichenbaum. When her explosives section ran into a German patrol in August 1943, shortly after the battle of Kosovo, and her comrades wanted to back off immediately, young Zenia screeched at them: "Cowards! Where are you running to? Forward! Forward!" She assumed command and her unit swooped down on the German ranks, making such an impression that they took to their heels. On March 23, 1943, one day before the Red Army arrived, Zenia Eichenbaum was killed in a gun battle with retreating German soldiers. She was posthumously honored as a "Heroine of the Soviet Union."[514]

The Radom area was the theater of operations for the Levi Group, a unit of the Communist Gwardia Ludowa, made up of Polish Jews. One of the lionesses (*levi* meaning "lion" in Hebrew) was Zofia Jamajka. Zofia, who came from a Hasidic family background, was fourteen when the Germans occupied Warsaw. She had to quit school, and the students' Spartakus club she was a member of was disbanded. A short time after the initial chaos, the first antifascist leaflets circulated in the city and Zofia, excited by the fact that there were actually people who were not resigned to their fate, set about successfully reorganizing the Spartakus club. After the setting up of the ghetto, she was delegated to attend a school training cadres for the active struggle, and went on to become the commander of an armed underground cell. Initially, there was no thought of armed struggle, because the priority was simple survival under the insufferable conditions in the ghetto. Zofia Jamajka took over responsibility of a group of children for one of the autonomous residents' committees, set up a people's canteen catering for the young, and also completed her schooling—illegally, since Jews were strictly banned from studies. When the first contacts from the Gwardia Ludowa arrived in the ghetto to recruit fighters for their partisan unit, Zofia immediately stepped forward and was just as quickly accepted.

She received a course of training in partisan warfare, and was trained in the use of all sorts of weapons, and as a field nurse—the Communist cadre training compulsory for all, including men. Although she did all that was asked of her, and although she had enlisted as a volunteer and had achieved her ambition, Zofia now hesitated and asked to be allowed to spend a little more time in the city. If she left for the forest, her parents would have had to pay the price: anybody quitting the ghetto was leaving her kin behind as hostages. Zofia knew that her parents would be shot as part of a collective reprisal, once it was discovered that she was gone. Sentiment prevented her from taking that step and she stayed in the city. Zofia's dilemma was cruelly resolved in July 1942, when her parents were deported to Treblinka, along with another 300,000 ghetto inhabitants who fell victim to the first extermination drive.

With a handful of comrades of both sexes, Zofia Jamajka departed for the forest that August. They had not gone far when they ran into a checkpoint, were arrested, and soon found themselves on a cattle-truck bound for Treblinka. It looked as if the end was nigh. During the journey through the open countryside, the guards opened the truck doors to dump corpses overboard. Weakened and half-dead in the cramped, filthy, stifling cattle-trucks, many of the occupants died en route before reaching their destination in the gas chamber. Zofia played dead and let herself be tossed out of the truck with the other corpses. She came out of that all right. With neither papers nor contacts, Zofia had no option but to make her way back to Warsaw. For a time, she was able to hide out in the Aryan sector of the city, thanks to help from a female comrade: she was issued phony papers and learned how to pass as a Catholic. Once her Aryan persona had been perfected and she knew the Our Father and the Hail Mary backwards and forwards, once she knew when to stand and when to kneel in church, and once it had become second nature to make the sign of the cross anytime that she was shocked by anything, the Gwardia Ludowa placed her in charge of publishing *Gwardist*, its illicit newspaper. In September 1942, the Gestapo traced the presses and arrested Zofia Jamajka at work. Even so, she managed to talk her way out of it, claiming that she was a poor orphan girl who had come to the city looking for work as a cleaning lady. It had never even occurred to her that she was cleaning a Communist den. Her phony papers withstood scrutiny, and Zofia was freed from Pawiak prison after three months.

Again with the aid of a female comrade, she eventually managed to reach the forests and, in December, became a member of the Levi unit. At first, Zofia worked as a liaison between the region's different partisan groups before moving on to set up a reconnaissance unit and participate in sabotage operations. Eventually, she was appointed to a special section for the assassination of spies and agents. When the Levi Group attacked the town of Gowarczow in January 1943, and took over the city for five hours—destroying both the police station and the main barracks, and making off with a list of spies and Gestapo provocateurs—Zofia Jamajka was in the forefront of the fighting.

On February 9, 1943, a German anti-partisan unit entered the area where the Levi Group was operating and forced that fifty-strong group of lions and lionesses to fall back. Their retreat was covered by two of the group's men plus Zofia Jamajka, who had turned eighteen and was in charge of a machine-gun. She let the Germans get within twenty meters and then opened fire. The entire group was able to get away, except Zofia and her two helpers, who died in a hail of gunfire. In April 1963, on the twentieth anniversary of the Warsaw ghetto uprising, the Polish government posthumously awarded Zofia Jamajka the Virtutis Militaris, one of the highest of its military honors.[515]

In the Vilna ghetto resistance, the FPO had had more women activists than was the norm—and in unusually high-ranking positions, at that. This did not change when, following the destruction of the ghetto, the FPO threw in its lot with the Soviet partisans. One of the FPO's leaders, Joseph Glazman, had quit Vilna in July 1943 and joined the partisans in the Narocz forest under commander Markov. With leave from Markov, the influx from Vilna set up a separate Jewish unit that they dubbed Mes't (Vengeance). A few weeks later, Markov disbanded Mes't: there were too many people in the group who had no military background, something he could not countenance in his battalion. The fighters among them were reassigned to a Belarussian detachment and the rest had to serve in an unarmed quarter-master unit. The ultimate implication of Markov's orders was that many of the Jewish combatants—particularly the women—were left without arms. They protested vehemently and some wept with anger. "We didn't come here to hide but to fight," they declared. "We paid a high price to get our weapons and you cannot steal them from us as if it were nothing! We proved our mettle as fighters well before we came to these forests!"[516] It did them no good. A few days later, tens of thousands of Germans started to comb through the forests. The partisans decided to withdraw: however, the commander in charge let only the Belarussians, and those Jews whose arms had not been confiscated, go with them. The rest were to try to conceal themselves. Anyone trying to join those leaving was deterred at gun-point. Desperate, the unarmed stragglers wandered through the swamps searching for somewhere safe they might go to ground. Over half of them fell into German hands; only one woman from Glazman's old unit survived. Only after this tragedy did Markov, who had returned to the Narocz area with his units, decide to absorb Jewish fighters of both sexes into his ranks unconditionally. He had some of the surviving children flown out to the unoccupied territories of the Soviet Union, where they awaited the end of the war.[517]

The band of FPO combatants led by Aba Kovner and Chenia Borowska set up an exclusively Jewish partisan unit in the Rudniki forests just thirty-five kilometers from Vilna. This group expanded rapidly until it numbered 250 women and men split into three battalions: Mstitel (The Avenger), Za pobedu (On to victory!), and Smert Faschizmu (Death to Fascism). Yiddish was the battalions' language of command, and their battle anthems were also in Yiddish: the group considered custody and preservation of Jewish culture as one its most important objectives. Its songs, such as *"Sog nit kejnmol as du gejst dem letztn weg"* (Never Say You're Off on Your Final Journey), spread beyond the borders of Lithuania, and are still being sung to this day. The FPO partisans also set up a family camp for refugees from Vilna and other Lithuanian cities, while the fighters of both sexes got on with their work. They mounted one their first spectacular operations in Vilna. Four partisans, including Vitka Kempner, contacted Sonia Madaysker, secured help from her underground Communist group, and carried out their plan by blowing up the power station and the city's water supply. The operation was a complete success. Everything in the city being brought to a standstill, and the German occupiers were confronted with absolute chaos. On its return journey, the sabotage group also freed sixty people from the Kailis labor camp and brought them back to the partisan camp. Meanwhile, their numbers had grown to 350 fighters, so many that a fourth battalion was set up, taking the name Borba (Struggle).

In the Rudniki area, it was hard to mount economic operations since the Germans kept the area under strict control and the rural population displayed an extremely anti-Semitic attitude. Every time they went in search of food, partisans ran the risk of skirmishes with German gendarmes or villager self-defense groups. This did not stop them from pursuing their aims—successfully. They sabotaged roads, bridges, and railway lines, blew up power stations, and repeatedly severed telephone links. Despite their tremendous effectiveness—or perhaps because of it— Yurgis, the commander-in-chief of the Lithuanian partisan movement, decided at the end of 1943 that the four battalions could not remain exclusively Jewish. Lithuanian partisans were appointed to them, non-Jews were placed in positions of command, and their staffs were reshuffled to incorporate Jews and non-Jews alike. Even so, the FPO fighters of both sexes managed to preserve their unit's Jewish character: both the Soviet and the Lithuanian comrades wound up singing anthems in Yiddish just like the Jews themselves.[518] A number of these partisans survived the war. Following the liberation, they emigrated to Israel and devoted themselves to documenting their struggles and their lives in the ghetto resistance and in the forests. The women also, like Vitka Kempner and Roza Korczak, spoke out, and thereby prevented the role of women in these struggles from sliding entirely into oblivion.

Niuta Tejtelbojm

"Little Flaxen-Haired Wanda."

The girl was quite pretty. And unbelievably young. Those long blond tresses—she looked like an Aryan woman straight out of a picture book. Even her flowery head scarf looked the part. She asked for the office of one of the higher-ranking officials. Right, lucky guy...

The men guarding the Gestapo building in Warsaw flashed her a complicit grin. The young woman—she couldn't have been more than sixteen—returned their grins and lowered her gaze, somewhat embarrassed. She stepped inside the building, made for the appointed room, knocked on the door, went inside, and stood there, shyly, on the threshold. The Gestapo official stood up, quite startled, and lightheartedly called out to her: "Don't tell me they have Loreleis in these parts too?" He never knew just how right he was in his error. "Lorelei" drew her revolver from her purse, took aim, and fired. The young woman then stepped out of the office, calmly shutting the door behind her, flashed the guard at the entrance another sparkling smile, and went on her way.[519]

The colleagues of the dead Gestapo officer did not have to unduly rack their brains to work out who had carried out this daring assassination. It was one of the terrorists most sought after by the Generalgouvernement, whose wanted poster hung in every government building, a price of 150,000 zloty on her head. Since the Germans had no idea what her real name was, she was being sought as "Little flaxen-haired Wanda."

Little Wanda's real name was Niuta Tejtelbojm, and she was twenty-four. Her hair was long enough that she could sit on it, and it never entered her mind to have it cut, since it made her look a lot younger than she was—and her enemies were always taken in by her luxuriant "Aryan" tresses. Niuta Tejtelbojm was born into a Hasidic family in Lodz in 1918. She attended a Polish secondary school, but rebelled against her strictly religious upbringing and joined an illegal

Communist school cell. She turned into one of its most active members, and her male and female colleagues used to describe her as "the firebrand." When the group was uncovered, Niuta was expelled from school, but still managed to enroll at Warsaw University where she studied History and Psychology. She dropped out in 1939, when her studies were rudely interrupted: the Germans had invaded Poland, and, a year later, Niuta Tejtelbojm was a captive of the ghetto like the rest of Warsaw's Jews.

At this point, she joined the Jewish wing of the PPR. From day one, she lived up to her nickname "firebrand." For a start, she taught herself how to use a gun, then trained her own cell, before finally taking it upon herself to educate a larger number of women in the secret arts of shooting and bomb-making. Some of these women would go on to become the most active fighters with the ZOB. One of her pupils would later recall Niuta's classes: "Nobody could have dreamt that, a short time ago, she herself had known nothing about weapons... And nobody equalled her skill at smuggling folk out of the ghetto and weapons and hand grenades in."[520]

In August 1942, the Gwardia Ludowa had set up its first support bases in the eastern districts of the Voivodia in Warsaw. One of their organizers was Niuta, who had joined the Gwardia Ludowa in the interim. Now she was in charge of contacts among the partisans, the ghetto, and the Aryan sector of the city—as well as smuggling people out of the ghetto and weapons in, as her pupil indicated. When the Germans mounted their first big extermination operation in July 1942, Niuta Tejtelbojm was ordered to move to the Aryan sector of the city to command a special resistance unit. She became a terrorist and adopted the name Wanda.

On October 8, 1942, Wanda's unit blew up the Warsaw-bound railroad at seven separate points. The occupying forces retaliated by hanging fifty prisoners, thirty-five of them Communists, and burying them in the Jewish cemetery: Jews and Communists, they made no distinction. On October 24, the Gwardia Ludowa took its revenge for the killing of the hostages. In a concerted operation, three details from Wanda's special unit attacked three targets simultaneously: the presses of the collaborationist daily newspaper *Nowy Kurier Warszawski*; the Café Mitropa in the central railway station, where they killed six German officers and wounded another fourteen; and the German café-club at the junction of Jerozolimski-Aleje and the Nowy Swiat, which was attacked with hand grenades, killing a further four German officers and injuring another eight. A couple of weeks later, the group carried out a hold-up of the Municipal Savings Bank in broad daylight, and vanished with upwards of a million zloty, without firing a single shot. The Gestapo machinery was mobilized, but there seemed no way of catching "little flaxen-haired Wanda." Quite the opposite. She lashed out again at the ranks of her pursuers. This time, she sought her target, a Gestapo officer, in his own home. When he saw the young woman standing before him wielding a revolver, the Aryan hero hid under his eiderdown in a panic. Wanda shot through the eiderdown feathers and, on this occasion too, she hit the mark.

Meanwhile, the Germans had entered the ghetto and the final extermination operation had begun. The ZOB, the Jewish fighting organization, rose in armed revolt. On the night of the first day, the leadership of the People's Guard were still debating how to assist the ghetto from the outside. After consultation with the ZOB, they decided to attack one of the gunnery emplacements that was keeping the fighters outside the ghetto at bay. This operation was entrusted to Wanda's special unit. On April 20, 1943, during a skirmish around the brush factory, a German heavy machine-gun emplacement opened up on the insurgents from Swietojerska Street. At 6:45 PM, Wanda's detail attacked this position, knocked out the machine-gun, and killed its crew: two Waffen-SS soldiers and two Polish policemen.

The Germans stepped up the hunt for "little flaxen-haired Wanda" even further. Wanda's comrades tried to persuade her to go to ground for a while or, at the very least, to take to the safety of the forest. Wanda refused to entertain the idea and carried on fighting. One day, as she was making her way home in July 1943, the Gestapo lay in wait for her in her digs. She tried to swallow poison, but failed. They tortured her for a period of days before she was finally executed. Shortly before her death, she managed to get a message to her comrades on the outside, male and female, reassuring them that she had named no one.

In the spring of 1945, on the second anniversary of the Warsaw ghetto uprising, Niuta Tejtelbojm was posthumously awarded the Grunwald Cross, one of the highest Polish military decorations.

Roza Robota

"I know what I've done and what lies in store for me."

The train carrying the Ciechánow Jews was bound straight for the ramp in Birkenau. Twenty-one-year-old Roza Robota knew the fate that awaited her and her companions-in-suffering. She was a member of the left-wing Zionist Pioneers of Hashomer Hatzair, and had assisted with organizing the resistance movement prior to the demolition of the ghetto. The Germans occupied Ciechánow within three days of their invasion of Poland, and now they were shipping the town's Jewish inhabitants to the gas chambers.[521]

While Roza's parents were being prodded towards the showers with the bulk of the deportees, SS men picked out Roza and a couple of other women: they would serve as slave laborers before going to their deaths. Roza was assigned a job in the garment section, while the rest of the women were forced to work for the Weichsel-Union-Werken, a Krupp subsidiary where some a thousand prisoners manufactured fuses for grenades. The women worked in the so-called gunpowder pavilion, the most insalubrious and strictly monitored section.

Roza Robota had not been in Birkenau long when she was contacted by the camp resistance. She was known as a reliable and courageous individual, so she was entrusted with one of the most dangerous missions: to secure explosives for the bombs needed for the planned uprising. On instructions from Israel Gutman and Joshua Leifer, two Jewish members of the resistance leadership, Noah Zabludowicz explained everything to Roza—whom he had known from Ciechánow—and asked if she was prepared to accept this mission. Roza Robota immediately answered that she was. At night, after work, Roza met secretly with the other women from Ciechánow, spoke to them about the planned revolt, and sought their assistance: they were to pilfer explosive materials during working hours and smuggle them out of the plant during the night shifts, which were not so closely monitored, for transmission to Roza.

The women were delighted to be able to do something, so it did not take much to win them over. "We can get hold of it and it is up to us alone," said one of them, Ester Wajsblum. "Thousands will perish, but perhaps somebody can be saved. It is incumbent upon us to create the conditions for a mass break out... We cannot go like sheep to the slaughter. We must put up a fight."[522]

From then on, twenty female Jewish slave laborers from the gunpowder pavilion at Weichsel-Union-Werken smuggled tiny pots of explosives out of the plant, night after night. They concealed them between tin plates or in the knots of their head scarves, undetected by the guards. Roza gathered up these nightly deliveries and passed them on to a male comrade from Ciechánow, after which they passed through a series of hands before reaching their destination with Filatov, a Russian prisoner of war and explosives expert in charge of assembling the bombs. Something always went wrong, forcing them to put off the uprising. The "special command" prisoners assigned to the work detail in the crematoria, ran out of patience. They were in the most desperate position. Every day, they crammed tons of corpses into the ovens and could endure the job no longer. Some of them had already taken their own lives. Their last remaining hope was that, by means of an uprising, they might at least spare the 400,000 Hungarian Jews who had arrived in Birkenau aboard one of the latest transports. When even this hope evaporated, they decided to take matters into their own hands, independently of the forever misfiring plans of the resistance leadership. On October 7, 1944, they revolted, killing a number of SS men and managing at least to blow up one of the four crematoria, leaving it permanently incapacitated. They then attempted to break out, but perished, every one of them, in a hail of gunfire.

The political department of the camp SS immediately opened its inquiries: the explosives trail inevitably led back to the Weichsel-Union-Werken. Three weeks later, having already arrested several female workers and released them again, they arrested three women from the gunpowder pavilion: Ester Wajsblum, Ella Gertner, and Regina Saphirstein—plus, for reasons unknown, Roza Robota, who was still working in the garment section. All four were savagely tortured, but the SS were particularly vicious towards Roza Robota, whom they believed—correctly—to have direct connections with the resistance. Day after, day she was taken to the basement of the feared Block 11, the

Auschwitz torture chamber. When she was only a heap of bloodied flesh unable even to walk, two female warders were brought in to continue her torture. Members of the camp resistance, with whom Roza had been in direct contact, prepared themselves for the worst. They knew that no one could withstand this torment. But Roza held out. Noah Zabludowicz, her old comrade from Ciechánow, persuaded Jacob, the *kapo* of Block 11, to let him into Roza's cell. Jacob got the guard drunk and took Noah down into the basement. Noah Zabludowicz, who survived Auschwitz, would later recount their meeting:

> I had the privilege of being the last person to see Roza a few days before she was executed. By night...I entered the bunker of Block 11 and saw the cells and the darkened corridors. I heard the screams of the condemned and shuddered in the depths of my being. Jacob escorted me to Roza's cell... Once my eyes had become used to the darkness, I was able to make out a figure draped in rags, stretched out on the cement floor. Its head turned to me. I was scarcely able to recognize her. She described the sadistic methods employed by the Germans during interrogations. The human being did not exist who could withstand that. She told me that she had taken the full blame, and that nobody else was in danger. She had betrayed no one. I attempted to console her, but she would not listen to me. "I know what I have done and what lies in store for me," she replied. All she asked was that the comrades should keep up the work. "Dying is easier," she said, "when one knows that the others will carry on."[523]

On January 6, 1945, six days before the liberation of Auschwitz by the Red Army, all four women were hanged in the Appellplatz (Parade Ground). Ester Wajsblum's sister, Hana, one of the slave laborers in the gunpowder pavilion, would later tell of her execution:

> They gave the order to "Fall in!" But it was only five o'clock in the morning... Suddenly, my eyes were drawn to the space between Blocks 4 and 5. What was behind this instruction?... Standing there, half asleep, I suddenly caught sight [of my sister]... Right after that, we heard the order: "Union forwards! Gunpowder section, one pace to

the front!"...I raised my head. I could make out the gallows a short distance away. I realized what was afoot... A silence descended upon the square. I could hear the quickened breathing, the suppressed sighs and tears. They began their walk. Heads held high, eyes staring forward into the distance, toward freedom. Freedom lost. The clatter of the stools as they were pulled out from under them. Their dying.[524]

The Road to Armed Resistance

"What else was there for me to do?"

1

"Why did I do it? What else was there for me to do? It was the only thing I could do!" That sentence, that seemingly banal statement linking Fifí Fernández de Velasco Pérez of Madrid to Truus Menger of Verhuizen, Dina Krischer of Nancy, Zala Sadolsek of Lobning, Gusta Drenger of Krakow, and Dora Goldkorn of Warsaw, linking the living and the dead, this statement flies in the face of everything normally said on this subject in the Federal Republic of Germany. The vast majority of those not directly affected, in Germany, by Nazi persecution, are unanimous: they knew nothing. Or if they did know something, there was nothing they could have done. Their cry of "What could we have done?" is, thus, at odds with "What else was there for us to do?"

The argument that—given the strength and perfection of Nazi controls—it was impossible to fight against them, seems more reasonable, more comprehensible than the "Despite everything!" stance. What was it that impelled people, impelled women, to embark upon a struggle with no prospect of success—from the point of view of anyone in her right mind—against an opponent outnumbering them a thousand-to-one? What was it that induced them to break with their lives, their education, their role, with everything that was regarded as normal in a woman, in order to continually risk their lives by stealing weapons, planting bombs, and shooting people? What induced them to walk away from their parents, their homes, their livelihoods, their familiar surroundings, in order to spend sleepless nights sheltering in some trench, enduring hunger and cold in some snow-blanketed partisan encampment, or fleeing like a cornered animal from one underground hideout to the next?

Most of these women were very young. Most of them had some history of political activity prior to the outbreak of the war. Many of them came from working-class backgrounds and, from a very early age, had known injustice and poverty. They had also grown up with minor demonstrations, strikes, and resistance. Many of them were Jewish and, thus, very personally affected by the new circumstances, the new order. Hardly any of them came from good bourgeois families, and, if they did, their world was abruptly and brutally shattered by the intrusion of those carrying out the Final Solution.

In the life of a woman in the 1930s and 1940s, there was no place for political activities, fighting, and comradeship with strange men. Whether she lived in Madrid, Amsterdam, or Warsaw, and no matter whether her origins were working-class or bourgeois, a young woman was raised to marry, have children, and rear them. She had a reputation to look out for, had to obey her father and be guided by her mother. There was nothing beyond family and home for her to take an interest in. In the book that he dedicated to these people, *Das ostjüdische Antlitz* (The Face of the Eastern Jew), Arnold Zweig, who was stationed in Lithuania as a First World War soldier and who witnessed the lives of the eastern Jews, wrote of the lot of the married women: "The world of books ceased to exist; the world of belief became their reality and compulsory fare; she had learned childcare as a girl, when she had to carry and look after the youngest of the family."[525]

Yet Zweig also notes that the younger women were turning their backs on this lifestyle. He made the acquaintance of one young woman who declined to accept society as it stood, and whose dreams were of revolution. The young people cited by Arnold Zweig, the onlooker, were not the offspring of the Jewish proletariat, but daughters and sons from good homes, students working towards their baccalaureate. These young Jews, according to Arnold Zweig, modelled themselves, not upon "the conquistadors and discoverers, with their legacy of slavery, murder, avarice, and all manner of injustices," nor upon the "rather phantasmagorical and insensitive Maccabees of history," but rather upon "revolutionaries in the protracted struggle for a life of dignity for human beings upon this earth, and involved in the fight underway in Russia. All of the murdered, the disappeared, the outlawed, and the fugitives, all active by word-of-mouth or with weapons in hand. And, when an open, serene faced girl...tight-lipped and head held high...gazed

upon all the pictures of socialist students, those open, serene faces...
and closed mouths; was it perhaps not inevitable that they would make
this resolution in their hearts: I undertake to live that life and do my
damnedest to be that way, too?"[526]

That flame was still burning in these women's daughters. They
were still in their girlhood when the Polish Jews found themselves persecuted in pogrom after pogrom; they had sampled anti-Semitism in what
was—up until that point—its most extreme form. The security and privi-
leges that their mothers had chosen to turn away from had long since
disappeared. It was the working-class girls who were pointedly affected
by the persecution, discrimination, and pogroms. Even so, knowledge
of injustice, be it third- or first-hand, is not automatically grounds for
rebelling. Especially not in a girl's case. But the image of the sheltered
daughter had long since died as a stereotype in the working-class areas
of Vilna and Warsaw. Daughters of the Jewish proletariat were already
putting in twelve or thirteen hours' work in factories and workshops:
what little money they earned as seamstresses or cleaners was sorely
needed at home. In the workplace, they passed around leaflets. Talk of
a strike was passed from person to person and, one day, there they were
in the crowd at some banned demonstration, running from the police,
finding places to hide, and learning when to keep their mouths closed.
Young female students would get wind of a cell at their high school
and began to watch for tell-tale gestures, unaccustomed expressions,
and leaflets surreptitiously left behind in the schoolyard. They would
indicate their interest and, one fine day, would be accosted by a fellow
student, who would invite them to go along with him to some meeting
of the Spartakus group or the left-wing Zionists' Pioneers. For a girl or
young woman, political activity was the only passport away from the
restricted, mundane rhythms of a predetermined woman's lot. In the
Communist Party's youth organization, the Bund's or the Hehalutz
movement's youth wings she would be among like-minded comrades
indisposed to accept the fate reserved for their class, their people, or
their sex. Instead of love stories, they would be reading the socialist classics; instead of looking after younger siblings or gutting herrings, these
young women could be debating a complete overhaul of their society.
The responsibility they were taking upon their shoulders was no longer
confined to changing the baby's diapers or keeping their hair shiny.
Now, they were part of the movement fighting to overthrow capitalist

rule, or to construct a new, classless society in Palestine. And it was partly up to them whether this dream would become a reality—mostly particularly up to them, their talents, their commitment, and their courage. "The day I was able to reestablish lost contact with my Spartakus group was one of the happiest days in my hard, tragic ghetto life," writes the Communist and ZOB fighter Dora Goldkorn, in her *Erinnerungen an dem Aufstand im Warschauer Ghetto* (Memoirs of the Warsaw Ghetto Uprising). "My whole being ached to be doing something."[527]

"Firebrand" is what her Spartakus comrades used to call young Niuta Tejtelbojm. When she suddenly found herself trapped inside the ghetto, her first reaction was to take up arms. She trained herself militarily and her next step was to pass on her recently acquired expertise to other young women.

The lives of the young women and men from the left-wing Zionist youth organizations also underwent a radical transformation. They had been working to build something, to create something, to make a contribution to a new life. The tasks that now fell to them spelled destruction and death. Gusta Drenger, from the liberal Zionist Akiva, is also writing on behalf of the others when she states in her *Tagebuch der Justyna* (Justyna's Journal):

> My God! Create? Destroy, destroy, and destroy again whatever the strength left in these young muscles would allow. For destruction was the only power they had left now. The only thing still worth a candle. Everything else would pass: only their destruction would endure. It was a paradox with few equals. The young and the able-bodied, with the potential to build new worlds, the ones who had for years, on a daily basis, been laying the foundations of belief in a well-rounded humanity, now had to make bloodshed, harrying activity, sabotage, rubble, destruction, and annihilation life's crowning achievement.[528]

They had been forced into this by the most inconceivable destruction, the most mind-boggling blood-letting, the systematic extermination of their entire people. The prospects before them were to confront death with silent resignation, or to use their own death to put a wrench in the works of a slick murder machine. Further degradation and torment, just to extend one's life of deportation after deportation by a couple of weeks or months, only to end one's days in the crematoria ovens of Chelmno, Treblinka, or Auschwitz, was too high a price to pay. Fleeing from one apartment to another; chasing after a labor permit; passing starving, begging children in the street day after day; listening to the screams of those driven mad by so much wretchedness; watching the murder of one's loved ones; seeing the killers smash small children's heads against a wall until their brains were spilled on the ground; hearing of mothers who had drowned their own children, lest they give away a hiding place with their crying; knowing that your own parents were at the embarkation point, waiting to be loaded on to trucks for deportation; surviving the slave labor, the hunger, and the disease—that was a life not worth living, a life on one's knees, a slave's life. Better to die, but to die fighting. That their fight might somehow succeed was almost more than they dared hope. "Victory," wrote Noemi Szac-Wajnkranc in her memoirs, *Im Feuer vergangen* (Vanished into the Flames), "could be one thing only: holding out for as long as possible and killing as many Germans as possible... Die! This is for my mother, my father, our children! I take aim at you! God grant that this bullet strikes home!"[529]

In the film *The Female Partisans of Vilna*, Vitka Kempner says, "We felt as if our lives were already forfeit. That simplified things for us."[530] And her comrade-in-arms, Chaya Lazar, mentions their meager arsenal— the light-bulb filled with explosives, the Molotov cocktail, "my very own hydrogen bomb, the most prized possession I could ever have owned."[531] Chayke Grossman, Vilna fighter and organizer of the Bialystok ghetto uprising, told American journalist Maria Syrkin, "We knew that our death did not spell the end, that our demise would become a symbol under which a new generation might be educated. That was what was on our minds in the ghettos. It was our Torah."[532]

Every one of these women was convinced in her heart of hearts that what she was doing was right and necessary, the only dignified, humane option. These sixteen-, seventeen-, and nineteen-year-old girls were not following in the footsteps of a fiancé or husband. They were not the appendages of some political activist, driven to activism because of the activism of their husbands. This decision was their own, this course was their own. And, for all their conviction, for all the contempt in which they held their own lives, it was a hard course.

Even though no man had a hand in their decision (or in deterring it), even if they had no children to be abandoned, there was still their parents. These young women felt great love, tenderness, and responsibility where their parents were concerned. The deportation of parents was what prompted many of them to finally take up arms. And those whose fathers and mothers were still living tortured themselves with the thought—the realistic thought—that they might be putting them in danger through their activities. Zofia Jamajka had already fulfilled all of the conditions required to go off with the partisans as a fully trained fighter and political officer, but stayed behind in Warsaw. She was afraid that the Germans might notice she had disappeared from the ghetto, and make her parents pay. Not until her mother and father were finally deported did Zofia make up her mind to take the trail into the forest. Gusta Drenger broke all of the rules of conspiracy in order to rescue her parents from the Krakow ghetto when the big drive began. Chayke Grossman took the risk of reporting late to her post when the fighting in the Bialystok ghetto started—an unforgivable breach for a fighter of her standing—so as to bid her elderly mother goodbye. In her memoirs, Dora Goldkorn describes one such tragedy, played out along pretty much similar lines in many families:

> One fine day, the father of our comrade Halinka Rochmann came up to the loft. The comrades standing guard outside our "factory" [a hideout where bombs and Molotov cocktails were made] spotted him and allowed him to pay a visit... Mr Rochmann [asked] his daughter tearfully to come home. "I'm all alone," he implored her, "like a hermit. Come with me. I have enough money left to save us both and settle in the Aryan sector." We could see that Halinka was in the throes of a difficult and painful tug-of-war. Alone, she was at war with herself and deeply pained. Even so, she resolutely refused her father's solicitations. "My life no longer belongs to you, Father, but to all of them" was Halinka's answer to her father's pleas. We went over to Halinka's desperate father and told him about how our life was now, about out tasks and our aims. We did all we could to comfort him in his wretchedness with friendly words. Mr Rochmann was, frankly, moved. He gave us a substantial sum of money, kissed his daughter goodbye, and left her with the words: "Take care of yourself, daughter. May God watch over you and help you along your life's new path."

Mr. Rochmann never saw his daughter again. He was a pious man and a very loving father. Before he left, he wished us heartfelt success in our work. Halinka was on the wracked with emotion the entire time, but valiantly held it all in until he left.[533]

Noemi Szac-Wajnkranc, who had made repeated unsuccessful attempts to rescue her parents from the Warsaw ghetto, subsequently discovered that her mother had died during the uprising.

I couldn't think about anything except my beloved mother who was scared of a piece of eggshell in her pancake, scared of dogs and scared of the sight of a gun, who had exhorted me a dozen times over before I left home, "Watch out for cars and trams!" and who took every setback suffered by me or my father as a catastrophe. That same mother was the first one to reach out to pick up a hand grenade, and the woman who said, "Work for the cause. Better to die by bullet, and not in the [gas] chambers anyway!"[534]

Julia Manzanal, Fifí Fernández de Velasco Pérez, and Rosario Sánchez, all of them militia women with whom I have conversed, had grown up in working-class barrios. Every one of them had been politicized well before the outbreak of civil war, and had been more or less actively involved in the Unified Socialist Youth (which was, in effect, Communist). Being still young girls, it was up to them to contribute to the family budget. They worked as seamstresses in factories and as street-sellers. At the age of fourteen, Julia, whose mother was separated, had already assumed the mantle of the head of the family. She loved her mother and still speaks of her with admiration and tenderness. Rosario's father, and Fifí's, were left-wing activists; not that they encouraged their daughters to get involved politically, but nor did they put any obstacles in their way when they made up their own minds.

Fifí was a rebel from a very early age, marauding around town with her brother, only to find that only she, as a girl, faced punishment for this. She kicked up a stink because the men of the family were served bigger portions than the women. She taught herself—surreptitiously— how to drive. In the Party youth organization, she was at last able to do everything that girls were forbidden: arrive at her own opinion and express it in public; stop putting up with injustices and fight them instead; and, yes, handle guns. Going off to the front was, as far as she was concerned, merely putting into practice everything that she had learned and practiced with great enthusiasm. It was also a chance to get out ridiculous dresses and take long, determined strides in men's trousers; to move freely and step outside the hated girlish role; to stop being treated like a tomboy, but rather as a *compañera* among *compañeros*.

Working in a factory and having family obligations, Julia had managed to stifle her yearnings for a bohemian lifestyle to some extent. She was what we today would describe as a social butterfly, flitting from bar to bar, dressed in the latest fashions and flirting with men. But she quickly discovered that a young woman had to pay a price for this sort of behavior. She was forever being pestered, subjected to sexual overtures, and even threats from men. She fought back and was outraged by the misunderstandings caused by her love of liberty and life of emotions. A young working-class woman who did not abide strictly by society's moral code was fair game. Once in the Communist Party youth organization, she learned there were other ways of breaking out of a monotonous and restrictive normality. Julia learned socialist theory and military skills: "I was so happy back then," she says to this day. She relished her man's uniform and wore her cap at a rakish angle.

Rosario was ambitious, not willing to work in the fields or stay in the village as a maid to her family. She wanted to learn a little and become a seamstress, but she also wanted to learn to type, do accounting, and get a broad education. In order to do that, she went directly to the capital city. Her parents let her go, even though they knew that the school she had applied to was a Communist Party training center. Rosario, who was rather aloof from politics, due to her father's fanatical behavior (he loved making an exaggerated public show of his republican beliefs), became politicized very gradually and tentatively. However, when the militiamen arrived at the school to recruit volunteers for the front, she was the first to raise her hand. She may have had doubts about their accepting girls, but not for a second did she have any doubts about what she herself wanted.

These girls were absolutely clear about the legitimacy and necessity of fighting fascists. They themselves had pushed for revolution and wanted to help effect a root and branch change in society and do away with all of injustices that had been their fate ever since childhood. They were well aware of their place and status. They could have just as easily held that status in the rearguard; they could have stuck to making food, stitching uniforms, collecting money, and tending the wounded. But that would have meant carrying on with the tiresome, routine, girlish existence, and ultimately, that would have amounted to their doing as their mothers had done—which is precisely what they were not willing to do. Going to the front, fighting with a weapon in hand was their only chance of effecting a radical change to their lives, even at the risk of those very same lives. These girls—Julia, Fifí, and Rosario—were caught up in the fight against fascism, not merely in their capacity as disciplined, politically aware Communists, cognizant of where their duty lay. They were not just doing it for the cause, but also for their own sakes—even though they may not have realized it then and might refuse to acknowledge it these days. They were grabbing their chance to enter forbidden territory, to shrug off the strait-jacket of their womanly lot, to gauge their own strength, and act.

Johanna Sadolsek, Zala during her partisan days, grew up in a family of women. She never knew her father, her grandfather was old and ailing, and her brother was away at the seminary. With help from Zala and an aunt, her mother and grandmother, between them, worked their small, heavily-mortgaged farm. Poverty, hard work, and discrimination left their mark on the teenaged Zala. In stocking feet—because she had no shoes—little Zala would trudge the long road to school, where she not only learned how to read and write, but also that the tongue with which she had been raised, Slovenian, was inferior, just as she herself was as a member of a scorned and oppressed ethnic group. She was forced to speak German and punished for any mistakes she might make in that unfamiliar tongue. Arriving home, where the tax collector might well have impounded their last remaining hen, she had to start to work immediately. At the age of seventeen, Zala formally took charge of the farmstead and became a peasant woman, being obliged to marry in order to do so. Nobody was interested in her feelings on the subject. Her workload was not reduced: indeed, it increased and, when her husband was called up, the entire responsibility fell upon Zala's shoulders. Yet her husband had—secretly—been politically active, and Zala had, for the first time, discovered that life as it stood did not necessarily have to be accepted.

Zala's marriage had not cost her independence: as the owner of a farm, she was still the boss and, as a farmer, it was almost impossible for her to change her job. Even so, she had become a more aware person, more interested in what was going on in the world outside her own potato patch. Contrary to her grandfather, who had swallowed the Nazi propaganda that poor farmers would have their debts relieved, Zala distrusted the Nazis, whose local representatives she had known, prior to the German annexation of Austria, as vitriolic enemies of the Slovene population. She monitored the behavior of the new (old) masters very closely and, with a mixture of curiosity and sympathy, listened to the rumors about Tito's Liberation Army, which had recently, it seemed, started to operate in Carinthia. Though still somewhat scared by these partisans, she realized—as did most Carinthian Slovenes—that these were her people. When she finally had her first encounter with them, she did not hesitate for a moment. The partisans needed help? Yes, of course, Zala would help them. The partisans wanted to talk to Zala? Zala answered their call. The partisans wanted Zala to mobilize the other women, and take charge of political and logistical matters? Zala was ready to do it. She reacted to her recruitment as if she had spent her whole life waiting for this moment. She was well aware that the fascists were her enemies. It was a matter of acute concern to her that the fascists meant to drive out the Slovene population, so she expected them to come looking for her and her family any day. Zala had it from reliable sources what the fascists did with the prisoners in the concentration camps, and this only fuelled her anger. There was only one thing that she had never previously imagined: that it was possible to fight back and beat this all-powerful enemy. And that was precisely what the partisans guaranteed.

There was nothing that could have stopped Zala after that. Especially now that she knew who her fellow-travellers were going to be. The female and male fighters of the Liberation Army were no strangers. Her own neighbor was one of them, the son of the farmer next door. And there were women in Tito's army. The group with which Zala started her fight against the Nazis was made up exclusively of women: her friends, neighbors, her sister-in-law. Added to the urge to do something, no doubt, there was the comfort of knowing and being able to trust her fellow-fighters, female and male alike. Risking her life on a daily basis now struck her as quite normal, an almost natural next step. She did not look upon herself as a heroine, merely as somebody doing what was expected in such matters. To end up swapping illegal leafleting for a gun was equally unremarkable. The Germans had discovered her, and she had managed to escape their clutches, so she naturally switched from covert to overt struggle, from logistical missions in the rearguard to an armed unit in the mountains. It never even occurred to her to consider going into hiding in the homes of friends or relatives, as others had done, and wait there for the war to end. Having to leave her child behind was terrible, but something she could get over. Zala knew that she could rely wholeheartedly on her mother. She would look after the boy, keep the farm running, and, as ever, carry on bringing food, clothing, and bandages to the partisans. Nothing, Zala knew, could ever break down their family unity. Anyway, her mother, despite being afraid for her, was proud of Zala, and would stick by her, no matter what. When the Germans attacked the farm, Zala's mother managed to escape, and she, too, joined the partisans.

Truus and Freddie Oversteegen grew up against a background of demonstrations, with their mother on social assistance, forever on the look-out for extra blankets, and with strangers always in hiding in their home. From a very early age, they learned that poverty was nothing to be ashamed of, that what little they had must to be shared out fairly, and that discretion was as essential a part of everyday life as brushing one's teeth. The pair had grown up fatherless, with a mother who loved them more than anything, she taught them about the root cause of injustice, that this had to be resisted, that solidarity outweighs all the goods and property in the world. Their mother, who all too often did not know what she was going to put on the table, inspired her daughters with a hunger for justice and human dignity. At the age of five, Truus overheard someone say, "All Reds ought to be strung up." When the terrified girl asked her mother who these Reds were, her mother responded, "Us." At the ages of ten and twelve, Freddie and Truus learned the meaning of fascism: it meant that people who were Communists or Jews had to spend the day stretched out on their family's dining room floor, not daring to venture out into the streets; it meant that these people had to leave their homeland and their homes, and now had nothing beyond what their mother could offer them.

By the time the Germans invaded the Netherlands, Truus and Freddie, sixteen and fourteen respectively, were already old hands at conspiracy. With a education like theirs, there certainly was not a lot that they could learn in the Communist Youth. At any rate, now there was an organization through which they could act immediately. Freddie and Truus were present when the triumphant leader of the Dutch Nazis suffered his first big defeat—when Mussert, backed by the might of the new masters, grabbed the microphone and, chest swollen with pride, was received in the main square in Haarlem by a deafening concerto from hundreds of bicycle bells. Not one word of Mussert's speech could be heard. Silence returned to the square only after it was announced that the Germans were coming and the rioters withdrew. By then, the square was almost empty, and the microphone cable had been cut. Truus and Freddie pedalled home, gratified, for the thing had worked to perfection, and the young people's action had become the talk of the day.

Back home, some people were sitting up in their dining room. Truus and Freddie wished the Jewish family "good *Shabbes*" just as casually as they would have said "Good night." Equally, it was second nature for the girls to watch the path to their house, and clear away any leftovers from the table as soon as their Jewish *onderduikers* had withdrawn into their hiding place. They handed out leaflets and the Communist Party's underground newspaper, *De Waarheid*. They stuck with their girl and boy colleagues from the Communist Youth, cycling out into the countryside with them, strolling through the meadows, having picnics, and chatting about the situation—who needed ration coupons for their *onderduikers*, who might lend a hand with printing the newspaper the next day, who could then ferry the bales out to the female and male distributors. They looked utterly innocent and saw it all as a sort of a game, an adventure, even though they understood their situation. When the game took a more serious turn, when they were recruited for special missions, for armed resistance, they did not think twice. The notion of killing a person was hard to get their heads around, but they were ready to kill the enemy, and those who supplied him with his victims. Not until they had fired their first shot, and hit the mark, would they fully comprehend what they had gotten themselves into.

They made their decision and held firm. They had known in advance that they would have to face the consequences. Truus had given up her job because she felt that her pride and dignity took priority over the much-needed income. The sexual predations of her boss at work had opened her eyes for the very first time to her status as a woman, which spelled humiliation and powerlessness. Her reaction to this was spontaneous: she fought back, physically, against the sexual harassment. Her behavior—unlike that of countless girls who endured such experiences out of fear and resignation—was understandable, as from a very early age, she had learned that man's dignity had to be defended. To Truus, of course, the term "man" also included women and girls. After all, it was a woman, her own mother, who had handed down this lesson, and she had never said anything about it not being applicable to persons of her own gender.

When her daughters signed on a really conspiratorial mission, she had left the decision up to her fifteen- and seventeen-year-old girls. Freddie and Truus chose the thorniest path, the most exciting, the most intense, the one they most admired. They had heard about the female partisans fighting in the Soviet Union against the Germans, and those young women represented their ideal of what a person ought to be. Now, they were being offered the chance to follow suit, to imitate their adored idols, to join the resistance's true elite while still in their girlhood.

Dina Lipka grew up not really knowing want, loved by her parents, in the bosom of a bourgeois and traditional, religiously observant family. It was taken for granted that the girls would go to high school: Dina did not have to struggle to be able to pursue her studies. However, the cracks soon appeared in this veneer of security. When Dina, whose parents came from Russia and Poland, attended school in France, the schoolmistress complained about Dina's inadequate command of the French language. Self-assured and keeping his cool, Dina's father retorted: "The girl speaks Russian, the girl speaks Polish, the girl speaks German. She will certainly succeed at learning French." But there was one thing that Dina had learned already: She was different. She was Jewish. Thanks to her family's traditionally matter-of-fact outlook, Dina saw her lot not as a disgrace, but as a honor. When the latent anti-Semitism of her French surroundings found itself boosted by the German occupiers' policy of extermination, Dina formed a self-defense squad at her school. Her world, which had withstood every adversity, finally came apart when, suddenly, Jewish colleagues stopped coming to class and Dina herself had to sew a yellow star on her overcoat.

She learned to despise those who presumed to humiliate others in this way, and to dispatch them to their deaths. As yet, Dina knew nothing of the gas chambers and crematoria, but she knew that her

Polish relations might well have lost their lives already, and that her family was in peril. Yet, instead of fear, it was hatred that welled up in her, along with a growing lust for revenge. She had never had any particular interest in politics, but now she felt that, as a Jew, it was calling to her. Given that the Jewish Communists were the resistance fighters who struck the most fear into the Germans, off she went to seek them out. She found them thanks to her instinct, as she says today. All that she knew was that the people living in the apartment above were Jews, and that these people had something to hide beyond their Jewishness. She was a hundred percent correct.

When Dina vanished, when she made up her mind to swap the semi-legal existence of an undercover Jew for an underground life as an armed resistance fighter, her mother knew why. Dina repeatedly trampled upon the most sacred laws of underground work in order to make surreptitious visits to her mother: "Even when she was in terror of death," Dina recounts, "I knew that I could have every confidence in her." It was her own fears with which she had to wrestle time and again, although they never got the better of her. The hatred she bore the murderers prevailed. Meanwhile, reports of concentration camps in Poland, reports of thousands living in hiding—like her own family—in thrall to fear and waiting for the nightmare to end, were also reaching France. This knowledge invested her with a strength far outweighing the instinct of self-preservation, for Dina could not live with this knowledge. The only way she could bear to go on living was by risking her life in order to destroy the occupiers' murder machine.

2

With the exception of the Spaniards, most of whom had received some military training in their youth organization, virtually none of these women had any experience with weapons or other military equipment. Like many others, they thought of strategy and tactics as political rather than military terms. It had never occurred to them that it would now be them taking the lives of others. Girls did not play at soldiers, girls did not take part in gang-fights in the street, and girls did not learn how to fight. True, Fifi and Truus had the occasional fights with boys, but they had always been conscious that they were breaking a taboo, doing something that was unseemly.

In the case of the young Jewish women, there was the additional consideration that they were part of a culture with a long tradition of anti-militarism, a world geared up for words rather than the machinery of war. In this regard, they were no different than their male comrades, and, in a way, this worked out to their advantage. In the left-wing Zionists groups and the Bund youth organization, men were no better than women in this crucial regard. Both were picking up weapons for the very first time in their lives, and both sexes learned together learned how to use them. Neither sex had the edge, for there was no one with years of experience: they were all complete novices. There were no notable differences in the Communist groups either. The experienced older female revolutionaries were well-versed in the use of a revolver, and they could pass this know-how on to their younger comrades, who thereby received the same training as the men. "Shooting practice was run-of-the-mill stuff to us," writes Dora Goldkorn in her *Memoirs of the Warsaw Ghetto Uprising,* where she also highlights the "grand, sacred mission."[535] The latter was doubtless also a factor, but, a few lines later, she hints at something else: delight at receiving such training, pride in their being allowed to grapple with something so serious and extraordinary as weapons.

These girls must have understood that military training as a decisive turning-point in their lives: as an irreversible radical break with the laws of femininity that had previously been foisted upon them as adolescent girls and by which, even as young Communists, they were still inhibited. Now, they were being taken seriously. Now, they were no longer just the future wives of Comrade Such-and-Such, but fighters in their own right. Dora Goldkorn again:

> I can still remember the first shooting lesson. There were five of us girls. I can see them all. Ludka Arbeijtsman from Wrona Street, a young student in the fourth year of her baccalaureate, the youngest of us, all bubbly enthusiasm and tenacity, was sitting just here. Beside her was Renia Niemiecka, who went through a lot of pain and tension on account of her father's religious conservatism. Over there, sat the bravest of us all, Esia Twerska from Vilna. And, lastly, there was Rózka Rosenfeld, the leader of our group. In front of us we had a wooden replica of a rifle. An instructor, Comrade Lena, had arrived to train us in the use of a rifle. We sat on the floor, started to practice with

the wooden replica, practiced our aim, but we looked upon such exercises as a bit of a game, and were visibly disappointed. We pressed for a real gun. Ludka refused even to pick up the wooden rifle. After some back and forth with the instructor, she eventually gave in and used diagrams to explain the workings of a revolver and hand grenade By the next hour of training, they brought us a real revolver and grenade.[536]

Training in the use of arms was the first step to underground work; the last, irrevocable step—in the ghettos—was the move into billets. Young women left home and moved into vacant apartments that, if at all possible, they ought never to leave, or leave only in disguise. They had to ensure that they were not recognized in the street by friends or acquaintances. The break with their previous existence was radical. They were turning their backs on everything daily life had been to them. They dyed their hair, carried false identity papers, and dressed up as Polish Aryan women when on a mission. The money they got from the organization was spent on food and the acquisition of arms: everything was shared by everyone. The comrades, female and male, were now one big family, offering one another encouragement and an emotional haven. In such communes, Dora Goldkorn recounts, there was no "room for hysteria, loss of heart, tittle-tattle, envy, squabbling, selfishness, or cowardice."[537]

Discipline took precedence over everything. Without an extremely big dose of it, they could never have persevered in their struggle in that sea of death of death and destruction. How many times must a Chayke, Zofia, Dora, or Niuta have been laid low by a secret despair, by the temptation to walk away from it all? In *Justyna's Journal*, Gusta Drenger tells how, once, she honestly wanted the Germans to catch her and be done with it. Life "amid the ruins" struck her as utter nonsense. Chayke Grossman recalls an attack of out-and-out defeatism. Following the crushing of the Bialystok ghetto, while on the run, she passed the embarkation point and felt an irresistible attraction to join the people waiting there and let herself be shipped off to the gas chambers with them. Utter exhaustion led these fighters in a hopeless struggle to dream of rest, and—as we know—death was the only rest on offer. At such times, when the struggle seemed pointless, the harsh discipline they had been taught was the only thing that saved them. They shrugged off the weakness and carried on. And, by carrying, on they rediscovered the sense of their struggle.

Like Zala, many other Titoist female partisans were peasants. They were no strangers to weapons; they had killed livestock and knew how to use a hunting gun. The rest of what they needed to fight was picked up from their unit. And they learned everything at once, including how to bed down on bare rock, fully-clothed and surrounded by men. Zala says that, at the start, she could not cope with the idea of spending the night sleeping, side-by-side with utterly strange men, and she refused to entertain the idea, making herself the butt of jokes. Once she realized nothing would happen—and that sexual harassment by male comrades-in-arms was subject to severe punishment—and once she had a chance to sample for herself the sexless climate of comradeship prevailing in the mountain camps, she felt deeply relieved. Nothing else struck her as so much of a problem. The absence of a change of clothes, the inadequate rations that could not fill her stomach were familiar enough things, since the situation was no better at home. Living with the lack of hygiene was a lot harder. Forever on the move, attacking and withdrawing, on long marches from one theater of operations to another, the female and male partisans would spend days, sometimes weeks, unable to wash their clothes, unable to so much as change their underwear, and this was particularly hard on the women who had their periods to contend with. Surrounded by men, simply keeping themselves clean became a problem, as was use of the—nonexistent—latrines.

The Spaniards had gone through the very same things in their Civil War. They had spent day after day in the trenches, covered in dirt, slipping cotton wool between their legs when no one was looking, and burying the bloodied wads in a hole under cover of the night. When battles dragged on and they could not find a chance to change their tampons, the blood would trickle down their trousers and harden. Fifi recounts that her thighs were often chapped for that very reason, and "stank" too. The only time they got a complete wash was when they were on leave from the front, but, as Julia puts it: "When did we ever get leave from the front?" They also had to get used to sleeping in the company of men, unable to take off so much as their boots.

Partisan women and front-line fighters alike were always exhausted. When there was no fighting to be done, there was sentry duty.

Rosario remembers that she soon learned to snatch two or three hours' sleep propped up against a tree. As in the ghetto resisters' communes, there was no place on the front lines in the Spanish sierras or in the mountains of Slovenia for "hysteria, squabbling, or selfishness." There was no place for weaknesses or for tantrums. And, if there was anyone who could indulge himself in weakness, rest assured it would be a man. The women knew that every shortcoming on their part would not be looked upon as a person failing, but rather as an original sin affecting their entire sex. A man breaking down in tears could expect to be comforted and hugged by his comrades. But women were afraid of being called cry-babies if they let a tear be seen: typical women. Mika Etchebéhère writes in her Spanish Civil War memoirs, *La guerra mía*, that, during a day-long bloody battle, she spent the entire time gritting her teeth until everybody finally fell asleep. Only then was she able to give free rein to her tears. Zala broke down just the once, when she heard the Germans' had attacked and torched her farmhouse, and deported her cousin. She did not know what had become of her mother, her son, or her grandmother, and feared the worst. She took herself off to a remote place, sat down on a boulder and wondered: What's the point of carrying on? Avenging them, was her commander's reply—he had followed her—to her unspoken question.

Truus and Freddie were given comprehensive training once they had decided upon armed resistance. They learned to shoot in a nearby forest. Later they also learned how to assemble bombs and place them on railway tracks. They could not carry on living at home, so moved to the home of a female comrade who was not on active service. After that, they had to move regularly. As terrorists of the first order, wanted throughout the land, they could not afford to let themselves be seen too often in one place. Sometimes, they had to live apart in the homes of strangers; sometimes they were together, or along with Hannie Schaft. They spent little of their time at home, their day being full of meetings, reconnaissance, operations, escape, and further meetings. In what free time they had left, they would distribute outlawed reviews, move Jewish *onderduikers* from one hideout to another, transport weapons and explosives. They did all of it in shabby clothing and threadbare overcoats, with a gun and bicycle, constantly on the move.

They knew what it was to go hungry. Their organization paid its female and male fighters only bare subsistence, and it was often the case that the money fell short even of that. Truus recounts how she often had a troubled conscience regarding her hosts, and preferred to eat a little less in order to avoid feeling that she was living off them. It was enough that her very presence should be putting their lives in jeopardy. A cup of ersatz tea and a crust of bread for breakfast, a couple of potatoes or some thin soup for dinner were often the only food the young women got. By night, whenever they happened to have nothing to do, they told each other stories and learned languages. When Truus and Freddie failed to take their lessons seriously and treated them as a diversion, Hannie was furious. "She was very stern," Truus explains, "wanting us to learn English for real, and not simply on a casual basis."

At night they shivered in their beds for want of enough blankets and, in the morning, they washed in cold water. Every venture into the street was a game of chance. What if someone recognized them? What if some traitor had betrayed them? What if the Germans came across their weapons during a search, or scrutinized their forged papers a little too closely? They had to have their eyes peeled at all times, even when they were not preparing or carrying out an operation. As resistance members, living outside the law, they did not need to do anything to be on the wanted list. Even if they were to be stopped while out for a harmless stroll, torture and death was in store for them once the Germans found out who had fallen into their clutches. Their lives were lived in permanent tension. Once, Truus collapsed in the middle of an operation. She lent on a house front, her cocked revolver in her pocket, and waited for some security service officer to open fire. Then, all of a sudden, she collapsed and lost consciousness. For some days, Truus was felled by a high fever. She thought that her number was up and was ashamed of having collapsed, ashamed of this unforgivable weakness. But when Hannie broke down, it was Truus who forced her to indulge this weakness. When it came to other people, she was well aware of how much a few tears could help.

Only briefly, though. A few moments of weakness had to bring a renewal of strength. Real weakness was something that these female resistance fighters could not afford. Even the tiniest mistake might give them away. Anyone who was really sick could not escape in time when an address turned problematic—when it came under surveillance. Anyone overly wrapped up in her own problems could not pay sufficient attention to her surroundings, and might easily walk into a trap, having failed to spot an informer, or a checkpoint. Whoever could not keep a cool head during an attack, might miss the target, and endanger herself and her comrades of both sexes.

Dina Lipka learned how to load, strip, and aim a handgun. She had never had anything like that in her grasp before, and was all concentration. She had no time for mistakes and could not spare a lot of time for practicing. She learned the necessary movements and, within a short time, was off on her first patrol, to get hold of a gun of her own.

She was scared. Scared because of the operation, and scared that it might be her turn to take a life. Only the deep-seated conviction that every shot was aimed at a genocidal killer—someone responsible for incredible suffering—and that every terrorist operation was designed to make it painfully apparent to the occupiers that they would be asked to pay for their crimes, made it possible for her to squeeze the trigger again, plant the bomb, and set the petrol can alight.

The rules of conspiracy were harsh. No friends, no family, no love. No going to the cinema, no parties, no eating out in restaurants with comrades. Just hard work and loneliness. Not that these rules were always observed. From time to time, riding roughshod over all caution, the "Jacquot Gang" would get together in its hideout. "We would eat and sing and chat with one another. But this happened only very occasionally. Not just because it broke the rules and was plainly, simply highly dangerous, but primarily because we did not have the time." There were rendezvous to be kept with strict punctuality. If anyone failed to make the daily rendezvous, it meant that she or he had been picked up. Nobody must create a misunderstanding by arriving late. There were weapons and explosives to be collected for upcoming operations, and *attentats* to be worked out and then carried out. Another day would go by, and the night hours were not for sleep, but for carrying out further acts of sabotage.

"We were forever hungry," Dina tells us. The organization paid its fighters of both sexes 2,500 francs per month, in addition to their rent and a couple of food ration coupons. This added up to the pay of an unskilled laborer, but it was not enough to live on, unless one had the time to spend hours on end queuing in the shops, travelling out into the countryside in search of food, or scouring the city to find the cheapest deals. "We were young," says Henri, "and ordinarily we would have frittered all our money away by the middle of the month." Dina disagrees: "I stretched it out exactly. Most of the time, I was the only one with any money left at the end of the month—in which case, I gave some to the others, of course." Food was a favorite topic among the fighters, on those rare occasions when they had the time and opportunity to sit down together. "We never talked about socialism or about politics, just about what we were going to eat after the liberation," explains Dina, with a laugh. Even so, they never kept one centime of the proceeds for themselves: "When we did a bank job, everything was handed over to the leadership. The money was destined for the struggle, for all of us."

3

Jews are cowardly, slavish, effeminate. Women are cowardly, inept, and like to be dominated. Jews cannot fight. Jews are people of letters, of the spoken word. They bear their fate with resignation. God puts them to a tough test as the chosen people, and they accept the ordeal. Women are born to create and preserve life. They are naturally predisposed to protecting it, not taking it. They are the better half of humanity.

There is no actual evidence to the contrary that could put paid to the myth that Jews behaved in a passive way and let themselves be led docilely, going willingly like sheep to the slaughter. Nor is there any actual evidence to the contrary to put paid to the myth that the real resistance to fascism—military resistance, armed resistance—was men's doing. But the reality struck terror into the Nazi murderers who came face to face with the actual facts: they came across fighting Jews and fighting women. Which left a lasting impression on them—unlike the many historians who, in their studies of the resistance, consistently ignore the Jews and women.

Might the knowledge that the victims fought back make it harder to ease a guilty conscience? Or is it easier to imagine a grey mass with heads hanging down, shuffling towards the gas chambers, offering no resistance, than a handful of desperate women and men brandishing Molotov cocktails and hurling themselves at the genocide's machine-guns? There is something intrinsically moving about victims. We can weep for them, share in their suffering, and surrender to emotion—before turning again to more important matters. It was horrific, but what could we have done? Being confronted with Jews who did something is less comfortable. It raises the issue of the Aryans who did nothing. It upsets the soothing image of the Jew of noble, intelligent aspect, going silently to his death. And gets us used to the idea that we need not accept things as they are, that fighting back is possible—even against an enemy who seems irretrievably superior—that survival at all costs need not be a human being's overriding goal.

The knowledge that there were women who took up arms and turned them on high-ranking male officers undermines the foundations of the patriarchal conception of sex roles. From right to left, from Church prelates through to leading lights of the feminist movement, work even now proceeds with a dogma upon which all are agreed: the dogma of woman's peaceable nature, of her vocation as the giver of life, as protectress of the young, as the victim. The dogma might include masculine aggression, but shies away from what that implies.

The bourgeois feminist contention that nationalism is merely an expression of a male politics—as far removed from women as the moon—and that nothing could, was, or should be done against it, is reemerging and acquiring fresh credibility in feminist circles. Women supposedly had enough on their plates just raising their family, in such hard times. This means that only men could afford the luxury—the price being paid by their partners—of taking part in the resistance. Quite apart from its implicit defamation, that assumption starts from the unspoken fact that it was only German—which is to say, Aryan— women who were completely de-politicized. The question of how a Jewish woman could have reared her family, and of where all these female Communists who could afford the luxury of resistance came from, is never answered—because it is never posed. The same goes for the question of how women conducted themselves in those countries under German occupation.

Even here, though, the myth endures. As a result, the image of the fighting woman is consistently occluded from Paris to Warsaw. And even the female historians are not free of it. In *Ils étaient juifs, résistants, communistes* (They Were Jews, Resisters, Communists), Annette Wievorka sets out to study the MOI resistance, describing the organization's female members primarily as auxiliaries and providers of cover. She devotes most of her attention to the activists who organized the infrastructures of the fighting groups and those who smuggled Jewish children out of the country—another important chapter about which historians say nothing. As yet, not enough documentary evidence has been amassed regarding these rescue operations that following rapid escape routes, crossed the whole of Europe. There has been no acknowledgment that this was due to the tireless efforts of women who, at the risk of their own lives, managed to save hundreds of victims from the clutches of genocide. And, of course, if any allusion is made to the role of women in the resistance, it is to roles that do not conflict with women's alleged innate disposition. Fighters like Jeanine Sontag, Simone Motta, and Olga Bancic merit little or no attention from Annette Wievorka. And Wievorka, who spent days researching in the Krischers' home in Nancy, rifling through their archives, completely ignores Dina Krischer. In her book, one will find detailed biographies of Henri Krischer, Herbert Herz, and Jacquot Szmulewicz, but the reader will not find out about women like Dina Lipka and Jacqueline Bloch who fought at their side.

If women had it in them to fight the German army, which was victorious on all fronts, and to sow fear and panic in the all-powerful, ruthless Gestapo, then women may also have it in them to stand up to less dangerous adversaries. If women have shown that they withstand equally well the drudgery of the trenches, the partisan encampment, and the outlaw life, then that certainly undermines the image of the weaker sex, in need of man's protection—at the cost of fewer rights, lower wages, less autonomy, and reduced entitlement to human dignity. As a result, when the fighting woman manages to break through the general amnesia, she is portrayed as a bloodthirsty brute. "Watch out for her: she has no respect for authority." These were not real women. "People thought that we went around like gunslingers, with a gun in each hand...bang, bang, bang!" says Truus Menger. Former comrades of Zala tell the comforting story of how she occasionally broke down and started to tremble. The women on the front lines in the Spanish Civil War were slandered and dismissed as whores. And partisan women like Zala have had to contend with similar notoriety. In any event, it could not have been normal women who quite simply refused to countenance a criminal and inhuman regime's imposition of its violence upon millions of people, who refused to look the other way and hope for the madness to stop some day, who refused to worry about her own safety and leave others to their fate, who refused to confine herself to an auxiliary role, serving up food and offering shelter.

Women like Fifi, Zala, Truus, Dina, and Niuta wanted something more. They wanted to give direct expression to their resistance, a resistance that was fuelled not just by an aversion to fascism, but rooted in a determined opposition to the way things were. These women's rebelliousness did not start once when the fascist generals mounted their coup or the Wehrmacht crossed the frontier. Long before that, they had come into conflict with a social order in which the few gave orders to the many, where there was someone on top and someone down below, an exploiter class and an exploited class, where people are classified as members of superior breeds and inferior breeds, where women have a lesser entitlement than men. They had joined forces with others to create a new society, where all differences would be eradicated. Fascism's extreme aggravation of the existing circumstances—the categorization of virtually the entire population of Europe as slave workers or overlords, some deserving to reproduce and some marked for extermination—catapulted them into an emergency situation that itself proved to be an opportunity. It was an opportunity to break once and for all with a pernicious and despised normality. They, who had, for quite some time, been trying to shrug off their everyday fetters, had a particular sensitivity to the heavy chains that the new regime meant to impose upon people in the conquered countries. This new and unprecedented menace also created a revulsion that led to the impulse to do something *now*. They were not cowed by the new masters' terror tactics, but rather galvanized by them, because they stirred an unexpected stubbornness within them.

If some of these girls threw in their lot with the armed resistance, not just out of political conviction, but also out of a certain quest for adventure, and a wish to break free of the stultifyingly restricted role of women, that in itself could not have sustained them for months and years at a time, day after day, through life on the front lines or as outlaws. The strength to carry on fighting as a wanted terrorist, under the noses of the enemy could not have derived from a lust for adventure alone. That strength was fuelled by a radical break with everything that society had to offer, with business as usual, with authority. These young women were trampling upon their allocated role, upon the law. They were breaking down the protective wall of instinctual of self-preservation. Their daring had taken them too far for them to want, or to be able, to turn back.

Another thing that kept the Jewish women fighters going, even in moments of darkest despair, was a burning lust for vengeance. This factor in particular is often dismissed with hindsight—not necessarily by the women concerned, but certainly by those who have written about them. From the humanistic point of view, vengeance is a negative impulse.

But the women fighters were good people—and good people fight for something: peace, liberation, a better world. From a socialist viewpoint, vengeance is equally illegitimate: it looks back, whereas the revolutionaries looks forward, toward a future yet to be forged. Not, of course, that vengeance is something peculiarly female. By virtue of their sex, women are good people and, as revolutionaries, their eyes are fixed on the future. From another angle, vengeance is seen as a rather grand (unsanctioned) passion, which is to say, a male passion. Finally, the motive of revenge, especially for women, is dismissed by some as petty-minded and tiresome. On all these grounds, generally speaking, vengeance is ruled out as a motivating factor in the resistance, and all the more where women's resistance is concerned.

"I defended my honor as a Jewish woman and I avenged our people," states Dina Krischer, calm, relaxed, proud. "Vengeance for the thousands upon thousands shot in the forests and murdered in the camps," pledged the women resisters in Warsaw, Vilna, and Bialystok. The eyes of these women were fixed upon more than a long-craved future that was the subject of heated discussions, a strategic objective still a long way off. They had more in mind than a socialist society that the survivors might some day build in Poland, France, and Palestine. They were also thinking about their parents quivering with fear in some cramped, dark hideout, the female and male comrades tortured in the Gestapo prisons, the school chums packed off to Auschwitz in cattle-trucks, the corpses in the lime pit, the ones asphyxiated in the gas chambers. It was on also on behalf of them that they reloaded their weapons, for them that they took aim, for them that they hit the target. And it was for them that they were risking their lives.

While the victims of torture and murder were not going to see that dreamed-of dawn, they could at least have their suffering and deaths avenged. Even if the killings could not be halted, the killers could at least be made to pay the price. Vengeance was a legitimate, invigorating basis upon which to carry on fighting in a bottomless pit of affliction and despair.

Vengeance and hatred. We may be sure that anyone unwilling to turn a blind eye to the fascist terror, but ready, instead, to embrace that confrontation, was not motivated solely by noble, high-minded sentiments. These female and male fighters were highly moral folk. They strove to distinguish between the instigators and those acting under orders. And they also strove not to act like their enemies. "I could never have killed a prisoner," said Fifi. Truus never lost sight of her mother's warning that not all Germans were Nazis. She never forgot the young partisan woman who explained, over Radio Moscow, how she was deeply affected by the fact that, in destroying a German tank, she was also destroying the life of its driver, a very young, terrified German soldier. Dina knew that the soldier she had shot at the previous day was overseeing the deportation of Jews from Lyon. Truus knew that the security service officer at whom she levelled her revolver would not be taking any more prisoners, would not be torturing or killing anybody else.

The future might well have been uncertain, but the enemy was in their country right now. Thinking himself invincible. Even though every *attentat*, every act of sabotage, every derailed train might only represent a pinprick in a tank, every single pinprick would eventually help destroy that tank. These young women could not have waited for the Allies or the Red Army to show up some day to drive the occupiers out of their homeland. They could not make do with preparing themselves for the day of liberation. Their radicality, their gravity, their hatred, and their thirst for revenge left them no option but to fight right then and there. Even in normal times, they had not been disposed to wait for things to change by themselves, but had taken their lives into their own hands and, thus, begun to change it for themselves. How could they be expected to bide their time now?

Every bullet that forced a Gestapo officer to his knees, armor-plated limousine or no, regardless of his arrogant smugness and in spite of his boundless power, was a victory scored against the rule of the overlords: it showed them that their fortress was not impregnable, that their invulnerability was mere illusion. With nothing more than a revolver, a hand grenade, and adamantine determination, a seventeen-year-old girl could score such a victory, and show the world that the brute was not all-powerful, that there was a point to carrying on with this unequal struggle. And every shot that inflicted a further wound upon the brute also struck home on behalf of those who would not live to see the conclusion of the struggle.

Endnotes

INTRODUCTION

1. Reuben Ainsztein, *Jewish Resistance in Nazi-Occupied Eastern Europe* (London: Elek,1974), 608.

2. Ibid., 598.

3. The allusion is to the leftwing Zionist Hehalutz (Pioneer) movement.

4. Kazimierz Moczarski, *Gespräche mit dem Henker. Dal Leben des SS-Gruppenführers und Generalleutnants der Polizei Jürgen Stroop* [Conversations with the Executioner: The Life of SS Gruppenführer and Police Divisional General Jürgen Stroop] (Frankfurt: Fischer, 1982), 177ff. The conversations were recorded in Mokotow prison near Warsaw.

5. Ibid., 178ff.

6. See *Carmagnole-Liberté*, the dossier drawn up by the Amicale du Bataillon Carmagnole-Liberté (Bourg-la-Reine, n.d.); and Rita Thalmann, "Une lacune de l'historiographie," in *Les Juifs dans la Résistance et la Libération*, ed. Association pour la recherche sur l'histoire contemporaine des Juifs [RHICOJ] (Paris: Editions du Scribe, 1985), 89.

7. Truus Menger, *Toen Niet, Nu Niet, Nooit* [Not Then, Not Now, Not Ever] (The Hague: Leopold, 1982). The references here are to the unpublished English translation (by Albert Boer), which is why I do not give page references. Truus Menger was also interviewed by the author in May 1987.

8. Raoul Hilberg, *Die Vernichtung der europaischen Juden. Die Gesamtgeschichte des Holocaust* [The Extermination of the European Jews: The Complete History of the Holocaust] (Berlin: Fischer, 1982). See also Ainsztein, *Jewish Resistance*; and Isaac Kowalski, ed., *Anthology on Armed Jewish Resistance, vol. 1* (New York: Jewish Combatants Publishers House, 1986), 11.

9. Rita Thalmann, "Une lacune," 89ff.

10. See Kowalski, vols. 1-3; and Ainsztein, *Jewish Resistance*.

11. See the references cited below in the footnotes on resistance in eastern Europe.

12. Bernhard Mark, *Der Aufstand in Warschauer Ghetto* [The Rising in the Warsaw Ghetto] (Berlin: Dietz, 1957).

13. Hanna Elling, *Frauen im deutschen Widerstand 1933–45* [Women in the German Resistance, 1933–45] (Frankfurt: Röderberg, 1978); Karin Berger, Elisabeth Holzinger, Lotte Podgornik, and Lisbeth N. Trallori, *Der Himmel ist blau. Kann sein. Frauen im Widerstand Österreich 1938–1945* [The Sky is Blue, Perhaps. Women in the Austrian Resistance, 1938–1945] (Vienna: Promedia, 1985) and *Ich gebe dir einen mantel, dass du ihn noch in Freiheit tragen kannst* [I Give to You an Overcoat: Maybe Someday You Can Wear It in Freedom] (Vienna: Promedia, 1987); Margarete Schütte-Lihotzky, *Erinnerungen aus dem Widerstand* [Memories of Resistance] (Hamburg: Konkret, 1985); and Gerda Szepansky, *Frauen leisten Widesrtand 1933–1945* [Women Putting Up Resistance, 1933-1945] (Frankfurt: Fischer, 1985).

14. See the documented discussion in RHICOJ; Lucien Steinberg, *La Révolte des Justes. Les Juifs contre Hitler* (Paris: Fayard, 1970); Dina and Henry Krischer, interview by author, Nancy, December 1987; Truus Menger; and Berger, et al.

15. Anne Grynberg and Alain Michel versus Adam Rayski in RHICOJ; and the author's interview with Dina and Henry Krischer.

16. See Adam Rayski in RHICOJ; Dina and Henry Krischer, interview by author, Nancy, December 1987; and Annette Wieviorka, *Ils étaient Juifs, Communistes, Résistants* (Paris: Denoel, 1986).

17. Dov Levin, *Fighting Back* (New York/London: Holmes and Meier, 1985); Yehuda Bauer, *They Chose Life* (New York/Jerusalem: The American Jewish Committee, 1973); and Shmuel Krakowski, *The War of the Doomed* (New York/London: Holmes and Meier, 1984).

18. Ibid.

19. Dora Schaul, *Résistance: Erinnerungen deutscher Antifaschisten* [Resistance: German Antifascists Remember] (Frankfurt: Dietz, 1973); *Österreicher im Exil. Frankreich 1938–1945* [Austrians in Exile: France, 1938–1945], published by the Dokumentationsarchiv des österreichischen Widerstandes, (Vienna and Munich, 1984); *Österreicher im Exil. Belgien 1938–1945* [Austrians in Exile: Belgium, 1938-1945], published by the Dokumentationsarchiv des österreichischen Widerstandes (Vienna and Munich, 1987).

20. Rita Thalmann, "Une lacune"; Sigrid Jacobeit, "Elsa Fugger," *Dachauer Hefte*, no. 3, (Dachau, 1987); and Vera Laska, *Women in the Resistance and Holocaust* (Connecticut: Greenwood, 1983).

21. Cited by Simone de Beauvoir in *The Second Sex*, trans. H.M. Parshley (New York: Penguin, 1972).

22. Yehuda Bauer, "By Force of Arms," in Kowalski, vol. 1, 49.

23. Jack Nusan Porter, "Jewish Women in the Resistance," in Kowalski, vol. 1, 293.

24. Yuri Suhl, "Roza Robota—Heroine of Auschwitz," in Yuri Suhl, ed., *They Fought Back* (New York: Schocken, 1967), 219ff.

25. Jacob Greenstein, "Children — Couriers in the Ghetto of Minsk," in Suhl, 241ff.

26. Rosario Sánchez Mora, interview by Pilar Panes Casas, Madrid, December 1987.

27. See Laska.

28. *Women in the Struggle for Social and National Equality Between the Two World Wars* (Belgrade 1977).

29. Army Group E High Command, Group ic/AO No 13000/44g., *Feind-Nachrichtenblatt (Griechische Banden)*, No 14, July–August 1944.

30. Bernard Mark, "The Herbert Baum Group," in Suhl, 55ff.

31. *Tagesrapport* [Daily Dispatches], no. 3, forwarded by the secret state police post in Cologne to the General Department of Reich Security — Iv Gst. of 20/xii/1944, Haupstaatsarchiv Düsseldorf, 74–78.

32. Here, see Ruben Ainsztein, op.cit., 795 et seq., and Vera Laska, op.cit.

RESISTANCE IN WESTERN EUROPE

33. Rosario Sánchez Mora, interview by Pilar Panes Casas, Madrid, December 1987.

34. See Karin Buselmeier and Clara Thalmann, "Interview über die Rolle der Frau in der Spanischen Revolution, 1936–1939" ["Interview on the Role of Women in the Spanish Revolution 1936-1939"], in *Frauen in der spanischen Revolution*, ed. Cornelia Krasser and Jochen Schmück (Berlin: Libertad, 1984); Franz Borkenau, *The Spanish Cockpit: An Eye-Witness Account of the Political and Social Conflicts of the Spanish Civil War* (London: Faber and Faber, 1937), quoted in Liz Willis, "Frauen in der Spanischen Revolution 1936–1939," in Krasser and Schmück, 41 ff.; George Orwell, *Homage to Catalonia* (New York: Penguin, 1977).

35. See Temma Kaplan, "Frauen und der spanische Anarchismus" ["Women and Spanish Anarchism"], in Krasser and Schmück, 15ff.

36. See Temma Kaplan, "Der Anarchismus in Spanien und die Frauenemanzipation" ["Anarchism in Spain and Female Emancipation"], in Krasser and Schmück, 34.

37. Ibid.

38. Ibid., 35.

39. Buselmeier and Thalmann, 65.

40. Ibid., 66.

41. See Mary Nash, *Mujeres Libres* (Barcelona: Tusquets, 1975); and Andreas Bohl, *Revolution in Spanien* (Munich: Andreas Bohl, 1984), 144ff.

42. See Bohl, 143ff.; and Lola Iturbe, "Mujeres Antifascistas/Mujeres Libres," in Krasser and Schmück, 86ff.

43. As quoted in ibid., 89.

44. Lucía Sánchez Saornil, "Die Frauenfrage in unseren Kreisen" ["The Women's Question in Our Circles"], in Krasser and Schmück, 82; and Nash, 43-61.

45. Buselmeier and Thalmann, 64ff.

46. See Borkenau, as quoted in Willis, 46.

47. See Willis, 43.

48. See Consuelo García, *Die Hand des Herzens. Leben und Kämpfe der Spanierin Soledad Real* [The Heart's Hand: The Life and Struggles of the Spaniard Soledad Real] (Munich: Autoren Edition, 1981), 57ff.

49. See Willis, 47.

50. Rosario Sánchez Mora, interview by Pilar Panes Casas, Madrid, December 1987.

51. See Orwell, as quoted in Willis, 49.

52. *Spain and the World*, July 19, 1937, as quoted in Willis, 53.

53. See Bohl, 150.

54. *Mujeres Libres*, "Las mujeres en los primeros días de lucha," no. 10, July 1937, as quoted in Nash, 91-92.

55. See Buselmeier and Thalmann, 168.

56. Ibid., 79.

57. Rosario Sánchez Mora, interview by Pilar Panes Casas, Madrid, December 1987.

58. See Mika Etchebéhère *La guerra mía. Eine Frau kämpft für Spanien* (My War: One Woman's Fight for Spain) (Frankfurt: Neue Kritik, 1980), 251ff.

59. Ibid., 56ff.

60. Ibid., 190ff.

61. Ibid., 249.

62. Ibid., 140ff.

63. Buselmeier and Thalmann, 76.

64. Julia Manzanal, interview by author, Madrid, June 1987.

65. Etchebéhère, 166.

66. Ibid., 67.

67. Ibid., 223.

68. Ibid., 180.

69. Ibid., 188.

70. Ibid., 194.

71. Ibid., 251.

72. Ibid.

73. See Clara and Pavel Thalmann, *Wo die Freiheit stirbt. Stationen eines politischen Kampfes* [Where Freedom Perished: Way-Stations of a Political Struggle] (Freiburg: Walter, 1974); Etchebéhère; Peter Weiss, *Die Asthetik des Widerstandes* [Aesthetics of Resistance] (Frankfurt: Suhrkamp, 1975); Orwell; Hans Magnus Enzensberger, *Der kurze Sommer der Anarchie* [Anarchy's Short Summer] (Frankfurt: Suhrkamp, 1972).

74. Rosario Sánchez Mora, interview by Pilar Panes Casas, Madrid, December 1987.

75. All information and verbatim quotations from Fidela Fernández de Velasco Pérez, aka Fifí, interview by author, Madrid, June 1987.

76. All details and direct quotations from Julia Manzanal, interview by author, Madrid, June 1987.

77. All details and direct quotations from Rosario Sánchez Mora, interview by Pilar Panes Casas, Madrid, December 1987.

78. See Karel Prusnik-Gasper, *Gemsen auf der Lawine* [Chamois in the Avalanche] (Ljubljana and Klagenfurt: Wieser, 1981), 113ff.

79. Unless otherwise indicated, on this and other matters see *Women in the Struggle for Social and National Equality Between the Two World Wars* (Belgrade, 1977).

80. As cited in the above.

81. See Teodor Domej, ed., *Vertreibung und Widerstand. Zum 40 Jahrestag der Vertreibung der Kärntner Slowenen und ihrer Eingliederung in den Kampf gegen Nazifaschismus* [Deportation and Resistance: In Commemoration of the 40th Anniversary of the Deportation of the Carinthian Slovenes and their Entry into the Struggle against Nazism] (Klagenfurt/Celovec: Zveza Slovenskih Izseljencev/Verband Ausgesiedelter Slowenen, 1982).

82. Ibid.

83. As quoted in *Women in the Struggle for Social and National Equality Between the Two World Wars*, 44.

84. Johanna Sadolsek-Zala, interview by author, Lobnig, near Eisenkappel, Carinthia, November 1987.

85. Ibid; see also Lisbeth N. Trallori, "Der 'verschwiegene' Widerstand" ["The Silenced Resistance"], *Zeitgeschichte* 12, no. 5 (February 1985).

86. As quoted in *Women in the Struggle for Social and National Equality Between the Two World Wars*, 54.

87. Ibid., 52.

88. Ibid., 49.

89. Unless otherwise indicated, for further details on this, and regarding the resistance of the Carinthian Slovenes, see Prusnik-Gasper; and Domej.

90. Rita Thalmann, "Les Femmes dans la Résistance Autrichienne," Austriaca, *Cahiers universitaires d'information sur l'Autriche* 9, no. 17, (November 1983), 89ff. Thalmann refers readers especially to Tilly Spiegel, *Frauen und Mädchen im österreichischen Widerstand* [Women and Girls in the Austrian Resistance] (Vienna/Frankfurt/Zurich, 1966); and Inge Brauneis, *Widerstand von Frauen in Österreich 1938–1945* [Women's Resistance in Austria, 1938–1945] (Dissertation, Vienna University, 1976).

91.Brauneis, as cited by Rita Thalmann, "Les Femmes," 90, 96.

92. Karel Prusnik-Gasper's book *Gemsen auf der Lawine* was first published in Ljubljana in 1958 under the original Slovene title *Gamsi na Plazu*.

93. Berger, et al.

94. Trallori, 151.

95. Unless otherwise indicated, the following details and direct quotations are from Johanna Sadolsek-Zala, interview by author, Lobnig, near Eisenkappel, Carinthia, November 1987.

96. Trallori, 153.

97. Unpublished transcript of Lisbeth N. Trallori's interview with Johanna Sadolsek [Zala] in 1982 for the book *Der Himmel is blau*, and for the film made by the same team of writers, *Küchengespräche mit Rebellinnen* [Kitchen Chats with Rebel Women] (Vienna: Medienwerkstatt Wien, 1984). Lisbeth N. Trallori was kind enough to make the transcript available to me. Hereafter, references to it will be abbreviated as: Trallori-Zala interview.

98. Trallori-Zala interview.

99. Trallori, 155.

100. See Trallori-Zala interview.

101. Prusnik-Gasper, 82ff.
102. Ibid., 87.
103. Trallori-Zala interview.
104. Ibid.
105. Ibid.
106. See Trallori, 160.
107. Ibid., 162.
108. Trallori-Zala Interview.
109. Prusnik-Gasper, 372ff.
110. Ibid.
111. Ibid.
112. Trallori-Zala interview.
113. Ibid.
114. Ibid.
115. Ibid.
116. Ibid.
117. Ibid.
118. Johanna Sadolsek-Zala in *Küchengespräche mit Ribellinnen*.
119. Trallori-Zala interview.
120. Truus Menger, interview by author, Verhuizen, Netherlands, May 1987.
121. Unless otherwise indicated, see, with regard to these and subsequent details of the Netherlands under the German occupation, Erich Koch "Unterdrückung und Widerstand" ["Oppression and Resistance"], *Dortmunder Vorträge*, no. 35 (n.d.); and *Texte zur Dauerausstellung* [Texts for a Standing Exhibition] (Amsterdam: Verzetsmuseum [Resistance Museum], n.d.).
122. See Annemarie de Wildt, *Je deed wat je doen moest. Vrouwen in verzet* [I Did What I Had to Do: Women in the Resistance] (Amsterdam: Self-published, 1985), unpaginated.
123. Ibid.
124. Ibid.
125. Ibid.
126. Ibid.
127. Truus Menger, interview by author, Verhuizen, Netherlands, May 1987.
128. All of the details and direct quotations in this chapter are from my interview with Truus Menger (née Oversteegen) and from the (unpublished) English translation of *Toen Niet, Nu Niet, Nooit*.
129 The author interviewed Dina Krischer in Nancy in December 1987. See also Dina Krischer, "Combattante à Carmagnole," in RHICOJ, 98ff.
130. *Carmagnole-Liberté*, the dossier drawn up by the Amicale du Bataillon Carmagnole-Liberté (Bourg-la-Reine, n.d.).
131. See, among others, Wieviorka; and David Douvette, "Une histoire controversée," in RHICOJ, 153ff.
132. Henri Krischer and Herbert Herz, interview by author, Nancy, December 1987; and Fred Kupferman "Introduction à un débat" in RHICOJ, 11..
133. Henri Krischer "Les barricades de la MOI," in RHICOJ, 174; plus the author's interview with Henri Krischer and Herbert Herz.
134. David Douvette, 153ff.; and Annie Kriegel, "La Résistance communiste," in *La France et la question juive 1940–1944: Acte du colloque du Centre de documentation juive contemporaine* (Paris: Sylvie Messinger, 1981), 354ff.
135. Ibid.
136. Ibid., 364.

137. Wieviorka, 28.

138. Marcel-Pierre Bernard, *Bouches du Rhône* (Dissertation, University of Provence, 1982), 180.

139. Kriegel, 356ff.; and Douvette, 154.

140. Ibid.

141. Kriegel, 357.

142. Bernard, 182.

143. Douvette, 155.

144. Wieviorka, 64ff.; and Henri Krischer and Herbert Herz, interview by author, Nancy, December 1987.

145. Wieviorka, 81.

146. Ibid., 87.

147. Ibid., 116ff.

148. Ibid., 23ff.

149. Stéphane Courtois, "Le 'Groupe Manouchian': Sacrifié ou trahi?" *Le Monde*, June 2–3, 1985.

150. Kriegel, 357.

151. Wieviorka, 23ff.

152. Ibid., 158.

153. "Quelques repères pour l'histoire," 15.

154. Abraham Lissner, "Diary of a Jewish Partisan," in Suhl, 283.

155. Ibid.

156. Ibid., 284.

157. Ibid.

158. "Quelques repères pour l'histoire," 15.

159. Wieviorka, 139ff.; and Rita Thalmann, "Une lacune," 92.

160. Ibid., 90; and Gisela Dreyer, *Unbekannter Widerstand —Weiblicher Widerstand. Frauen in der französischen Résistance* [The Unknown Resistance—Women's Resistance: Women in the French Resistance], transcript of a program from the SFB Berlin radio and television channel.

161. Wieviorka, 21ff.

162. Rita Thalmann, 91.

163. Jacques Ravine, *La Résistance organisée des Juifs* (Paris: Julliard, 1973), as cited by Rita Thalmann, "Une lacune," 91.

164. David Diamant, *Les Juifs dans la Résistance 1940–44* (Paris: Le Pavillon, 1971), as cited by Rita Thalmann, "Une lacune," 91.

165. Rita Thalmann, "Une lacune," 90.

166. Dreyer.

167. Rita Thalmann, "Une lacune," 90ff.

168. Ania Francos, *Il était des femmes dans la Résistance* (Paris: Stock, 1971).

169. Lissner, "Diary," 287ff.

170. Ibid., 289; and Rita Thalmann, "Une lacune," 93.

171. Lissner, "Diary," 289ff

172. Abraham Lissner, *Un franc-tireur juif raconte* (Paris: Self-published, 1972), 90ff.; and Rita Thalmann, "Une lacune," 93.

173. *Service Liquidateur du Front National (OS-FN-FTPE)*, Marcel Mugnier, Paris 1969, Archives of Dina and Henri Krischer, Nancy.

174. *Résistance*, Frankfurt 1975, 210ff.

175. *Service Liquidateur*.

176. Rita Thalmann, "Une lacune," 93.

177. Ibid.

178. Ibid., 93ff.

179. Wieviorka, 252; and Catherine Varlin, "Une ville engloutie: La résistance des femmes juives," in RHICOJ, 101ff.

180. Lissner, "Diary," 291.

181. Courtois.

182. Ibid.

183. Wieviorka, 178ff.

184. As cited by Courtois.

185. Wieviorka, 231ff.

186. As cited by Courtois.

187. Adam Rayski, "Il faut réconstituer par le menu cette histoire tragique," *Le Monde*, June 19, 1985.

188. Courtois.

189. Henri Krischer, "Le Bataillon FTP-MOI Carmagnole-Liberté," *La Presse Nouvelle*, September 1985.

190. Ahlrich Meyer "Résistance und Klassenkampf" ["Resistance and Class Struggle"], *Die Tageszeitung*, May 11, 1987.

191. Dina and Henri Krischer, Herbert Herz, Jacquot Szmulewicz, and others, interview by author, Nancy, December 1987.

192. Ibid.

193. Henri Krischer, "Les barricades," 176.

194. Dina Krischer, interview by author, Nancy, December 1987.

195. *Exposition (de la) Mairie de Vénissieux*, September 1985.

196. Wieviorka, 195.

197. *Exposition (de la) Mairie de Vénissieux*.

198. Henri Krischer and Herbert Herz, interview by author, Nancy, December 1987.

199. Douvette, 155.

200. Henri Krischer, 175ff.

201. *Exposition (de la) Mairie de Vénissieux*.

202. Dina Krischer, 98; and Dina Krischer, interview by author, Nancy, December 1987.

203. Henri Krischer and Herbert Herz, interview by author, Nancy, December 1987.

204. Dina Krischer, interview by author, Nancy, December 1987.

205. Léon Landini, "Quelques mots d'histoire sur Carmagnole-Liberté," in *Exposition (de la) Mairie de Vénissieux*.

206. Ibid.

207. On this and all other subsequent Carmagnole operations, see Carmagnole-Liberté dossier.

208. For this and subsequent details on Jeanine Sontag, see *Broschüre der Amicale Carmagnole-Liberté zum Gedächtnis von Jeanine Sontag* [Amicale Carmagnole-Liberté Dossier Commemorating Jeanine Sontag] (Bourg-la-Reine, n.d.); and author's Dina and Henri Krischer, interview by author, Nancy, December 1987.

209. *Exposition (de la) Mairie de Vénissieux*.

210. Dina and Henri Krischer and Herbert Herz, interview by author, Nancy, December 1987.

211. Ibid.

212. Ibid.

213. *Exposition (de la) Mairie de Vénissieux*.

214. Ibid.

215. Dina and Henri Krischer and Herbert Herz, interview by author, Nancy, December 1987.

216. See *Carmagnole-Liberté* dossier.

JEWISH RESISTANCE IN EASTERN EUROPE

217. Bauer, "By Force of Arms," 44ff.

218. Israel Gutman, "Youth Movements in the Underground and the Ghetto Revolts," in Meir Grubsztein, ed. *Jewish Resistance during the Holocaust: Proceedings of the Conference on Manifestations of Jewish Resistance* (Jerusalem: Yad Vashem Studies, 1971).

219. Ainsztein, *Jewish Resistance*, 551ff.

220. Cited in ibid., 489.

221. Ibid., 481.

222. Ibid., 518ff.

223. Ibid., 463ff.

224. Ibid., 477ff.

225. With regard to this profile of the official Polish resistance, I am basing my comments essentially on Ainsztein, *Jewish Resistance*, 396ff. See also Bernard Mark, *Der Aufstand*; and Yitzhak Arad, "Introduction," in Kowalski, vol. 1, 17ff.

226. As cited by Ainsztein.

227. Ibid.

228. Ibid.

229. Ibid.

230. Ibid.

231. Bernard Mark, *Der Aufstand*, 26.

232. Ibid.

233. Vladka Meed, *On Both Sides of the Wall* (Tel Aviv: Beit Lohamei Hagetaot and Hakibbutz Hameuchad, 1973), 246.

234. Ibid., 246ff.

235. Marie Syrkin, *Blessed is the Match* (New York: Jewish Publication Society, 1947), 199ff.

236. Emanuel Ringelblum, *Notes from the Warsaw Ghetto* (New York: Schocken, 1975), 273ff.

237. Arad, "Introduction," 19.

238. Ainsztein, *Jewish Resistance*, 55.

239. Ibid., 564.

240. Ibid.

241. Gutman, 265.

242. Ainsztein, *Jewish Resistance*, 590, 602.

243. Ibid., 602.

244. Ibid., 600.

245. Arad, "Introduction," 21; and Ainsztein, *Jewish Resistance*, 600ff.

246. John Bunzl, *Klassenkampf in der Diaspora* [Class Struggle in the Diaspora] (Vienna: Europa, 1975), 62ff.

247. Ibid., 101ff.

248. Ibid., 152.

249. Ibid., 111ff.

250. Ibid., 108.

251. Gutman, 261.

252. Ibid., 262; and Syrkin, 194ff.

253. Ibid., 196.

254. Gutman, 263.

255. Ibid., 266ff.

256. Ibid., 271. See also Ainsztein, *Jewish Resistance*, 565.

257. Ibid.; and Syrkin, 197ff.

258. As cited by Gutman, 271ff.

259. Gutman, 271.

260. Arad, "Introduction," 24.

261. Gutman, 276.

262. As cited by Gutman, 276ff.; and Chayke Grossman, "The Days of the Uprising," in Kowalski, vol. 3, 538ff.

263. Gutman, 278; Arad, "Introduction," 23; Yitzhak Zuckerman, "Twenty Five Years after the Warsaw Ghetto Revolt," in Grubsztein, 27; Moshe Kahanowitz, "Why No Separate Jewish Partisan Movement Was Established in World War II," in Kowalski, vol. 3, 26ff.

264. Ainsztein, *Jewish Resistance*, 551.

265. Bernard Mark, *Der Aufstand*, 15.

266. Ainsztein, *Jewish Resistance*, 551.

267. Ibid.

268. Bernard Mark, *Der Aufstand*, 17.

269. Ibid., 19.

270. Ibid., 20.

271. Ibid.

272. Ibid., 24; and Ainsztein, *Jewish Resistance*, 554.

273. Bernard Mark, *Der Aufstand*, 23.

274. Ibid., 20ff.

275. Ibid., 21.

276. Ainsztein, *Jewish Resistance*, 555.

277. Ibid.

278. Ibid., 564.

279. Ibid., 565ff.; Bernard Mark, *Der Aufstand*, 142.

280. Bernard Mark, *Der Aufstand*, 40.

281. Ainsztein, *Jewish Resistance*, 573ff.; Bernard Mark, *Der Aufstand*, 56; and Meed, 90.

282. Bernard Mark, *Der Aufstand*, 61; and Ainsztein, *Jewish Resistance*, 575.

283. Ainsztein, *Jewish Resistance*, 574ff.

284. Ibid., 577ff.

285. Ibid., 591.

286. As quoted, ibid., 578ff.

287. Ibid., 588.

288. Ibid., 589.

289. Ibid., 591.

290. Ibid., 592.

291. Meed, 71ff.

292. Ibid., 72.

293. Ainsztein, *Jewish Resistance*, 592.

294. Ibid.

295. As quoted by Ainsztein, *Jewish Resistance*, 593.

296. Ibid.

297. Bernard Mark, *Der Aufstand*, 138ff.; and Ainsztein, *Jewish Resistance*, 594. Mark and Ainsztein both give the names only of the male members of the leadership. However, in the short biographies of Zivia Lubetkin written by Isaac Kowalski (*Armed Jewish Resistance*, vol.

1, 151) and Jack Nusan Porter (ibid., 293), and in the book published by the Kibbutz Lahomeit Haggetaot, *Zeugnisse Uberlebender* [Survivors' Testimonies] (in Kowalski, vol. 3, 614), there are references to Zivia Lubetkin having been a co-founder of the Antifascist Bloc and the ZOB, and on the ZOB leadership.

298. Bernard Mark, *Der Aufstand*, 138ff.; and Ainsztein, *Jewish Resistance*, 594.

299. Bernard Mark, *Der Aufstand*, 147ff.; and Ainsztein, *Jewish Resistance*, 598.

300. Meed, 156.

301. Ibid., 156ff.

302. Ainsztein, *Jewish Resistance*, 600.

303. Ibid., 604.

304. Ibid., 606.

305. As cited by Bernard Mark, *Der Aufstand*, 169.

306. Ainsztein, *Jewish Resistance*, 607.

307. Ibid., 608. See also Bernard Mark, *Der Aufstand*, 175.

308. Bernard Mark, *Der Aufstand*, 175.

309. Ibid., 175ff.; and Ainsztein, *Jewish Resistance*, 608, ff.

310. Ibid., 609.

311. Ibid., 617.

312. Ibid., 609.

313. Ibid.

314. Ainsztein, *Jewish Resistance*, 622; and Bernard Mark, *Der Aufstand*, 231.

315. Ibid., 187.

316. Zuckerman, 31.

317. Emanuel Ringelblum, 326.

318. Meed, 171.

319. Cited by Bernard Mark, *Der Aufstand*, 226.

320. Ainsztein, *Jewish Resistance*, 621ff.; and Bernard Mark, *Der Aufstand*, 244ff.

321. Ainsztein, *Jewish Resistance*, 618.

322. Marek Edelman, "The Ghetto Fights," in Kowalski, vol. 3, 88.

323. Bernard Mark, *Der Aufstand*, 239ff.

324. Ainsztein, *Jewish Resistance*, 624.

325. Ibid., 625ff.

326. Ibid., 626.

327. Ibid.

328. Ibid., 628.

329. Edelman, 92.

330. Cited in Bernard Mark, *Der Aufstand*, 264.

331. As quoted, ibid., 283.

332. As quoted, ibid., 263.

333. As cited by Ainsztein, *Jewish Resistance*, 652.

334. Teletype message sent by Stroop on May 3, 1943 to General Kröger, the SS and Police commander in the East, in Krakow, as cited by Bernard Mark, *Der Aufstand*, 358.

335. Moczarski, 177ff.

336. Cited by Bernard Mark, *Der Aufstand*, 317.

337. Bernard Mark, *Der Aufstand*, 300; and Ainsztein, *Jewish Resistance*, 364ff.

338. See, among others, Meed, 196ff.

339. Ainsztein, *Jewish Resistance*, 642ff.

340. Bernard Mark, *Der Aufstand*, 338.

341. Ainsztein, *Jewish Resistance*, 658.

342. Bernard Mark, *Der Aufstand*, 345.
343. Ibid., 353.
344. Ibid., 363.
345. Ibid.
346. Ibid., 372ff.
347. Ibid., 382.
348. Cited by Ainsztein, *Jewish Resistance*, 661.
349. Bernard Mark, *Der Aufstand*, 406.
350. Zivia Lubetkin, "The Polish Uprising," in Kowalski, vol. 1, 152, 155.
351. Ibid., 155.
352. Ibid., 157ff.
353. Dov Levin, "Participation of the Lithuanian Jews in the Second World War," in Kowalski, vol. 1, 272.
354. Yitzhak Arad, *Ghetto in Flames* (Jerusalem: Ahva Cooperative Printing Press, 1980), 9.
355. Ainsztein, *Jewish Resistance,*, 486.
356. Ibid.
357. Arad, *Ghetto in Flames*, 20ff.
358. Dov Levin, "Participation of the Lithuanian Jews," 286.
359. Ibid., 287.
360. Arad, *Ghetto in Flames*, 21ff.
361. Ainsztein, *Jewish Resistance*, 489.
362. Ibid., 487ff.
363. Ibid., 494.
364. Arad, *Ghetto in Flames*, 108ff.
365. Ibid., 75; and Ainsztein, *Jewish Resistance*, 486.
366. Ibid, 505ff.; and Arad, *Ghetto in Flames*, 124ff.
367. Ainsztein, *Jewish Resistance*, 488.
368. Arad, *Ghetto in Flames*, 193ff.
369. Ainsztein, *Jewish Resistance*, 489.
370. Arad, *Ghetto in Flames*, 229.
371. Ibid., 231ff.
372. Ibid., 189; and Ainsztein, *Jewish Resistance*, 497.
373. Ibid., 490; and Arad, *Ghetto in Flames*, 234.
374. Ibid., 239ff.
375. Ibid., 255.
376. Ibid., 257; and Ainsztein, *Jewish Resistance*, 494.
377. Ibid, 501ff.
378. Arad, *Ghetto in Flames*, 243ff.
379. Ainsztein, *Jewish Resistance*, 500.
380. Arad, *Ghetto in Flames*, 244.
381. Ibid., 498ff.
382. Ibid., 496ff.
383. Arad, *Ghetto in Flames*, 245ff.
384. Arad, *Ghetto in Flames*, 260ff.; and Ainsztein, *Jewish Resistance*, 502. See also Yehuda Bauer, "They Chose Life," in Kowalski, vol. 1, 49; and Abraham Foxman, "The Resistance Movement in the Vilna Ghetto" (after a report by Abraham Suckewer), in Kowalski, vol. 1, 152.
385. Arad, *Ghetto in Flames*, 347.
386. Ibid.

387. Ibid., 241. See also Foxman, 151.
388. Arad, *Ghetto in Flames*, 253; and Ainsztein, *Jewish Resistance*, 387ff.
389. Arad, *Ghetto in Flames*, 316.
390. Ainsztein, *Jewish Resistance*, 491.
391. Arad, *Ghetto in Flames*, 375ff.
392. Ainsztein, *Jewish Resistance*, 512; and Arad, *Ghetto in Flames*, 387ff.
393. Ainsztein, *Jewish Resistance*, 513.
394. Arad, *Ghetto in Flames*, 399.
395. Ainsztein, *Jewish Resistance*, 513.
396. Arad, *Ghetto in Flames*, 409.
397. Ibid.
398. Ainsztein, *Jewish Resistance*, 514.
399. Ibid., 515. See also Arad, *Ghetto in Flames*, 410ff.
400. As cited by Arad, *Ghetto in Flames*, 433ff.
401. Ibid.
402. Ibid., 423ff.
403. Ibid., 432ff. See also Ainsztein, *Jewish Resistance*, 516.
404. Cited by Arad, *Ghetto in Flames*, 433ff.
405. Arad, *Ghetto in Flames*, 433; and Ainsztein, *Jewish Resistance*, 517.
406. Ainsztein, *Jewish Resistance*, 517.
407. Ibid., 518.
408. Ibid., 518ff.
409. Ibid., 519ff.
410. Ibid., 522ff.
411. Ibid., 524.
412. Ibid., 525ff.
413. Ibid., 529ff.
414. Ibid., 531ff.
415. Ainsztein, "The Bialystok Ghetto Revolt," in Suhl, 139ff.
416. Ainsztein, *Jewish Resistance*, 533.
417. Ibid., 534.
418. As cited by Ainsztein, *Jewish Resistance*, 535.
419. Ainsztein, *Jewish Resistance*, 535ff.
420. Ibid., 537.
421. Ibid., 538.
422. Grossman, 534.
423. Ainsztein, *Jewish Resistance*, 539.
424. Grossman, 543.
425. Quoted in Ainsztein, *Jewish Resistance*, 539.
426. Grossman, 538ff.
427. Ainsztein, *Jewish Resistance*, 540ff.
428. Grossman, 542.
429. Ainsztein, *Jewish Resistance*, 541.
430. Grossman, 542ff.
431. Ibid., 544ff.
432. Ainsztein, *Jewish Resistance*, 542.
433. Ibid.
434. Ibid., 542ff.
435. Ibid., 543ff.

436. Grossman, 546ff.

437. Ibid., 547.

438. Ibid.

439. Ainsztein, *Jewish Resistance*, 544.

440. Ibid.

441. Ibid. 545.

442. Ibid.

443. Ainsztein *Jewish Resistance*, 824ff.

444. Ibid., 825ff.

445. Ibid., 830ff.; and Shmuel Krakowski "The Jewish Fighting Organization in Cracow" (excerpted from *The War of the Doomed*), in Kowalski, vol. 3. 137.

446. Krakowski, "Jewish Fighting Organization," 137; and Ainsztein, *Jewish Resistance*, 832, 836.

447. Ainsztein, *Jewish Resistance*, 831.

448. Krakowski, "Jewish Fighting Organization," 138; and Ainsztein, *Jewish Resistance*, 838.

449. Ibid., 826.

450. Ibid., 833.

451. Quoted in ibid., 840.

452. Ainsztein, *Jewish Resistance*, 837ff.; and Krakowski, "Jewish Fighting Organization," 139.

453. Ainsztein, *Jewish Resistance*, 829, 833.

454. Cited by Ainsztein, *Jewish Resistance*, 834ff.

455. Ainsztein, *Jewish Resistance*, 835.

456. Krakowski, "Jewish Fighting Organization," 139.

457. Ainsztein, *Jewish Resistance*, 841ff.

458. Ibid., 843ff.; and Krakowski, "Jewish Fighting Organization," 140.

459. Quoted by Sefer Hapartisanim, in Kowalski, vol. 2, 112ff.

460. Ainsztein, *Jewish Resistance*, 844ff.

461. Quoted by Hapartisanim, 113.

462. Krakowski, "Jewish Fighting Organization," 140; and Ainsztein, *Jewish Resistance*, 848.

463. Quoted by Krakowski, "Jewish Fighting Organization," 140ff.

464. Ainsztein, *Jewish Resistance*, 849.

465. Ibid., 826ff.

466. Ibid., 849.

467. Krakowski, 141ff.

468. Joseph Tennenbaum, "Underground," in Kowalski, vol. 3, 312.

469. Ainsztein, *Jewish Resistance*, 463ff.; and Laster Eckman and Chaim Lazar, "The Jewish Resistance," in Kowalski, vol. 1, 315.

470. Eckman and Lazar, 314.

471. Ainsztein, *Jewish Resistance*, 465ff.

472. Ibid., 466.

473. Ibid., 463, 464, 467.

474. Eckman and Lazar, 315.

475. Ainsztein, *Jewish Resistance*, 472.

476. Ibid., 469.

477. Ibid.

478. Ibid.

479. Ibid., 470.

480. Ibid., 471.

481. Ainsztein, *Jewish Resistance*, 474; and Eckman and Lazar, 318.
482. Ibid., 318ff.
483. Ibid., 319.
484. Ainsztein, *Jewish Resistance*, 464.
485. Cited by Eckman and Lazar, 318ff.
486. Cited, ibid., 323ff.
487. Ainsztein, *Jewish Resistance*, 477.
488. Eckman and Lazar, 322.
489. Ibid.
490. Ibid., 320; and Ainsztein, *Jewish Resistance*, 480ff., 482.
491. Eckman and Lazar, 324ff.; Isaac Kowalski, "Interview with Kube's Assassin," in Kowalski, vol. 2, 376ff.; and Porter, 293.
492. Ainsztein, *Jewish Resistance*, 483.
493. Eckman and Lazar, 327ff.
494. Ainsztein, *Jewish Resistance*, 483.
495. Ibid., 483ff.
496. Ibid., 484..

WITH THE PARTISANS

497. Shalom Cholawski, *Soldiers from the Ghetto* (San Diego/New York/London: Barnes, 1980), 89ff.
498. Arad, *Ghetto in Flames*, 450ff.; and Ainsztein, *Jewish Resistance*, 390ff.
499. See Ainsztein, *Jewish Resistance*, 279ff.; Arad, *Ghetto in Flames*, 450ff.; Arad, "Introduction," 26ff.; Moshe Kahonowitz, "Why No Separate Jewish Partisan Movement Was Established during World War II," in Kowalski, vol. 3, 26ff.; Levin, *Fighting Back*, 179ff.; and Krakowski, *The War of the Doomed*.
500. Ainsztein, *Jewish Resistance*, 279ff.
501. Ibid., 281, 285ff.
502. See Levin, *Fighting Back*, 179ff.; Meed, 280ff.; Syrkin, 242ff.; and Krakowski, *The War of the Doomed*. See also Primo Levi, *If Not Now, When* (New York: Summit Books, 1985).
503. Ainsztein, *Jewish Resistance*, 303ff.; and Arad, "Introduction," in Kowalski, vol.1, 26ff.
504. As above, ibid.
505. Arad, "Introduction." See also Primo Levi, and statements from surviving female and male FPO fighters in Aviva Kempner and Josh Waletzky's film *Partisans of Wilna* (New York: Icarus Films, 1985).
506. Porter, 291ff.; and Syrkin, 242ff.
507. Krakowski, *The War of the Doomed*, 28.
508. Porter, 292.
509. Syrkin, 247ff.
510. Cited by Syrkin, 251ff.
511. V.A. Andreyev "In the Forests of Bryansk," in Kowalski, vol. 2, 545ff.
512. Ibid., 547.
513. Cholawski, 96ff.
514. Ainsztein, *Jewish Resistance*, 335.
515. Krakowski, *The War of the Doomed*, 106ff.; Levin, *Fighting Back*, 179ff.; and especially Esther Mark, "Zofia Jamajka," in Suhl, 77ff.
516. Levin, *Fighting Back*, 184.
517. See ibid., 184ff.; Arad, *Ghetto in Flames*, 450ff.; and Ainsztein, *Jewish Resistance*, 309ff.

518. See the sources cited above, plus the declarations of the surviving FPO fighters in Kempner and Waletzky's film *Partisans of Wilna*.

519. For biographical details regarding Niuta Tejtelbojm, see Ainsztein, *Jewish Resistance*, 634ff.; Bernard Mark Der Aufstand, 98ff.; Yuri Suhl, "Little Wanda with the Braids," in Suhl, 51ff.; and Porter, 293ff.

520. Cited by Suhl, 52.

521. For biographical details of Roza Robota see Ainsztein, *Jewish Resistance*, 800ff.; Suhl, 219ff.; Porter, 294, Hana Wajsblum, "Widerstand in Auschwitz," *Dachauer Hefte*, no. 3 (November 1987), 248ff. (The original document is filed under reference number 033/144-3-6 in the Yad Vashem archives.)

522. As cited by Wajsblum, 251.

523. As cited by Suhl, 22ff.

524. Wajsblum, 252.

THE ROAD TO ARMED RESISTANCE.

525. Arnold Zweig and Herman Struck, *Das ostjüdische Antlitz* (Wiesbaden: Fourier, 1988), 111.

526. Ibid., 130ff.

527. Dora Goldkorn, "Erinnerungen an den Aufstand im Warschauer Ghetto," in *Im Feuer vergangen*, compiled by Arnold Zweig (Berlin [GDR]: Rütten & Loening, 1960), 587.

528. Gusta Dawidsohn-Draengerowa "Tagebuch der Justyna," in *Im Feuer vergangen*, 184.

529. Noemi Szac-Wajnkranc, "Im Feuer vergangen," in *Im Feuer vergangen*, 531.

530. Kempner and Waletzky.

531. Ibid.

532. Syrkin, 234.

533. Goldkorn, 588.

534. Szac-Wajnkranc, 536.

535. Goldkorn, 588.

536. Ibid., 588ff.

537. Ibid., 594.

Index

51 Group (all Jewish partisan unit) 240–241

A

Accolades 11
Ackelsberg, Martha v
Adamowicz, Irene 195
Akiva 159, 174, 215–216
Alicante 49
Altman, Tosia 185
Anarchists xxi, 18, 19
Andreyev, V.A. 239
Anielewicz, Mordecai 170, 174, 181
Anthology on Jewish Armed Resistance xxviii
Antifascist Bloc 174
Antifascist Struggle Bloc 205, 208–209
Antifascist Women's Front 52, 54, 67, 73
    Zena Danas (magazine) 55
Armée Juive xvii, xix
Assassinations xix, 85, 90, 91, 92, 97, 115–116, 143, 174, 246
Austria 60

B

Bancic, Olga 113, 275
Baran, Debora 184
Bauminger, Heshik 216
Berson, Dora 145, 229
Biala, Khaya 210
Bialystok 143, 169, 202
    Bialystok Antifascist Bloc 203
Bialystok ghetto uprising 204–205, 210–214

Binnenlandse Strijdkrachten (BS) 86, 100–102
Birkenau, resistance in 249–252
Bloch Schynckmann, Jacqueline 136–137, 140, 275
    photo 137
Boczow, Wolf 114
Boraks, Edek 203
Bór-Komorowski, General 146, 147–148
Borkowska, Anna 192
Borowska, Chenia 192, 193, 195, 200, 234, 244
Bouhuys, Mies xxiv
Brander, Chawa 184
Brojdo, Ber 175
Brzezinska, Zocha 184
Bund, The 158, 161, 169–170, 174
    Za Nasza i Wasza Wolnosz (paper) 168
    Zukunft (Youth group) 203
Butbinik, Celia 228

C

Carinthia 51, 55, 60
Carinthian Fatherland Service 60
Cheigham, Rachel xix
Chico (Julia Manzanal) 37
Children 111, 196–197
    rescue of xii, xiv, 97–101
Cholawski, Shalom 240
CIF 32
CNT-FAI 19
Cohn, Marianne xiv
Communist Party 192, 202–203
Communist Party of Yugoslavia 52

The Kate Sharpley Library

Comrades and Friends,

The Kate Sharpley Library was named in honor of Kate Sharpley, a First World War anarchist and anti-war activist, one of the countless "unknown" members of our movement so often ignored by "official historians" of anarchism. The Library was founded in South London in 1979 and reorganized in 1991.

We have over 12,000 English language books, pamphlets and periodicals on anarchism, including complete or near complete runs of *Black Flag*, *Direct Action* (from 1945 onwards), *Freedom, Man, Spain and the World, Woman Rebel, Freedom* (USA), *Why, The Blast, Spanish Revolution*, and a host of others. We have an equally strong collection of posters, leaflets, manuscripts, letters, and internal records, including reports from the IWA (AIT/IAA), the Anarchist Federation of Britain (1945-1950), the Syndicalist Workers Federation (1950-1979), Cienfuegos Press, ASP, and records from many more groups and organizations. Our foreign language sections covers a similar range of material in over thirty languages including many rare pamphlets and newspapers.

We regularly publish new research on lost areas of anarchist history, as well as historically important documents from the past. Our aim is to give, as Pietro Gori writes, "flowers for the fallen" and allow the movement of today to learn from the past. Any movement that ignores its own history deserves what it gets!! The Kate Sharpley Library is always on the lookout for relevant material, and we ask all anarchist groups and publications to add our name to their mailing list. This is a rare opportunity to keep your history alive. We also appeal to all comrades and friends to donate suitable material to the Library. If you are reading this, that includes you!! ALL donations of anarchist material are welcome, as are financial contributions since our only income is from individual donations and sales. We have, and will continue to have, NO state support.

Please contact us if you would to use our facilities and collection. We publish a regular bulletin of library news and historical articles (many never published in English before). For details of our publications, please write to us at info@katesharpleylibrary.net or:

KSL	KSL
B.M Hurricane	PBM #820
London	2425 Channing Way
WC1N3XX	Berkeley, CA 94704
UK	USA

Friends of AK Press

AK Press is a worker-run co-operative that publishes and distributes radical books, visual & audio media, and other mind-altering material. We're a dozen people who work long hours for short money, because we believe in what we do. We're anarchists, which is reflected both in the books we publish and in the way we organize our business. All decisions at AK Press are made collectively—from what we publish to what we carry for distribution. All the work, from sweeping the floors to answering the phones, is shared equally.

Currently, AK Press publishes about twenty titles per year. If we had the money, we would publish forty titles in the coming year. New works from new voices, as well as a growing mountain of classic titles that, unfortunately are being left out of print.

All these projects can come out sooner with your help. With the Friends of AK Press program, you pay a minimum of $25 per month (of course, we welcome larger contributions), for a minimum three month period. All the money received goes directly into our publishing funds. In return, Friends automatically receive (for the duration of their membership), one FREE copy of EVERY new AK Press title (books, dvds, and cds), as they appear. As well, Friends are entitled to a 10% discount on everything featured in the AK Press Distribution Catalog and on our website—thousands of titles from the hundreds of publishers we work with. We also have a program where groups or individuals can sponsor a whole book. Please contact us for details. To become a Friend, go to: http://www.akpress.org.

Also available from AK Press

PETER KROPOTKIN—The Conquest of Bread
SAUL LANDAU—A Bush & Botox World
JOSH MACPHEE & ERIK REULAND (eds)—Realizing the Impossible: Art Against Authority
RICARDO FLORES MAGÓN—Dreams of Freedom: A Ricardo Flores Magón Reader
NESTOR MAKHNO—The Struggle Against The State & Other Essays
SUBCOMANDANTE MARCOS—¡Ya Basta!
G.A. MATIASZ—End Time
CHERIE MATRIX—Tales From the Clit
ALBERT MELTZER—Anarchism: Arguments For & Against
ALBERT MELTZER—I Couldn't Paint Golden Angels
JESSICA MILLS—My Mother Wears Combat Boots
RAY MURPHY—Siege Of Gresham
NORMAN NAWROCKI—Rebel Moon
MICHAEL NEUMANN—The Case Against Israel
CRAIG O'HARA—The Philosophy Of Punk
ANTON PANNEKOEK—Workers' Councils
ABEL PAZ (CHUCK MORSE, translator)—Durruti in the Spanish Revolution
BEN REITMAN—Sister of the Road: The Autobiography of Boxcar Bertha
PENNY RIMBAUD—The Diamond Signature
PENNY RIMBAUD—Shibboleth: My Revolting Life
RUDOLF ROCKER—Anarcho-Syndicalism
RUDOLF ROCKER—The London Years
RAMOR RYAN—Clandestines: The Pirate Journals of an Irish Exile
RON SAKOLSKY & STEPHEN DUNIFER—Seizing the Airwaves
ROY SAN FILIPPO—A New World In Our Hearts
MARINA SITRIN—Horizontalism: Voices of Popular Power in Argentina
ALEXANDRE SKIRDA—Facing the Enemy: A History Of Anarchist Organisation From Proudhon To May 1968
ALEXANDRE SKIRDA—Nestor Makhno: Anarchy's Cossack
VALERIE SOLANAS—Scum Manifesto
CHRIS SPANNOS (ed)—Real Utopia
JEFFREY ST. CLAIR—Born Under a Bad Sky
CJ STONE—Housing Benefit Hill & Other Places
ANTONIO TELLEZ—Sabate: Guerilla Extraordinary
MICHAEL TOBIAS—Rage and Reason
SETH TOBOCMAN—Disaster and Resistance
JIM TULLY—Beggars of Life: A Hobo Autobiography
TOM VAGUE—Televisionaries
JAN VALTIN—Out of the Night
RAOUL VANEIGEM—A Cavalier History Of Surrealism
FRANÇOIS EUGENE VIDOCQ—Memoirs of Vidocq: Master of Crime
MARK J. WHITE—An Idol Killing
JOHN YATES—Controlled Flight Into Terrain
JOHN YATES—September Commando

CDs
MUMIA ABU JAMAL—All Things Censored Vol.1
JUDI BARI—Who Bombed Judi Bari?
JELLO BIAFRA—Become the Media
JELLO BIAFRA—In the Grip of Official Treason
NOAM CHOMSKY—Case Studies in Hypocrisy
NOAM CHOMSKY—The Imperial Presidency
NOAM CHOMSKY—New War On Terrorism: Fact And Fiction
NOAM CHOMSKY—Propaganda and Control of the Public Mind
NOAM CHOMSKY & CHUMBAWAMBA—For A Free Humanity: For Anarchy
CHUMBAWAMBA—A Singsong and A Scrap
WARD CHURCHILL—Doing Time: The Politics of Imprisonment
WARD CHURCHILL—In A Pig's Eye
ANGELA DAVIS—The Prison Industrial Complex
THE EX—1936: The Spanish Revolution
NORMAN FINKELSTEIN—An Issue of Justice
ROBERT FISK—War, Journalism, and the Middle East
FREEDOM ARCHIVES—Chile: Promise of Freedom
FREEDOM ARCHIVES—Prisons on Fire: George Jackson, Attica & Black
    Liberation
FREEDOM ARCHIVES—Robert F. Williams
JAMES KELMAN—Seven Stories
TOM LEONARD—Nora's Place and Other Poems 1965–99
CASEY NEILL—Memory Against Forgetting
GREG PALAST—Live From the Armed Madhouse
UTAH PHILLIPS—I've Got To know
UTAH PHILLIPS—Starlight on the Rails box set
DAVID ROVICS—Behind the Barricades: Best of David Rovics
ARUNDHATI ROY—Come September
HOWARD ZINN—Heroes and Martyrs: Emma Goldman, Sacco & Vanzetti,
    and the Revolutionary Struggle
HOWARD ZINN—A People's History of the United States
HOWARD ZINN—People's History Project Box Set
HOWARD ZINN—Stories Hollywood Never Tells

DVDs
NOAM CHOMSKY—Imperial Grand Strategy
NOAM CHOMSKY—Distorted Morality
STEVEN FISCHLER & JOEL SUCHER—Anarchism in America/Free Voice
    of Labor
ARUNDHATI ROY—Instant-Mix Imperial Democracy
ROZ PAYNE ARCHIVES—What We Want, What We Believe: The Black Panther
    Party Library (4 DVD set)
HOWARD ZINN & ANTHONY ARNOVE (ed.)—Readings from Voices of a
    People's History of the United States